THE FESTAL MENAION

The Service Books of the Orthodox Church

The Festal Menaion

translated from the original Greek

by

MOTHER MARY

of the Orthodox Monastery of the Veil of the Mother of God
Bussy-en-Othe, France

and

ARCHIMANDRITE KALLISTOS WARE

Spalding Lecturer in Eastern Orthodox Studies
University of Oxford

with an introduction by

ARCHPRIEST GEORGES FLOROVSKY

Emeritus Professor of Eastern Church History
Harvard University

FABER AND FABER
24 Russell Square
London

First published in 1969
by Faber and Faber Limited
24 Russell Square London WC1
Made and printed in Great Britain by
William Clowes and Sons, Limited
London and Beccles

SBN 571 08687 x

CONTENTS

CONTENTS

PREFACE

Today, more than ever before, there is a compelling need for Orthodox liturgical texts in the English language. In preparing the present volume, the translators have been concerned to meet the needs of at least three different groups:

First, we have had in mind the situation of the younger generation within the Orthodox emigration, most of whom are obliged at the present time to attend services in a tongue that is not their own. In Great Britain, in the United States, Canada, and Australia, there are today many thousands of Orthodox Christians—and before long their total number will be reckoned in millions—whose primary language is English, and who can no longer fully understand services performed in Greek, Slavonic, Romanian, or Arabic. In most parishes, however, the chief language used in public worship is still that of the Mother Country. Without translations which they can consult at home or take to church, these English-speaking Orthodox are being spiritually starved, cut off as they are from a full participation in communal prayer.

In the second place, we have kept in view the needs of parishes as well as individuals. In America and elsewhere, an appreciable number of Orthodox parishes—although still only a minority—have now begun to use English in their public worship; and translations are thus required not only for private consultation but for liturgical use. The employment of English at Orthodox services cannot but increase enormously during the next thirty years; besides English-language parishes, before long there will doubtless be

English-speaking Orthodox monasteries. These parishes and monastic centres will require texts that are suitable for reading aloud and singing; and the monasteries will want, in addition, an English version that is as complete as possible.

Nor, in the third place, is it the Orthodox alone who need such translations. Never before has the Orthodox Church possessed so many friends in other Christian communions: and by far the best way in which these non-Orthodox can come to understand the faith and life of Orthodoxy is by sharing in its liturgical worship. Abstract explanations are not enough: as Philip said to Nathanael, 'Come and see' (John 1:46). Only too often, however, these friends of Orthodoxy have been deterred by the sad lack of adequate translations.

This threefold situation has been constantly in our minds as we prepared the present version. We are deeply conscious of its many defects. We have made every effort to provide a text that is dignified and accurate; but the task of translating the Orthodox service books is beset by formidable difficulties, and it is impossible to hope for anything that approaches perfection. Greek liturgical poetry at its best combines a marvellous beauty of language with a rigorous precision in theological expression. Much of that beauty and that precision is inevitably lost in the transition from Greek to English, and no one can be more vividly aware of this than the translators themselves. On many occasions we have been tempted to give up in discouragement. But always one thing has led us to persevere—our knowledge that on the practical level there is an urgent and specific need for English texts.

So voluminous are the Orthodox service books that it will require many years of work by different translators before a full English version is made available. So far as our own contribution is concerned, we have chosen to begin with the Twelve Great Feasts, which—next to the supreme festival of Easter—occupy a place of outstanding importance within the

Orthodox calendar. This book contains the special offices for nine of the twelve: of these nine, all are 'fixed', that is, occurring upon the same date each year, and the texts for all nine are found in the same set of service books, the Menaia.[1] The remaining three of the Great Feasts are 'movable', and depend on the date of Easter.

There is little necessity to underline the profound significance, both devotionally and theologically, of the feasts included in this volume. It contains the texts for Christmas, Epiphany, the Annunciation, and the Presentation of Our Lord in the Temple (the 'Meeting'), which express the true Orthodox faith concerning the Incarnation of the Saviour. It contains the office of the Transfiguration, which is essential for any proper understanding of the Orthodox doctrine of 'Divine Light' and mystical prayer. It contains the office for the Exaltation of the Cross, which deserves to be studied with care by all who imagine that Orthodoxy concentrates solely upon the risen Christ, to the neglect of Christ crucified. It contains the services for the Nativity of the Holy Virgin, for her Entry into the Temple and her Dormition: without a knowledge of these three offices, it is impossible to appreciate the true character of Orthodox devotion to the Mother of God.

The texts for each feast are here given *in full*. This has been a fundamental principle in our work. We have not sought to make a selection, using our own private judgement to decide what is of greater or lesser importance: but we have attempted to render in its integrity all that stands written in the Greek and Slavonic service books. To some this will seem an unrealistic attitude, for almost everywhere in the Orthodox Church today the services are abbreviated. But we are translators, not liturgical reformers: some abbreviation may be generally necessary, but it is not for us, as translators, to pre-determine what form the abbreviation shall in fact take.

[1] On the Orthodox service books, see Appendix II (pp. 535–43).

Furthermore, the portions habitually omitted often include texts of great value, both from the literary and from the doctrinal viewpoint; and it seemed to us vitally important that all this material should be made accessible in English.

The basis of our translation is the original Greek: this has been compared everywhere with the Slavonic, and at times with the Romanian. The edition of the Menaia that we have normally employed is that issued at Athens by the publishing organization *Phos*, under the auspices of the 'Christian Union of Young Workers' (12 volumes, 1960–61). On occasion we have adopted alternative readings found in the edition published at Rome by the Press of the Propaganda (6 volumes, 1888–1901); or else we have followed the older Orthodox editions printed at Venice in the last century. There exists, unfortunately, no fully critical edition of the Menaia—nor, indeed, of any major service book used by the Orthodox Church. In particular, the attributions of authorship given at the head of the canons and of other compositions are frequently open to question. In the present edition these traditional attributions are for the most part retained, although we recognize that many of them must be viewed with caution.

The rubrics and liturgical directions, as given in the Greek and Slavonic books, are often brief to the point of obscurity; and at times we have thought it wise to expand and clarify them. On matters of ritual we have adopted as our guide the Typikon of St. Sabas, followed by the Greek-speaking Churches up to 1888, and still in use within the Russian Church.[1] It has not been possible to note all the discrepancies between the Greek and Slavonic Menaia, but a number of the more significant divergences are mentioned.

We have deliberately reproduced the directions in the Menaia or the Typikon concerning fasting, even though these regulations are now widely disregarded by Orthodox in the

[1] On the question of the Typikon, see further below (pp. 541–3).

western world. But whether or not contemporary Orthodox choose to keep the fasts, it seems only right that they should be reminded what the traditional rules in fact demand.

The Tones[1] are indicated throughout, as in the Greek and Slavonic Menaia. It was our original intention to mark divisions in those texts which are normally chanted, so as to facilitate singing: but we decided that this was impracticable, since there exists a great variety of Church music within the Orthodox communion, and no one system of pointing would prove universally convenient. It seems best to leave individual choir masters free to insert their own pointing.

In course of time English-speaking Orthodox will doubtless evolve a musical tradition of their own, which will take its place alongside those of Greece, Russia, and the other Orthodox nations. As yet no such tradition has had time to develop: and Orthodox of English language must therefore draw for the present upon some existing musical heritage within Orthodoxy. The best adapted for this purpose seems to be that of Russia. Byzantine chant is too intricate: if it is to be used, then the stress and rhythm of the Greek original must be preserved almost exactly in English translation, and this raises insuperable difficulties. But Russian music is far more flexible; and in particular the simpler Russian monastic chants can easily be adapted to an English text. We have kept this possibility in mind as we made our translations.

No attempt has been made to reproduce the acrostics which abound in the Greek canons, and all allusions to these acrostics have therefore been omitted.

So far as the general style of our translation is concerned, after much experimenting we decided to take as our model the language of the Authorized Version (the King James Bible). This, we realize, is a controversial decision. Many of our readers will probably feel that, if the liturgical texts

[1] For the meaning of this and other technical terms, see the Glossary in Appendix III (pp. 544-62).

are to come alive for people today, they must be rendered in a more contemporary idiom. To this it must be answered that the Greek used in the canons and hymns that are here translated was *never* a 'contemporary' or 'spoken' language. The Byzantine hymnographers wrote in a liturgical style that was consciously 'artificial', even though it was never intentionally obscure or unintelligible. As we see it, the language of the Authorized Version is best adapted to convey the spirit of the original liturgical Greek. We do not dispute the necessity for more modern translations of Scripture, and their great value—in certain contexts: but for our present purpose it was the Authorized Version that provided what we most required. For three centuries and more the Authorized Version, and along with it the Anglican Book of Common Prayer, have provided the words with which English-speaking peoples throughout the world have addressed God; and these two books have become a part not only of our literary but of our spiritual inheritance. So long as certain archaisms of language and construction are avoided, the English of the King James Bible is still easily understood.

To ensure a certain consistency of diction, we have in general refrained from using words that do not occur in the Authorized Version. But it has not been possible to adhere to this principle inflexibly. In particular, the Greek liturgical texts often use technical terms taken not from Scripture but from the Fathers: and in many cases no equivalent could be found for these in the vocabulary of the King James Bible.

In common with the Commission for the Anglican Revised Psalter,[1] we have not tied ourselves to rendering each word in the original by the same English word throughout. Here our practice agrees with that of St. Jerome, who, for example,

[1] *The Revised Psalter: the amended text as approved by the Convocations of Canterbury and York in October 1963* (London, S.P.C.K., 1964), p. viii.

in the Vulgate rendering of the Epistles, translated the Greek verb *evdokein* in no less than ten different ways. To quote an eminent translator of the Scriptures, Mgr. Ronald Knox: 'Every common word in every living language has, not one meaning, but a quantity of shades of meaning. . . . Words are not coins, dead things, whose value can be mathematically computed. You cannot quote an exact English equivalent for a French word, as you might quote an exact English equivalent for a French coin. Words are living things, full of shades of meaning, full of associations.'[1]

Quotations from Scripture are normally taken from the Authorized Version. This raises some difficulty where the Old Testament is concerned, for here the Orthodox Church uses the Greek text of the Septuagint, which often differs considerably from the Hebrew text upon which the Authorized Version is based. Unfortunately there exists no satisfactory English translation of the Septuagint as a whole; and we felt it entirely beyond our present resources to attempt a new rendering of our own. With reluctance we decided eventually upon a compromise. In the case of complete Psalms or full-length Lessons from the Old Testament, as a rule the text of the Authorized Version is reproduced without change. But for single verses of Scripture, inserted between stichera or the like, we have made our own translation from the Greek, while keeping always as close as possible to the Authorized Version. Since the verse of Scripture and the accompanying sticheron are often directly related, the link between them would at times be destroyed if we had everywhere followed the Authorized Version without adaptation.

Throughout the book, the Psalm numbering is that of the Septuagint.[2]

[1] R. A. Knox, *On Englishing the Bible* (London, 1949), pp. 10–11.

[2] For the differences between this and the Hebrew numbering, see p. 530.

The material in the Orthodox service books falls into two clearly defined categories. First, there is a Scriptural 'stratum'—readings from the Psalter and other parts of the Old Testament, from the Epistles and the Gospels. Alongside this, there is a non-Scriptural 'stratum', consisting in religious poetry—canons, stichera, kontakia, sessional hymns, and the like. The contents of this present volume belong for the most part to the latter category. Yet even this second 'stratum' is in its deeper reality profoundly Scriptural, being everywhere permeated with Biblical images and phraseology: indeed, the Orthodox service books as a whole are in the last analysis little else than one vast and extended meditation upon Holy Scripture. Many of the liturgical texts become unintelligible if the underlying references to the Bible are not appreciated. We have therefore indicated the more important of these references in footnotes, without attempting to list them exhaustively.

In addition to the actual translations, much explanatory material is to be found in the introductory sections and in the appendixes. We are happy to include, in the first place, an introduction by Archpriest Georges Florovsky, Emeritus Professor of Eastern Church History at Harvard University, describing the spirit of liturgical piety which prevails within the Orthodox Church. Then follows an introductory section by the two translators, of a more technical character, concerning the particular texts contained in this volume. Among other things we have provided a series of analytical plans giving in summary form the structure of the Byzantine Liturgy and the offices. These are intended as a general guide: certain possible variations of minor importance have been omitted; also no mention is made of the special rules observed during Lent. After this comes a section on the 'Common of the Vigil', giving the unchanging parts of the Vigil Service, whether on a feast or on an ordinary Sunday.

Among the four appendixes, we would direct attention

especially to the third, which supplies the meaning of technical terms not explained elsewhere in the text.

Our purpose in all this explanatory matter has not been to enter into historical discussions—save only to a very limited degree—still less, to suggest liturgical reforms, but simply to describe the Orthodox practice as it exists at the present time. We have deliberately placed all this supplementary material either at the beginning or at the end of the volume, and not in the main body of the text. This is because we hope that the work may be employed not only as a book for study but as a book for prayer: and it would not be correct, in the sections of this volume intended for use as a service book, to insert any expressions of personal opinion. This is the reason, for example, why the explanations of each feast are not printed immediately in front of the feast concerned, but are all grouped together in the introduction. In the actual text of the offices, footnotes are restricted almost entirely to Scriptural references, with an occasional indication of the difference between the Greek and the Slavonic.

The services contained in this volume have, to our knowledge, appeared in English only once before, in a book that has long been out of print: *The Ferial Menaion or the Book of Services for the Twelve Great Festivals and the New Year's Day*, translated by N. Orloff (London, 1900). Professor Orloff has here rendered the literal sense of the original with conscientious accuracy: but he was translating into a language not his own and, as so often in such a situation, the resulting English version is so eccentric in style—and at times altogether grotesque and ludicrous—that it cannot decently be used in public worship.[1] The well-known *Service*

[1] Orloff, who was Professor at King's College, London, produced two other volumes of translations: *Octoechos or the Book of Eight Tones* (London, 1898); *The General Menaion* (London, 1899). Regrettably these display the same stylistic defects as his *Ferial Menaion*.

Book of Miss I. F. Hapgood, issued with the blessing of Patriarch Tikhon and widely employed by the Orthodox of America, includes no more than short extracts from the texts of the Great Feasts. Fuller texts for Vespers and for Lauds at Mattins may be found in the work of Father Seraphim Nassar, *Divine Prayers and Services*, but this generally omits the canons.

In the translation of the canons, we have been greatly helped by two works: St. Nicodemus of the Holy Mountain, *'Εορτοδρόμιον* (Venice, 1836), and Professor Evgraf Lovyagin, of the St. Petersburg Theological Academy, *Bogosluzhebnye kanony na slavyanskom i russkom yazike* (St. Petersburg, 1867). The schematic plans for the services are based partly upon K. Nikolsky, *Posobie k izucheniyu ustava bogosluzheniya pravoslavnoi Tserkvi* (St. Petersburg, 1900), and also upon E. Mercenier, F. Paris, and G. Bainbridge, *La prière des églises de rite byzantin* (3 volumes, 2nd edition: Chevetogne, 1947–53). This last work we have also found a valuable aid in preparing the introduction and notes.

The translators desire to express their profound gratitude to all who have assisted them. The translation has been undertaken in very close co-operation with Mother Eudoxia, Abbess of the Monastery of the Veil of the Mother of God, Bussy-en-Othe, who has offered advice and help on innumerable points, great and small. We owe more to her than we can readily express, and without her constant encouragement the work would certainly never have been brought to completion. Our sincere thanks are due also to various sisters and friends of the community for their generous help in typing, arranging, and checking the manuscript. Father Kallistos wishes also to thank the Abbot and brethren of the Monastery of St. John the Theologian, Patmos, for the kind hospitality which they extended to him while he was engaged on the revision of the translation. He is especially indebted to Archimandrite Jeremias, Ecclesiarch of the Monastery, who explained to him many of the intricate points concerning the structure of the services. Finally we are extremely grateful to Archpriest Georges Florovsky for his introductory essay.

The Forefeast of the Annunciation
24 March/6 April 1968
Bussy-en-Othe

MOTHER MARY
ARCHIMANDRITE KALLISTOS

THE WORSHIPPING CHURCH

Pray without ceasing
I Thess. 5:17

(i) COMMUNITY AND RETREAT

There is an essential duality in Christian existence.

Christianity stands by personal faith and commitment, and yet Christian existence is intrinsically corporate: to be Christian means to be in the Community, in the Church and of the Church. However, personality should never be simply submerged in the collective. The Church consists of responsible persons. The simile of the Body should never be misinterpreted and pressed too far. The Church is composed of unique and irreplaceable personalities which can never be regarded merely as elements or cells of the whole, because each individual is in direct and immediate union with Christ and His Father—the personal is not to be dissolved in the corporate. Christian 'togetherness' should not degenerate into a kind of impersonalism.

The first followers of Jesus, in the 'days of His flesh', were not isolated individuals engaged in their private quest for truth. They were Israelites—and our Lord Himself used to declare that He was 'not sent but unto the lost sheep of the house of Israel' (Matt. 15:24); and the Twelve were ordered by Him to go precisely to these lost sheep, and to avoid the Gentiles and the Samaritans (Matt. 10:5, 6). The first followers of Jesus were regular members of an established and instituted Community—'the House of Israel', 'the Chosen People' of God—and they were waiting 'for the consolation of Israel', according to the Prophecy and Promise. In a sense, a 'Church' already existed when Jesus began His ministry. It was Israel, the People of the Covenant. His preaching was first addressed to the members of this Community. He never addressed individuals as individuals. The existing Covenant was the constant background of His preaching. The Sermon on the Mount was not addressed to an occasional crowd of accidental listeners, but rather to an 'inner circle' of those who were already following Jesus in the anticipation—or with the conviction—that He was the 'One who should come', that is, the Messiah. 'The Little Flock', that community which Jesus had gathered around Himself, was, in fact, the faithful 'Remnant' of Israel, a re-constituted 'People of God'. It was reconstituted by the Call of God, by the announcement of the Kingdom, by the 'Good News' of salvation. And yet to this call each person has to respond individually, by an act of personal faith. This personal response in faith, however, incorporates the believer into the Community. Or rather it is an existential pre-requisite of incorporation which is effected and completed in Baptism, by the grace of God. Yet one has first to believe and to commit oneself with the oath of allegiance, and then to be baptized. The 'faith of the Church' must be always personally appropriated, and continually maintained by spiritual effort.

The two aspects of Christian existence—personal and corporate—are linked together inseparably. One is saved only in the Community, and yet salvation is mediated always through personal faith and obedience.

This basic duality of Christian existence is conspicuously reflected in the realm of worship. Christian worship is at once personal and corporate, although these two aspects may be at times in tension.

There are in the Gospel two significant passages concerning prayer, and they may seem to guide the worshipper in opposite directions.

In the Sermon on the Mount the multitude were exhorted to pray 'in secret', in seclusion or in solitude. Of course, this injunction was directed primarily against 'the hypocrites', against those who displayed a pretentious ostentation in worship—'in the corners of the streets, that they may be seen of men'; and a similar warning was extended also to almsgiving. Yet there is a deeper dimension to this invitation to 'secrecy', or privacy, in prayer. Indeed, prayer is intrinsically a *personal* act, or rather a personal *action*. It is always a person who prays. It is an intimate encounter of persons with the Living God, and, obviously, there should be no witnesses at this encounter: 'enter thy closet . . . shut thy door . . .'. One has to stand before God, alone, face to face: 'pray to Thy Father *which is in secret* . . .'. One has *to retire* for worship, or even to be secluded. And yet, paradoxically, even in this retirement or seclusion, in the solitude of one's closet, one can pray only as a member of the redeemed Community, be it the Israel of old or the Church of Christ. Indeed, no true worshipper can ever forget that *his* Father is also the *common* Father of all believers and of the whole human race. As Christians we are instructed to call in worship on *Our Father*, who is also 'the Father of our Lord Jesus Christ'. No true Christian can pray *only for himself*, even in his closet. Comprehensiveness in prayer is the mark of spiritual health and maturity. In its compass and content Christian prayer can never be strictly 'private', although it must be always personal. Moreover, Christians should be fully aware of the ultimate ground of their privilege to pray—it is precisely their membership in the Community, in the Church of Christ.

On another occasion our Lord was speaking to the disciples of the mystery of joined prayer. Believers—'two or three' of them—may 'agree' to pray for certain things in common. And then the ultimate mystery of worship is manifested: 'for where two or three are gathered together in My name, there am I in the midst of them'. This 'agreement' is not just an occasional human assent. The 'gathering' in the name of Christ is itself a gift of the Spirit. And it presupposes a kind of spiritual preparation or training. The praying heart must be enlarged to the measure of Christ's love for man. Only in the spirit of Christ's love can individuals truly come together, so that they meet as 'brethren', that is, as brethren in Christ.

Prayer 'in secret' and prayer 'in common' actually belong to each other inseparably as aspects of the same devotional commitment and action. There is no choice: they must be practised together. Indeed, it is the rule of the Church that believers should prepare themselves for corporate worship by their personal devotions 'at home', 'in the closet'. It is spiritually dangerous to ignore this regulation. But it is no less dangerous to be so much absorbed in 'home devotions' that the urge to join with brethren in corporate worship expires or is reduced: for the climax of Christian worship—and also its centre—is the Holy Communion in which Christ Himself appears in the midst of those gathered in His name. In any case, as St. Cyprian used to explain to his flock, Christian prayer is essentially the 'prayer of the people', since 'we—the whole people—are one'. Accordingly, the goal and measure of Christian worship is *unanimity*—'with one heart and one mouth'. And we Christians must be ever grateful for the grace given to us—'with one accord to make our common supplications' unto our Father in Heaven.

(ii) REMEMBRANCE AND THANKSGIVING

Christian worship is essentially an 'encounter'. Moreover, it is also a 'dialogue'. There are always two partners in worship. The worshipper is always expecting an answer. 'Give ear, O Lord, unto my prayer; and attend to the voice of my supplication. In the day of my trouble I will call upon Thee; for Thou wilt hear me' (Ps. 85:6–7). As the prophet put it, 'I am a God at hand, and not a God far off' (Jer. 23:23, quoted by St. Cyprian in his treatise on the Lord's Prayer). The initiative is divine. We call on God because He has called us first. Thus Christian worship is a *response* to the call or 'challenge' of God. We pray because the initiative has been taken by God, and we are made aware of that divine initiative through the testimony of Scripture. We call on God whom we are given to know—because He has revealed Himself through the ages, in special events, through special messengers, and finally in His Only-begotten Son, our Beloved Lord Christ Jesus. He first called upon the people He had created, and He called upon them because He created man for His own purpose, shaping him in His own image, imprinting His similitude on every man. He has disclosed Himself in that marvellous history which is recorded on the pages of the Holy Writ. But He has done much more than that. The Son of God came down to dwell among men for their salvation. The climax of God's revelation is 'the Gospel of Jesus Christ, the Son of God'. It is the story of an Encounter, of a personal conversation with men of One who was Divine and who for our sake, 'for us men and for our salvation', had become or 'was made' man. Always Christians pray to God 'through Jesus Christ our Lord'. And this reference is crucial and decisive. One comes to the Father only through the Son, 'who has declared Him' (John 1:18). As Christians, we call on God *whom we know*—from His mighty deeds of our salvation in Christ. Accordingly, there are always two major emphases in Christian worship: *remembrance* and *thanksgiving*—*anamnesis* and *eucharistia*. They belong together inseparably.

The starting point of Christian worship is *commemoration* or *remembrance*. The Christian Faith itself is primarily an obedient and grateful *recognition* of the mighty and saving deeds of God which culminated in the 'coming down' of the Son of God. God has acted, once for all. Man now has to acknowledge God's gracious action and to testify to His love and glory. Christian worship is only possible in the context of God's *historic Revelation*, in the perspective of 'Sacred History' which is precisely the 'History of Salvation'. Accordingly, it is determined and characterized by certain 'credal assumptions' in which we assess and interpret, in the light of faith, God's deeds and purposes. Already under the Old Dispensation the whole structure of Jewish worship was essentially 'historic'. The memory of God's mighty deeds in the past dominates the Psalter, that exemplary 'Book of Prayers' which has retained its central place also in the worship of the Christian Church, public and 'private'. Certainly, this 'memory' has been reassessed and reinterpreted in the light of the New Dispensation. But the same sense of history has been emphatically retained. The Living God to whom prayers were addressed by the Jews under the Law has now disclosed His ultimate concern 'in these last days'. The same Living God who chose Israel to be His servant and His people, has finally manifested His unfailing love for man in a more excellent way in Christ Jesus. The Old Covenant was finally superseded by the New, but this New Covenant 'in Christ' was, in fact, but the climax and consummation of the Old. This intimate connection between the two is strongly emphasized in the *Magnificat* and *Nunc dimittis*, those great and triumphant scriptural hymns of the Church. The worship of the Church was built on old foundations. The Church took over the sacred memories of Ancient Israel and it still devoutly recalls the mighty deeds of God under the Old Dispensation. The reminiscences of the Old, understood as a prophetic anticipation, reappear in many Christian hymns and prayers. Moreover, the Church has retained the old liturgical scheme or pattern of 'remembrance' and 'recital'. *Lectio divina*, the recitation of Scripture, is still an integral and organic part of Christian worship, including both the New and the Old Testaments. It is significant that especially on great occasions of liturgical commemoration numerous readings from the Old Testament are prescribed—to emphasize the unity and continuity of 'Sacred History'. On these great days the worship of the Church has most conspicuously an historical dimension. Christian faith and hope are rooted in Sacred History. Prophecy and Gospel belong inseparably together, as promise and consummation. 'God who at sundry times and in divers manners spake in time past unto the fathers by the prophets, hath in these last days spoken unto us by the Son whom He hath appointed heir of all things, by whom also He made the worlds' (Hebr. 1 : 1–2).

This *historic character* of Christian worship is clearly expressed in the structure of the liturgical year. From early times there was in the Church a yearly commemoration of the crucial *Triduum*—from Cross to Resurrection—as well as a weekly commemoration of the Resurrection, on each 'Lord's Day'. Gradually a comprehensive scheme of yearly commemorations was elaborated; actually every day has now its own 'memory'. This Christian calendar has obviously a vital theological significance and many theological implications. Day by day the Church looks back to its past. The calendar testifies to the *sanctification of time*. The Church lives in the dimension of sacred memories, while at the same time looking equally to the future.

No doubt, the consummation was much greater than the promise, and its mystery passed all expectations and all understanding. Nevertheless it was precisely a 'consummation' and also—in a sense—a 'recapitulation'. Paradoxically at one and the same time it abrogated the Old and confirmed its perennial significance. The very nature of Sacred History has been radically and profoundly changed, and yet it is still the same continuing history. Abraham is still 'the father of all believers', not only in the Old Israel but in the Christian Church. The saints of the Old Dispensation found their place in the Christian calendar. Since the coming of Christ, by virtue of the Incarnation, God is now guiding His People as it were 'from the inside', and no more 'from the outside', as happened *sub umbraculo legis*. The Christian remembrance is much more than just a memory or reminiscence. Indeed, Christians are bound to look back to the mighty events which are the foundation of their faith and hope: Incarnation, Cross and Resurrection, Pentecost. But these individual events of the past are, at the same time, paradoxically present in the Church here and now. The Incarnation of the Word is at once an historic event of the past which can and should be 'remembered' in the ordinary way, and also *an abiding presence* of the Lord which can be directly perceived and recognized at all times and at any particular time by the eye of faith, in the Church. This changes radically the meaning and character of *anamnesis* in Christian worship. There is much more than merely an enlargement or extension of common historical perspective. The *accomplishment* of the Promise was not just an extra event in the homogeneous sequence of happenings. It was an 'event' indeed, but it was an event *which never passes*. Of course, it can be dated with a certain measure of chronological accuracy, and we are actually counting 'the years of the Lord', *anni Domini*—from Christ's Nativity at Bethlehem, *post Christum natum*. Yet that which is 'remembered' is also actually present, and will be present 'unto the ages of ages'—till He comes again. For even before He comes He is already present in the Church. It is precisely His abiding presence which makes the Church what it is, that is, the Body of Christ. Now this mysterious presence of Christ—in the Church and within the world—has been *inaugurated in history*, by a sovereign intervention of God, by a decisive revelatory 'earthquake', to use the bold expression of St. Gregory of Nazianzus. The acknowledgement of the Presence is inseparably coupled with the memory of the Past. This paradoxical coincidence of Past and Present constitutes the distinctive and unique characteristic of the Christian 'memory', which reaches its culmination in the Eucharistic *anamnesis* or 'commemoration'.

The Holy Eucharist is the centre of Christian worship. An elaborate cycle of daily offices has been built, in the course of time, around this centre of devotion. Moreover, the Eucharist is not only a particular 'office' or *akolouthia*, but primarily a sacrament, a *mysterion*. Now the Eucharistic rite is obviously an *anamnesis*, a 'Memorial of the Lord', performed 'in His memory', according to His ordinance. But, on the other hand, it is undoubtedly not a mere commemoration of the Last Supper. In fact, it *is* the Last Supper itself. Christ Himself is actually *present* in the sacred rite, both as its supreme and perennial minister and as the victim, 'for Thou Thyself both offerest and art offered'. In the strong words of St. John Chrysostom, each Eucharistic celebration *is* actually *the Last Supper* itself, in its full reality, without any diminution. '*This table is the same as that and has nothing less*' (*In Matt. hom.* 82). 'The offering is the same, whether it be offered by some ordinary man, or by Paul or Peter. That which Christ gave to His disciples, and that which the priests minister now is the same. This is in no wise inferior to that, because it is not men that sanctify even this, but the Same who sanctified the one sanctifies the other also' (*In II Tim. hom.* 2). *There is no difference*, St. John concluded. The Eucharistic Sacrament is neither a mere remembrance nor a 'repetition' of the Last Supper. It is rather its 'manifestation' or extension. Worshippers are, as it were, *taken back* to the Upper Room and made participants of the same sacred Supper. This paradoxical nature of sacramental *anamnesis*, which is at the same time an actual and immediate encounter, or rather communion, with the ever abiding Lord, discloses the ultimate mystery of Christian existence. The Body is never separated from the Head. The Church is more than just an assembly of believers, of those who believe and acknowledge the mighty deeds of God 'in ages past', including the times of the Gospel. It is above all the Body of Christ, a corporation of them who dwell in Him and in whom Christ Himself is dwelling and abiding, according to His own solemn promise. There is in the Church a certain mysterious *continuity between Christ the Saviour and Christians*—who are being saved precisely as 'members' of His Body—whatever the manner in which we may attempt to comprehend and to explain this ultimate mystery, the mystery of the Church. St. John Chrysostom once endeavoured to describe this mystery in daring words, speaking in the person of Christ Himself: 'I pursued thee, I ran after thee, that I might overtake thee. I united and joined thee to Myself. . . . Above I hold thee, and below I embrace thee. . . . . I descended below. I not only am mingled with thee, I am entwined in thee. . . . Things united remain yet in their own limits, but I am interwoven with thee. I would have no more division between us. I will that we both be one' (*In I Tim. hom.* 15, *sub fine*). St. John had in mind precisely the mystery of Communion.

Indeed, the Eucharistic *anamnesis* is also a *koinonia*, communion, encounter. Those who 'remember' or 'commemorate' the Lord, according to His ordinance, are not 'outside Him' but 'in Him', *in Christo*, as branches of a vine. They belong to His 'fulness', to the *pleroma* which is the Church (Eph. 1:22, 23). In no sense are Christians outsiders. They are members of Christ. Christian worship is the worship of those who are inside. It is significant that this great mystery of our Lord's Presence has been from the earliest Christian times described as *Eucharist*, that is, *Thanksgiving*. The major prayer in the rite, the *anaphora*, is precisely an elaborate *anamnesis* or recollection of the *Magnalia Dei*, from Creation itself up to the Last Supper and

Christ's solemn injunction 'to do it in His remembrance'. The Sacrament is assessed in a wide perspective of the History of Salvation. Yet it is an *anamnesis in the form of thanksgiving*, *eucharistia*. Gratitude is the proper response of man to the benevolence or *philanthropia* of God. As a response of man to the saving Providence of God, especially to the mystery of our Redemption, by Jesus Christ and in Him, and to the unfathomable gift of New Life in the Spirit, Christian worship is primarily an expression of grateful acknowledgement, of praise and adoration. It culminates ultimately in *doxology*. It is significant that we are directed to conclude our prayers and intercessions with doxologies: '*for all glory, honour, and worship befitteth Thee* . . .'. It should be also our starting point: *Hallowed be Thy Name* is the first and introductory petition of the Lord's Prayer and only then do intercessions follow.

(iii) ENCOUNTER AND DIALOGUE

Worship is the norm of Christian existence. It should be the constant disposition or attitude of the Christian man. Indeed, to worship God means precisely to be aware of His presence, to dwell constantly in this presence. It is through worship that the 'new man' is being formed in the believer, and the baptismal grace of adoption is actualized. The Christian man must be always in the state of worship, whether it is expressed in words or not. In its essence worship is the orientation of man towards God. *Into Thy hands I commend my spirit*. . . .

Prayer is a bounden duty of believers. Faith and worship cannot be separated. But prayer is also a daring endeavour, inasmuch as it is also a spiritual urge of those who believe. One meets God always with awe and trembling, if also with love and adoration. In prayer one has to begin with an act of detachment—'to lay aside all the cares of this life'. In no sense is this an easy task, especially when we want to present precisely these 'cares'—our troubles and needs—to Him, in search for help and illumination. That is why we are instructed to pray 'in the closet', in retirement, in retreat from 'the world'. However, the walls of the chamber, the shut door, and any other external fences, cannot by themselves prevent distraction or dissipation. This can be achieved only by an intense internal effort, by steady and continuous training, by a total reorientation of one's life. But detachment is not indifference. God Himself is not indifferent to man's needs or 'cares'.

It has been often suggested, by many authorities and expert masters of spiritual life, that 'prayer books', the fixed formularies of worship, are only intended for the beginners. This is undoubtedly true, if the statement is properly understood. Fixed formulae are, of course, no more than a means towards something much greater. Yet they are an appropriate means. It is spiritually dangerous to neglect the 'books', to dispense with them hastily, and to indulge arbitrarily in extempore improvisations of one's own composition. It is more than merely a question of discipline. The settled formulae not only help to fix the attention, but also feed the heart and mind of worshippers, offering topics for meditation and reminding them of the mighty deeds of God. There is no room for psychologism or subjectivism in Christian worship. The goal and purpose of worship is the '*prayer of the mind*', to the complete exclusion of all 'passions'. Serenity is here the measure. *Let all human flesh be silent, and with awe and trembling stand*. . . .

There is in the Church a fixed rule or order of worship, even for prayer 'in the closet'. And it is our duty to follow it. Of course, there must be more than a mere recitation: the words must come from the heart, and the heart may also find its own words. But spontaneous prayer can come only after an assiduous training. A sound balance should be maintained between 'recitation' and 'improvisation' in worship, although obviously there can be no formal rules for this. The purpose of training is to introduce the worshipper into a 'conversation' with God, to guide him into 'encounter' with the Living God. It is significant that most of the Church's offices, including the rule for prayers at home, begin with a most daring appeal to the Holy Spirit, the Heavenly King: *Come and abide in us*. In fact, it is an anticipation of our ultimate and final goal—*to acquire the Holy Spirit of God*. The end is paradoxically anticipated from the very beginning. The search for the Spirit is the moving force of worship. It may happen that at a certain moment in worship the Spirit starts speaking in our hearts. Then one has to stop and listen. 'The Spirit itself beareth witness with our spirit that we are the children of God. . . . The Spirit itself maketh intercession for us with groanings which cannot be uttered' (Rom. 8:16,26). At this point prayer, in the ordinary sense of the word, ceases. As St. Seraphim of Sarov said, one can no more ask, 'Come and abide in us', when the Spirit has already come and speaks in the heart. One can but receive the visitation with joy, but also with humility. Of course, the Spirit manifests itself only in the souls which have been prepared by a long and steady exercise in devotion. There is no room for human 'improvisation'. It is the Spirit that improvises.

At this very point the crucial problem arises: in what manner can and should we correlate these personal devotions 'in the closet' with the corporate worship in the community? The encounter with God, while praying 'in the closet', is certainly the core of worship. It is a genuine encounter and a communion with God. What, then, is missing here? Why and how should this intimate encounter with the Living God in the secrecy of the closet be supplemented by participation in the public and corporate worship of Community? These are not idle or vain questions. They are of immense practical importance, especially urgent and burning in our own time. Nor are they simple questions which would admit of a general and unvarying solution. In fact, there is a constant tension in the devotional practice of individual Christians between 'private devotions' and 'corporate worship', and it can be overcome only by an intensive meditation on the articles of faith. A certain tendency towards a peculiar kind of spiritual 'individualism' seems to be inherent in the practice of solitary prayer, if only subconsciously. Now it is indeed true that 'in the closet' the worshipper enters into an intimate and direct conversation with the Living God and acquires the Holy Spirit. It is this intimate encounter with God which is usually stressed in our current manuals of spiritual life. At the same time, of course, it is always assumed that those who worship 'in the closet' are members of the Church. But this aspect of the matter is not always sufficiently emphasized. In fact, Christians are only entitled to pray as members of the Community. This is not only an objective presupposition, but an internal spiritual condition, an integral part of their devotional orientation. 'Private devotions' are inevitably but a preparation for, and a sequel to, 'corporate worship'. They always are pointing beyond themselves. *Prayer is intrinsically subordinate to sacraments.* It is possible only on the basis of our sacramental incorporation into the Body of Christ, through Holy Baptism. Accordingly, the ultimate 'encounter' is realized also in a *sacramental* way, in the mystery of the Holy Eucharist. All 'private devotions' must be consciously directed towards this sacramental goal. It is highly significant that Nicolas Cabasilas wrote his great book *Life in Christ* in the form of a treatise on sacraments—the triad of the sacraments of initiation: Baptism, Chrismation, Eucharist. The root of Christian existence is there, and of Christian worship too. One should also remember at this point Father John of Kronstadt and his teaching.

For Cabasilas, the Eucharist is an '*ultimate mystery*', a sacramental consummation, 'the goal and term of life'. The Eucharist is the summit of Christian pilgrimage. And when this final stage of sacramental life has been achieved, there is nothing else that man may desire or need. In this mystery or sacrament, not only are the gifts of the Spirit granted and received, but the Risen Lord Himself is present. One cannot move farther. When Christ is in us, what else can we seek? Christ abides in the communicants. This is a 'perfect sacrament', more perfect than any other, the beginning and the end of all blessings, the ultimate goal of all human aspirations. God is united with us 'in a most perfect union', and nothing can be more perfect than this marvellous conjunction. . . . Cabasilas was here following in the steps of St. John Chrysostom, with his daring Eucharistic realism. The same experience of intimate communion with Christ is expressed in those remarkable prayers which the Church orders to be recited before and after communion by all participants. There is more than an encounter: there is union and communion.

In the Eucharist those who are separated and estranged from each other by human frailty are brought together into the perfect and intimate unity of the One Body in Christ. Human exclusiveness and the mutual impenetrability of men are overcome. The faithful are 'co-members' of each other through Christ in the Church, or even 'con-corporeal' with each other and with Christ in His Body, to use the phrase of St. Cyril of Alexandria. In the Eucharist the essential unity of Christians finds its perfect expression. This unity is not restricted or confined to those who are taking actual part in a particular celebration on a particular day. Each celebration is in reality universal, and the Eucharist is ever one. Christ is never divided. Every Liturgy is celebrated in communion with the whole Church, Catholic and Universal. It is celebrated in the name, and by the authority, of the whole Church. Spiritually in every celebration the whole Church, 'the whole company of heaven', takes an invisible, yet real, part. This unity extends not only to all places but also to all times. It includes all generations and all ages. The living and the departed are to be 'commemorated' at every celebration of the Divine Liturgy. It is not only a remembrance, in a narrow and psychological sense of the word, not only a witness of our human sympathy and concern, but rather an insight into the universal fellowship of all believers, living and departed, in Christ, the common Risen Lord. In this sense, the Eucharist is a manifestation of the mystery of the Church, or rather of the mystery of the Whole Christ. As has been already stated, every celebration is identical with the Last Supper. It is in the Eucharist that the Church is aware and conscious of her profound unity and anticipates her final perfection in the age to come. The Eucharist is not only an expression of our human fellowship and of our human brotherhood, but above all an expression or an image of the divine mystery of our Redemption. It is a mystery of Christ. Every time that the Eucharist is celebrated, we witness to and we live in this perfect unity, initiated and inaugurated by the Incarnate and Risen Lord. We pray in the name of all mankind, of all those who have been called and have responded to the call. We pray as the Church—the whole Church is praying with us, or rather *in us* and through us.

Of course, one has to be spiritually prepared for this participation in the mystery of the Worshipping Church, cleansed and purified. Worship in 'the closet' is indispensable. But it can be consummated only in the common celebration of the ultimate mystery of Christ, in communion with all our brethren.

The story of Redemption is not yet completed. Rooted in the commemoration of the past, Christians are living still in expectation: the Kingdom is still to come. Yet, on the other hand, the Church herself is the token of this glorious consummation and from the early times she has prayed for its fulfilment: 'As this broken bread was scattered upon the mountains, and was gathered together and became one, so let Thy Church be gathered together from the ends of the earth into Thy Kingdom' (*Didache*, ix. 4).

GEORGES FLOROVSKY

THE ORTHODOX SERVICES AND THEIR STRUCTURE

(i) The Five Cycles

From the liturgical viewpoint the life of an Orthodox Christian is composed of various cycles.

First of all, there is the great cycle embracing a man's whole life from birth to death, from cradle to coffin. This consists in actions which are not repeated, but occur once only during the earthly existence of each person: baptism; chrismation or confirmation; burial. To this cycle belong also the sacraments or sacramental blessings which confer special grace for a particular office or vocation within the Christian community: marriage; monastic profession; holy orders.[1]

At the other extreme from this major sequence involving a Christian's entire life, there is the daily cycle of prayers and praises offered by the Church once in every twenty-four hours. In the liturgical life of Orthodoxy, as with the Jews and other ancient peoples, the day is considered to begin at sunset. Accordingly the Church observes the following order:

[1] Certain minor qualifications must be added. Under exceptional circumstances, chrismation may be repeated: for instance, an Orthodox who has apostatized to Islam is received back into the Church by anointing with chrism. Second marriages occur after the death of the other partner or, less commonly, after divorce: but this is in some measure a departure from the strict norm. There are various degrees in monastic profession and holy orders: but no single degree is ever repeated, each being conferred once for all.

Vespers (Gk. ἑσπερινός; Slavonic, *vechérnya*)
Compline (Gk. ἀπόδειπνον; Slavonic, *povechérie*)
Midnight Office or Nocturns (Gk. μεσονυκτικόν; Slavonic, *polúnoshchnitsa*)
Mattins (Gk. ὄρθρος; Slavonic, *útrenya*)
First Hour
Third Hour
Sixth Hour
Ninth Hour

Such is the basic daily pattern. To complete the series there may be added:

(i) The 'Interhours'. During certain periods of fasting, each of the Hours (Gk. ὧραι; Slavonic, *chasý*) is followed by an intermediate office or 'Interhour' (Gk. μεσώριον; Slavonic, *mezhdochásie*).

(ii) The Offices for the Blessing of the Table (a) at midday (b) in the evening.

(iii) Morning and Evening Prayers, and the general commemoration of the Living and the Dead which has its own liturgical form. These are of a more informal character than the other offices. They are read by lay people before the icons in their own homes; in monasteries they are sometimes recited by each member of the community individually in his or her cell, while in other cases they take a corporate form and are read aloud in chapel.

The Holy Liturgy is frequently included in this daily cycle: its place is normally after the Sixth Hour, but during fasts it is celebrated after Vespers. It is somewhat misleading, however, to treat the Liturgy as part of the daily cycle. In the first place, it is not in fact prescribed to be celebrated each day: according to Orthodox practice, except in cathedrals and large monasteries a daily Eucharist has always been the exception rather than the rule. Secondly, and more important, the Eucharist in its deeper reality does not properly belong to the 'liturgy of time', and therefore stands apart from the daily cycle. The celebration of the Lord's Supper is always an 'eschatological' event, in which the *eschaton*, the Age to Come, breaks in upon this present age: and so, although occurring in time, it transports the participants to a point altogether outside time—to the 'heavenly places' where there is no past, present, or future, but only the eternal Now. The Eucharist, then, cannot simply be integrated into the temporal sequence nor set on a level with daily offices such as Mattins and Vespers.

Connected with the Liturgy is the service of the Typika (Gk. *τυπικά*; Slavonic, *izobrazítelnaya*), which is sometimes read after the Sixth Hour on days when there is no celebration of the Eucharist.[1] On occasion it may also precede the Liturgy.

Obviously the great majority of Orthodox are not able to participate in the whole of the daily cycle. It is usually performed in its entirety only in monasteries, and even here there may be considerable abbreviations. In many parish churches Vespers and Mattins are not celebrated daily, but only at weekends and at major feasts. On working days a devout lay Christian will be content to read the Morning and Evening Prayers, in a shorter or a fuller form according to the time at his disposal.

Between these two extremes—the daily sequence, and that of a man's entire life—there are three intermediate cycles which together comprise the Church's Year:

(i) The weekly cycle of the Eight Tones.
(ii) The annual cycle of movable feasts, centred upon Easter.
(iii) The annual cycle of fixed feasts, commencing on 1 September.

In daily worship these three cycles are combined together

[1] During fasts, after the Ninth Hour.

and superimposed one upon another, thus endowing the liturgical year with a constant and unfailing variety. The material for each cycle is contained in a special book or set of books:

the weekly cycle in the Octoechos;
the annual cycle of movable feasts in the Triodion and the Pentekostarion;
the annual cycle of fixed feasts in the twelve volumes of the Menaia.[1]

(ii) The Great Feasts

Among the festivals of the Christian Year, a place of preeminent honour belongs naturally to Easter Day, the 'feast of feasts'. Next in importance come the Twelve Great Feasts, divided into two groups: Feasts of the Mother of God, and Feasts of the Lord.[2] If a Feast of the Mother of God falls on a Sunday, the special texts for the feast are combined with the Sunday office of the Resurrection, taken from the Octoechos; but in the case of a Feast of the Lord all texts for Sunday are omitted.

Feasts of the Mother of God (Gk. *Θεομητορικαὶ ἑορταί*):

1. The Birth of the Theotokos (8 September).
2. The Entry of the Theotokos into the Temple (21 November).
3. The Meeting of Our Lord (2 February).[3]
4. The Annunciation (25 March).

[1] On these and the other service books, see Appendix II, pp. 535–43, where the disposition of these three cycles is further explained.

[2] The list of Twelve Great Feasts that follows reflects the normal Orthodox practice; but—particularly in iconographic representations of the Twelve Feasts—variations in the list sometimes occur.

[3] Western 'Presentation' or 'Purification'. Sometimes reckoned as a Feast of the Lord.

5. The Dormition of the Theotokos (15 August).[1]

Feasts of the Lord (Gk. *Δεσποτικαὶ ἑορταί*):

1. The Exaltation of the Cross (14 September).
2. Christmas (25 December).
3. Theophany (6 January).
4. Palm Sunday (one week before Easter).
5. The Ascension of Our Lord (40 days after Easter).
6. Pentecost (Trinity Sunday: 50 days after Easter).[2]
7. The Transfiguration of Our Lord (6 August).

As can be seen, three out of these Twelve Great Feasts are movable, forming part of the annual Easter cycle, while the remaining nine are fixed and belong to the cycle of the Menaia. It is the texts for these nine fixed feasts that are contained in the present volume.

Each of the nine feasts in question is preceded by a period of preparation, known as the forefeast; two of them are also preceded by a special fast.[3] Three are followed, on the next

[1] Western 'Assumption'.

[2] In the east the feast of the Trinity is observed on the day of Pentecost itself, not—as in the west—a week later.

[3] Four special fasts are observed in the Byzantine liturgical year:

(i) The Christmas Fast, beginning on 15 November.
(ii) The Great Fast (Lent), beginning seven weeks before Easter. The Great Fast, strictly defined, ends on the Saturday of Lazarus (the day before Palm Sunday): Holy Week itself, although likewise observed as a fast, stands apart from the six preceding weeks of Lent, and is regarded as occupying a distinctive and unique position within the Church's Year.
(iii) The Fast of the Apostles, varying in length between one and six weeks: it begins on the Monday after All Saints (the Monday eight days after Pentecost) and ends on the eve of the feast of Sts. Peter and Paul (29 June).
(iv) The Dormition Fast, beginning on 1 August and ending on the eve of the feast of the Dormition (15 August).

In addition, all Wednesdays and Fridays are days of fasting, except:

(a) between Christmas and Theophany

day, by a distinctive commemoration known as a Synaxis (Slavonic, *Sobór*); and all except one are followed by a period termed the afterfeast, during which the festival continues to be observed. The last day of the afterfeast—the day on which the festival finally closes—is called the apodosis (Slavonic, *otdánie*).

In detail the arrangements for each feast are as follows:

(i) †The Birth of the Theotokos (8 September).[1]
- One day of forefeast (7 September).
- Memorial of Sts. Joachim and Ann, the parents of the Theotokos (9 September).
- Four days of afterfeast (9–12 September).

(ii) †The Exaltation of the Cross (14 September).
- One day of forefeast (13 September).
- Seven days of afterfeast (15–21 September).

(iii) †The Entry of the Theotokos into the Temple (21 November).
- One day of forefeast (20 November).
- Four days of afterfeast (22–25 November).

(iv) †Christmas (25 December).
- Fast of forty days, commencing 15 November.
- †Five days of forefeast (20–24 December).[2]
- †Special observance (*paramoni*; Slavonic *navechérie*) on the eve of the feast (24 December).
- †Synaxis of the Theotokos (26 December).

(b) during the week after the Sunday of the Publican and the Pharisee (the third week before Lent)
(c) during Easter week
(d) during the week after Pentecost.

The Exaltation of the Cross (14 September), the eve of Theophany (5 January), and the Beheading of St. John the Baptist (29 August) are also fasts.

[1] The symbol † indicates that the texts for the day in question are included in the present volume.

[2] Only the texts for the last day of the forefeast—24 December—are included in this volume.

Six days of afterfeast (26–31 December).
General dispensation from all fasting until 4 January inclusive.

(v) †Theophany (6 January).
†Four days of forefeast (2–5 January).[1]
†Special observance (*paramoni*) on the eve of the feast (5 January).
†Synaxis of St. John the Baptist (7 January).
Eight days of afterfeast (7–14 January).

(vi) †The Meeting of Our Lord (2 February).
One day of forefeast (1 February).
Memorial of Sts. Simeon and Ann (3 February).
Seven days of afterfeast (3–9 February).[2]

(vii) †The Annunciation (25 March).
One day of forefeast (24 March).
†Synaxis of the Archangel Gabriel (26 March).[3]

(viii) †The Transfiguration of Our Lord (6 August).
One day of forefeast (5 August).
Seven days of afterfeast (7–13 August).

(ix) †The Dormition of the Theotokos (15 August).
One day of forefeast (14 August).
Eight days of afterfeast (16–23 August).

The pattern of services varies in the case of particular feasts:

(A) *On 8 and 14 September, 21 November, 2 February, 6 and 15 August*

1. Small Vespers

[1] Only the texts for the last day of the forefeast—5 January—are included in this volume.

[2] Depending upon the closeness of the feast to the beginning of Lent, the afterfeast may be shortened or omitted altogether.

[3] Only the texts for Vespers of the Synaxis are included. The feast closes either on 25 March itself, or on the day of the Synaxis, 26 March.

2. Vigil:[1] Great Vespers with Lity
   Mattins
   First Hour
3. Third and Sixth Hour
   Liturgy
4. Ninth Hour[2]

(B) *Christmas and Theophany*[3]

1. On the Eve:
   A. Royal Hours
      Typika

[1] Here, and throughout this volume, in the case of all Great Feasts we have assumed as our norm the observance of a vigil (Gk. *ἀγρυπνία*; Slavonic, *vsénoshchnoe bdénie*). This is in fact the standard practice in Russian churches, whether parochial or monastic. Among the Greeks, vigils are held at Great Feasts by certain monasteries, but not as a rule in the parishes.

If there is a vigil:

(i) Small Vespers are recited earlier in the afternoon. (In practice they are scarcely, if ever, said outside monasteries.)

(ii) The vigil begins with Great Vespers or Great Compline, as the case may be, together with the Lity; this is followed immediately by Mattins and then the First Hour.

(iii) Small Compline and the Midnight Office are not read.

If there is no vigil:

(i) Small Vespers are not read.

(ii) Great Vespers with the Lity are celebrated on their own. In the morning Mattins are sung, followed immediately by the First, Third, and Sixth Hours, and the Liturgy. (According to the present practice in Greek parishes, the Hours are omitted and the Liturgy follows at once upon Mattins.)

(iii) Small Compline and the Midnight Office are read as usual. But if Great Compline is prescribed, Small Compline is not used.

[2] Read immediately before Vespers. On 14 September and 6 August at the Vespers following (i.e. the second Vespers of the Feast) a Great Prokimenon is sung, except on Saturday evenings.

[3] Should these feasts fall on Sunday or Monday, the arrangements are different (see pp. 352–3, 337–8).

B. Great Vespers
Liturgy of St. Basil
(Theophany: Great Blessing of the Waters)

2. Vigil: Great Compline with Lity
Mattins
First Hour
3. Third and Sixth Hours
Liturgy of St. John Chrysostom
(Theophany: Great Blessing of the Waters)
4. Ninth Hour[1]

(C) *The Annunciation*

Here the rules are of great complexity.[2] If the feast itself falls on a weekday in Lent (Tuesday to Friday inclusive), then the arrangements are thus:

1. On the Eve: Great Vespers
(Liturgy of the Presanctified)[3]
2. Vigil: Great Compline with Lity
Mattins
First Hour
3. Third, Sixth, and Ninth Hours
Great Vespers
Liturgy of St. John Chrysostom

(iii) The Background and Meaning of the Feasts

It lies far beyond the scope of these introductory notes to discuss in full the theological significance of the liturgical

[1] Read immediately before Vespers. At the second Vespers of the Feast, Great Prokimenon, except on Saturday evenings.

[2] For details, see pp. 435–7.

[3] The Liturgy of the Presanctified is celebrated when the eve of the feast falls on Wednesday or Friday (also on certain other days: see p. 435).

texts that follow. We have simply attempted to provide certain general indications for those unfamiliar with Orthodox worship, more especially in the case of such feasts as make use of non-Scriptural material.

(i) *The Birth of the Theotokos* (8 September). The texts for this day are based largely on the *Book of James* or *Protevangelion*, a work dating from the second century A.D., and recounting the nativity and early years of the Blessed Virgin Mary.[1] According to the story there recorded, Mary's parents, Joachim and Ann, remained childless for many years. Both were true servants of God, righteous and devout: but their prayers for a child were not answered. One day, when Joachim came to make his offering in the temple, to his humiliation he was turned away by the High Priest, who reproached him sharply for his lack of children. In discouragement and bitterness Joachim retired into the desolate hill country, among the shepherds and their flocks, in order to hide his shame. As he was praying there to God, it chanced that his wife Ann was praying at the very same time in the garden of their house at Jerusalem. An angel appeared to them both, announcing that Ann should bear a child, whose name was to become illustrious throughout all the world. Ann promised to offer her child, boy or girl, as a gift to the Lord. All his depression gone, Joachim returned home in haste; his wife, anxious to share the good news with him, ran out of the house and they met at the city gate. In due course the angel's promise was fulfilled, and Ann bore a daughter, Mary.

The Orthodox Church does not place the *Protevangelion* of James on the same level as Holy Scripture: it is possible, then, to accept the spiritual truth which underlies this narrative, without necessarily attributing a literal and historical exactness to every detail. The deeper meaning of

[1] English translation in M. R. James, *The Apocryphal New Testament* (Oxford, 1924), pp. 39–49.

the story is not difficult to appreciate. It makes clear that, from the moment of her birth and even long before it, the Mother of God was specially consecrated to the Holy Trinity, elect and marked out by God. The Incarnation was not a casual and fortuitous event but the fruit of lengthy preparation, something ordained from before all ages in the providence of God. And so, at her first entry into the world, she who was chosen to be the instrument of this mystery was to an especial degree the object of God's ever-watchful care. Such is the inner truth underlying the infancy narratives of Our Lady; and such also is the point repeatedly stressed in the liturgical texts for the day—that Mary was 'foreordained before the womb as Mother of our God' (Great Vespers, aposticha).

The Theotokos, we have said, was marked out and chosen by God 'from the moment of her birth *and even long before it*.' From one point of view the whole history of the Old Covenant points forward to her: and for this reason the Orthodox Church constantly discerns, throughout the pages of the Old Testament, veiled references and allusions to the Theotokos. The long sequence of patriarchs, prophets, priests, and kings reaches its culmination in the daughter of Joachim and Ann. Born under the Old Covenant, she is the last and greatest of the righteous men and women of Israel: in her is summed up all the holiness and faith of God's chosen people, the children of Abraham. When she answered at the Annunciation, 'Be it unto me according to thy word', she spoke not only for herself, but as their representative, in the name of them all. Forming as she does the link between the Old and the New, between the Law and Grace, it is most important not to isolate her from her context within Israel after the flesh.[1]

[1] This is one of the reasons why Orthodox feel reservations about the Roman Catholic dogma of the Immaculate Conception.

Another 'link figure' between the Old and the New—though in a different way from the Theotokos—is the Forerunner, St. John the Baptist.

Since the Church's Year begins on 1 September, the Nativity of the Theotokos is the first Great Feast in the annual cycle. Its position at this point is appropriate. The birth of Mary may be seen as marking the inauguration of the scheme of salvation: with her birth we begin already to look forward to the birth of her Son, and so to the redemption that He accomplished in the flesh. 'The preordained tabernacle of our reconciliation with God now begins to be' (Mattins, First Canon, Canticle Eight). 'Today grace begins to bear its first fruits' (Great Vespers, sticheron on *Lord, I have cried*).

The feast of Our Lady's Nativity—as the texts for the day abundantly indicate—is above all else an occasion of great joy. The birth of a child is rightly a cause for happiness to the mother and father, particularly when they have begun to despair of ever having children. In Mary's case, however, the parents' rejoicing is shared by all creation, for her birth foreshadows the universal salvation that is to come. 'Thy birth, O Theotokos, has brought joy to all the inhabited earth' (troparion of the feast); 'Let there be common joy in the world among angels and mankind' (second exapostilarion).

One fundamental truth is plainly expressed in the liturgical material for 8 September. Mary's link with her Son, her place within the saving and redemptive mission of Christ, is never for one moment forgotten. Mary is honoured by the Church, not primarily for herself, but as Mother of the Lord—because it was within her womb that the hypostatic union between God and man was brought to pass. The many titles given to the Theotokos in the services for the day —'Temple and Throne of God', 'Bridge of Life', 'Mystical Paradise', 'living Pavilion of the glory of God'—all alike serve to illustrate this vital truth. Always Mary is venerated because of the Child that she bore: Mother and Son are not to be separated, but Mariology is to be understood as an extension of Christology.

(ii) *The Exaltation of the Cross* (14 September). In the liturgical observances of Good Friday the Church views the Crucifixion within its original setting, as an event in the first Holy Week at Jerusalem. At the feast of the Exaltation, by contrast, the Cross is regarded rather in its effects upon the subsequent history of the Church. On Good Friday the note is predominantly—though never exclusively—one of sorrow and mourning; on 14 September the Cross is commemorated in a spirit of triumph, as a 'weapon of peace and unconquerable ensign of victory' (kontakion of the feast).

The services for the day allude in particular to four themes:

(a) There are constant references to the vision of the Cross seen by the Emperor Constantine in the year 312, shortly before his victory over Maxentius.

(b) The feast of the Exaltation recalls more especially the finding of the True Cross by Constantine's mother, St. Helen. As the news of the discovery spread through the Holy City, vast crowds gathered to venerate the Cross of the Lord. The Patriarch of Jerusalem, St. Makarios, carried it up into a pulpit: and when the people saw it lifted on high, they all began to cry out, again and again, *Kyrie eleison*, 'Lord, have mercy'—an event recalled in the service of the day, with the frequent repetition of *Kyries* at the ceremony of Exaltation.

(c) The feast on 14 September also commemorates the second great Exaltation of the Cross, at Constantinople in 629. The True Cross had fallen into the hands of the Persians in 614, when they captured the Holy City of Jerusalem. It was subsequently recovered by the Emperor Heraclius and brought to the capital, Constantinople, where it was triumphantly exalted in the Great Church of Agia Sophia.[1]

(d) Finally, there are allusions to an event which is now more specifically commemorated on 13 September: the

[1] i.e. Holy Wisdom: often termed 'St. Sophia' or 'Sancta Sophia' by English writers.

Dedication of the Church of the Resurrection, built by Constantine on the site of the Holy Sepulchre and completed in 335.

In the title of the feast, the Exaltation is termed 'universal'. This is an essential element in the meaning of the festival: the power of the Cross extends to every part of the universe, and the salvation which it brings embraces the entire creation. That is why, in the ceremony of Exaltation, the priest turns in blessing towards each point of the compass: 'The four ends of the earth, O Christ our God, are sanctified today' (troparion at the ceremony of Exaltation).

(iii) *The Entry of the Theotokos into the Temple* (21 November). This feast takes up the story of Mary's infancy from the *Protevangelion* of James, at the point where it was left by the previous feast of Our Lady's Nativity (8 September). When Mary was three years old, Joachim and Ann decided that the time had come to fulfil their promise and to offer her to the Lord. Joachim gathered the young girls of the neighbourhood to form an escort, and he made them go in front of Mary, carrying lighted torches. Captivated by the torches, the young child followed joyfully into the temple, not once looking back at her parents nor weeping as she was parted from them. Such was precisely Joachim's plan: he wished her to go to her new home in gladness, not in sorrow. The High Priest Zacharias—future father of John the Baptist—received her and set her to dwell in the Holy of Holies, where she was fed miraculously by the hand of an angel. In the words of the *Protevangelion*, 'The Lord put grace upon her, and she danced with her feet, and all the house of Israel loved her.' So she remained in the temple until the age of twelve, when Zacharias betrothed her to Joseph.

As with the feast of the birth of the Theotokos, what matters is not the historical exactness of the story but its inner meaning. This account of Mary's Entry into the temple and of her dwelling there signifies her total dedication to God, in readiness for her future vocation as Mother of the Incarnate Lord. At the Annunciation, the Holy Spirit overshadowed her at the word of the angel and she conceived the Saviour; but the Spirit had also dwelt within her from infancy, preparing her in body and soul to be a fitting tabernacle for the Deity—a living Temple, a personal Holy of Holies. Such is basically the spiritual meaning of the feast. Its chief theme is this indwelling grace of the Spirit, present and active within her from her earliest moments. As one of the texts for the day expresses it, speaking not of the Annunciation but of her Entry into the temple: 'All the powers of heaven stood amazed, seeing the Holy Spirit dwell in thee' (Great Vespers, theotokion before the entrance).

Along with Mary's Nativity on 8 September, her Entry into the temple is a feast of anticipation. 'Today is the foreshadowing of the good pleasure of God, and the herald of the salvation of men' (troparion of the feast). As we show honour to Mary 'the child of God', we look forward always to the Incarnation of Christ. We look forward, more specifically, to the feast of Christmas which is to follow in little more than a month; and for this reason some of the Christmas hymns are already sung in advance, during the course of today's canon.

(iv) *The Nativity of Christ* (25 December). The two feasts of Christ's birth and of His baptism are so closely linked together as to form in reality one single and undivided observance. The Church's Year contains accordingly two great moments, two 'poles': the first is Easter; the second, Christmas and Theophany.

Before Christmas, as before Easter, there is a lengthy and elaborate period of preparation. Christmas is preceded by a fast corresponding to Lent and lasting for forty days. On the Sundays immediately before 25 December, there are special commemorations which emphasize the link between the Old

Covenant and the New. The second Sunday before Christmas—the Sunday of the Forefathers—calls to remembrance the ancestors of Christ according to the flesh, whether before or under the Law. The Sunday that follows is still broader in scope, commemorating all the righteous men and women who pleased God from the beginning of time, from the days of Adam the first man down to Joseph, the betrothed of the Mother of God. Approaching Christmas in this way, the worshipper is enabled to see the Incarnation, not as an abrupt and irrational intervention of the divine, but as the culmination of a long process extending over thousands of years. It was the translators' original intention to include the services for these two Sundays in the present volume, for they constitute a marvellous summary of the history of God's people: unfortunately reasons of space rendered this impossible.

The forefeast of Christmas commences on 20 December, and from this point onwards most of the texts are directly concerned with Christ's Nativity. Once more, considerations of space made it necessary to omit all but the last day of the forefeast. On Christmas Eve (24 December)—which is known by the special title *paramoni* (Gk. *παραμονή*; Slavonic, *navechérie*)[1]—the services take an exceptional form. The Hours are unusually long and are termed the Great or Royal Hours, since they were attended in the Byzantine period by the Emperor and court. They are followed by Great Vespers and the Liturgy of St. Basil.

On Christmas Day itself the services commemorate not only the birth of Christ in Bethlehem and the adoration of the shepherds, but also the arrival of the Magi with their gifts of gold, frankincense, and myrrh. The story of the three Wise Men (Matthew 2:1–12), which in the Roman and

[1] This term is applied in particular to the eves of Christmas and Theophany. *Παραμονή*, a watch or vigil, is derived from *παραμένειν*, to wait.

Anglican use is appointed for 6 January, is read in the Byzantine rite on the morning of 25 December.

The familiar and homely elements of the Nativity story—the baby wrapped in swaddling clothes and laid in a manger, the ox and the ass beside Him, the shepherds watching with their flocks by night—are by no means forgotten in the Orthodox hymns for this day. But the main centre of interest lies elsewhere: not in these picturesque details, touching though they may be, not simply in the humanity of the child Jesus, but rather in the paradoxical union of that humanity with the divinity. 'A young child, the pre-eternal God' (kontakion of the feast): this is the supreme and crucial meaning of Christmas. Without ceasing to be what He is from all eternity—true God—One of the Trinity yet became truly and entirely man, born as a baby from a human mother.

It is to this theme, under ceaselessly varying forms, that the liturgical texts of the day continually revert—to the *contrast* between the divine and the human in the one Person of the Incarnate Christ. He who formed the world now Himself 'takes form' as a creature; the Creator makes Himself to be created; 'He who holds the whole creation in the hollow of His hand today is born of the Virgin' (Christmas Eve, Ninth Hour); 'older than ancient Adam', He lies in His mother's arms; the Lord of Glory, who 'looses the tangled cords of sin', is wrapped in swaddling bands; He who is the divine Reason (*Logos*) rests in a manger of beasts without reason (*aloga*); He is fed with milk who gives food to all the universe. Passages such as these are more than a rhetorical *tour de force*: they are intended to make the members of the Church realize, in some small measure, how strange and amazing a thing it is that God should become very man. As the worshipper stands in spirit beside the crib, it is not enough for him to see, lying in the straw, 'gentle Jesus meek and mild'; he must see more than this—

the Son of God, begotten of His Father before all ages, Light from Light, true God from true God.

The days following Christmas are associated with the two who were nearest to God at His Nativity—His mother and His foster-father. 26 December is the Synaxis of the Mother of God, while the first Sunday after Christmas commemorates 'Joseph the Betrothed', along with David, the ancestor of Our Lord, and St. James 'the Brother of God' (Gk. Ἀδελφόθεος).[1] Other events connected with Christ's infancy are remembered on 29 December (the Massacre of the Innocents) and 1 January (the Circumcision of Our Lord). Although the afterfeast of Christmas concludes on 31 December, the spirit of the festival extends until the eve of Theophany, all fasting being suspended in the ten days that follow Christmas.

(v) *Theophany* (6 January). In the eastern tradition this feast celebrates Our Lord's baptism in Jordan, not the adoration of the Magi. The general pattern of services is the same as at Christmas, with a special *paramoni* and the reading of the Royal Hours on 5 January, which is observed as a strict fast. Theophany is marked, however, by a distinctive ceremony, not held at Christmas—the Great Blessing of the Waters. This is performed twice, on 5 January after the Liturgy, and on 6 January at the end of Mattins or (more usually) after the Liturgy. The first blessing is held in church; the second, if possible, in the open air beside a river or spring, or at the sea shore. In countries where the winter is of extreme severity holes are dug in the ice of the frozen rivers. During recent years in England, the Greeks have established the custom of blessing the sea at Margate, with the bishop present and large numbers of the clergy. The culminating moment in this ceremony of blessing occurs

[1] See Mark 6:3, Acts 1:14, etc. 'Brother' is here understood by Orthodox to mean half-brother (perhaps child of Joseph by a previous marriage); or else cousin or other close relative.

when the officiating priest plunges or throws the Cross three times into the water, thus recalling the triple immersion of Christ in the Jordan, as well as the triple immersion which every Orthodox Christian undergoes at his own baptismal initiation. Lest the phrase 'Great Blessing of the Waters' be misunderstood, it should immediately be emphasized that the blessing is effected, not by the officiating priest and the people who are praying with him, but by Christ Himself, who is the true celebrant in this as in all the mysteries of the Church. It is Christ who has blessed the waters once for all at His baptism in the Jordan: the liturgical ceremony of blessing is simply an extension of Christ's original act. This is a point of primary importance, about which more must be said shortly.

The basic meaning of the feast as a whole is summed up in its title *Epiphany*, 'manifestation', or more specifically *Theophany*, 'manifestation of God'. Christ's baptism in the Jordan is a 'manifestation of God' to the world, in the first place because it forms the beginning of Our Lord's public ministry; but secondly, and in a deeper sense, because at this baptism there was granted to the world a revelation of the Holy Trinity. All three Persons were made 'manifest' together: the Father testified from on high to the divine Sonship of Jesus; the Son received His Father's testimony; and the Spirit was seen in the form of a dove, descending from the Father and resting upon the Son. This threefold disclosure is the subject of the troparion of the feast:

> When Thou, O Lord, wast baptized in the Jordan,
> The worship of the Trinity was made manifest.
> For the voice of the Father bore witness unto Thee,
> Calling Thee the beloved Son,
> And the Spirit in the form of a dove
> Confirmed His word as sure and steadfast.
> O Christ our God, who hast appeared and enlightened the world,
> Glory to Thee.

This theme of 'manifestation' or 'revelation' is expressed in particular under the symbolism of light: in the words of the troparion just quoted, Christ has 'appeared and *enlightened* the world'. Thus, besides the title 'Theophany', 6 January is known also as the 'Feast of Lights' (Gk. '*Εορτὴ τῶν Φώτων*). The Church celebrates on this day the illumination of the world by the light of Christ: 'Light from Light, Christ our God has shone upon the world, God made manifest' (Mattins of the feast, first sticheron at Lauds); 'Thou broughtest light to all things by Thine Epiphany' (Mattins of the feast, ypakoë); 'Ye that lie in darkness, leap for joy, for a great light has now appeared to you' (Mattins on 5 January, Canon, Canticle Nine).

Manifestation, illumination—with these two ideas there goes a third: renewal, regeneration, re-creation. Christ's baptism in Jordan renews our nature, for it is the prelude to our baptism in the font; and it renews and regenerates, not our human nature only, but the whole material creation.

To understand this idea of renewal, it is helpful to begin by asking a question which is, in fact, posed repeatedly in the texts for the feast. Why was Christ baptized? We are baptized because we are sinful: we go down dirty into the water, and we emerge cleansed. But what need had Christ, who is sinless, to undergo baptism in the Jordan? To this, the liturgical texts answer: 'Though as God He needs no cleansing, yet for the sake of fallen man He is cleansed in the Jordan' (Mattins of the feast, First Canon, Canticle Five); 'As man He is cleansed that I may be made clean' (Compline on 5 January, Canon, Canticle One). 'For the sake of sinful man': in reality it is not He who is cleansed in the Jordan but we ourselves. In taking manhood upon Him at His Incarnation, Our Lord assumed a representative rôle: He became the New Adam, summing up the whole human race in Himself, just as the first Adam summed up and contained all mankind in himself at the Fall. On the Cross, although sinless, Jesus Christ suffered and died for the sins of all humanity; and in the same way at His baptism, although sinless, He was cleansed for all men's sins. When He went down into the Jordan, as the New Adam He carried us sinful men down with Him: and there in the waters He cleansed us, bearing each of us up once more out of the river as a new creature, regenerate and reconciled.

In Christ's baptism at the hands of John, our own baptismal regeneration is already accomplished by anticipation. The many celebrations of the Eucharist are all a participation in the single and unique Last Supper; and in a similar way all our individual baptisms are a sharing in the baptism of Christ—they are the means whereby the 'grace of Jordan' is extended, so that it may be appropriated by each one of us personally. As an indication of the close connection between Christ's baptism and our baptism, it may be noted that the prayer at the Great Blessing of the Waters on Theophany is almost identical with the prayer of blessing said over the font at the sacrament of baptism.

But Christ's descent into the river has also a further significance. When Christ went down into the waters, not only did He carry us down with Him and make us clean, but He also made clean the nature of the waters themselves. As the troparion of the forefeast puts it, 'Christ has appeared in the Jordan to sanctify the waters'. The feast of Theophany has thus a cosmic aspect. The fall of the angelic orders, and after it the fall of man, involved the whole universe. All God's creation was thereby warped and disfigured: to use the symbolism of the liturgical texts, the waters were made a 'lair of dragons'. Christ came on earth to redeem not only man, but—through man—the entire material creation. When He entered the water, besides effecting by anticipation our rebirth in the font, he likewise effected the cleansing of the waters, their transfiguration into an organ of healing and grace.

If water acts as a means of grace pre-eminently in the sacrament of baptism, it is also used as a means of sanctification on many other occasions as well. That is why Orthodox are encouraged to drink from the water that has been blessed at Epiphany and to sprinkle themselves with it; they take it also to their homes, and keep it there to use from time to time. In all this they are not guilty of superstition. If they act so, it is because they are convinced that in virtue of Christ's Incarnation, of His Baptism and Transfiguration, all material things can be made holy and 'spirit-bearing'. 'At Thine appearing in the body, the earth was sanctified, the waters blessed, the heaven enlightened' (Compline on 5 January, Canon, Canticle Four). This, then, is part of the meaning of Theophany: in the eyes of one who is a Christian, nothing should ever appear trivial or mean, for the redemptive and transforming grace of the Saviour extends to all things, however outwardly despicable.

At Theophany there is the same emphasis as at Christmas upon Christ's self-emptying—upon the contrast between the inward glory which as God He never ceased to possess, and His entire humility as man. God by nature, in His self-abasement He did not refuse baptism from John: 'As a servant Thou dost bow Thy head beneath the hand of the servant' (Compline on 5 January, Canon, Canticle One); 'One of the Trinity bowed His head and received baptism' (Mattins of the feast, First Canon, Canticle Nine). To emphasize the point more vividly, constant references are made to the bewilderment and hesitation of the Baptist: 'The Forerunner was seized with trembling and cried aloud, saying: "How shall the lamp illuminate the Light? How shall the servant set his hand upon the Master? O Saviour, who takest away the sin of the world, sanctify both me and the waters"' (Blessing of the Waters). This theme is specially developed on the day following the feast, which is observed as the Synaxis of St. John the Baptist.

(vi) *The Meeting of Our Lord* (2 February). This festival, known in the west as the Presentation of Christ in the Temple or the Purification of the Blessed Virgin Mary, in the east bears the title 'Meeting' (Gk. '*Υπαπαντή*; Slavonic, *Srétenie*)—the meeting, that is, of Christ with His people. Our Lord, brought to the temple by His mother and by Joseph, now meets His chosen people in the persons of Simeon the Elder and Ann the Prophetess. This feast forms the conclusion of the Nativity sequence, which opened some eighty days earlier with the beginning of the Christmas fast.

At the Meeting, as at Christmas and Theophany, the Church thinks about the *kenosis*, the deep self-emptying of the Incarnate Word. He who is Giver of the Law is Himself obedient to the Law: 'Today He who once gave the Law to Moses on Sinai submits Himself to the ordinances of the Law, in His compassion becoming for our sakes as we are' (Vespers, Lity). The texts for this day are based for the most part upon Simeon's Song, *Nunc Dimittis*: they speak of the salvation that Christ has come to confer, of the glory and light of revelation that have been granted through His Incarnation.

(vii) *The Annunciation* (25 March). 'The Incarnation', it has been rightly said, 'was not only the work of the Father, of His Power and His Spirit: it was also the work of the will and the faith of the Virgin.'[1] On the feast of the Annunciation, therefore, Orthodoxy commemorates not only the divine initiative, whereby God in His lovingkindness took flesh from a Virgin; it commemorates also the human response, whereby Mary freely accepted the vocation set before her. God always respects human liberty; and so, when He elected to become man, He desired to do so with the willing agreement of her whom He chose as His mother. 'Behold the handmaid of the Lord; be it unto me according

[1] Nicolas Cabasilas, *On the Annunciation*, 4 (*Patrologia Orientalis*, XIX, Paris, 1926, p. 488).

to thy word' (Luke 1:38): Mary's answer to the angel was not a foregone conclusion. She could have refused: she was not a passive instrument but an active participant, with a free and positive part to play in God's scheme of salvation.

To make abundantly clear the voluntary character of her choice, the Canon for the Annunciation takes the form of a dialogue between the Virgin and Gabriel. Mary's doubts are set forth with the utmost directness, we see all her incredulity and her embarrassment; and this is done in order to make clear that she acted in full freedom, consciously and deliberately accepting the will of God. When, on this and other feasts, the Orthodox Church shows honour to the Mother of God, it is not just because God chose her but also because she herself chose aright.

(viii) *The Transfiguration* (6 August). This is a feast that enjoys far greater prominence in Orthodoxy than in western Christendom. In the Roman rite, the Transfiguration is merely a 'double of the second class', while the Anglican Prayer Book of 1662 does not even provide a special Collect, Epistle, or Gospel for this day.[1] But in the Orthodox tradition 6 August is reckoned as one of the Twelve Great Feasts, of such importance that it supplants the Sunday office entirely.

The Transfiguration is *par excellence* the feast of Christ's divine glory. Like Theophany, it is a feast of light: 'Today on Tabor in the manifestation of Thy Light, O Word, Thou unaltered Light from the Light of the unbegotten Father, we have seen the Father as Light and the Spirit as Light, guiding with light the whole creation' (exapostilarion). Nor is this the only parallel between the two feasts. Like Theophany,

[1] This omission has been rectified in the 1928 Book, as also in the revisions of the Book of Common Prayer used in many parts of the Anglican Communion overseas. One of the best studies in English on the Transfiguration is in fact from the pen of an Anglican: A. M. Ramsey (Archbishop of Canterbury), *The Glory of God and the Transfiguration of Christ* (London, 1949).

although less explicitly, the Transfiguration is a revelation of the Holy Trinity. On Tabor, as at the baptism in Jordan, the Father speaks from heaven, testifying to the divine Sonship of Christ: and the Spirit is also present, on this occasion not in the likeness of a dove, but under the form of dazzling light, surrounding Christ's person and overshadowing the whole mountain. This dazzling light is the light of the Spirit.[1]

The Transfiguration, then, is a feast of divine glory—more specifically, of the glory of the Resurrection. The ascent of Mount Tabor came at a critical point in Our Lord's ministry, just as He was setting out upon His last journey to Jerusalem, which He knew was to end in humiliation and death. To strengthen His disciples for the trials that lay ahead, He chose this particular moment to reveal to them something of His eternal splendour, 'as far as they were able to bear it' (troparion of the feast). He encouraged them—and all of us—to look beyond the suffering of the Cross to the glory of the Resurrection.

The light of the Transfiguration, however, foreshadows not only Christ's own Resurrection on the third day, but equally the Resurrection glory of the righteous at His Second Coming. The glory which shone from Jesus on Tabor is a glory in which all mankind is called to share. On Mount Tabor we see Christ's human nature— the human substance which He took from us—filled with splendour, 'made godlike' or 'deified'. What has happened to human nature in Christ can happen also to the humanity of Christ's followers. The Transfiguration, then, reveals to us the full potentiality of our human nature: it shows us the glory which our manhood once possessed and the glory which, by God's grace, it will again recover at the Last Day.

This is a cardinal aspect of the present feast, to which the

[1] See Mattins, Second Canon, Canticle Six, third troparion.

liturgical texts frequently revert. At His Transfiguration, it is said, the Lord 'in His own person showed them the nature of man, arrayed in the original beauty of the Image' (Great Vespers, aposticha). 'Today Christ on Mount Tabor has changed the darkened nature of Adam, and filling it with brightness He has made it godlike' (Small Vespers, aposticha). 'Thou wast transfigured upon Mount Tabor, showing the exchange mortal men will make with Thy glory at Thy second and fearful coming, O Saviour' (Mattins, sessional hymn).

The feast of the Transfiguration, therefore, is not simply the commemoration of a past event in the life of Christ. Possessing also an 'eschatological' dimension, it is turned towards the future—towards the 'splendour of the Resurrection' at the Last Day, towards the 'beauty of the divine Kingdom' which all Christians hope eventually to enjoy.

(ix) *The Dormition of the Theotokos* (15 August). Although the western title of this feast—the 'Assumption' —is sometimes employed by Orthodox, in the service books it is simply designated 'Falling Asleep' or 'Dormition' (Gk. *Κοίμησις*; Slavonic, *Ouspénie*).

As with the Nativity (8 September) and the Entry of the Mother of God (21 November), the texts for 15 August are based primarily on non-Biblical material.[1] At the time of her death, so it is believed, the Mother of God was living in the house of St. John on Mount Zion. The Twelve were preaching the Gospel in different parts of the world; but so that they might see the Virgin once again before her death, all of them except Thomas were carried miraculously on clouds to the Holy City. Besides the Twelve, the Apostle Paul, together

[1] For an analysis of the early tradition concerning the death and assumption of the Blessed Virgin Mary, see P. Voulet, S.J., *S. Jean Damascène : Homélies sur la Nativité et la Dormition* (*Sources Chrétiennes*, 80: Paris, 1961), pp. 24–36.

with the bishops Dionysios the Areopagite, Hierotheos, and Timothy, were also present at her bedside. As they stood round her, the Holy Virgin commended her spirit into the keeping of her Son and God: and He Himself descended from heaven and took her soul up with Him in His arms.[1] Led by Peter, the apostles sang funeral hymns in her honour, and carried her body down to the valley of Cedron, close to Gethsemane, where she was laid in a tomb specially prepared for her. The Jews tried to interrupt the funeral procession, one of them even attempting to upset the bier: his hands were cut off by an angel, but he was subsequently healed. Thomas arrived on the third day after the burial. Since he was anxious to look for a last time on the Theotokos, the apostles opened the tomb—and found it empty.

Without insisting on the literal truth of every element in this account, Orthodox tradition is clear and unwavering in regard to the central point: the Holy Virgin underwent, as did her Son, a physical death, but her body—like His—was afterwards raised from the dead and she was taken up into heaven, in her body as well as in her soul. She has passed beyond death and judgement, and lives wholly in the Age to Come. The Resurrection of the Body, which all Christians await, has in her case been anticipated and is already an accomplished fact. That does not mean, however, that she is dissociated from the rest of humanity and placed in a wholly different category: for we all hope to share one day in that same glory of the Resurrection of the Body which she enjoys even now.

Indeed, so far from being separated, Our Lady remains always most intimately linked to mankind—linked through her urgent and unceasing intercession on our behalf. 'Lady, behold thy Son . . . Behold thy mother' (John 19:26–27).

[1] In icons of the Dormition Christ is seen standing above the bier, while Mary's soul rests in His arms, in appearance like a small child wrapped in white.

The Church has long seen, in these words of Our Lord from the Cross, the giving to Mary of a universal motherhood: she is mother not to John only, but to all the children of God. Dwelling in heaven with Jesus, her care as mother remains undiminished, and embraces the universe: 'In giving birth, O Theotokos, thou hast retained thy virginity, and in falling asleep thou hast not forsaken the world' (troparion of the feast). In heaven, as on earth, the Mother of God continues 'ever watchful in her prayers, and in her intercession lies unfailing hope' (kontakion of the feast).

The preceding pages have indicated only a very small part of the rich and many sided teachings to be found in the liturgical texts for the Great Feasts. These texts are not to be approached simply as pieces of 'devotional' poetry, designed to move and edify the worshipper. They are, on the contrary, intensely *theological*—a primary and essential source for any understanding of the faith. No real insight into Orthodox theology is possible without a proper knowledge of Orthodox worship. It is no coincidence that the very word 'Orthodoxy' should mean not only 'right belief' but 'right praise' or 'glory'. The core of Orthodox tradition is to be found in the service books: *lex orandi lex est credendi*—we express our faith in our prayers. In 1950, when Pope Pius XII proclaimed the dogma of the Bodily Assumption of Our Lady, members of the Roman Catholic hierarchy in France approached Metropolitan Vladimir, Russian Exarch in Western Europe for the Ecumenical Patriarchate, inquiring what the belief of the Orthodox might be on this matter. In answer the Metropolitan urged them to read the Orthodox office of the Dormition, used on 15 August; and he said that he had nothing to add to what was written there.

Those unfamiliar with Orthodox worship may at first be surprised at the large amount of repetition that occurs in the services. They will find that things are appointed to be said or sung three or more times, while throughout the canons and other hymns the same basic ideas, in varying images and terminology, are repeated again and again. This constant reiteration, so far from indicating poverty of thought or a liturgical garrulousness, is designed to serve a definite purpose. Orthodoxy makes little or no use of that form of spiritual recollection known in the west as 'meditation', when a period of time is set aside each day for systematic thought upon some chosen theme. Its place is taken in the Orthodox Church by corporate liturgical worship. As an Orthodox Christian stands in church, hour by hour, during the vigil of some Great Feast or at the services on an ordinary day, he hears the same necessary and saving truths continually underlined, now in one way and now in another. In this fashion the theological significance of the different mysteries of the faith is deeply and indelibly impressed upon his mind, becoming almost second nature; and if he prays with attention during his time of corporate worship, he has no need for a special period of discursive meditation to emphasize their meaning still more. The words that are read and sung in church are by themselves sufficient to provide him with abundant nourishment for his life in Christ.

In the true Orthodox tradition there is no divorce between theology and worship, between private meditation and public prayer. All genuine worship, while embracing the emotions, must also be reflective, intelligent, and essentially theological; for, as the Fathers expressed it, we are the 'logical sheep' of Christ. And at the same time all genuine theology must be a living theology—not an abstract exercise of the reasoning powers, but a vision of God's kingdom, attained first and foremost through liturgical celebration.

Such is the viewpoint from which the texts in this present volume must be understood.

(iv) Plans of the Services

Variable parts of the service (i.e., which change according to the feast or commemoration of the day, or according to the tone of the week) are printed in capital letters.

A. *Great Vespers at a vigil*	B. *Great Vespers not at a vigil*[1]
Blessing by priest: *Glory to the holy, consubstantial, life-giving, and undivided Trinity*	Blessing by priest: *Blessed is our* (
Psalm of Introduction (Psalm 103)	Psalm of Introduction (Psalm 103)
Great Litany	Great Litany
Reading from the Psalter[5] Small Litany	Reading from the Psalter[5] Small Litany
Lord, I have cried, with STICHERA	*Lord, I have cried*, with STICHER
Entrance *O joyful light*	Entrance *O joyful light*
1. PROKIMENON 2. LESSONS from the Old Testament[6]	1. PROKIMENON 2. LESSONS from the Old Test
Litany of Fervent Intercession, *Let us all say, with all our soul*	Litany of Fervent Intercession, *Let us all say, with all our soul*
Vouchsafe, O Lord	*Vouchsafe, O Lord*
Litany of Fervent Intercession, *Let us complete our evening prayer to the Lord*	Litany of Fervent Intercession, *Let us complete our evening praye Lord*
Lity, with STICHERA Litany, *O Lord, save Thy people*[6]	Lity, with STICHERA Litany, *O Lord, save Thy people*[6]

ily Vespers on ordinary s	D. *Small Vespers before a vigil*[2]	E. *Great Vespers followed by the Liturgy*[3]
ssing by priest: *ssed is our God*[4]	Blessing by priest: *Blessed is our God*	1. Blessing by priest: *Blessed is the Kingdom* 2. *O heavenly King* 3. Trisagion, etc., and Lord's Prayer
lm of Introduction alm 103)	Psalm of Introduction (Psalm 103) *Kyrie eleison* (3 times) *Glory be to the Father . . .* *Both now . . .*	Psalm of Introduction (Psalm 103)
eat Litany		Great Litany
ading from the Psalter[5] all Litany		
d, *I have cried*, with CHERA	*Lord, I have cried*, with STICHERA	*Lord, I have cried*, with STICHERA
oyful light	*O joyful light*	Entrance with Book of Gospels *O joyful light*
OKIMENON	PROKIMENON	1. PROKIMENON 2. LESSONS from the Old Testament
		Small Litany[7]
chsafe, O Lord	*Vouchsafe, O Lord*	
any of Fervent Intercession, *Let us complete evening prayer to the d*		

A. *Great Vespers at a vigil*	B. *Great Vespers not at a vigil*
APOSTICHA	APOSTICHA
Song of Simeon Trisagion, etc., and Lord's Prayer	Song of Simeon Trisagion, etc., and Lord's Prayer
APOLYTIKION	APOLYTIKION
Blessing of Bread[8]	Blessing of Bread[8]
Conclusion of the service: 1. Psalm 33:1–10 2. Blessing by priest	Conclusion of the service: 1. Blessing by priest 2. Prayer for Orthodox Christians 3. Dismissal by priest

NOTES

[1] In the Greek practice, Great Vespers are often celebrated on their own; according to the normal Russian rules, Great Vespers always form part of a vigil. In the Greek practice, there is sometimes a Lity at Great Vespers, even though there is no vigil; but according to the normal Russian rules, a Lity occurs only at a vigil.

[2] i.e. when Great Vespers are to be sung later in the evening, as part of the vigil.

[3] i.e. on the eves of Christmas and Theophany, except when these feasts fall on Sunday or Monday; also on the feast of the Annunciation (25 March), except when this is a Saturday or Sunday.

Daily Vespers on ordinary days	D. *Small Vespers before a vigil*	E. *Great Vespers followed by the Liturgy*
APOSTICHA	APOSTICHA	
Song of Simeon Trisagion, etc., and Lord's Prayer	Song of Simeon Trisagion, etc., and Lord's Prayer	
APOLYTIKION THEOTOKION	APOLYTIKION	
Litany of Fervent Intercession, *Have mercy upon us, O God*	Litany, *Have mercy upon us, O God*[9]	
Conclusion of the service: 1. Blessing by priest 2. Prayer for Orthodox Christians 3. Dismissal by priest	Conclusion of the service: Dismissal by priest	

[4] If the Ninth Hour is read immediately before Vespers, we begin as specified above in the chart. Otherwise, we begin as follows:

1. Blessing by priest: *Blessed is our God*
2. *O heavenly King*
3. Trisagion, etc., and Lord's Prayer

Kyrie eleison (12 times)
O come, let us worship. . . .

And then the Psalm of Introduction.

[5] On certain days there is no reading from the Psalter, in which case the Small Litany is also omitted. At Great Vespers, if there is a reading from the Psalter, it is always *Blessed is the man . . .* (the first kathisma; sometimes only the first portion of the first kathisma).

[6] On certain days only.

[7] After this we continue as in the Liturgy of St. Basil or St. John Chrysostom, as the case may be: trisagion, prokimenon, epistle, etc.

[8] On days when there is a Lity.

[9] As at the beginning of Mattins: type C, opening section, §5.

COMPLINE

A. Great Compline

I. 1. Blessing by priest: *Blessed is our God.*
   2. *O heavenly King.*
   3. Trisagion, etc., and Lord's Prayer.

II. *First Part*
   1. Reading from the Psalter: Psalms 4, 6, 12.
      Psalms 24, 30, 90.
      God is with us.
      Three troparia, beginning *Now that I have passed through the day.*
      Hymn to the angels and saints, *The bodiless powers of the cherubim.*
      Nicene Creed.
      Hymn to the saints, *O all-holy Lady Theotokos.*
   2. Trisagion, etc., and Lord's Prayer.
   3. TROPARION of the feast or TROPARIA of the day.
   4. Prayer.

III. *Second Part*
   1. Reading from the Psalter: Psalms 50, 101.
      The Prayer of Manasses.
   2. Trisagion, etc., and Lord's Prayer.
   3. KONTAKION of the feast or appointed TROPARIA.
   4. Prayer.

IV. *Third Part*
   1. Reading from the Psalter: Psalms 69, 142.
      Small Doxology.[1]
   2. Trisagion, etc., and Lord's Prayer.

[1] On the eve of Great Feasts, here follows the Lity. The remainder of Great Compline is not said, but the service concludes as at Vespers.

3. Troparion *Lord of Hosts*, with Psalm 150.
   Other troparia.
4. Prayer of the Hours.

V. *Conclusion of the service*
1. Prayer to the Holy Virgin.
   Evening Prayer to Christ.
   Prayer to the Holy Trinity.
2. Dismissal by priest.
3. Mutual forgiveness.
4. Final Litany, *Let us pray for the peace of the world.*

B. Small Compline

I. 1. Blessing by priest: *Blessed is our God.*
2. *O heavenly King.*
3. Trisagion, etc., and Lord's Prayer.

II. Reading from the Psalter: Psalms 50, 69, 142.
Small Doxology.
Nicene Creed.
CANON of the Theotokos or CANON appointed for the day.
It is meet.

III. Trisagion, etc., and Lord's Prayer.

IV. KONTAKION of the feast or TROPARION of the day, etc.

V. Prayer of the Hours.

VI. Conclusion of the service.
1. Prayer to the Holy Virgin.
   Evening Prayer to Christ.
   Prayer to the Holy Trinity.
2. Dismissal by priest.
3. Mutual forgiveness.
4. Final Litany, *Let us pray for the peace of the world.*

ORTHODOX SERVICES AND THEIR STRUCTURE

MIDNIGHT OFFICE

I. 1. Blessing by priest: *Blessed is our God.*
   2. *O heavenly King.*
   3. Trisagion, etc., and Lord's Prayer.

II. *First Part*
   1. Reading from the Psalter: Psalm 50.
      On weekdays: Psalm 118 (kathisma 17).
      On Saturday: Psalms 64–69.
      On Sunday: CANON and troparia to the Holy Trinity.
   Nicene Creed.[1]
   2. Trisagion, etc., and Lord's Prayer.
   On Sunday, the YPAKOË.[2]
   3. Troparia.[1]
   4. Prayer of the Hours.[1]
   Other prayers.[1]

III. *Second Part*[1]
   1. Reading from the Psalter: Psalms 120, 133.
   2. Trisagion, etc., and Lord's Prayer.
   3. Troparia.
   4. Prayers.

IV. *Conclusion of the service*
   1. Dismissal by priest.
   2. Mutual forgiveness.
   3. Final Litany, *Let us pray for the peace of the world.*

[1] Omitted on Sunday.

[2] On Sundays, after the ypakoë there follows *Kyrie eleison* (40 times); *Glory be to the Father . . . Both now . . .; Greater in honour than the cherubim . . .; In the Name of the Lord, give the blessing, Father;* Priest, *God be merciful unto us . . .;* prayer to the Holy Trinity; and then the conclusion of the service as in Section IV.

PLANS OF THE SERVICES

MATTINS

A. *Mattins at a vigil on a feast*[1]	B. *Mattins at a vigil on Sunday*[1]	C. *Mattins on an ordinary day (not at a vigil)*
		Opening of the service: 1. Blessing by the priest: *Blessed is our God* 2. Psalms 19 and 20 3. Trisagion, etc., and Lord's Prayer 4. Troparia 5. Litany, *Have mercy upon us, O God* 6. Blessing by the priest: *Glory to the holy, consubstantial, life-giving, and undivided Trinity*
The Six Psalms	The Six Psalms	The Six Psalms
Great Litany *The Lord is God*, and the TROPARION of the feast (3 times)	Great Litany *The Lord is God*, and the appointed TROPARIA	Great Litany *The Lord is God*, and the appointed TROPARIA
Reading from the Psalter: 1. First reading Small Litany SESSIONAL HYMN 2. Second reading Small Litany SESSIONAL HYMN 3. Polyeleos MEGALYNARION[3] Small Litany SESSIONAL HYMN 4. Hymn of degrees: first antiphon in Tone Four	Reading from the Psalter: 1. First reading Small Litany SESSIONAL HYMN 2. Second reading Small Litany SESSIONAL HYMN 3. Psalm 118 or polyeleos Evlogitaria of the Resurrection Small Litany YPAKOË 4. HYMN OF DEGREES in tone of the week	Reading from the Psalter: 1. First reading SESSIONAL HYMN 2. Second reading SESSIONAL HYMN 3. Third reading[2] SESSIONAL HYMN
1. PROKIMENON 2. *Let everything that hath breath* 3. GOSPEL	1. PROKIMENON 2. *Let everything that hath breath* 3. GOSPEL 4. *We have seen the Resurrection of Christ*	
Psalm 50 TROPARIA	Psalm 50 TROPARIA	Psalm 50

A. *Mattins at a vigil on a feast*[1]	B. *Mattins at a vigil on Sunday*[1]	C. *Mattins on an ordinary day (not at a vigil)*
Litany, *O Lord, save Thy people*	Litany, *O Lord, save Thy people*	
The CANON: 1. Canticles One and Three Small Litany YPAKOË or SESSIONAL HYMN 2. Canticles Four, Five, and Six Small Litany KONTAKION and IKOS SYNAXARION[4] 3. Canticles Seven, Eight, and Nine Small Litany EXAPOSTILARION	The CANON: 1. Canticles One and Three Small Litany SESSIONAL HYMN 2. Canticles Four, Five, and Six Small Litany KONTAKION and IKOS SYNAXARION[4] 3. Canticles Seven, Eight, and Nine Small Litany *Holy is the Lord our God* EXAPOSTILARION	The CANON: 1. Canticles One and Three Small Litany SESSIONAL HYMN 2. Canticles Four, Five, and Six Small Litany KONTAKION and IKOS SYNAXARION[4] 3. Canticles Seven, Eight, and Nine Small Litany EXAPOSTILARION
Lauds, with STICHERA	Lauds, with STICHERA	Lauds
Great Doxology TROPARION of the feast	Great Doxology TROPARION according to the tone of the week	Small Doxology
Litany of Fervent Intercession: 1. *Have mercy upon us, O God* 2. *Let us complete our morning prayer to the Lord*	Litany of Fervent Intercession: 1. *Have mercy upon us, O God* 2. *Let us complete our morning prayer to the Lord*	Litany of Fervent Intercession: *Let us complete our morning prayer to the Lord*
		APOSTICHA Trisagion, etc., and Lord's Prayer TROPARION of the day THEOTOKION Litany of Fervent Intercession, *Have mercy upon us, O God*
Conclusion of the service: 1. Blessing by priest 2. Prayer for Orthodox Christians 3. Dismissal by priest	Conclusion of the service: 1. Blessing by priest 2. Prayer for Orthodox Christians 3. Dismissal by priest	Conclusion of the service: 1. Blessing by priest 2. Prayer for Orthodox Christians 3. Dismissal by priest[5]

1 If there is no vigil, Mattins begins as in C.

2 Sometimes there are only two readings from the Psalter (see p. 534).

3 In the Slav use only.

4 In the Greek use (see p. 558).

5 The dismissal is omitted if the First Hour follows immediately after Mattins.

PLANS OF THE SERVICES

HOURS

A. On Ordinary Days

I. 1. Blessing by priest: *Blessed is our God.*
  2. *O heavenly King.*
  3. Trisagion, etc., and Lord's Prayer.[1]

II. Reading from the Psalter. *O come, let us worship . . .*
  First Hour: Psalms 5, 89, 100.
  Third Hour: Psalms 16, 24, 50.
  Sixth Hour: Psalms 53, 54, 90.
  Ninth Hour: Psalms 83, 84, 85.

III. 1. TROPARION of the day.
  2. Theotokion.
  3. Verses from Scripture.

IV. Trisagion, etc., and Lord's Prayer.

V. KONTAKION of the day.

VI. Prayer of the Hours.

VII. Dismissal by priest and final prayer.

B. The Royal Hours on the eves of Christmas and Theophany

I. (as in A).

II. Reading from the Psalter.[2]

III. 1. TROPARION of the day.

[1] I. 1–3 are omitted, if the Hour in question follows immediately on a previous office: e.g. when the First Hour is read after Mattins, or the Sixth Hour is read after the Third.

[2] In each Royal Hour, two of the Psalms are different from those read normally at the Hours, but one Psalm remains the same (Psalms 5, 50, 90, and 85 respectively).

2. Theotokion.
3. STICHERA of the feast, with verses from Scripture.
4. Scriptural readings:
   PROKIMENON
   LESSON from the Old Testament
   EPISTLE
   GOSPEL
5. Verses from Scripture.

IV–VII. (as in A).

TYPIKA

I. Psalms 102 and 145.
O Only-begotten Son and Word of God.

II. The Beatitudes.
Troparia and verses.
Nicene Creed.[1]
Prayer for forgiveness.

III. Lord's Prayer.

IV. KONTAKION of the feast or TROPARION of the day, etc.

V. Prayer to the Holy Trinity.
Blessed be the Name of the Lord.[1]
Psalm 33.[1]
It is meet.
Dismissal by priest.

DIVINE LITURGY

I. *PREPARATION*
1. Vesting of the ministers.

[1] If the Liturgy is to be celebrated later, this is omitted.

2. Preparation of the Holy Gifts (Prothesis or Proskomidia).

II. *LITURGY OF THE CATECHUMENS*

A. Opening of the service (Enarxis):
1. Blessing by priest.
2. Great Litany.
3. First ANTIPHON or first Psalm of the Typika (Psalm 102).
   Small Litany.
4. Second ANTIPHON or second Psalm of the Typika (Psalm 145).
   O Only-begotten Son and Word of God.
   Small Litany.
5. Third ANTIPHON with TROPARION of the feast; or the Beatitudes with the appointed TROPARIA.

B. Small Entrance.
Introit, *O come, let us worship.*
(On certain days only: special INTROIT).

C. TROPARIA and KONTAKIA of the day.

D. Trisagion.

E. Readings from Scripture:
1. PROKIMENON.
2. EPISTLE.
3. Alleluia, with the appointed VERSES.
4. GOSPEL.

F. Prayer for the Church:
1. Litany of Fervent Intercession, *Let us all say, with all our soul.*
2. Litany for the catechumens; dismissal of the catechumens.

III. *LITURGY OF THE FAITHFUL*

A. Two Litanies for the faithful.

B. Great Entrance, before and after which is sung the Hymn of the Cherubim.

C. Litany of Fervent Intercession, *Let us complete our prayer to the Lord.*

D. Kiss of Peace.

E. Nicene Creed.

F. Eucharistic Prayer (Anaphora):
   1. Opening dialogue between priest and people (or choir).
   2. Eucharistic Prayer, with responses by people (or choir):
      Thanksgiving
      Anamnesis
      Epiclesis
   3. Intercession for the Church, and singing of *It is meet*, or of the HYMN to the Holy Virgin appointed for the day.
   4. Conclusion of the Eucharistic Prayer, and blessing by priest.

G. Litany, *Having commemorated all the saints.*

H. Lord's Prayer.

I. Elevation and fraction of the Consecrated Gifts; the choir sings the COMMUNION VERSE.

J. Communion:
   1. Communion of clergy.
   2. Communion of people; hymn to the Holy Trinity; and hymn *Let our mouth be filled with Thy praise.*
   3. Litany of thanksgiving.

K. Conclusion of the service:
   1. Prayer behind the ambon.
   2. Final blessing and dismissal.
   3. Distribution of antidoron; reading of Psalm 33:11–22.

THE COMMON OF THE VIGIL

Great Vespers

Priest: Glory to the holy, consubstantial, life-giving, and undivided Trinity, always, now, and ever, and unto the ages of ages.

Choir: Amen.

Priest: O come, let us worship God our King.
O come, let us worship and fall down before Christ our King and our God.
O come, let us worship and fall down before Christ Himself, our King and our God.

Psalm of Introduction (Psalm 103). This is usually sung in the shortened form:[1]

Bless the Lord, O my soul:
Blessed art Thou, O Lord.
Bless the Lord, O my soul:
O Lord my God, Thou art very great:
Thou art clothed with honour and majesty.
The waters stand above the mountains.
O Lord, how marvellous are Thy works:
In wisdom hast Thou made them all.
Glory to Thee, O Lord, who hast made them all.
Glory be to the Father . . . Both now . . .
Alleluia, alleluia, alleluia, glory be to Thee, O God (*3 times*).

Great Litany: In peace let us pray to the Lord . . .

[1] Slav use.

Reading from the Psalter. The first kathisma is usually sung in the shortened form:[1]

Blessed is the man that hath not walked in the counsel of the ungodly: alleluia, alleluia, alleluia.

For the Lord knoweth the way of the righteous, and the way of the ungodly shall perish: alleluia, alleluia, alleluia.

Serve the Lord with fear and rejoice in Him with trembling: alleluia, alleluia, alleluia.

Blessed are all they that put their trust in Him: alleluia, alleluia, alleluia.

Arise, O Lord; save me, O my God: alleluia, alleluia, alleluia.

Salvation belongeth unto the Lord; Thy blessing is upon Thy people: allelulia, allelulia, alleluia.

Glory be to the Father, and to the Son, and to the Holy Spirit: both now, and ever, and unto the ages of ages. Amen.

Alleluia, alleluia, alleluia, glory be to Thee, O God (*3 times*).

Glory be to Thee, O God.

Small Litany: Again and again in peace let us pray to the Lord . . .

Lord, I have cried (*Psalms 140, 141, 129, 116*) *in the appointed tone. This is usually sung in the shortened form:*

Lord, I have cried unto Thee, hear me: hear me, O Lord. Lord, I have cried unto Thee, hear me: give ear to the voice of my prayer when I cry unto Thee. Hear me, O Lord.

Let my prayer be set forth in Thy sight as incense: and let the lifting up of my hands be an evening sacrifice. Hear me, O Lord.

If there are ten stichera:

Bring my soul out of prison, that I may praise Thy Name.

The righteous shall compass me about, until Thou recompense me.

[1] Slav use.

If there are eight stichera:

Out of the depths have I cried unto Thee, O Lord: Lord, hear my voice.

Let Thine ears be attentive to the voice of my supplication.

If Thou, Lord, shouldest mark iniquities, O Lord, who shall stand? But there is forgiveness with Thee.

For Thy Name's sake have I waited for Thee, O Lord: my soul hath waited for Thy word, my soul hath hoped in the Lord.

From the morning watch until the night, from the morning watch let Israel trust in the Lord.

For with the Lord there is mercy, and with Him is plenteous redemption: and He shall redeem Israel from all his iniquities.

O praise the Lord, all ye nations: praise Him, all ye people.

For His merciful kindness is great towards us: and the truth of the Lord endureth for ever.

Glory be to the Father . . . Both now . . .

On Saturday evenings, except when it is a Great Feast, here follows the dogmatikon in the tone of the week.

Entry. Deacon: Wisdom. Let us attend.

Evening Hymn:

O joyful light of the holy glory of the immortal Father, heavenly, holy, blessed, Jesus Christ: now that we are come to the setting of the sun and behold the evening light, we sing in praise to God the Father, Son, and Holy Spirit. It is meet at all times to praise Thee in hymns with happy voice, O Son of God who grantest life: therefore the world gives Thee glory.

Prokimenon according to the day of the week. On Saturday evening (Psalm 92):

TONE SIX

Deacon: The Lord is King, and hath put on glorious apparel.

This is repeated by the Choir.

℣ 1. *Deacon:* The Lord hath put on His apparel and girded Himself with strength.

Choir: The Lord is King, and hath put on glorious apparel.

℣ 2. *Deacon:* He hath made the world so sure that it cannot be moved.

Choir: The Lord is King, and hath put on glorious apparel.

℣ 3. *Deacon:* Holiness becometh Thine house, O Lord, for ever.

Choir: The Lord is King, and hath put on glorious apparel.

Deacon: The Lord is King,

Choir: And hath put on glorious apparel.

On Sunday evening (Psalm 133):

TONE EIGHT

Behold now, bless the Lord, all ye servants of the Lord.

℣. Ye that stand in the house of the Lord, in the courts of the house of our God.

On Monday evening (Psalm 4):

TONE FOUR

The Lord will hear me when I cry unto Him.

℣. Thou hast heard me when I called, O God of my righteousness, Thou hast set me at liberty when I was in trouble.

On Tuesday evening (Psalm 22):

TONE ONE

Thy mercy, O Lord, shall follow me all the days of my life.

℣. The Lord is my shepherd, therefore shall I lack nothing: He hath made me to lie down in green pastures.

On Wednesday evening (Psalm 53):

TONE FIVE

Save me, O God, for Thy Name's sake, and judge me by Thy might.

℣. Hear my prayer, O God, and hearken unto the words of my mouth.

On Thursday evening (Psalm 120):

TONE SIX

My help cometh even from the Lord, who hath made heaven and earth.

℣. I lifted up mine eyes unto the hills, from whence my help shall come.

On Friday evening (Psalm 58):

TONE SEVEN

Thou art my Defender, O God, and Thy mercy shall go before me.

℣. Deliver me from mine enemies, O God, and ransom me from those that rise up against me.

On Great Feasts and on certain lesser feasts, Lessons from the Old Testament are now read.

Litany: Let us all say, with all our soul . . .

Evening Prayer. The Reader:

Vouchsafe, O Lord, to keep us this evening without sin. Blessed art Thou, O Lord God of our fathers, and praised and glorified is Thy Name for evermore. Amen.

O Lord, let Thy mercy lighten upon us, as our trust is in Thee.

Blessed art Thou, O Lord: teach me Thy statutes.

Blessed art Thou, O Master: make me to understand Thy statutes.

Blessed art Thou, O Holy One: enlighten me with Thy statutes.

O Lord, Thy mercy is for ever: despise not the works of Thine hands. Unto Thee is due praise, unto Thee is due song, unto Thee is due glory, to the Father, and to the Son, and to the Holy Spirit, now, and ever, and unto the ages of ages. Amen.

Litany: Let us complete our evening prayer to the Lord . . .

On Great Feasts and on certain lesser feasts, here follows the Lity.

The Aposticha.

The Song of Simeon (Luke 2:29–32). Reader or Choir:

Lord, now lettest Thou Thy servant depart in peace, according to Thy word: for mine eyes have seen Thy salvation, which Thou hast prepared before the face of all people: a light to lighten the Gentiles, and the glory of Thy people Israel.

The Reader continues:

Holy God, Holy and Mighty, Holy and Immortal, have mercy upon us (*3 times*).

Glory be to the Father . . . Both now . . .

Most Holy Trinity, have mercy upon us.

O Lord, cleanse our sins.

O Master, forgive our transgressions.

O Holy One, visit and heal our infirmities, for Thy Name's sake.

Kyrie eleison, Kyrie eleison, Kyrie eleison.

Glory be to the Father . . . Both now . . .

The Lord's Prayer: Our Father . . .

Priest: For Thine is the kingdom, the power, and the glory, of the Father, and of the Son, and of the Holy Spirit, now, and ever, and unto the ages of ages. Amen.

Apolytikion. On Saturdays,[1] *the following hymn to the Mother of God:*

Hail, Theotokos Virgin, Mary full of grace, the Lord is with thee. Blessed art thou among women, and blessed is the fruit of thy womb: for thou hast borne the Saviour of our souls (*3 times*).

If it is a Great Feast of Our Lord or of the Mother of God, the troparion of the Feast (3 times).

On other feasts, the troparion of the Feast twice, and then once, Hail, Theotokos Virgin, Mary full of grace . . .[1]

If there is a Lity, the Blessing of the Bread now takes place.

Then the Choir sings: Blessed be the Name of the Lord, from henceforth and for evermore (*3 times*).

And the Priest gives the Blessing: May the blessing and the mercy of the Lord come upon you . . .

Mattins

The Six Psalms.

Great Litany: In peace let us pray to the Lord . . .

Then are sung the following verses from Psalm 117:

Deacon: The Lord is God and hath appeared unto us: blessed is He that cometh in the Name of the Lord.

[1] Slav use.

℣1. O give thanks unto the Lord, and call upon His holy Name.

Choir: The Lord is God . . .

℣2. *Deacon:* All the nations compassed me about, but in the Name of the Lord have I driven them back.

Choir: The Lord is God . . .

℣3. *Deacon:* I shall not die, but live, and declare the works of the Lord.

Choir: The Lord is God . . .

℣4. *Deacon:* The stone that the builders rejected, the same is become the chief corner-stone: this is the Lord's doing, and it is marvellous in our eyes.

Choir: The Lord is God . . .

Then the Choir sings the appointed troparia:

On Sundays, the troparion (apolytikion) of the Resurrection in the tone of the week (twice), and the Sunday theotokion in the tone of the week (once).

On Great Feasts, the troparion (apolytikion) of the Feast (3 times).

On other feasts, the troparion (apolytikion) of the day (twice), and the Sunday theotokion in the same tone as the troparion of the day (once).

First reading from the Psalter.
Small Litany.
Sessional Hymn or Hymns.
Second reading from the Psalter.[1]
Small Litany.[1]
Sessional Hymn or Hymns.

[1] Often omitted.

On Sundays, Psalm 118 or the polyeleos (Psalms 134 and 135); on Great Feasts, the polyeleos. The polyeleos is usually sung in the shortened form:[1]

Praise ye the Name of the Lord, praise Him, O ye servants of the Lord. Alleluia, alleluia, alleluia.

Ye that stand in the house of the Lord, in the courts of the house of our God. Alleluia, alleluia, alleluia.

Blessed is the Lord from Zion, who dwelleth in Jerusalem. Alleluia, alleluia, alleluia.

O give thanks unto the Lord, for He is good: for His mercy endureth for ever. Alleluia, alleluia, alleluia.

O give thanks unto the God of heaven: for His mercy endureth for ever. Alleluia, alleluia, alleluia.

On Great Feasts and on certain lesser feasts, here follows the megalynarion.[1]

On Sundays only, the Choir sings the Evlogitaria of the Resurrection:

TONE FIVE

Blessed art Thou, O Lord: teach me Thy statutes.

The company of angels was amazed, beholding Thee, O Saviour, numbered among the dead, who hast destroyed the power of death and raised up Adam with Thyself, setting all men free from hell.

Blessed art Thou, O Lord: teach me Thy statutes.

'Why mingle ye sweet-smelling ointment with tears of pity, O ye women disciples?' cried the angel who shone as lightning within the tomb to the women bearing myrrh. 'Behold the tomb and understand: for the Saviour has risen from the grave.'

Blessed art Thou, O Lord: teach me Thy statutes.

The women bearing sweet-smelling ointment hastened early in the morning to Thy tomb, lamenting; but the angel

[1] Slav use.

arose before them and he said: 'The time for lamentation has ceased; weep not: but tell the apostles of the Resurrection.'

Blessed art Thou, O Lord: teach me Thy statutes.

The women bearing sweet-smelling ointment came to Thy tomb, O Saviour. But they heard an angel say to them: 'Why count ye the Living among the dead? For as God He has risen from the tomb.'

Glory be to the Father, and to the Son, and to the Holy Spirit.

We worship the Father together with His Son and the Holy Spirit, the Holy Trinity, One in Essence, and we cry with the seraphim: Holy, Holy, Holy art Thou, O Lord.

Both now, and ever, and unto the ages of ages. Amen.

O Virgin, who hast borne the Giver of Life, thou hast delivered Adam from sin, and to Eve thou hast brought joy in place of sorrow. He who took flesh from thee, who is both God and man, has raised up once more those who had fallen from life.

Alleluia, alleluia, alleluia, glory be to Thee, O God (*3 times*).

Small Litany.

On Sundays, the ypakoë from the Octoechos; otherwise, the appointed Sessional Hymn or Hymns.

On Sundays, the Hymn of Degrees in the tone of the week; otherwise, the first antiphon of the Hymn of Degrees in Tone Four, as follows:

From my youth up many passions have made war against me: but do Thou help and save me, O my Saviour.

Ye that hate Zion, ye shall be put to shame by the Lord: as grass in the fire shall ye be withered up.

Glory be to the Father . . . Both now . . .

By the Holy Spirit is every soul filled with life: through purification it is raised on high and made bright by the Three-fold Unity in a holy mystery.

Then follows the prokimenon: on Sundays, in the tone of the week; on feasts, as appointed.

Deacon: Let us pray to the Lord.
Choir: Kyrie eleison.
Priest: For holy art Thou, O our God . . .
Deacon: Let everything that hath breath praise the Lord.
This is repeated by the choir.
Deacon: Praise God in His saints: praise Him in the firmament of His power.
Choir: Let everything that hath breath praise the Lord.
Deacon: Let everything that hath breath
Choir: Praise the Lord.
Deacon: And that He will count us worthy . . .

Reading of the Gospel.

On Sundays the Choir sings the Hymn of the Resurrection:

We have seen the Resurrection of Christ; let us worship the holy Lord Jesus, who alone is without sin. We venerate Thy Cross, O Christ, and we praise and glorify Thy holy Resurrection. For Thou art our God: we know no other save Thee; upon Thy Name we call. Come, all ye faithful, let us venerate the holy Resurrection of Christ: for lo, through the Cross joy has come to all the world. Ever blessing the Lord, we sing the praises of His Resurrection: for He endured the Cross on our behalf, and has destroyed death by death.

Then Psalm 50 is read, and after it the following is sung on Sundays:

Glory be to the Father, and to the Son, and to the Holy Spirit.

At the prayers of the apostles, O merciful Lord, cleanse me from the multitude of my transgressions.

Both now, and ever, and unto the ages of ages. Amen.

At the prayers of the Theotokos, O merciful Lord, cleanse me from the multitude of my transgressions.

Have mercy upon me, O God, according to Thy loving kindness: according to the multitude of Thy tender mercies blot out my transgressions.

Jesus has risen from the tomb as He foretold, granting us life eternal and great mercy.

On Great Feasts, Jesus has risen from the tomb . . . *is replaced by a sticheron of the Feast; and special texts for the Feast may also be appointed in place of the verses,* At the prayers of the apostles . . . *and* At the prayers of the Theotokos . . .

Litany: O Lord, save Thy people . . .

Then follows the Canon. After the third canticle, Small Litany followed by the appointed Sessional Hymns or Ypakoë. After the sixth canticle, Small Litany followed by the Kontakion and Ikos. At the end of the eighth canticle we say, We praise, bless, and worship the Lord; we extol and exalt Him above all for ever; *and then the Katavasia.*

After this, on Great Feasts we sing the irmos and troparia of the ninth canticle, accompanied by one or more special megalynaria. Otherwise, we sing the Magnificat as follows:[1]

Deacon: Let us honour in hymns and magnify the Theotokos and Mother of the Light.

And the Choir sings the Song of the Theotokos (Luke 1: 46–55):

My soul doth magnify the Lord, and my spirit hath rejoiced in God my Saviour.

Greater in honour than the cherubim, and past compare more glorious than the seraphim, thou who without corruption hast borne God the Word: verily the Theotokos, thee do we magnify.

[1] If a Great Feast of the Mother of God falls on a Sunday, the Magnificat is sung in the normal way.

For He hath regarded the low estate of His handmaiden: for, behold, from henceforth all generations shall call me blessed.

Greater in honour than the cherubim . . .

For He that is mighty hath done to me great things, and holy is His Name: and His mercy is on them that fear Him from generation to generation.

Greater in honour than the cherubim . . .

He hath showed strength with His arm; He hath scattered the proud in the imagination of their hearts.

Greater in honour than the cherubim . . .

He hath put down the mighty from their seats and exalted them of low degree: He hath filled the hungry with good things and the rich He hath sent empty away.

Greater in honour than the cherubim . . .

He hath holpen His servant Israel, in remembrance of His mercy: as He spake to our fathers, to Abraham and to his seed for ever.

Greater in honour than the cherubim . . .

The irmos and the remainder of the ninth canticle are then read or sung.

Small Litany.

Then follows, on Sundays only:

Deacon: Holy is the Lord our God.
Choir: Holy is the Lord our God.
Deacon: For holy is the Lord our God.
Choir: Holy is the Lord our God.
Deacon: Over all men is our God.
Choir: Holy is the Lord our God.

Exapostilarion of the Sunday or of the Feast.

Lauds (Psalms 148, 149, 150). These are usually sung in the shortened form:

Let everything that hath breath praise the Lord. Praise the Lord from the heavens: praise Him in the heights. To Thee is due praise, O God.

Praise Him, all ye angels of His: praise Him, all His hosts. To Thee is due praise, O God.

And we continue at this point, or a few verses later, according to the number of stichera to be sung:

To execute upon them the judgement written: this honour have all His saints.

Praise God in His saints: praise Him in the firmament of His power.

Praise Him for His mighty acts: praise Him according to His excellent greatness.

Praise Him with the sound of the trumpet: praise Him with the psaltery and harp.

Praise Him with the timbrel and dance: praise Him with the stringed instruments and organs.

Praise Him upon the well-tuned cymbals: praise Him upon the loud cymbals. Let everything that hath breath praise the Lord.

And on Sundays two verses are added:[1]

Arise, O Lord my God, lift up Thine hand: forget not Thy poor for ever (*Psalm* 9:33).

I will praise Thee, O Lord, with my whole heart: I will speak of all Thy marvellous works (*ibid.*, 2).

Glory be to the Father . . .

On Sundays, the Gospel sticheron follows here.

Both now . . .

On Sundays, the following hymn to the Theotokos is sung:

[1] When a Great Feast of the Mother of God falls on Sunday, these two verses are replaced by the verses sung at the aposticha of Vespers. If a Great Feast of the Lord falls on Sunday, the two verses are omitted.

Most blessed art thou, O Virgin Theotokos, for through Him who took flesh from thee, is hell led captive, Adam recalled from the dead, the curse made void, Eve set free, and we are given life. Therefore we cry aloud in praise: Blessed art Thou, O Christ our God, who hast so been pleased: Glory to Thee.

The Great Doxology:

Priest: Glory to Thee who hast shewed us the light.

Choir: Glory to God in the highest and on earth peace, good will among men.

We praise Thee, we bless Thee, we worship Thee, we glorify Thee, we give thanks to Thee for Thy great glory.

O Lord God, heavenly King, God the Father Almighty; O Lord, the Only-begotten Son, Jesus Christ; and Thou, O Holy Spirit.

O Lord God, Lamb of God, Son of the Father, that takest away the sin of the world, have mercy upon us, Thou that takest away the sins of the world.

Receive our prayer, Thou that sittest at the right hand of the Father, and have mercy upon us.

For Thou only art holy, Thou only art the Lord, O Jesus Christ, to the glory of God the Father. Amen.

Every day I will bless Thee, and praise Thy Name for ever and ever.

Vouchsafe, O Lord, to keep us this day without sin.

Blessed art Thou, O Lord God of our Fathers, and praised and glorified is Thy Name for evermore.

O Lord, let Thy mercy lighten upon us, as our trust is in Thee.

Blessed art Thou, O Lord: teach me Thy statutes (*3 times*).

O Lord, Thou hast been our refuge from generation to generation. I said: Lord, have mercy upon me; heal my soul, for I have sinned against Thee.

O Lord, unto Thee I have fled for refuge: teach me to do

Thy will, for Thou art my God. For with Thee is the fountain of life, and in Thy light shall we see light. Continue Thy mercy unto those that know Thee.

Holy God, Holy and Mighty, Holy and Immortal, have mercy upon us (*3 times*).

Glory be to the Father . . . Both now . . .

Holy and Immortal, have mercy upon us.

And we end by singing more solemnly:

Holy God, Holy and Mighty, Holy and Immortal, have mercy upon us.

Then the Choir sings the appointed troparion. On Sundays, if the tone of the week is the 1st, 2nd, 3rd, or 4th, we sing:[1]

TONE FOUR

Today is salvation come unto the world. Let us sing praises to Him who rose from the tomb, the Author of our life. For, destroying death by death, He has given us victory and great mercy.

If the tone of the week is the 5th, 6th, 7th, or 8th, we sing:

TONE EIGHT

Rising from the tomb and bursting the bonds of hell asunder, Thou hast destroyed the sentence of death, O Lord, delivering all men from the snares of the enemy. Appearing to Thine apostles, Thou hast sent them forth to preach, and through them Thou hast given Thy peace to the inhabited earth, O Thou who alone art rich in mercy.

But on Great Feasts, in place of the above the troparion of the Feast is sung once.

On other feasts, the troparion of the day is sung once, followed by the Sunday theotokion in the same tone as the troparion of the day.

[1] In the Slav use the rules are as follows:
1st, 3rd, 5th, or 7th Tone: *Today is salvation come . . .*
2nd, 4th, 6th, or 8th Tone: *Rising from the tomb . . .*

Two Litanies: Have mercy upon us, O God, *and* Let us complete our morning prayer to the Lord.

Deacon: Wisdom. *Choir:* Give the blessing.

Priest: Blessed be He Who Is . . .

Choir: Confirm, O Lord, the holy Orthodox faith of Orthodox Christians unto the ages of ages.

Priest: Most holy Theotokos, save us.

Choir: Greater in honour than the cherubim . . .

Priest: Glory to Thee, O Christ our God and our Hope, glory to Thee.

Choir: Glory be to the Father . . . Both now . . .
Kyrie eleison, Kyrie eleison, Kyrie eleison.
Father, give the blessing.

Priest: May Christ our true God . . . (*On Sundays*, May He who rose from the dead . . .; *and on Great Feasts, the special Dismissal of the Feast, when such is appointed.*)

The First Hour is then read.

8 SEPTEMBER

THE BIRTH OF OUR MOST HOLY LADY THE THEOTOKOS

Small Vespers

On Lord, I have cried, *four stichera are sung:*

TONE ONE

(*to the special melody*, O purest Virgin, thou joy of the heavenly hierarchies . . .)

℣. From the morning watch until the night, from the morning watch let Israel trust in the Lord (*Psalm* 129:6).

Joachim and Ann keep festival, having brought into the world the only Theotokos, first fruit of our salvation. With them we celebrate the feast today, blessing the pure Virgin from the root of Jesse.[1]

℣. For with the Lord there is mercy, and with Him is plenteous redemption: and He shall redeem Israel from all his iniquities (*ibid.*, 7–8).

From Ann today has sprung forth a rod,[2] a branch given by God, even the Theotokos, salvation of men. From her, in manner past understanding, is born the Maker of all, who in His goodness purges all the indignity of Adam.

℣. O praise the Lord, all ye nations: praise Him, all ye people (*Psalm* 116:1).

The Maiden in whom God came to dwell, the pure Theotokos, glory of the prophets, the daughter of David, is

[1] Isaiah 11:10.

[2] Isaiah 11:1.

born today of Joachim and Ann sober in spirit; and by her birthgiving she overthrows the curse of Adam that weighed upon us.

℣. For His merciful kindness is great towards us: and the truth of the Lord endureth for ever (*ibid.*, 2).

The soil which formerly was barren gives birth to fertile ground, and nourishes with milk the holy fruit sprung from her sterile womb. Dread wonder: she who sustains our life, who received within her body the Bread of Heaven, feeds at her mother's breast.

Glory be to the Father . . . Both now . . .

TONE TWO

Come, all ye who love virginity, and who are friends of purity: come ye and welcome with love the boast of virgins. She is the fountain of life that gushes forth from the flinty rock;[1] She is the Bush[2] springing from barren ground and burning with the immaterial fire that cleanses and enlightens our souls.

Aposticha:

TONE TWO

(*to the special melody*, O house of Ephratah . . .)

The Virgin, offspring of Joachim and Ann, has appeared to men, releasing all from the bonds of sin.

℣. Hearken, O daughter, and consider, and incline thine ear (*Psalm* 44:11).

The barrenness of Ann has truly been revealed as an overshadowed mountain,[3] from which salvation has been granted to all the faithful.

[1] Exodus 17:6.

[2] Exodus 3:2.

[3] The reference is to Habakkuk 3:3, 'God shall come from Teman, and the Holy One from the mountain overshadowed by the forest.' In Orthodox hymnography this text is commonly applied to the Mother of God.

℣. Even the rich among the people shall entreat thy favour (*ibid.*, 13).

The most holy Virgin, having broken the bonds of the barrenness of Ann, has come forth to men, bestowing remission.

Glory be to the Father . . . Both now . . .

SAME TONE

O ye faithful, let us come, glorifying the Maiden. For from a barren mother has she been born, renewing our nature that had grown barren.

Apolytikion (troparion) of the feast, Thy birth, O Theotokos, has brought joy (*p. 107*), *and Dismissal.*

Great Vespers

We sing Blessed is the man (*the first portion of the first kathisma*).

On Lord, I have cried, *eight stichera are sung:*

TONE SIX

(*by Sergios*)

℣. Out of the depths have I cried unto Thee, O Lord: Lord, hear my voice (*Psalm*, 129:1–2).

Today God who rests upon the spiritual thrones has made ready for Himself a holy throne upon earth. He who made firm the heavens in His wisdom has prepared a living heaven in His love for man. For from a barren root He has made a life-giving branch spring up for us, even His Mother. God of wonders and hope of the hopeless, glory be to Thee, O Lord.

℣. Let Thine ears be attentive to the voice of my supplication (*ibid.*, 2).

Today God who rests upon the spiritual thrones . . .

℣. If Thou, Lord, shouldest mark iniquities, O Lord, who shall stand? But there is forgiveness with Thee (*ibid.*, 3–4).

This is the day of the Lord: rejoice, ye people. For lo, the Bridal Chamber of the Light, the Book of the Word of Life, has come forth from the womb, and the East Gate, newly born, awaits the entrance of the Great Priest.[1] She alone brings into the world the one and only Christ, for the salvation of our souls.

℣. For Thy Name's sake have I waited for Thee, O Lord: my soul hath waited for Thy word, my soul hath hoped in the Lord (*ibid.*, 5–6).

Although by the will of God other women who were barren have brought forth famous offspring, yet among all such children Mary has shone most brightly with divine glory. For, herself born wondrously of a barren mother, she bore in the flesh the God of all, in fashion surpassing nature, from a womb without seed. She is the only gateway of the Only-begotten Son of God, who passed through this gate, yet kept it closed:[2] and having ordered all things in His own wisdom He has wrought salvation for all mankind.

℣. From the morning watch until the night, from the morning watch let Israel trust in the Lord (*ibid.*, 6).

(*by Stephen of the Holy City*)

Today the barren gates are opened and the virgin Door of God comes forth. Today grace begins to bear its first fruits, making manifest to the world the Mother of God, through whom things on earth are joined with heaven, for the salvation of our souls.

℣. For with the Lord there is mercy, and with Him is plenteous redemption: and He shall redeem Israel from all his iniquities (*ibid.*, 7–8).

Today the barren gates are opened . . .

℣. O praise the Lord, all ye nations: praise Him, all ye people (*Psalm* 116:1).

Today is the beginning of joy for all the world; today the winds blow that bring tidings of salvation. The barrenness of

[1] Ezekiel 44:1–3.
[2] Ezekiel, *loc. cit.*

our nature has been loosed: for the barren woman is revealed as mother of her who, after bearing the Maker, still remained Virgin. From her He who is God by nature takes what is alien to Him and makes it His own; through her Christ works salvation for those gone astray in the flesh, He who loves mankind and is the Deliverer of our souls.

℣. For His merciful kindness is great towards us: and the truth of the Lord endureth for ever (*ibid.*, 2).

Today Ann the barren gives birth to the Child of God, foreordained from all generations to be the habitation of the King of all and Maker, Christ our God, in fulfilment of the divine dispensation. Through her we children of earth have been formed anew, and restored from corruption to life without end.

Glory be to the Father . . . Both now . . .

Today God who rests upon the spiritual thrones, *the first sticheron (p. 100).*

Entrance, O joyful light, *and prokimenon of the day.*

Lessons:

Reading from Genesis (28: 10–17).

And Jacob went out from Beersheba, and went toward Haran. And he lighted upon a certain place, and tarried there all night, because the sun was set; and he took of the stones of that place, and put them for his pillows, and lay down in that place to sleep. And he dreamed, and behold a ladder set up on the earth, and the top of it reached to heaven: and behold the angels of God ascending and descending on it. And, behold, the Lord stood above it, and said, I am the Lord God of Abraham thy father, and the God of Isaac: the land whereon thou liest, to thee will I give it, and to thy seed; and thy seed shall be as the dust of the earth, and thou shalt spread abroad to the west, and to the east, and to the north, and to the south: and in thee and in thy seed shall all the families of the earth be blessed. And, behold, I am with thee, and will keep thee in all places whither thou goest, and will bring thee again into this land; for I will not leave thee, until I have done that which I have spoken to thee of. And Jacob awaked out of his sleep, and he said, Surely the Lord is in this place; and I knew it not. And he was afraid, and said, How dreadful is this place! this is none other but the house of God, and this is the gate of heaven.

Reading from the Prophet Ezekiel (43:27–44:4).

And it shall be, that upon the eighth day, and so forward, the priests shall make your burnt offerings upon the altar, and your peace offerings; and I will accept you, saith the Lord God. Then He brought me back the way of the gate of the outward sanctuary which looketh toward the east; and it was shut. Then said the Lord unto me, This gate shall be shut, it shall not be opened, and no man shall enter in by it; because the Lord, the God of Israel, hath entered in by it, therefore it shall be shut. It is for the prince; the prince, he shall sit in it to eat bread before the Lord; he shall enter by the way of the porch of that gate, and shall go out by the way of the same. Then brought He me the way of the north gate before the house: and I looked, and, behold, the glory of the Lord filled the house of the Lord.

Reading from Proverbs (9:1–11).

Wisdom hath builded her house, she hath hewn out her seven pillars: she hath killed her beasts; she hath mingled her wine; she hath also furnished her table. She hath sent forth her maidens: she crieth upon the highest places of the city, Whoso is simple, let him turn in hither: as for him that wanteth understanding, she saith to him, Come, eat of my bread, and drink of the wine which I have mingled. Forsake the foolish, and live; and go in the way of understanding. He that reproveth a scorner getteth to himself shame: and he that rebuketh a wicked man getteth himself a blot. Reprove not a scorner, lest he hate thee: rebuke a wise man, and he will love thee. Give instruction to a wise man, and he will be yet wiser: teach a just man, and he will increase in learning. The fear of the Lord is the beginning of wisdom: and the knowledge of the holy is understanding. For by me thy days shall be multiplied, and the years of thy life shall be increased.

At the Lity:

TONE ONE

(by Stephen of the Holy City)

O ye people, today is come to pass the first fruit of our salvation. For lo, she who was foreordained from generations of old as Mother and Virgin and Receiver of God, comes forth in birth from a barren woman: a flower has blossomed from Jesse, and from his root a branch has sprung.[1] Let Adam our forefather be glad and let Eve rejoice with great joy. For behold, she who was made from the rib of Adam plainly declares her daughter and descendant blessed. 'For', says she, 'unto me is born deliverance, through which I shall be set free from the bonds of hell.' Let David rejoice, striking upon the harp, and let him bless God: for lo, the Virgin comes forth from a barren rock, for the salvation of our souls.

TONE TWO

Come, all ye who love virginity, and who are friends of purity: come ye and welcome with love the boast of virgins. She is the fountain of life that gushes forth from the flinty rock;[2] she is the Bush[3] springing from barren ground and burning with the immaterial fire that cleanses and enlightens our souls.

[1] Isaiah 11:1.
[2] Exodus 17:6.
[3] Exodus 3:2.

SAME TONE

(by Anatolios)

What is this sound of feasting that we hear? Joachim and Ann mystically keep festival. 'O Adam and Eve', they cry, 'rejoice with us today: for if by your transgression ye closed the gate of Paradise to those of old, we have now been given a glorious fruit, Mary the Child of God, who opens its entrance to us all.'

SAME TONE

She who was preordained to be the Queen of all and habitation of God, has come forth today from the barren womb of joyful Ann. She is the divine sanctuary of the eternal Essence; through her cruel hell has been trampled under foot, and Eve with all her line is established secure in life. It is meet and right that we should cry aloud to her: 'Blessed art thou among women, and blessed is the fruit of thy womb.'[1]

Glory be to the Father . . . Both now . . .

TONE EIGHT

(by Sergios of the Holy City)

On this solemn day of our feast let us strike the spiritual harp: for today is born of the seed of David the Mother of Life, who destroys the darkness. She is the restoration of Adam and the recalling of Eve, the fountain of incorruption and the release from corruption: through her we have been made godlike and delivered from death. Let us, the faithful, cry to her with Gabriel: 'Hail, thou who art full of grace: the Lord is with thee,[2] through thee granting us great mercy.'

[1] Luke 1:42.
[2] Luke 1:28.

Aposticha:

TONE FOUR

(*by Patriarch Germanos*)

The Joy of all the world has shone forth upon us, the far-famed Virgin sprung from righteous Joachim and Ann. On account of her exceeding goodness she is become the living Temple of God, and is in truth acknowledged as the only Theotokos. At her prayers, O Christ our God, send down peace upon the world and on our souls great mercy.

℣. Hearken, O daughter, and consider, and incline thine ear (*Psalm* 44:11).

As foretold by the angel, today hast thou come forth, O Virgin, the all-holy offspring of righteous Joachim and Ann. Thou art a heaven and the throne of God, and a vessel of purity, proclaiming joy to all the world, O Protector of our life. Thou dost destroy the curse and givest blessing in its place. Therefore on this feast of thy birth, O Maiden called by God, intercede that our souls be given peace and great mercy.

℣. Even the rich among the people shall entreat thy favour (*ibid.*, 13).

Today let Ann, barren and childless, clap her hands with joy. Let things on earth put on their bright array; let kings dance and priests make glad in hymns of blessing; let the whole world keep feast. For lo, the Queen and spotless Bride of the Father has blossomed from the root of Jesse. No more shall women bear children in sorrow: for joy has put forth its flower, and the Life of men has come to dwell in the world. No more are the gifts of Joachim turned away: for the lament of Ann is changed to joy. 'Let all the chosen Israel rejoice with me', she says: 'for behold, the Lord has given me the living Pavilion of His divine glory, unto the joy and gladness of us all and the salvation of our souls'.

Glory be to the Father . . . Both now . . .

TONE EIGHT

(by Sergios of the Holy City)

Come, all ye faithful, and let us run to the Virgin: for lo, today is born she who was foreordained before the womb as Mother of our God. She is the treasure of virginity, the rod of Aaron[1] springing from the root of Jesse, the preaching of the prophets, offshoot of the righteous Joachim and Ann. She is born, and with her is the world become new again. She is born, and the Church clothes herself in majesty. She is the holy Temple, the Receiver of the Godhead: the instrument of virginity, the Bridal Chamber of the King, wherein was accomplished the marvellous mystery of the ineffable union of the natures which come together in Christ. Worshipping Him, we sing the praises of the all-spotless birth of the Virgin.

Apolytikion (troparion) of the feast:

TONE FOUR

Thy birth, O Theotokos, has brought joy to all the inhabited earth: for from thee has shone forth the Sun of Righteousness, Christ our God. He has loosed us from the curse and given the blessing; He has made death of no effect, and bestowed on us eternal life.

And the Dismissal.

Mattins

After the first reading from the Psalter, sessional hymn:

TONE FOUR

Cry out, O David: what has God sworn to thee? 'What God swore to me He has now fulfilled,' said he: 'from the fruit of my loins He has given the Virgin. From her the

[1] Numbers 17:8 (17:23, Septuagint).

Creator, Christ the New Adam, is born, a King to sit upon my throne. Today He reigns, whose rule cannot be shaken.'[1] The barren woman bears the Theotokos who sustains our life.

Glory be to the Father . . . Both now . . .

Repeat.

After the second reading from the Psalter, sessional hymn:

SAME TONE

From the root of Jesse and from the loins of David, Mary, the Child of God, is born unto us today, and the whole creation is made new and godlike. Rejoice together, heaven and earth: praise her, ye kindreds of the nations. Joachim is glad and Ann rejoices as she cries: 'The barren woman bears the Theotokos who sustains our life.'

Glory be to the Father . . . Both now . . .

Repeat.

After the polyeleos, the megalynarion:[2]

We magnify thee, O most holy Virgin, and we honour thy holy parents and praise thine all-glorious Nativity.

℣. Lord, remember David and all his meekness (*Psalm* 131:1).

We magnify thee . . .

℣. Arise, O Lord, into Thy rest: Thou and the Ark of Thy holiness (*ibid.*, 8).

We magnify thee . . .

Glory be to the Father . . . Both now . . .

Alleluia, alleluia, alleluia, glory be to Thee, O God (*3 times*).

We magnify thee . . .

[1] Psalm 88:4–5.

[2] In the Slav use only.

Sessional hymn:

TONE EIGHT

Let the heavens rejoice and let the earth be glad. For the Heaven of God, the divine Bride, is born on earth according to the promise. The barren woman gives suck to her child Mary, and Joachim rejoices at this birth, saying: 'A rod is born unto me, and from it the flower that is Christ shall blossom from the root of David.[1] Marvellous in truth is this wonder.'

Glory be to the Father . . . Both now . . .

Repeat.

The first antiphon of the hymn of degrees in Tone Four.

Prokimenon: *TONE FOUR*

I will make thy name to be remembered in all generations (*Psalm* 44:18).

℣. My heart is inditing a good matter (*ibid.*, 2).

Let everything that hath breath . . .

READING FROM THE HOLY GOSPEL ACCORDING TO LUKE (1:39–49, 56).

And Mary arose in those days, and went into the hill country with haste, into a city of Judah; and entered into the house of Zacharias, and saluted Elisabeth. And it came to pass, that, when Elisabeth heard the salutation of Mary, the babe leaped in her womb; and Elisabeth was filled with the Holy Ghost: and she spake out with a loud voice, and said, Blessed art thou among women, and blessed is the fruit of thy womb. And whence is this to me, that the mother of my Lord should come to me? For, lo, as soon as the voice of thy salutation sounded in mine ears, the babe leaped in my womb for joy. And blessed is she that believed: for there shall be a performance of those things which were told her from the

[1] Isaiah 11:1.

Lord. And Mary said, My soul doth magnify the Lord, and my spirit hath rejoiced in God my Saviour. For He hath regarded the low estate of His handmaiden: for, behold, from henceforth all generations shall call me blessed. For He that is mighty hath done to me great things; and holy is His name. And Mary abode with her about three months, and returned to her own house.

Psalm 50.

Glory be to the Father . . .
At the prayers of the Theotokos . . .
Both now . . .
At the prayers of the Theotokos . . .
Have mercy upon me . . .
The Joy of all the world has shone forth upon us, *the first sticheron of the aposticha at Vespers* (*p.* 106).

Two Canons are used: the first, by St. John of Damascus, in eight troparia, including the irmos, and the second, by St. Andrew of Crete, in six, likewise including the irmos. Before the troparia we say Most holy Theotokos, save us.

Canticle One

First Canon

TONE TWO

(**Irmos**) Come, O ye people, and let us sing a song to Christ our God, who divided the sea and through it led His people, whom He had brought out of Egyptian bondage: for He has been glorified.

Come, O ye faithful, rejoicing in the divine Spirit, and let us honour in hymns the ever-Virgin Maid, who has come forth today from a barren woman, for the salvation of mortal men.

Hail, holy Mother and handmaid of Christ our God, who

hast restored to mankind its original blessedness. We all glorify thee in song as is right.

Today the Bridge of Life is born. Through her mortal men, fallen into hell, find their way up again, and they glorify in song Christ the Giver of life.

Second Canon

TONE EIGHT

(**Irmos**) He who shattered the enemy with His mighty arm and made Israel pass through the Red Sea, His praises let us sing as our Deliverer and God, for He has been glorified.

Let all the creation dance for joy and let David also be glad: for of his tribe and seed has come forth a rod that bears as flower the Lord and Deliverer of all.

The Holy of Holies is placed as an infant in the holy sanctuary, to be reared by the hands of an angel. Let us all feast with faith the day of her nativity.

Ann, the barren and sterile, was not childless before God: for she was foreordained from many generations to become mother of the pure Virgin, from whom the Maker of all creation sprang forth in the form of a servant.

Thou alone, O Sheep without blemish, from thy womb hast offered to Christ, the Lamb of God, our substance to be His fleece: therefore in our hymns we all honour thee on this day of thy nativity from Ann.

Glory be to the Father . . .

I glorify the Three without beginning, I sing the praises of the Holy Trinity, I proclaim Three coeternal in one essence: for a single God is glorified in Father, Son, and Holy Spirit.

Both now . . .

Who has ever beheld a child whom no father begat reared on His Mother's milk? Or where has a virgin Mother ever been seen? Truly, O pure Mother of God, in manner past understanding thou hast fulfilled both these marvels.

Katavasia,[1] *TONE EIGHT*

Inscribing the invincible weapon of the Cross upon the waters, Moses marked a straight line before him with his staff and divided the Red Sea, opening a path for Israel who went over dry-shod. Then he marked a second line across the waters and united them in one, overwhelming the chariots of Pharaoh.[2] Therefore let us sing to Christ our God, for He has been glorified.

Canticle Three

First Canon

(**Irmos**) O Lord, who hast put sin to death by the wood of the Cross, establish us in Thee and graft Thy fear in our hearts, as we sing Thy praise.

Having lived without reproach before the Lord, the holy parents brought forth the salvation of all, giving birth to her that bore our Creator and our God.

The Lord, who is a spring of life to all, led forth the Virgin from a barren womb. Into her He deigned to enter, preserving her virginity inviolate after childbirth.

Today let us exalt the fruit of Ann, Mary, who brought forth the life-giving Cluster: let us sing her praises as Theotokos, Protector and Helper of us all.

Second Canon

(**Irmos**) My heart is established in the Lord, my horn is exalted in my God, my mouth is enlarged over mine enemies: I have rejoiced in Thy salvation.

Blessed is thy womb, O Ann sober in spirit, for it brought forth the fruit of virginity, even her that without seed bore Jesus, the food and the Deliverer of creation.

[1] The katavasia at the end of each canticle is taken from the feast of the Exaltation of the Cross, which is to follow shortly (14 September).

[2] Exodus 14:21–29.

The whole creation calls thee blessed, O ever-Virgin born today of Ann: thou spotless branch of the root of Jesse, that brought forth Christ as flower.

O undefiled Theotokos, thy Son has set thee higher than all creation; He magnifies thy birth from Ann and fills all with gladness on this day.

Glory be to the Father . . .

We worship Thee, O Father, who in essence art without beginning, we sing the praises of Thine everlasting Son, and we venerate the coeternal Spirit: for the Three are by nature One God.

Both now . . .

O undefiled Theotokos, who hast borne the Light-giver and the Cause of the Life of men, thou art revealed as the Treasure of our Life and Gateway of the Light which no man can approach.

(**Katavasia**) The rod of Aaron is an image of this mystery, for when it budded it showed who should be priest.[1] So in the Church, that once was barren, the wood of the Cross has now put forth flower, filling her with strength and steadfastness.

Ypakoë

TONE TWO

The Prophet spoke of the holy Virgin as the Gate through which none might pass, save our God alone.[2] Through her did the Lord go, from her did the Most High come forth, yet left her still sealed, delivering our life from corruption.

Alternatively, this sessional hymn may be said:

TONE FOUR

Mary, the Virgin and in truth the Theotokos, has shone upon us today as a cloud of light, and from her righteous

[1] Numbers 17:8.
[2] Ezekiel 44:1–3.

parents she goes forth unto our glory. Adam is no more condemned, Eve is set free from bonds. Therefore with boldness we cry aloud to her who alone is pure: 'Thy birth brings tidings of joy to all the inhabited earth.'

Glory be to the Father . . . Both now . . .

Repeat.

Canticle Four

First Canon

(**Irmos**) I have heard the tidings of Thy dispensation, O Lord, and I have glorified Thee, who alone lovest mankind.

We sing Thy praises, O Lord, who hast given to all the faithful a haven of salvation, even her that bore Thee.

Christ shewed thee forth to all, O Bride of God, as the boast and strength of those who sing with faith the praises of Thy mystery.

Absolved of sin by thy supplications, O Lady who hast not known wedlock, gratefully we call thee blessed.

Second Canon

(**Irmos**) I heard tidings of Thee, O Lord, and was afraid: that Thou, the eternal God, in Thine ineffable counsel hast taken flesh and gone forth from the Virgin. Glory to Thee, O Christ, glory to Thy might.

Let us, the faithful, glorify the all-holy birth of the Theotokos in psalms and hymns: let us worship with faith the God who never lies, and who swore of old to David to give him a fruit of his loins.[1]

O Lord, Thou hast opened the womb of Sarah, giving her Isaac as fruit in her old age.[2] Today, O Saviour, Thou hast likewise given to godly Ann a fruit born from her womb, even Thine own Mother without spot.

[1] Psalm 88:4–5.
[2] Genesis 21:1–3.

'O Lord, Thou hast hearkened to my prayer,' let Ann exclaim. 'Thou hast granted me today the fruit of the promise, her that among all generations and women was foreordained to be Thy pure and undefiled Mother.'

Today the inhabited earth rejoices with thee, O holy Ann. For thou hast borne as blossom the Mother of its Redeemer, even her who brought forth the Rod of our strength from the root of Jesse, and who bore Christ as flower.

Glory be to the Father . . .

O Trinity without beginning, I glorify Thee, undivided in essence, and with my tongue of clay I cry aloud as the cherubim: Holy, Holy, Holy, is He who is and remaineth ever the one eternal God.

Both now . . .

O Undefiled, in thy birth are now fulfilled the prophecies of those inspired by God, who in their faith called thee Tabernacle and Gate, spiritual Mountain, Bush and Rod of Aaron sprung from the root of David.[1]

(**Katavasia**) O Lord, I have heard the mystery of Thy dispensation: I have considered Thy works, and I have glorified Thy Godhead.

Canticle Five

First Canon

(**Irmos**) Thou hast scattered the dim shades of dark sayings, and hast illuminated the hearts of the faithful by the coming of the truth through the Child of God: guide us also by Thy light, O Christ.

O ye people, let us sing the praises of the Cause of all things, who caused Himself to become like unto us. Counted worthy to behold the images that prefigured Him, the pro-

[1] Exodus 26:1; Ezekiel 44:1–3; Daniel 2:45; Exodus 3:2; Numbers 17:8.

phets rejoiced: and now they enjoy as fruit His manifest salvation.

The shoot of the sapless rod revealed unto Israel the chosen priest;[1] and now in fashion marvellous the all-glorious Offspring from a barren womb shows forth the shining glory of her parents.

Second Canon

(**Irmos**) O Lord our God, grant us peace; O Lord our God, make us Thine own. O Lord, none other do we know save Thee, and we call upon Thy Name.

Undefiled was thy Nativity, O Virgin undefiled: ineffable was thy conception and thy travail. Past speech was thy child-bearing, O Bride unwedded; for it was God, who has entirely clothed Himself in me.

Let the ranks of angels make glad today; let the children of Adam dance and sing. For the Rod is born, from whom as flower sprang forth Christ, the only Deliverer of Adam.

Today at thy birth Eve is loosed from her condemnation; Adam also is loosed from the ancient curse and he cries to thee, O undefiled Maiden: 'Through thee have we been delivered from corruption.'

Glory be to thee, who today hast glorified her that was barren. For she has borne, according to the promise, the ever-green Rod from which Christ, the flower of our life, sprang forth.

Glory be to the Father . . .

We worship Thee, O undivided Trinity, without beginning, uncreated, coeternal, one in nature, marvellously proclaimed to all eternity in one essence and three Persons.

Both now . . .

Thy womb has become a Holy Table; thy purity has remained untouched, O Virgin, as it was before. Christ the

[1] Numbers 17:8.

Sun has come forth from thee as a bridegroom from his chamber.[1]

(Katavasia) O thrice-blessed Tree, on which Christ the King and Lord was stretched! Through thee the beguiler fell, who tempted mankind with the tree. He was caught in the trap set by God, who was crucified upon thee in the flesh, granting peace unto our souls.

Canticle Six

First Canon

(Irmos) Jonah cried aloud unto the Lord from the belly of the whale: 'Do Thou lead me up from the bottom of hell, I pray, that with a voice of praise and in the spirit of truth I may sacrifice to Thee as my Deliverer.'

In their barren affliction the holy parents of the Mother of God cried aloud unto the Lord; and they brought her forth for the common salvation and glory of all generations.

The holy parents of the Mother of God received from heaven a gift worthy of God, a Throne higher than the very cherubim[2]—she who in childbirth bore the Word and the Creator.

Second Canon

(Irmos) As the waters of the sea, the waves of life toss me, O Thou who lovest man. But as Thou hast brought Jonah from the whale, O compassionate Lord, do Thou bring my life out of corruption.

We sing the praises of thy holy birth and venerate thy conceiving without seed, O Maiden, Bride of God and Virgin; and with us the ranks of angels and the souls of the saints dance for joy.

[1] Psalm 18:6.

[2] A reference to two visions of God in the Old Testament: Isaiah 6:1 and Ezekiel 1:4.

Thy wise parents, O Undefiled, brought thee, who art the Holy of Holies, as an offering to the house of the Lord, there to be reared in holiness and made ready to become His Mother.

Let both barren and mothers dance for joy; make bold and leap up in gladness, O ye childless. For the barren and childless woman brings forth the Theotokos, who is to deliver Eve from her pains in travail and Adam from the curse.[1]

I hear David singing to thee: 'Virgins shall be brought after thee, they shall be brought into the temple of the King.'[2] And with him I also sing thy praises, O daughter of the King.

Glory be to the Father . . .

In thee, O Undefiled, is the mystery of the Trinity praised and glorified. For the Father was well pleased with thee, and in thee the Word made His tabernacle among us, and the Holy Spirit overshadowed thee.

Both now . . .

Thou art become a golden censer,[3] for the Fire made His tabernacle in thy womb, even the Word from the Holy Spirit; and He was seen in the form of a man, O pure Mother of God.

(**Katavasia**) Jonah stretched out his hands in the form of a cross within the belly of the sea monster, plainly prefiguring the redeeming Passion. Cast out from thence after three days, he foreshadowed the marvellous Resurrection of Christ our God, who was crucified in the flesh and enlightened the world by His Rising on the third day.

[1] Genesis 3:16–19.
[2] Psalm 44:15–16.
[3] 1 Kings 7:50 (Hebrew); Hebrews 9:4.

Kontakion

TONE FOUR

(by Romanos the Melodist)

O Undefiled, by thy holy Nativity Joachim and Ann were set free from the reproach of childlessness, and Adam and Eve from the corruption of death. Delivered from the guilt of sin, Thy people keep the feast as they sing unto thee: The barren woman bears the Theotokos who sustains our life.

Ikos

The prayer and groaning of Joachim and Ann at their barrenness and childlessness have proved acceptable, and have come unto the ears of the Lord; and they have put forth a fruit that brings life to the world. The one offered his prayer in the mountain, the other bore her reproach in the garden. But with joy the barren woman bears the Theotokos who sustains our life.

Canticle Seven

First Canon

(**Irmos**) The bush on the mountain that was not consumed by fire, and the Chaldean furnace that brought refreshment as the dew, plainly prefigured thee, O Bride of God. For in a material womb, unconsumed thou hast received the divine and immaterial fire. Therefore we cry aloud unto Him who was born of thee: O God of our fathers, blessed art Thou.

Of old the giver of the Law[1] was unable to understand the invisible manifestation of thy great mystery, O all-holy Lady, though he was taught through symbols not to think earthly thoughts: therefore, astonished at this wonder, he said: 'O God of our fathers, blessed art Thou.'

[1] Moses (Exodus 3:2).

Inspired by God, the divine choir[1] spoke of thee in prophecy as the Mountain, the Gate of heaven, and the spiritual Ladder: for out of thee was hewn a stone, not cut by hand of man; and thou art the gate through which passed the Lord of wonders, the God of our fathers.

Second Canon

(**Irmos**) The furnace of the Chaldeans, flaming with fire, was bedewed by the presence of the Spirit of God, and the Children sang aloud: 'O God of our fathers, blessed art Thou.'

O Undefiled, we feast and venerate with faith thy holy birth according to the promise: for thereby, through Christ's appearance, we have been delivered from Adam's ancient curse.

Now Ann makes glad and cries aloud exulting: 'Though barren, I have given birth to the Mother of God, through whom the condemnation of Eve has been remitted, and all her pains in travail.'

Adam is set free and Eve dances for joy, and in spirit they cry aloud to thee, O Theotokos: 'By thee, through Christ's appearance, we have been delivered from Adam's ancient curse.'

O ye that are barren and without posterity, O ye unfruitful souls, make haste, for Ann has many children now and she is full of joy. O ye mothers, dance and exult with the Mother of God.

Glory be to the Father . . .

Let us glorify the Father, the Son, and the Spirit, in unity of Godhead, the most holy Trinity, undivided, uncreated, coeternal and in essence one.

Both now . . .

Thou alone, a Virgin after childbirth, hast borne God; thou hast renewed our nature by thy bearing, O Mary. Thou

[1] The patriarchs and prophets of the Old Testament: see Daniel 2:45; Genesis 28:12–17; Ezekiel 44:2.

hast released Eve from the ancestral curse, O pure Mother of God.

(Katavasia) The senseless decree of the wicked tyrant, breathing forth threats and blasphemy hateful to God, confused the people. Yet neither the fury of wild beasts nor the roaring of the fire could frighten the three Children: but standing together in the flame, fanned by the wind that brought refreshment as the dew, they sang: 'Blessed art Thou and praised above all, O our God and the God of our fathers.'

Canticle Eight

First Canon

(Irmos) Long ago in the furnace of the Children hast Thou prefigured Thine own Mother, O Lord. For this image delivered them from the fire, and they walked in the midst of it unconsumed. Thou hast manifested her today to the ends of the earth: her praises do we sing and we exalt her above all for ever.

The preordained tabernacle of our reconciliation with God now begins to be. It is she who shall bear unto us the Word, appearing in the material substance of the flesh. He has brought us from not being into being: His praises do we sing and we exalt Him above all for ever.

Ann's barrenness was transformed, thereby destroying the world's barrenness in good things; and this wonder plainly foreshadowed Christ's coming to dwell with mortal men. He has brought us from not being into being: His praises do we sing and we exalt Him above all for ever.

Second Canon

(Irmos) Thou who coverest Thy high places with the waters, and settest the sand as a bound to the sea,[1] Thou

[1] Psalm 103:3; Jeremiah 5:22.

who dost compass all things, the sun sings Thy praises, the moon gives Thee glory, every creature offers his hymn unto Thee, his Author and Creator, for ever.

Thou who hast wrought wonders for the barren womb of Ann, Thou who hast opened her childless side and given her fruit, Thou art the holy God, Thou art the Son of the Virgin: Thou hast taken flesh from her, the ever-flowering Virgin and Theotokos.

Thou who dost seal the deep and open it again, who bringest water in the clouds and givest showers of rain, Thou, O Lord, hast made to flower an undefiled fruit from the barren root of holy Ann, even the Rod that is the Theotokos.

Thou hast loosed the unbreakable bonds of childlessness. Thou hast given the barren woman a fertile offspring and a glorious fruit. Of that same offspring Thou hast Thyself become the Son and shoot: when Thou camest to dwell among us, O merciful Lord, Thou hast chosen her as Thy Mother according to the flesh.

Husbandman of our thoughts and gardener of our souls, Thou hast made the barren earth fertile. Thou hast turned the ground that once was parched into fruitful land, rich in corn and bearing fruit. From holy Ann Thou hast made to blossom an undefiled fruit, the Theotokos.

We bless the Lord, Father, Son, and Holy Spirit.

O Trinity supreme in being, Unity without beginning, the multitudes of angels sing Thy praises and tremble before Thee. Heaven, earth, and the depths stand in awe of Thee, men bless Thee, fire is Thy servant, all things created obey Thee in fear, O Holy Trinity.

Both now . . .

O strangest of tidings! God has become the Son of a woman. The birth was without seed, the Mother knew not a man, and the Child she bore is God. O dread sight! O strange conceiving by the Virgin! O nativity beyond speech! Indeed all these things are past sight and mind.

We praise, bless, and worship the Lord: we extol and exalt Him above all for ever.

(**Katavasia**) O ye Children, equal in number to the Trinity, bless ye God the Father and Creator; sing ye the praises of the Word who descended and changed the fire to dew; and exalt ye above all for ever the most Holy Spirit, who gives life to all.

Canticle Nine

First Canon

The Magnificat and Greater in honour than the cherubim *are not sung. Before the irmos and each of the troparia we sing the megalynarion:*

Magnify, O my soul, the most glorious birth of the Mother of God.

(**Irmos**) From thy virgin womb the Light that was before the sun, even God who has shone forth upon us, took flesh ineffably, coming to dwell among us in the body. Thee, then, O blessed and all-holy Theotokos, do we magnify.

He who made springs of water gush forth from the rock for the disobedient people,[1] unto our joy gives thee to the obedient gentiles as fruit from a barren womb. Thee, then, O undefiled Mother of God, as is meet and right, do we magnify.

Thou art our deliverer from the sharp punishment of old, the restoration of our mother Eve, the cause of the reconciliation of our kind to God, the bridge that leads us to the Maker; thee, then, O Theotokos, do we magnify.

Second Canon

Megalynarion sung before the irmos and the troparia:

Magnify, O my soul, the Virgin Mary, born of a barren womb.

[1] Exodus 17:6.

(Irmos) Virginity is alien to motherhood, and child-bearing is a thing strange to virgins: yet in thee, O Theotokos, both are to be found. Therefore we and all the nations of the earth without ceasing call thee blessed.

O Mother of God, thou hast inherited according to the promise a birth worthy of thy purity. For as a God-given fruit hast thou been granted to her who before was fruitless. Therefore we and all the nations of the earth without ceasing call thee blessed.

Fulfilled is the prophecy of him that cried aloud, saying: 'I will raise up the tabernacle of holy David that is fallen.'[1] Thee, O Undefiled, did his words prefigure, through whom the dust of man has been wholly refashioned into a body for God.

We venerate thy swaddling clothes, O Theotokos: we glorify the Lord who gave thee as fruit to her that before was childless. He has opened by a miracle the barren womb of Ann: for, as almighty God, He does whatsoever pleases Him.

O holy Ann, mother of the Virgin, thou hast put forth from thy womb, against all hope, a virgin flower according to the promise, a divine bud pure and beautiful. Therefore as the root of our life do we call thee blessed.

Glory be to the Father . . .

It is alien to evil-doers to glorify the Trinity that has no beginning, Father, Son, and Holy Spirit, the uncreated and sovereign Power that founded the whole world by an act of His might.

Both now . . .

Thou hast contained in thy womb, O Virgin Mother, one of the Trinity, Christ the King, whose praises all creation sings and before whom the thrones on high tremble. O all-venerated Lady, entreat Him for the salvation of our souls.

[1] Amos 9: 11.

(**Katavasia**) O Theotokos, thou art a mystical Paradise, who untilled hast brought forth Christ. He has planted upon earth the life-giving Tree of the Cross: therefore at its Exaltation on this day, we worship Him and thee do we magnify.

(**Another Katavasia**) Today the death that came to man through eating of the tree, is made of no effect through the Cross. For the curse of our mother Eve that fell on all mankind is destroyed by the fruit of the pure Mother of God, whom all the powers of heaven magnify.

Exapostilarion

The ends of the inhabited earth greatly rejoice today at thy birth, O Mary, Maiden, Mother of God and Bride who knowest not wedlock: for thereby thou hast removed the painful reproach of thy parents' childlessness and the curse on childbirth which our mother Eve brought on herself (*twice*).

Glory be to the Father . . . Both now . . .

Be renewed, O Adam, and be magnified, O Eve; ye prophets, dance with the apostles and the righteous; let there be common joy in the world among angels and mankind. For the Theotokos is born today of righteous Joachim and Ann.

Lauds. Four stichera are sung:

TONE EIGHT[1]

(*to the special melody*, O marvellous wonder . . .)

℣. Praise Him for His mighty acts: praise Him according to His excellent greatness (*Psalm* 150:2).

O marvellous wonder! The fount of life is born of a barren woman, and grace begins gloriously to bear its fruit. Rejoice, O Joachim, inspired by God, who hast become the father of the Theotokos: there is no other father in mankind like unto thee. For through thee has been given to us the Maiden in

[1] In certain editions, Tone One.

whom God came to dwell, the Tabernacle of God, the most holy Mountain.

℣. Praise Him with the sound of the trumpet: praise Him with the psaltery and harp (*ibid.*, 3).

O marvellous wonder! The fount of life . . .

℣. Praise Him with the timbrel and dance: praise Him with the stringed instruments and organs (*ibid.*, 4).

O marvellous wonder! At the behest of the Almighty Maker of all, a fruit has shone forth from a barren womb, that has wholly ended the world's barrenness in good. Ye mothers, dance with the mother of the Theotokos and cry: 'Hail, thou who art full of grace: the Lord is with thee,[1] granting great mercy to the world through thee.'

℣. Praise Him upon the well-tuned cymbals: praise Him upon the loud cymbals. Let everything that hath breath praise the Lord (*ibid.*, 5–6).

Living pillar of chastity and bright vessel shining with grace, Ann the glorious has brought into the world an offspring that is truly the divine flower of virginity, and who bestows the beauty of virginity on all who are virgins and desire this gift of grace, granting great mercy to the faithful.

Glory be to the Father . . . Both now . . .

TONE SIX

This is the day of the Lord: rejoice, ye people. For lo, the Bridal Chamber of the Light, the Book of the Word of Life, has come forth from the womb, and the East Gate, newly born, awaits the entrance of the Great Priest.[2] She alone brings into the world the one and only Christ, for the salvation of our souls.

Great Doxology and Dismissal.

[1] Luke 1:28.
[2] Ezekiel 44:1–3.

Liturgy

The Typika (Psalms 102 and 145) and the Beatitudes. With the Beatitudes are sung four troparia from Canticle Three of the first Canon of the feast (p. 112) and four troparia from Canticle Six of the second Canon (pp. 117–8).

Alternatively, according to the modern Greek practice, the following antiphons may be sung.[1]

Antiphon One

TONE TWO

℣. 1. Lord, remember David and all his meekness (*Psalm* 131:1).

At the prayers of the Theotokos, save us, O Saviour.

℣ 2. Lo, we heard of it at Ephratah: we found it in the fields of the wood (*ibid.*, 6).

At the prayers of the Theotokos . . .

℣ 3. Glorious things are spoken of thee, O city of God (*Psalm* 86:3).

At the prayers of the Theotokos . . .

℣ 4. God is in the midst of her; she shall not be moved: God shall help her, and that right early (*Psalm* 45:6).

At the prayers of the Theotokos . . .

Glory be to the Father . . . Both now . . .

At the prayers of the Theotokos . . .

Antiphon Two

SAME TONE

℣ 1. The Lord hath sworn in truth unto David; and He will not turn from it (*Psalm* 131:11).

[1] On this and other feasts of the Mother of God (21 November, 2 February, 25 March, 15 August), the Slav service books and the older editions of the Greek service books prescribe the Typika and the Beatitudes, antiphons being provided only for the feasts of Our Lord.

O Son of God, wonderful in Thy saints, save us who sing to Thee: alleluia.

℣ 2. Of the fruit of thy body will I set upon thy throne (*ibid.*).

O Son of God . . .

℣ 3. There will I make the horn of David to bud: I have ordained a lamp for mine anointed (*ibid.*, 17).

O Son of God . . .

℣ 4. For the Lord hath chosen Zion: He hath desired it for His habitation (*ibid.*, 13).

O Son of God . . .
Glory be to the Father . . . Both now . . .
O Only-begotten Son and Word of God . . .

Antiphon Three

TONE FOUR

℣ 1. Here will I dwell: for I have desired it (*Psalm* 131:14).

The troparion of the feast, Thy birth, O Theotokos, has brought joy (*p. 107*).

℣ 2. The Most High hath sanctified His tabernacle (*Psalm* 45:5).

The troparion of the feast.

℣ 3. Holy is Thy temple, and wonderful in righteousness (*Psalm* 64:5–6).

The troparion of the feast.

After the introit, the troparion of the feast (*p. 107*); Glory be to the Father . . . Both now . . .; *the kontakion of the feast* (*p. 119*).

Prokimenon: *TONE THREE*

My soul doth magnify the Lord, and my spirit hath rejoiced in God my Saviour (*Luke* 1:46–47).

℣. For He hath regarded the low estate of His handmaiden: for, behold, from henceforth all generations shall call me blessed (*ibid.*, 48).

READING FROM THE EPISTLE OF PAUL TO THE PHILIPPIANS (2:5–11).

Brethren, let this mind be in you, which was also in Christ Jesus: who, being in the form of God, thought it not robbery to be equal with God: but made Himself of no reputation, and took upon Him the form of a servant, and was made in the likeness of men: and being found in fashion as a man, He humbled Himself, and became obedient unto death, even the death of the cross. Wherefore God also hath highly exalted Him, and given Him a name which is above every name: that at the name of Jesus every knee should bow, of things in heaven, and things in earth, and things under the earth; and that every tongue should confess that Jesus Christ is Lord, to the glory of God the Father.

Alleluia, TONE EIGHT

℣ 1. Hearken, O daughter, and consider, and incline thine ear (*Psalm* 44:11).

℣ 2. Even the rich among the people shall entreat thy favour (*ibid.*, 13).

READING FROM THE HOLY GOSPEL ACCORDING TO LUKE (10:38–42; 11:27–28).

At that time Jesus entered into a certain village: and a certain woman named Martha received Him into her house. And she had a sister called Mary, which also sat at Jesus' feet, and heard His word. But Martha was cumbered about much serving, and came to Him, and said, Lord, dost Thou not care that my sister hath left me to serve alone? bid her therefore that she help me. And Jesus answered and said unto her, Martha, Martha, thou art careful and troubled about many things: but one thing is needful: and Mary hath chosen that good part, which shall not be taken away from her. And it came to pass, as He spake these things, a certain woman of the company lifted up her voice, and said unto Him, Blessed is the womb that bare Thee, and the paps which Thou hast sucked. But He said, Yea rather, blessed are they that hear the word of God, and keep it.

In place of It is meet, *we sing the megalynarion* Magnify, O my soul, the Virgin Mary, born of a barren womb, *and the irmos from Canticle Nine of the second Canon* *(p. 124)*.

Communion verse:

I will receive the cup of salvation, and call upon the Name of the Lord (*Psalm* 115:4).

If the feast falls on a day of fasting (i.e. a Wednesday or Friday), fish, wine, and oil are allowed, but meat and animal products (eggs, milk, butter, and cheese) are not permitted.

Because of its nearness to the feast of the Exaltation of the Cross, the feast of the Birth of the Theotokos is observed for five days only, the apodosis falling on 12 September. On that day all the office of the feast is repeated, omitting only the entrance, lessons, lity, and blessing of bread at Vespers; and the polyeleos and Gospel at Mattins. In the reading of the Psalter at Vespers, the normal kathisma appointed for the day is used.

14 SEPTEMBER

THE UNIVERSAL EXALTATION OF THE PRECIOUS AND LIFE-GIVING CROSS

Small Vespers

Before the beginning of Vespers, the priest puts the Holy Cross on a tray decorated with branches of basil or flowers, and places it on the table of the Prothesis.

On Lord, I have cried, *four stichera are sung:*

TONE FOUR

Lifted high upon the Cross, O Master, with Thyself Thou hast raised up Adam and the whole of fallen nature. Therefore, exalting Thine undefiled Cross, O Thou who lovest mankind, we ask Thee for Thy strength from above, crying: O God Most High, in Thy mercy save those who honour the sacred, light-giving and divine Exaltation of Thy Cross (*twice*).

With the psalmist, O Master, do we now behold the footstool on which Thine undefiled feet rested,[1] Thy precious Cross, exalted this day with love. And with devotion lifting it on high, we beseech Thee, crying: O Thou who hast sanctified all men by Thy divine Cross, make us sharers in Thine ineffable compassion and Thy grace.

As an unconquerable token of victory, an invincible shield and a divine sceptre, we worship Thy most Holy Cross, O Christ, whereby the world has been saved and Adam filled with joy. With the whole assembly of those born on earth we

[1] Psalm 98:5.

honour it, singing its praises, and as we celebrate its divine Exaltation, we entreat Thee for forgiveness.

Glory be to the Father . . . Both now . . .

TONE TWO

(*by the Emperor Leo*)

O three-branched Cross of Christ, thou art my strong protection. Sanctify me by thy might, that I may venerate and glorify thee in faith and love.

Aposticha:

TONE TWO

(*to the special melody*, O house of Ephratah . . .)

The Cross of Christ is exalted today, the life-giving Wood on which was fastened in the flesh He who restores all mankind.

℣. Exalt ye the Lord our God: and worship at His footstool, for He is holy (*Psalm* 98:5).

As we behold the Wood of the Cross exalted on high, let us magnify God who in His goodness was crucified upon it in the flesh.

℣. God is our King of old: working salvation in the midst of the earth (*Psalm* 73:12).

Hail! Cross of the Lord, divine protection of the faithful, invincible rampart, raising us up from earth.

Glory be to the Father . . . Both now . . .

SAME TONE

Come ye, and let us all kiss with joy the Wood of salvation, on which was stretched Christ the Redeemer.

Apolytikion (troparion) of the feast, O Lord, save Thy people *(p. 141), and Dismissal.*

After the conclusion of Small Vespers, the priest and the deacon put on their vestments. The deacon censes the Holy Cross which rests on the table of the Prothesis, and says:

Father, give the blessing.

The priest:

Blessed is our God . . .

Then are said the trisagion, etc., and the Lord's Prayer, followed by the troparion of the feast, O Lord, save Thy people (*p. 141*); Glory be to the Father . . . Both now . . . ; *and the kontakion of the feast,* Lifted up of Thine own will (*p. 148*).

The priest places the tray with the Cross on his head. Preceded by lighted candles and by the deacon who censes the Cross, he goes to the Holy Table, laying the Cross down on it in the centre, the Book of the Gospels being set upright at the back of the altar. A candle is lit and left burning in the sanctuary.

Great Vespers

No reading from the Psalter.

On Lord, I have cried, *eight stichera are sung:*

TONE SIX

(*to the special melody,* Having set all your hope on the things of heaven . . .)

The Cross is raised on high, and urges all the creation to sing the praises of the undefiled Passion of Him who was lifted high upon it. For there it was that He killed our slayer, and brought the dead to life again: and in His exceeding goodness and compassion, He made us beautiful and counted us worthy to be citizens of heaven. Therefore with rejoicing let us exalt His Name and magnify His surpassing condescension (*3 times*).

Moses prefigured thee, O precious Cross, when he stretched out his hands on high and put Amalek the tyrant to flight.[1]

[1] Exodus 17:10–14.

Thou art the boast of the faithful and succour of the persecuted, the glory of the apostles, the champion of the righteous, and the preserver of all the saints. Therefore, beholding thee raised on high, creation rejoices and keeps feast, glorifying Christ, who in His surpassing goodness through thee has joined together that which was divided (*3 times*).

O most venerable Cross, attended by ranks of rejoicing angels, thou art exalted today, and by divine command thou dost lift up again all those who, through the stealing of the fruit, had been made outcasts and were sunk in death. Therefore, embracing thee in faith with heart and lips, from thee we draw sanctification and we cry aloud: Exalt ye Christ, the God most good, and venerate His divine footstool (*twice*).[1]

Glory be to the Father . . . Both now . . .

TONE TWO

Come, all ye peoples, and let us venerate the blessed Wood, through which the eternal justice has been brought to pass. For he who by a tree deceived our forefather Adam, is by the Cross himself deceived; and he who by tyranny gained possession of the creature endowed by God with royal dignity, is overthrown in headlong fall. By the blood of God the poison of the serpent is washed away; and the curse of a just condemnation is loosed by the unjust punishment inflicted on the Just. For it was fitting that wood should be healed by wood, and that through the Passion of One who knew not passion should be remitted all the sufferings of him who was condemned because of wood. But glory be to Thee, O Christ our King, for Thy dread dispensation towards us, whereby Thou hast saved us all, for Thou art good and lovest mankind.

[1] Psalms 98:5; 131:7.

Entrance, O joyful light, *and prokimenon of the day*.[1]

Lessons:

READING FROM EXODUS (15:22–16:1).

Moses brought Israel from the Red Sea, and they went out into the wilderness of Shur; and they went three days in the wilderness, and found no water. And when they came to Marah, they could not drink of the waters of Marah, for they were bitter: therefore the name of it was called Marah. And the people murmured against Moses, saying, What shall we drink? And he cried unto the Lord; and the Lord showed him a tree, which when he had cast into the waters, the waters were made sweet: there He made for them a statute and an ordinance, and there He proved them, and said, If thou wilt diligently hearken to the voice of the Lord thy God, and wilt do that which is right in His sight, and wilt give ear to His commandments, and keep all His statutes, I will put none of these diseases upon thee, which I have brought upon the Egyptians: for I am the Lord that healeth thee. And they came to Elim, where were twelve wells of water, and threescore and ten palm trees: and they encamped there by the waters. And they took their journey from Elim, and all the congregation of the children of Israel came unto the wilderness of Sin, which is between Elim and Sinai.

READING FROM PROVERBS (3:11–18).

My son, despise not the chastening of the Lord; neither be weary of His correction: for whom the Lord loveth He correcteth, even as a father the son in whom he delighteth. Happy is the man that findeth wisdom, and the man that getteth understanding. For the merchandise of it is better than the merchandise of silver, and the gain thereof than fine gold. She is more precious than rubies: and all the things

[1] If the feast falls on Saturday, at Vespers on Friday evening the Great Prokimenon is sung, *Our God is in heaven and on earth* (see p. 390).

thou canst desire are not to be compared unto her. Length of days is in her right hand; and in her left hand riches and honour. Her ways are ways of pleasantness, and all her paths are peace. She is a tree of life to them that lay hold upon her: and happy is everyone that retaineth her.

READING FROM THE PROPHET ISAIAH (60:11–16).

Thus saith the Lord: Therefore thy gates shall be open continually, O Jerusalem; they shall not be shut day nor night; that men may bring unto thee the forces of the Gentiles, and that their kings may be brought. For the nation and kingdom that will not serve thee shall perish; yea, those nations shall be utterly wasted. The glory of the Lebanon shall come unto thee, the fir tree, the pine tree, and the box together, to beautify the place of My sanctuary; and I will make the place of My feet glorious. The sons also of them that afflicted thee shall come bending unto thee; and all they that despised thee shall bow themselves down at the soles of thy feet; and they shall call thee, The city of the Lord, The Zion of the Holy One of Israel. Whereas thou hast been forsaken and hated, so that no man went through thee, I will make thee an eternal excellency, a joy of many generations. Thou shalt also suck the milk of the Gentiles, and shalt suck the breast of kings: and thou shalt know that I the Lord am thy Saviour and thy Redeemer, the Mighty One of Jacob.

At the Lity:

TONE ONE

(*by Andrew of Jerusalem*)

Today the holy words of David have truly received their fulfilment: for lo, in the sight of all the world we venerate the footstool of Thine undefiled feet.[1] And putting our hope in the shadow of Thy wings,[2] we cry aloud unto Thee, all-compassionate Lord: May the light of Thy countenance be

[1] Psalm 98:5.
[2] Psalm 56:2.

marked as a sign upon us,[1] and do Thou exalt the horn of Thine Orthodox people, by the Exaltation of Thy precious Cross, O Christ of many mercies.

SAME TONE

The Tree of true life was planted in the place of the skull, and upon it hast Thou, the eternal King, worked salvation in the midst of the earth.[2] Exalted today, it sanctifies the ends of the world, and the Church of the Resurrection celebrates its dedication. Angels in heaven greatly rejoice and men upon earth make glad, crying aloud with David and saying: Exalt ye the Lord our God and worship at His footstool, for He is holy, granting the world great mercy.

SAME TONE

Prefiguring Thy Cross, O Christ, Jacob the Patriarch, when he gave the blessing to his descendants, laid his hands crosswise upon their heads.[3] And today as we exalt Thy Cross, O Saviour, we cry: Give victory to Thine Orthodox people[4] as Thou once gavest it to Constantine.

TONE TWO

(*by Theophanes*)

Divine treasure hidden in the earth, the Cross of the Giver of Life appeared in the heavens to the godly King,[5] and its inscription spiritually signified his victory over the enemy. Rejoicing with faith and love, inspired by God he made haste to raise on high the Cross which he had seen in his vision; and with great zeal he brought it forth from the bosom of the earth, for the deliverance of the world and the salvation of our souls.

[1] Psalm 4:7.
[2] Psalm 73:12.
[3] Genesis 48:14.
[4] Literally, 'our Orthodox King'.
[5] St. Constantine the Great.

SAME TONE

(by Cyprian)

The crossing of his hands by the Patriarch Jacob at the blessing of his children foreshadowed the mighty token of Thy Cross. Having it as our safeguard that cannot be overthrown, we drive out with invincible strength the hosts of demons; and casting down by it the arrogance of Belial, we put to flight the all-destroying power of hateful Amalek.[1] And now that it is lifted on high, we the faithful offer it in piety to Thy goodness for the cleansing of our sins, crying aloud in all the fulness of our voices: Have mercy, O Lord, made flesh of the Virgin: O Thou who art good, take pity on the works that Thou hast fashioned in Thy wisdom.

SAME TONE

(by the Emperor Leo)

O three-branched Cross of Christ, thou art my strong protection. Sanctify me by thy might, that I may venerate and glorify thee in faith and love.

TONE FOUR

Let us make glad today and sing in honour of the feast, and with joyful face and tongue openly cry aloud: O Christ, for us Thou hast accepted condemnation, being spat upon and scourged; Thou wast wrapped in a purple robe, and hast gone up upon the Cross. Seeing Thee, the sun and the moon hid their light, the earth quaked in fear, and the veil of the temple was rent in twain. Do Thou Thyself now grant us Thy precious Cross as guardian and protector and driver away of demons, that embracing it, we may all cry aloud: Save us, O Cross, by thy might. Make us holy by thy splendour, O precious Cross, and strengthen us through thine Exaltation: for thou hast been given to us as the light and salvation of our souls.

[1] Exodus 17:10–14.

SAME TONE

(*by Anatolios*)

O Cross, sign radiant with light among the stars, thou hast in prophecy revealed a trophy of victory to the godly King; and when his mother Helen found thee, she displayed thee in the sight of all the world. And today the choirs of the faithful shout aloud as they raise thee up on high: Enlighten us by thy brightness, O life-giving and all-venerable Cross: make us holy by thy might, and lifted on high before the battle line, strengthen us through thine Exaltation.

Glory be to the Father . . . Both now . . .

SAME TONE

(*by Anatolios*)

Moses prefigured the power of the precious Cross, O Christ, when he put to flight Amalek, his adversary, in the wilderness of Sinai: for when he stretched out his arms in the form of a cross, the people became strong again.[1] And now the fulfilment of these images has come to pass for us. Today is the Cross exalted and devils are put to flight; today the whole creation is set free from corruption: for through the Cross every gift of grace has shone upon us. Therefore all of us rejoicing fall before Thee, saying: How marvellous are Thy works, O Lord:[2] glory to Thee!

Aposticha:

TONE FIVE

(*to the special melody*, Hail! life-giving Cross . . .)

Hail! life-giving Cross, unconquerable trophy of godliness, door to Paradise, succour of the faithful, rampart set about the Church. Through thee corruption is utterly destroyed,

[1] Exodus 17:10–14.

[2] Psalm 103:24.

the power of death is swallowed up, and we are raised from earth to heaven: invincible weapon, adversary of devils, glory of martyrs, true ornament of saints, haven of salvation bestowing on the world great mercy.

℣. Exalt ye the Lord our God: and worship at His footstool, for He is holy (*Psalm* 98:5).

Hail! Cross of the Lord: through thee mankind has been delivered from the curse. Shattering the enemy by thine Exaltation, O Cross all-venerable, thou art a sign of true joy. Thou art our help, thou art the strength of kings, the power of righteous men, the majesty of priests. All who sign themselves with thee are freed from peril. Thou rod of strength under which we like sheep are tended, thou art a weapon of peace round which the angels stand in fear. Thou art the divine glory of Christ, who grants the world great mercy.

℣. God is our King of old: working salvation in the midst of the earth (*Psalm* 73:12).

Hail! guide of the blind, physician of the sick and resurrection of all the dead. O precious Cross, thou hast lifted us up when we were fallen into mortality. Through thee corruption has been destroyed, and incorruption has flowered forth; we mortal men are made divine and the devil is utterly cast down. Seeing thee exalted by the hands of bishops on this day, we exalt Him who was lifted high upon thee, and we venerate thee, plenteously drawing from thee great mercy.

Glory be to the Father . . . Both now . . .

TONE EIGHT

(by John the Monk)

Today, O Christ our God, we sinners venerate with unworthy lips Thy precious Cross, which Moses once prefigured in himself, when he overthrew Amalek and put him to flight; and which David the psalmist commanded to be venerated as Thy footstool.[1] We cry aloud to Thee that wast pleased to be crucified upon it: O Lord, with the thief count us worthy of Thy Kingdom.[2]

Apolytikion (troparion) of the feast:

TONE ONE

O Lord, save Thy people and bless Thine inheritance, granting Orthodox Christians victory over their enemies,[3] and guarding Thy commonwealth with Thy Cross.

And the Dismissal.

Mattins

After the first reading from the Psalter, sessional hymn:

TONE ONE

We venerate the wood of Thy Cross, O Thou who lovest mankind, for upon it Thou, the Life of all, wast nailed. O Saviour, Thou hast opened Paradise to the thief who turned to Thee in faith, and Thou hast counted him worthy of blessedness when he confessed to Thee crying, 'O Lord remember me'.[4] Accept us like him, as we cry: We all have sinned, in Thy merciful kindness despise us not.

Glory be to the Father . . . Both now . . .

Repeat.

After the second reading from the Psalter, sessional hymn:

TONE SIX

No sooner had the wood of Thy Cross been set up, O Christ our Lord, than the foundations of death were shaken.

1 Exodus 17:10–14; Psalm 98:5.
2 Luke 23:42.
3 Literally, 'granting the kings victory over barbarians'.
4 Luke 23:42–43.

For that which hell had swallowed eagerly, it let go in trembling. Thou hast shown us Thy salvation, O Holy One, and we glorify Thee. Have mercy upon us, O Son of God.

Glory be to the Father . . . Both now . . .

Repeat.

After the polyeleos, the megalynarion:[1]

We magnify Thee, O Christ the Giver of life, and we honour Thy precious Cross, whereby we have been saved from the bondage of the enemy.

℣. O Lord, judge them that offend me: fight against them that fight against me (*Psalm* 34:1).

We magnify Thee . . .

℣. Take hold of shield and buckler, and stand up for mine help (*Psalm* 34:2).

We magnify Thee . . .

Glory be to the Father . . . Both now . . .

Alleluia, alleluia, alleluia, glory be to Thee, O God (*3 times*).

We magnify Thee . . .

Sessional hymn:

TONE EIGHT

In times past Joshua, the son of Nun, stretched out his arms crosswise, O my Saviour, mystically prefiguring the sign of the Cross: and the sun stood still until he had defeated the enemy that resisted Thee, O God.[2] And now this same sun is darkened, seeing Thee upon the Cross destroying the power of death and despoiling hell.

Glory be to the Father . . . Both now . . .

Repeat

[1] In the Slav use only.

[2] Joshua 10:12–13.

The first antiphon of the hymn of degrees in Tone Four.

Prokimenon: *TONE FOUR*

All the ends of the earth have seen the salvation of our God (*Psalm* 97 : 3).

℣. Sing unto the Lord a new song, for He hath done marvellous things (*ibid.*, 1).

Let everything that hath breath . . .

READING FROM THE HOLY GOSPEL ACCORDING TO JOHN (12 : 28–36).

The Lord said, Father, glorify Thy name. Then came there a voice from heaven, saying, I have both glorified it, and will glorify it again. The people therefore, that stood by, and heard it, said that it thundered: others said, An angel spake to Him. Jesus answered and said, This voice came not because of Me, but for your sakes. Now is the judgement of this world: now shall the prince of this world be cast out. And I, if I be lifted up from the earth, will draw all men unto Me. This He said, signifying what death He should die. The people answered Him, We have heard out of the law that Christ abideth for ever: and how sayest Thou, The Son of man must be lifted up? who is this Son of man? Then Jesus said unto them, Yet a little while is the light with you. Walk while ye have the light, lest darkness come upon you: for he that walketh in darkness knoweth not whither he goeth. While ye have light, believe in the light, that ye may be the children of light.

We have seen the Resurrection of Christ *is sung after the Gospel as on Sundays, whatever the day of the week on which the feast falls.*

Psalm 50.

Glory be to the Father . . .

TONE TWO

O three-branched Cross of Christ, thou art my strong protection. Sanctify me by thy might, that I may venerate and glorify thee in faith and love.

Both now . . .

Repeat.

Have mercy upon me . . .

TONE SIX

O Cross of Christ, thou hope of Christians, thou guide of those who have gone astray, haven of the storm-tossed, victory in warfare, firm foundation of the inhabited earth, physician of the sick, and resurrection of the dead: Have mercy upon us.

The Canon of the feast, by St. Cosmas. In each canticle, the irmos is repeated, and then twelve troparia are read. Before the troparia we say, Glory to Thy precious Cross, O Lord.

TONE EIGHT

Canticle One

(**Irmos**) Inscribing the invincible weapon of the Cross upon the waters, Moses marked a straight line before him with his staff and divided the Red Sea, opening a path for Israel who went over dry-shod. Then he marked a second line across the waters and united them in one, overwhelming the chariots of Pharaoh.[1] Therefore let us sing to Christ our God, for He has been glorified.

In times past Moses, standing between the two men of God,[2] prefigured in his person the undefiled Passion. Forming a cross with his outstretched hands, he raised a standard of victory and overthrew the power of all-destroying Amalek. Therefore let us sing to Christ our God, for He has been glorified.

[1] Exodus 14:21–29.
[2] Aaron and Hur (Exodus 17:10–14).

Moses set upon a wooden pole a cure against the deadly and poisonous bite of the serpents: for crosswise upon the wood —as a symbol of the Cross—he placed a serpent that creeps about the earth, and thereby he triumphed over calamity.[1] Therefore let us sing to Christ our God, for He has been glorified.

Heaven showed the Cross as sign of victory to Constantine, the holy king and upholder of the faith. Through it the proud insolence of his enemies was cast down, deceit was overthrown, and the divine faith was spread to the ends of the earth. Therefore let us sing to Christ our God, for He has been glorified.

(**Katavasia**) Inscribing the invincible weapon of the Cross upon the waters. . . .

Canticle Three

(**Irmos**) The rod of Aaron is an image of this mystery, for when it budded it showed who should be priest.[2] So in the Church, that once was barren, the wood of the Cross has now put forth flower, filling her with strength and steadfastness.

The rock that was struck and gushed forth water for a hard-hearted and disobedient people,[3] made manifest the mystery of the Church, chosen by God: for the Cross is her strength and steadfastness.

When the spear pierced Thine immaculate side, water flowed forth with blood, thereby establishing Thy New Testament, and washing sin away.[4] For the Cross is the glory of the faithful, the strength and steadfastness of kings.

(**Katavasia**) The rod of Aaron is an image of this mystery . . .

[1] Numbers 21 : 8–9; John 3 : 14.
[2] Numbers 17 : 8.
[3] Exodus 17 : 1–6.
[4] John 19 : 34; Matthew 26 : 28; Luke 22 : 20.

Sessional hymn

TONE EIGHT

In Paradise of old, the wood stripped me bare, for by giving its fruit to eat, the enemy brought in death. But now the wood of the Cross that clothes men with the garment of life has been set up in the midst of the earth, and the whole world is filled with boundless joy. Beholding it exalted, O ye people, let us with one accord raise in faith our cry to God: Thy house is full of glory.[1]

Glory be to the Father . . . Both now . . .

Repeat.

Canticle Four

(**Irmos**) O Lord, I have heard the mystery of Thy dispensation: I have considered Thy works, and I have glorified Thy Godhead.

In days of old Moses transformed with wood the bitter wells in the wilderness, prefiguring the bringing of the Gentiles to the true faith through the Cross.[2]

Jordan received into its deep bosom a sharp axe, and then was forced by a stick of wood to give it back again,[3] thus betokening the cutting of error by the Cross and baptism.

The people of Israel, a sacred army drawn up in four divisions, marched in this figure before the ark of the testimony, gaining glory by their ranks formed in the sign of the Cross.[4]

Stretched out in wondrous fashion, the Cross sent forth rays as the sun, and the heavens declared the glory of our God.[5]

[1] 3 Kings (1 Kings) 8:11; Isaiah 6:1.
[2] Exodus 15:23–25.
[3] 4 Kings (2 Kings) 6:4–7.
[4] Numbers 2.
[5] Psalm 18:2.

(**Katavasia**) O Lord, I have heard the mystery of Thy dispensation . . .

Canticle Five

(**Irmos**) O thrice-blessed Tree, on which Christ the King and Lord was stretched! Through thee the beguiler fell, who tempted mankind with the tree. He was caught in the trap set by God, who was crucified upon thee in the flesh, granting peace unto our souls.

Thou Wood famous in song, O Cross on which Christ was outstretched, the whirling sword that guarded Eden was afraid of thee; and the dread cherubim gave way before Christ who was crucified upon thee, granting peace unto our souls.[1]

The powers from beneath the earth, our adversaries, tremble when they see the sign of the Cross displayed in the air wherein they dwell; and the multitude of the inhabitants of heaven, together with those born on earth, bow the knee before Christ who grants peace unto our souls.[2]

Shining with pure rays, the holy Cross sheds its divine light upon the peoples darkened by the beguilement of error, and it reconciles them to Christ who was crucified upon it, granting peace unto our souls.

(**Katavasia**) O thrice-blessed Tree, on which Christ the King and Lord . . .

Canticle Six

(**Irmos**) Jonah stretched out his hands in the form of a cross within the belly of the sea monster, plainly prefiguring the redeeming Passion. Cast out from thence after three days, he foreshadowed the marvellous Resurrection of Christ our

[1] Genesis 3 : 24.
[2] Philippians 2 : 10; Ephesians 2 : 2.

God, who was crucified in the flesh and enlightened the world by His Rising on the third day.

Bent with age and wasted by sickness, Jacob was straightened when he crossed his hands,[1] showing thereby the power of the life-giving Cross. For God, who was crucified upon it in the flesh, thereby wrote anew the letter of the old Law written in shadows, and drove away the soul-destroying disease of error.

Holy Israel, by laying his hands crosswise on the heads of the young, signified that the people serving under the Law should enjoy for a time the honour due to the firstborn. When suspected of error in so doing, he changed not the life-giving figure: for, cried he, the newly-planted people of Christ our God, fortified by the Cross, shall take the higher place.[2]

(**Katavasia**) Jonah stretched out his hands in the form of a cross . . .

Kontakion

TONE FOUR

Lifted up of Thine own will upon the Cross, do Thou bestow Thy mercy upon the new commonwealth that bears Thy Name. Make the Orthodox people[3] glad in Thy strength, giving them victory over their enemies: may Thy Cross assist them in battle, weapon of peace and unconquerable ensign of victory.

Ikos

He who was caught up in the third heaven to Paradise,[4] and who heard unspeakable and divine words which it is not lawful for the human tongue to utter, wrote to the Galatians

[1] To bless his grandsons Ephraim and Manasseh (Genesis 48 : 14).
[2] Genesis 48 : 14–19.
[3] Literally, 'our faithful kings'.
[4] St. Paul (2 Corinthians 12 : 2–4).

—as lovers of the Scriptures, you have read His words and know—'But God forbid', said he, 'that I should glory save in the Cross of our Lord Jesus Christ'[1] on which He killed our passions by His Passion. Let us, then, firmly hold fast to the Cross of the Lord, the glory of us all: for this Wood is our salvation, weapon of peace and unconquerable ensign of victory.

Canticle Seven

(**Irmos**) The senseless decree of the wicked tyrant, breathing forth threats and blasphemy hateful to God, confused the people. Yet neither the fury of wild beasts nor the roaring of the fire could frighten the three Children: but standing together in the flame, fanned by the wind that brought refreshment as the dew, they sang: 'Blessed art Thou and praised above all, O our God and the God of our fathers.'

The first man, through eating from the tree, went to dwell in corruption: condemned to shameful banishment from life, he fell prey to bodily corruption, which he transmitted to all our kind like some pollution from disease. But the inhabitants of the earth, finding restoration in the wood of the Cross, cry aloud: Blessed art Thou and praised above all, O our God and the God of our Fathers.

The breaking of the law of God came through disobedience, and the untimely partaking of the fruit of the tree brought death to mortal men. Henceforth the tree of precious life was kept under guard, until the confession of the good thief[2] opened the path of access to it once again, as he perished in agony, crying: 'Blessed art Thou and praised above all, O our God and the God of our Fathers.'

Israel, foreseeing the future, did reverence to the top of

[1] Galatians 6:14.
[2] Luke 23:42.

Joseph's staff,[1] revealing how in times to come the most glorious Cross should be the safeguard of royal power. For it is a triumphal glory to kings, and a light to those who cry with faith: Blessed art Thou and praised above all, O our God and the God of our fathers.

(**Katavasia**) The senseless decree of the wicked tyrant . . .

Canticle Eight

(**Irmos**) O ye Children, equal in number to the Trinity, bless ye God the Father and Creator; sing ye the praises of the Word who descended and changed the fire to dew; and exalt ye above all for ever the most Holy Spirit, who gives life to all.

At the exaltation of the Wood that is sprinkled with the blood of the incarnate Word of God, sing praises, ye powers of heaven, feasting the restoration of mortal men. Ye people, venerate the Cross of Christ, whereby resurrection has been granted to the world unto all ages.

Ye earthly dispensers of grace, reverently exalt with your hands the Cross on which hung Christ our God, and the lance that pierced the body of God the Word. Let all the nations see the salvation of God and glorify Him unto all ages.

Ye faithful Christian kings, forechosen by divine decree, rejoice. Receiving from God the Precious Cross, make this victorious weapon your glory, for by it the tribes of the enemy that rashly seek battle are scattered unto all ages.

(**Katavasia**) O ye Children, equal in number to the Trinity . . .

Canticle Nine

The Magnificat and Greater in honour than the cherubim *are not sung, but before the irmos and the troparia we sing the megalynarion:*

[1] Genesis 47:31 (Septuagint).

Magnify, O my soul, the most precious Cross of the Lord.

(**Irmos**) O Theotokos, thou art a mystical Paradise, who untilled hast brought forth Christ. He has planted upon earth the life-giving Tree of the Cross: therefore at its Exaltation on this day, we worship Him and thee do we magnify.

Let all the trees of the wood rejoice,[1] for their nature is made holy by Christ, who planted them in the beginning and who was outstretched upon the Tree. At its Exaltation on this day, we worship Him and thee do we magnify.

The Cross is raised up as a sacred horn of strength to all God's people, upon whose foreheads it is marked. Thereby are all the horns of the spiritual powers of wickedness crushed.[2] At its Exaltation on this day, we worship Him and thee do we magnify.

Another Canon

Before the irmos and the troparia we sing:

Magnify, O my soul, the Exaltation of the life-giving Cross of the Lord.

(**Irmos**) Today the death that came to man through eating of the tree, is made of no effect through the Cross. For the curse of our mother Eve that fell on all mankind is destroyed by the fruit of the pure Mother of God, whom all the powers of heaven magnify.

Not suffering the deadly bitterness of the tree still to remain, Thou hast utterly destroyed it through the Cross. In like manner of old did wood once destroy the bitterness of the waters of Marah,[3] prefiguring the strength of the Cross that all the powers of heaven magnify.

Through the Cross, O Lord, today Thou hast raised us up again, who were plunged continually in the gloom of our

[1] Psalm 95:12.
[2] Psalm 74:10.
[3] Exodus 15:23–25.

forefather. Unrestrained greed thrust down our nature into error: but now we have been restored to our full inheritance by the light of Thy Cross which we, the faithful, magnify.

To show the world, O Lord, the figure of the Cross, reverenced in all places as most glorious, Thou hast formed it in the sky, shining with boundless light, unconquerable armour for the King.[1] This holy Cross do all the powers of heaven magnify.

Katavasia

The two irmoi, each preceded by its megalynarion:

O Theotokos, thou art a mystical Paradise . . .
Today the death that came to man . . .

Exapostilarion

TONE TWO

The Cross is the guardian of the whole earth; the Cross is the beauty of the Church. The Cross is the strength of kings; the Cross is the support of the faithful. The Cross is the glory of angels and the wounder of demons (*twice*).

Glory be to the Father . . . Both now . . .

Today the Cross is exalted and the world is sanctified. For Thou who art enthroned with the Father and the Holy Spirit hast spread Thine arms upon it, and drawn the world to knowledge of Thee, O Christ. Make worthy of divine glory those that have put their trust in Thee.

Lauds. Four stichera are sung:

TONE EIGHT

(*to the special melody*, O marvellous wonder . . .)

O marvellous wonder! The most holy Cross, the life-giving Tree, is lifted up on high today and shown to the

[1] Constantine.

world. All the ends of the earth give glory, all the devils are affrighted. How great a gift is here bestowed on mortal men! Through Thy Cross save our souls, O Christ, Thou who alone art full of compassion (*twice*).

O marvellous wonder! The Cross which carried the Most High as a cluster of grapes full of life is seen today exalted high above the earth. Through the Cross we all are drawn to God, and death has been for ever swallowed up. O undefiled Wood! Through thee we enjoy the immortal fruit of Eden, as we glorify Christ.

O marvellous wonder! The length and breadth of the Cross is equal to the heavens, for by divine grace it sanctifies the whole world. By the Cross barbarian nations are conquered, by the Cross the sceptres of kings are confirmed. O divine ladder! By thee we go up to heaven, exalting Christ the Lord in song.

Glory be to the Father . . . Both now . . .

TONE SIX

Today the Cross of the Lord goes forth, and the faithful welcome it with love; and they receive healing of soul and body and of every weakness. Let us kiss it with joy and fear: with fear, for we are unworthy because of sin; with joy, for upon it Christ the Lord was in His great mercy crucified, who grants the world salvation.

Great Doxology

During the Doxology the priest puts on all his vestments, and stands with the incense before the Holy Table, on which lies the Precious Cross, upon a tray with branches of basil or flowers. When the choir begins to sing Holy God, *he goes round the Holy Table, censing the Cross from the four sides. Then, while the choir sings the concluding* Holy God *to a slow and solemn melody, he takes the Cross with the tray and, placing it upon his head, he proceeds round the Holy Table and out of the sanctuary through the north door. The Cross is preceded by processional candles and the exapteryga, and by the deacon with the incense. The priest stops in front of the Royal Doors, facing to the east, and when the final* Holy God *has ended, he says:*

Wisdom, let us attend.

The choir then sings the troparion of the feast, O Lord, save Thy people *(p. 141), 3 times.*

The priest proceeds to the centre of the church, and places the Cross on a table or analogion specially prepared for it: and he censes the Cross from the four sides of the table.

The priest makes three prostrations, whatever day it may be, and, taking the precious Cross with the branches of basil, he faces towards the east, raises it above his head, and says in a loud voice:

Have mercy upon us, O God, according to Thy great mercy; we pray Thee, hear and have mercy.

The choir sings Kyrie eleison *a hundred times. The priest makes the sign of the Cross three times with the precious Cross, and then slowly bends to the ground with it, after which he slowly rises again, finally raising the Cross once more above his head. As the choir comes to the end of the first hundred* Kyrie eleison, *the priest lowers the Cross to the level of his chest, and once more makes the sign of the Cross with it three times.*

Then he stands on the right side of the table and, facing towards the north, he says:

Again we pray for all pious and Orthodox Christians.

And he raises the Cross as before, while the choir sings the second hundred Kyrie eleison.

He then stands on the east side of the table and, facing towards the west, he says:

Again we pray for our Archbishop (*name*) and for all our brethren in Christ.

The choir sings the third hundred Kyrie eleison, *while he raises the Cross as before.*

He then goes to the left side of the table and, turning towards the south, he says:

Again we pray for the souls of all Orthodox Christians, for their health and salvation, and the remission of their sins.

The choir sings the fourth hundred Kyrie eleison, *as he raises the Cross a fourth time.*

Finally he returns to the front of the table and, facing towards the east again, he says:

Again we pray for all who serve or have served in this holy church (*or* monastery), for their health and salvation, and the remission of their sins.

The choir sings the final hundred Kyrie eleison, *while the Cross is elevated for the fifth and last time.*[1]

Holding the Cross above his head, the priest sings the kontakion of the feast, Lifted up of Thine own will upon the Cross *(p. 148), and makes the sign of the Cross once more over the people.*

Then the priest lays the Cross on the table and sings once:

TONE SIX

We venerate Thy Cross, O Master, and we glorify Thy holy Resurrection.

This is repeated twice by the choir.

Meanwhile the priest makes two prostrations in front of the Cross and kisses it, after which he makes a third prostration. The Cross is then venerated by the other clergy in order of rank and by all the faithful, each making three prostrations, two before venerating the Cross, and one after.

[1] In the Russian Church this ceremony of the fivefold Exaltation of the Cross is normally performed only in cathedrals and monasteries, while in ordinary parish churches the Veneration of the Cross takes place without the Exaltation. In the Russian practice, during the five hundred *Kyrie eleison*, the priest faces in the following order: east, south, west, north, and again east.

During the veneration of the Cross, the choir sings the following:

TONE TWO

(by the Emperor Leo)

Come, ye faithful, and let us venerate the life-giving Wood, on which Christ, the King of Glory, stretched out His hands of His own will. To the ancient blessedness He raised us up, whom the enemy had before despoiled through pleasure, making us exiles far from God. Come, ye faithful, and let us venerate the Wood, through which we have been counted worthy to crush the heads of our invisible enemies. Come, all ye kindred of the nations, and let us honour in hymns the Cross of the Lord. Hail, O Cross, complete redemption of fallen Adam. With thee as their boast, our faithful kings laid low by thy might the people of Ishmael. We Christians kiss thee now with awe, and glorifying God who was nailed upon thee, we cry: O Lord, who on the Cross wast crucified, have mercy upon us, for Thou art good and lovest mankind.

TONE FIVE

Come, ye people, and looking on this marvellous wonder, let us venerate the might of the Cross. For a tree put forth the fruit of death in Paradise; but life is the flower of this Tree on which the sinless Lord was nailed. Reaping incorruption from it, all the nations cry: O Thou who through the Cross hast laid death low and set us free, glory to Thee.

SAME TONE

O God, fulfilled are the words of Thy prophets Isaiah and David, saying: 'All the nations shall come and worship before Thee, O Lord.'[1] For behold, O Thou who art good, the people filled with Thy grace in Thy courts at Jerusalem. O Thou who hast endured the Cross for us and hast brought us life by Thy Resurrection, guard us and save us.

[1] Psalm 85:9; Isaiah 66:23.

TONE SIX

Today is lifted up from the hidden places of the earth the Tree of life on which Christ was nailed, confirming our faith in the Resurrection. And exalted on high by priestly hands, it proclaims His Ascension into heaven, whereby our nature, lifted from its fallen state on earth, is made a citizen of heaven. Therefore let us cry in thanksgiving: O Lord who wast raised upon the Cross, Thou hast raised us with Thyself; count worthy of the joy of heaven those that praise Thee.[1]

SAME TONE

The four ends of the earth, O Christ our God, are sanctified today by the Exaltation of Thy Cross with its four arms: and with it is the horn of Thy faithful people[2] exalted, who thereby dash in pieces the horns of their adversaries. Great art Thou, O Lord, and marvellous in Thy works: glory to Thee.

SAME TONE

The sayings of the prophets foretold the holy Wood, whereby Adam was set free from the ancient curse of death. And today, at the Exaltation of the Cross, all creation raises its voice, asking of God plenteous mercy. O Master, who alone art boundless in compassion, be our atonement and save our souls.

TONE EIGHT

O God, fulfilled are the words of Thy prophet Moses, saying: 'Ye shall see your life hang before your eyes'.[3] Today the Cross is exalted and the world is set free from error. Today the Church of Christ's Resurrection celebrates its dedication, and the ends of the earth rejoice greatly; with cymbals like David, they offer Thee their song, saying: O

[1] This piece is not found in the Slavonic books.
[2] Literally, 'our faithful kings'.
[3] Deuteronomy 28:66 (Septuagint).

God, Thou hast worked salvation in the midst of the earth[1] through the Cross and the Resurrection, whereby Thou hast saved us, O Thou who art good and lovest mankind. Glory be to Thee, O all-powerful Lord.

SAME TONE

Today the Master of the Creation and the Lord of Glory is nailed to the Cross, and His side is pierced; and He who is the sweetness of the Church, tastes gall and vinegar. A crown of thorns is put upon Him who covers heaven with clouds; He is clothed in a cloak of mockery. He who formed man with His hands, is struck by a hand of clay. He who wrappeth the heaven in clouds, is smitten upon His back. He accepts spitting and scourging, reproach and buffeting; and all these things my Deliverer and God endures for me that am condemned, that in His compassion He may save the world from error.[2]

Glory be to the Father . . . Both now . . .

SAME TONE

Today He Who is by nature unapproachable, becomes approachable for me, and suffers His Passion, thus setting me free from passions. He who grants light unto the blind is spat upon by the mouths of the transgressors, and He gives His back to scourging for the sake of those that are captive. When the pure Virgin, His Mother, beheld Him upon the Cross, she cried out in pain: 'Woe is me, my Child: why hast Thou done this? Thou, whose beauty was fairer than that of all mortal men, dost appear without life and form, having neither shape nor comeliness. Woe is me, O my Light. I cannot bear to look upon Thee sleeping, and I am

[1] Psalm 73:12.

[2] This and the following troparion are taken from the Triodion (Veneration of the Cross on the third Sunday in Lent). They are used on 14 September only in the Slav practice.

wounded in my innermost self, a harsh sword pierces my heart.' I sing the praises of Thy Passion, I venerate Thy merciful kindness: glory to Thee, O longsuffering Lord.

And the Dismissal.

Liturgy

Antiphon One

TONE TWO

℣ 1. My God, my God, look upon me: why hast Thou forsaken me? (*Psalm* 21 : 2)

At the prayers of the Theotokos, save us, O Saviour.

℣ 2. The words of my transgressions are far from my salvation (*ibid.*).

At the prayers of the Theotokos . . .

℣ 3. O my God, I cry in the daytime, but Thou hearest not (*ibid.*, 3).

At the prayers of the Theotokos . . .

℣ 4. But Thou, the praise of Israel, dwellest in the sanctuary (*ibid.*, 4).

At the prayers of the Theotokos . . .
Glory be to the Father . . . Both now . . .
At the prayers of the Theotokos . . .

Antiphon Two

SAME TONE

℣ 1. O God, why hast Thou cast us off for ever? (*Psalm* 73 : 1)

O Son of God, crucified in the flesh, save us who sing to Thee: alleluia.

℣ 2. Remember Thy congregation, which Thou hast purchased of old (*ibid.*, 2).

O Son of God . . .

℣ 3. This is Mount Zion wherein Thou hast dwelt (*ibid.*).

O Son of God . . .

℣ 4. God is our King of old: working salvation in the midst of the earth (*ibid.*, 12).

O Son of God . . .
Glory be to the Father . . . Both now . . .
O Only-begotten Son and Word of God . . .

Antiphon Three

TONE ONE

℣ 1. The Lord reigneth, let the people rage: He sitteth upon the cherubim, let the earth be moved (*Psalm* 98 : 1).

The troparion of the feast, O Lord, save Thy people (*p. 141*).

℣ 2. The Lord is great in Zion: and He is high above all the people (*ibid.*, 2).

The troparion of the feast.

℣ 3. Let them give thanks to Thy great name: for it is holy (*ibid.*, 3).

The troparion of the feast.

Introit:

Exalt ye the Lord our God: and worship at His footstool, for He is holy (*Psalm* 98 : 5).

O Son of God, crucified in the flesh, save us who sing to Thee: alleluia.[1]

The troparion of the feast (p. 141); Glory be to the Father . . . Both now . . .; *the kontakion of the feast (p. 148).*

In place of the trisagion is sung:

We venerate Thy Cross, O Master: and we glorify Thy holy Resurrection (*3 times*).
Glory be to the Father . . . Both now . . .
And we glorify Thy holy Resurrection.

[1] In the Slav use, *O Son of God* . . . is sung only at pontifical services.

We venerate Thy Cross, O Master: and we glorify Thy holy Resurrection.

Prokimenon: *TONE SEVEN*

Exalt ye the Lord our God: and worship at His footstool, for He is holy (*Psalm* 98 : 5).

℣. The Lord reigneth, let the people rage (*ibid.*, 1).

READING FROM THE FIRST EPISTLE OF PAUL TO THE CORINTHIANS (1 : 18–24).

Brethren, the preaching of the Cross is to them that perish foolishness; but unto us which are saved it is the power of God. For it is written, I will destroy the wisdom of the wise, and will bring to nothing the understanding of the prudent. Where is the wise? Where is the scribe? Where is the disputer of this world? Hath not God made foolish the wisdom of this world? For after that in the wisdom of God the world by wisdom knew not God, it pleased God by the foolishness of preaching to save them that believe. For the Jews require a sign, and the Greeks seek after wisdom: but we preach Christ crucified, unto the Jews a stumbling block, and unto the Greeks foolishness; but unto them which are called, both Jews and Greeks, Christ, the power of God, and the wisdom of God.

Alleluia, TONE ONE

℣ 1. Remember Thy congregation, which Thou hast purchased of old (*Psalm* 73 : 2).

℣ 2. God is our King of old: working salvation in the midst of the earth (*ibid.*, 12).

READING FROM THE HOLY GOSPEL ACCORDING TO JOHN (19 : 6–11, 13–20, 25–28, 30–35).

At that time the chief priests and elders of the people took counsel against Jesus to put Him to death. And they came to Pilate, saying, Crucify Him, crucify Him. Pilate saith unto them, Take ye Him, and crucify Him: for I find no fault in Him. The Jews answered him, We have a law, and by our law He ought to die, because He made Himself the Son of God. When Pilate therefore heard that saying, he was the more afraid; and went again into the judgement hall, and saith unto Jesus, Whence art Thou? But Jesus gave him no answer. Then saith Pilate unto Him, Speakest Thou not unto me? Knowest Thou not that I have power to crucify Thee, and have power to release Thee? Jesus answered, Thou couldest have no power at all against Me, except it were given thee from above. When Pilate therefore heard that saying, he brought Jesus forth, and sat down in the judgement seat in a place that is called the Pavement, but in the Hebrew, Gabbatha. And it was the preparation of the passover, and about the sixth hour: and he saith unto the Jews, Behold your King! But they cried out, Away with Him, away with Him, crucify Him. Pilate saith unto them, Shall I crucify your King? The chief priests answered, We have no king but Caesar. Then delivered he Him therefore unto them to be crucified. And they took Jesus, and led Him away. And He bearing His cross went forth into a place called the place of a skull, which is called in the Hebrew, Golgotha: where they crucified Him, and two others with Him, on either side one, and Jesus in the midst. And Pilate wrote a title, and put it on the cross. And the writing was, Jesus of Nazareth the King of the Jews. This title then read many of the Jews: for the place where Jesus was crucified was nigh to the city: and it was written in Hebrew, and Greek, and Latin. Now there stood by the cross of Jesus His mother, and His mother's sister, Mary the wife of Cleophas, and Mary Magdalene. When Jesus therefore saw His mother, and the disciple standing by, whom He loved, He saith unto His mother, Woman, behold thy son! Then saith He to the disciple, Behold thy mother! And from that hour that disciple took her unto his own home. After this, Jesus, knowing that all things were now accomplished, bowed His head, and gave up the ghost. The Jews, therefore, because it was the preparation, that the bodies should not remain upon the cross on the sabbath day (for that sabbath day was an high day), besought Pilate that their legs might be broken, and that they might be taken away. Then came the soldiers, and brake the legs of the first, and of the other which was crucified with Him. But when they came to Jesus, and saw that He was dead already, they brake not His legs: but one of the soldiers with a spear pierced His side, and forthwith came there out blood and water. And he that saw it bare record, and his record is true.

In place of It is meet, *we sing the megalynarion and first irmos from Canticle Nine of the Canon (p. 151).*

Communion verse:

The light of Thy countenance is marked upon us, O Lord (*Psalm* 4:7).

Whatever the day of the week on which the Exaltation of the Cross occurs, even Saturday or Sunday, it is observed as a fast: neither meat, fish, nor animal products are eaten, but oil and wine may be used.

The apodosis of the feast falls on 21 September. On that day all the office of the feast is repeated, omitting only the entrance, lessons, lity, and breaking of bread at Vespers; and the polyeleos and Gospel at Mattins, together with the ceremonies of the Exaltation and Veneration of the Cross.

After the conclusion of the Liturgy, the priest comes out from the sanctuary with the censer, preceded by the deacon with a candle. He goes to the centre of the church, where the Cross is resting on a table, and he censes the precious Cross. Then he takes it with the tray and, placing it on his head, he carries it into the sanctuary, the deacon going in front and censing the Cross. Then the priest places the Cross on the Holy Table and censes it from the four sides, going round the Holy Table.

21 NOVEMBER

THE ENTRY OF THE MOST HOLY THEOTOKOS INTO THE TEMPLE

Small Vespers

On Lord, I have cried, *four stichera are sung:*

TONE ONE

(*to the special melody*, O purest Virgin, thou joy of the heavenly hierarchies . . .)

Having received the fruit of the promise come from the Lord, today in the temple Joachim and Ann offered the Mother of God as an acceptable sacrifice; and Zacharias the great High Priest received her with his blessing (*twice*).

Into the holy places the Holy of Holies is fittingly brought to dwell, as a sacrifice acceptable to God. The virgins adorned by virtues go before her carrying torches, and offer her to God as a most sacred Vessel.

Let the gate of the temple wherein God dwells be opened: for Joachim brings within today in glory the Temple and Throne of the King of all, and he consecrates as an offering to God her whom the Lord has chosen to be his Mother.

Glory be to the Father . . . Both now . . .

TONE SIX[1]

David prophesied concerning thee, O Undefiled, foretelling thine entry and thy consecration in the temple.[2]

[1] In some editions of the service books, Tone Eight.

[2] Psalm 44:15–16.

Keeping this feast today, the ends of the earth glorify thee, O far-famed Lady. Zacharias rejoices as he receives thee at thine entry this day into the temple, thou Mother of the Word of life, who, Virgin before childbirth, hast remained after childbirth Virgin. The Holy of Holies is filled with exultation as it welcomes thee, who dost sustain our life. Therefore we also cry to thee in song: Entreat thy Son and our God on our behalf, that we may be granted great mercy.

Aposticha:

TONE TWO

(*to the special melody*, O house of Ephratah . . .)

O ye gates of the sanctuary, into the Holy of Holies receive ye a Virgin, the spotless Tabernacle of God the Almighty.

℣. Virgins shall be brought to the King after her: her companions shall be brought unto Thee (*Psalm* 44:15).

Ye virgins, joyfully bearing torches, attend the pure Virgin on her way, as she enters the Holy of Holies, the Bride of the King of all.

℣. With gladness and rejoicing shall they be brought: they shall be brought into the temple of the King (*ibid.*, 16).

The living Bridal Chamber of God the Word receives bread from the hands of a divine angel, as she dwells in the Holy of Holies.

Glory be to the Father . . . Both now . . .

SAME TONE

The three-lamped Light, making thee burn, O Theotokos, in the temple of His glory, sends thee heavenly food, and magnifies thee.

Apolytikion (troparion) of the feast, Today is the foreshadowing of the good pleasure (*p. 172*), *and Dismissal.*

Great Vespers

We sing Blessed is the man (*the first portion of the first kathisma*).

On Lord, I have cried, *eight stichera are sung:*

TONE ONE

(*to the special melody*, O marvellous wonder . . .)

Today let us, the faithful, dance for joy, singing to the Lord with psalms and hymns, venerating His hallowed Tabernacle, the living Ark, that contained the Word who cannot be contained. For she, a young child in the flesh, is offered in wondrous fashion to the Lord, and with rejoicing Zacharias the great High Priest receives her as the dwelling place of God (*twice*).

Today the living Temple of the holy glory of Christ our God, she who alone among women is pure and blessed, is offered in the temple of the Law, that she may make her dwelling in the sanctuary. Joachim and Ann rejoice with her in spirit, and choirs of virgins sing to the Lord, chanting psalms and honouring His Mother (*twice*).

Thou, O Virgin Mother of God, art she whom the prophets proclaimed. Thou art the glory of the apostles and the pride of martyrs, the restoration of all who dwell on earth: for through thee we are reconciled to God. Therefore we honour thy coming into the temple of the Lord; and saved by thine intercession, with the angel we all cry to thee: 'Hail! Most Holy'.

TONE FOUR

Led by the Holy Spirit, the holy Maid without spot is taken to dwell in the Holy of Holies. By an angel is she fed, who is in truth the most holy Temple of our Holy God. He has sanctified all things by her entry, and has made godlike the fallen nature of mortal men.

The young girls rejoice today, and with their lamps in hand they go in reverence before the spiritual Lamp, as she enters into the Holy of Holies. They foreshadow the brightness past speech that is to shine forth from her and to give light by the Spirit to those that sit in the darkness of ignorance.[1]

Ann the all-blessed cried out rejoicing: 'O Zacharias, take her whom the prophets of God proclaimed in the Spirit, and lead her into the holy temple, there to be brought up in reverence, that she may become the divine Throne of the Master of all, His Palace, His resting-place, and His dwelling filled with light.'

Glory be to the Father . . . Both now . . .

TONE EIGHT

After thy birth, O Lady and Bride of God, thou hast gone to dwell in the temple of the Lord, there to be brought up in the Holy of Holies, for thou art thyself holy: and Gabriel then was sent to thee, O Virgin all-undefiled, to bring thee food. All the powers of heaven stood amazed, seeing the Holy Spirit dwell in thee. Therefore, O Mother of God without stain or blemish, glorified in heaven and on earth, save our kind.

Entrance, O joyful light, *and prokimenon of the day.*

Lessons:

Reading from Exodus (40:1–5, 9–10, 16, 34–35).

And the Lord spake unto Moses, saying, On the first day of the first month shalt thou set up the tabernacle of the tent of the congregation. And thou shalt put therein the ark of the testimony, and cover the ark with the veil. And thou shalt bring in the table, and set in order the things that are to be set in order upon it; and thou shalt bring in the candlestick, and light the lamps thereof. And thou shalt set the altar

[1] Isaiah 9:2.

of gold for the incense before the ark of the testimony, and put the hanging of the door to the tabernacle. And thou shalt take the anointing oil and anoint the tabernacle, and all that is therein, and shalt hallow it, and all the vessels thereof; and it shall be holy. And thou shalt anoint the altar of the burnt offering, and all the vessels, and sanctify the altar: and it shall be an altar most holy. Thus did Moses: according to all that the Lord commanded him, so did he. Then a cloud covered the tent of the congregation, and the glory of the Lord filled the tabernacle. And Moses was not able to enter into the tent of the congregation, because the cloud abode thereon, and the glory of the Lord filled the tabernacle.

Reading from the Third Book of Kings (1 Kings 7:51; 8:1, 3–4, 5, 6–7, 9–11).

So was ended all the work that king Solomon made for the house of the Lord. Then Solomon assembled the elders of Israel, and all the heads of the tribes, the chief of the fathers of the children of Israel, unto Jerusalem, that they might bring up the ark of the covenant of the Lord out of the city of David, which is Zion. And all the elders of Israel came, and the priests took up the ark. And they brought up the ark of the Lord, and the tabernacle of the congregation, and all the holy vessels that were in the tabernacle, even those did the priests and the Levites bring up. And king Solomon, and all the congregation of Israel, that were assembled unto him, were with him before the ark. And the priests brought in the ark of the covenant of the Lord unto His place, into the oracle of the house, to the most holy place, even under the wings of the cherubims. For the cherubims spread forth their two wings over the place of the ark, and the cherubims covered the ark and the staves thereof above. There was nothing in the ark save the two tables of stone, which Moses put there at Horeb, when the Lord made a covenant with the children of Israel, when they came out of the land of Egypt.

And it came to pass, when the priests were come out of the holy place, that the cloud filled the house of the Lord, so that the priests could not stand to minister because of the cloud: for the glory of the Lord had filled the house of the Lord.

READING FROM THE PROPHET EZEKIEL (43:27–44:4. *See p. 103*).

At the Lity:

TONE ONE

(*by George of Nicomedia*)

Today let heaven above greatly rejoice and let the clouds pour down gladness[1] at the mighty acts, exceeding marvellous, of our God. For behold, the Gate that looks towards the east,[2] born according to the promise from a fruitless and barren womb, and dedicated to God as His dwelling, is led today into the temple as an offering without blemish. Let David greatly rejoice, striking his harp. 'Virgins', said he, 'shall be brought to the King after her, her companions shall be brought unto Thee.[3] Within the tabernacle of God, within His place of propitiation, she shall be brought up, to become the dwelling place of Him who was begotten of the Father without change before all ages, for the salvation of our souls.'

TONE FOUR

(*by the same*)

Today the Theotokos, the Temple that is to hold God, is led into the temple of the Lord, and Zacharias receives her. Today the Holy of Holies rejoices greatly, and the choir of angels mystically keeps feast. With them let us also celebrate the festival today, and let us cry aloud with Gabriel: Hail,

[1] Isaiah 45:8.
[2] Ezekiel 44:1–3.
[3] Psalm 44:15.

thou who art full of grace: the Lord is with thee, He who has great mercy.[1]

SAME TONE

Come, all ye peoples, and let us praise her who alone is undefiled: she who was foretold by the prophets and offered in the temple, the Mother preordained before all ages, who in the last times has been shown forth as Theotokos. O Lord, at her intercession grant us Thy peace and great mercy.

Glory be to the Father . . . Both now . . .

TONE FIVE

(*by Leo the Master*)

A day of joy has dawned, and a feast worthy of all reverence. For today she who was Virgin before childbirth, and remained Virgin after bearing child, is offered in the temple. The venerable Zacharias, father of the Forerunner, cried aloud rejoicing: 'The Expectation of those in affliction, herself holy, is come to the holy temple, there to be consecrated as dwelling-place of the Almighty.' Let Joachim the forefather be glad and let Ann rejoice exceedingly, for they have offered unto God, as a three year old victim of sacrifice, the Queen without blemish. Rejoice with them, O ye mothers; ye virgins, dance for joy, and ye barren, be of good cheer. For the preordained Queen of all has opened the Kingdom of Heaven unto us. Rejoice and be exceeding glad, ye peoples.

Aposticha:

TONE FIVE

(*to the special melody*, Hail, life-giving Cross . . .)

Heaven and earth rejoice, beholding the spiritual Heaven, the only Virgin without blemish, enter the house of God,

[1] Luke 1:28.

there to be reared in reverence. To her Zacharias in amazement cried: 'O Gate of the Lord! Unto thee I open the gates of the temple: rejoice and go round it in gladness. For I know and believe that the deliverance of Israel shall now come to dwell openly in our midst, and that from thee shall be born God the Word, who grants the world great mercy.'

℣. Virgins shall be brought to the King after her: her companions shall be brought unto Thee (*Psalm* 44:15).

Ann, truly blessed by God's grace, led with gladness into the temple of the Lord the pure and ever-Virgin, who is full of grace, and she called the young girls to go before her, lamps in hand. 'Go, Child', she said, 'to Him who gave thee unto me; be unto Him an offering and a sweet smelling incense. Go into the place which none may enter: learn its mysteries and prepare thyself to become the pleasing and beautiful dwelling-place of Jesus, who grants the world great mercy.'

℣. With gladness and rejoicing shall they be brought: they shall be brought into the temple of the King (*ibid.*, 16).

The most holy Virgin, Temple that is to hold God, is dedicated within the temple of the Lord; and young girls, bearing lamps, now go before her. Her noble parents, Joachim and Ann, leap for joy and dance, for they have borne her that is to bear the Creator; and she, the All-Pure, with rejoicing goes round the divine habitations and is fed by the hands of an angel. She it is that shall become Mother of Christ, who grants the world great mercy.

Glory be to the Father . . . Both now . . .

TONE SIX

(by Sergios of the Holy City)

Today let us, the arrays of the assembled faithful, triumph in spirit and reverently praise the Child of God, Virgin and Theotokos, as she is offered in the temple of the Lord: she who was forechosen from all generations to be the dwelling-place of Christ, the Master and God of all. O virgins bearing lamps, go ye before her, honouring the majestic advance of the ever-Virgin. Ye mothers, setting aside every sorrow, follow them in gladness, singing the praises of her who became the Mother of God and mediator of joy for the world. With the angel joyfully let us all cry 'Hail!' to her that is full of grace and ever intercedes for our souls.

Apolytikion (troparion) of the feast:

TONE FOUR

Today is the foreshadowing of the good pleasure of God and the herald of the salvation of men. The Virgin is revealed in the temple of God, and beforehand she announces Christ to all. Let us therefore cry to her with mighty voice: Hail! Thou fulfilment of the Creator's dispensation.

And the Dismissal.

Mattins

After the first reading from the Psalter, sessional hymn:

TONE ONE

The fruit of righteous Joachim and Ann is brought as an offering to God in the holy sanctuary, she who sustains our life, a young child in the flesh; and she receives the blessing of Zacharias the priest. Let all of us in faith call her blessed, for she is the Mother of the Lord.

Glory be to the Father . . . Both now . . .

Repeat.

After the second reading from the Psalter, sessional hymn:

TONE FOUR

Before thy conception, O pure Virgin, thou wast consecrated to God; and now after thy birth thou art offered as a gift to Him, in fulfilment of thy parents' promise. To the divine temple thou art brought, thyself a Temple truly divine, innocent from the time thou wast a babe; thou hast appeared in the sanctuary accompanied by brightly burning lamps, who art the Receiver of the Divine Light that no man can approach. Magnificent in truth is thine entry, O only Bride of God and ever-Virgin.

Glory be to the Father . . . Both now . . .

Repeat.

After the polyeleos, the megalynarion:[1]

We magnify thee, O most holy Virgin, Maiden chosen of God, and we honour thine entry into the temple.

℣. Great is the Lord and greatly to be praised: in the city of our God and in His holy mountain (*Psalm* 47 : 2).

We magnify thee . . .

℣. Holy is Thy temple, and wonderful in righteousness (*Psalm* 64 : 5–6).

We magnify thee . . .

Glory be to the Father . . . Both now . . .

Alleluia, alleluia, alleluia, glory be to Thee, O God (*3 times*).

We magnify thee . . .

Sessional hymn: *TONE EIGHT*

Let David the Psalmist greatly rejoice, let Joachim and Ann be glad, for a holy child has come forth from them, Mary the Lamp that bears the Divine Light; and she rejoices as she enters the temple. The son of Barachias,[2] beholding her, gave her his blessing and cried out in joy: 'Hail! Thou wonder of all the world.'

Glory be to the Father . . . Both now . . .

Repeat.

[1] In the Slav use only.
[2] Zacharias (Matthew 23 : 35).

The first antiphon of the hymn of degrees in Tone Four.

Prokimenon: TONE FOUR

Hearken, O daughter, and consider, and incline thine ear (*Psalm* 44:11).

℣. My heart is inditing a good matter (*ibid.*, 2).

Let everything that hath breath . . .

READING FROM THE HOLY GOSPEL ACCORDING TO LUKE (1:39–49, 56. *See p. 109*).

Psalm 50.

Glory be to the Father . . .

TONE TWO

Today the living Temple of the great King enters the temple to be prepared as a divine dwelling-place for Him. O ye people, rejoice exceedingly.

Both now . . .

Repeat.

Have mercy upon me . . .

Today the Theotokos, the Temple that is to hold God, *the second of the stichera sung at the Lity (p. 169).*

Two Canons are used, the first by George of Nicomedia and the second by Basil the Monk. Before the troparia we say Most holy Theotokos, save us.

Canticle One

First Canon

TONE FOUR

(**Irmos**) I shall open my mouth and the Spirit will inspire it, and I shall utter the words of my song to the Queen and

Mother: I shall be seen radiantly keeping feast and joyfully praising her entry.

We know that thou, O All-Undefiled, art a treasury of wisdom and a never-failing fountain of grace. We therefore pray thee, O Lady, let fall some drops of knowledge upon us, that we may sing thy praises for ever.

Thou who art honoured, O Most Holy, far above the heavens, thou who art both Temple and Palace, thou art dedicated in the temple of God, to be prepared as a divine dwelling-place for His coming.

She who made the light of grace shine forth, the Theotokos, has illuminated all men and brought them together to adorn with songs her most radiant triumph. O come, let us join them and hasten to her.

Having opened the gates of the temple of God, the Glorious Gate[1] through which human thoughts cannot pass now urges us to enter with her and to delight in her divine marvels.

Second Canon

TONE ONE

(**Irmos**) Let us all sing a triumphant song unto God who has done wondrous things with His mighty arm, and has saved Israel: for He has been glorified.

Let us this day hasten together to the Theotokos, honouring her in songs, and let us keep spiritual feast. For she is offered in the temple as a gift to God.

Let us praise in songs the glorious advance of the Theotokos. For today as a precious gift she is prophetically offered in the temple, who is herself a Temple of God.

Ann without reproach greatly rejoiced, offering her child in the temple as a precious gift to God, while Joachim, bright with joy, kept feast with her.

[1] Ezekiel 44:1–3.

David the forefather praised thee of old in hymns, O Virgin Bride of God, calling thee Daughter of Christ the King:[1] Him thou hast borne as Mother and thou hast fed Him as thy child.

The Theotokos, when she was three years old after the flesh, was led to the Lord; and Zacharias, the priest of God, received her in the temple with rejoicing and established her there.

Ye virgins carrying lamps, be of good cheer today and begin the song; ye mothers, join them in praises to the Queen and Mother, as she enters the temple of Christ the King.

Glory be to the Father . . .

O Trinity, one in essence, Father, Word, and Holy Spirit, with faith we glorify Thee as Maker of all, and in reverence we cry: Save us, O God.

Both now . . .

The King and God goes forth wearing the purple dyed from thy blood, O All-Undefiled. He has renewed all mankind in His compassion.

Katavasia,[2] *TONE ONE*

Christ is born, give ye glory. Christ comes from heaven, meet ye Him. Christ is on earth, be ye exalted. O all the earth, sing unto the Lord, and sing praises in gladness, O ye people, for He has been glorified.

Canticle Three

First Canon

(**Irmos**) O Mother of God, thou living and plentiful fount, give strength to those united in spiritual fellowship,

[1] Psalm 44: 14.

[2] The feast of the Entry of the Mother of God falls within the Christmas fast, and so the katavasia at the end of each canticle is taken from the office for Christmas.

who sing hymns of praise to thee: and on this day of thy venerable entry, vouchsafe unto them crowns of glory.

Today has the temple become a wedding adornment and a fair chamber for the Virgin, as it receives the living Bridal Chamber of God, pure and without spot, she who shines more brightly than all the creation.

David, leading the dance, leaps in gladness and rejoices with us, and thee, O undefiled and all-pure Virgin, he calls the Queen, clad in raiment of many-coloured needlework, standing in the temple before the King and God.[1]

From Eve of old the transgression came upon mankind, and now from Eve's stock has flowered forth our restoration and incorruption, even the Theotokos, who is brought today into the house of God.

The hosts of angels and the multitude of all mankind dance today before thy face, O all-pure Lady, and carrying lamps they go before thee, proclaiming thy greatness in the house of God.

Second Canon

(**Irmos**) Let my heart be established in Thy will, O Christ my God, who hast established the second heaven above the waters, and hast founded the earth upon the floods, in Thine almighty power.[2]

O ye who love the feasts, celebrate and be glad in spirit, exulting today in the holy feast of the Daughter of the King and the Mother of our God.

Be glad today, O Joachim, and rejoice exceedingly in spirit, O Ann, who now present unto the Lord your daughter, as a three-year old victim of sacrifice, holy and utterly without spot.

[1] 2 Kings (2 Samuel) 6:14–16; Psalm 44:14.
[2] Genesis 1:7; Psalm 23:2.

Dwelling-place of God, the Theotokos Mary, three years old after the flesh, is offered in the holy temple, and the virgins her companions, carrying lamps, go before her.

The ewe-lamb of God without spot, the dove without blemish,[1] the tabernacle that is to hold God, the sanctuary of the glory, has chosen to dwell in the holy temple.

Three years old in the flesh and many years old in spirit, more spacious than the heavens and higher than the powers above, let the Bride of God be praised in song.

Celebrating the coming of the Theotokos into the sanctuary, let us too, carrying lamps today in spirit, go in joy with the virgins to the temple.

Ye priests of God, clothe yourselves by grace in righteousness, going in joy to meet the Daughter of the King and God as she enters the Holy Place.

Glory be to the Father . . .

The Father is Light, His Son is Light, and the Spirit, the Comforter, is Light: for, shining forth as from one sun, the Trinity divinely illuminates and preserves our souls.

Both now . . .

The prophets proclaimed thee in ages past, speaking of thee as ark of holiness, golden censer, candlestick, and table;[2] and we sing thy praises as the Tabernacle that held God.

(**Katavasia**) To the Son who was begotten of the Father without change before all ages, and in the last times was without seed made flesh of the Virgin, to Christ our God let us cry aloud: Thou hast raised up our horn, holy art Thou, O Lord.

Sessional hymn

TONE FOUR

Cry out, O David, what is this present feast? Is it for her

[1] Numbers 6:14; Leviticus 14:10,22.

[2] Psalm 131:8; 1 Kings 7:50 (Hebr.); Hebrews 9:4; Exodus 25:23,31.

of whom thou hast sung in the Book of Psalms, calling her Daughter, Child of God and Virgin, saying: 'Her companions the virgins that follow her shall be mystically led unto the King?'[1] Make this feast to be held in honour throughout all the world by those who cry: The Theotokos is come among us, mediator of salvation.

Glory be to the Father . . . Both now . . .

Repeat.

Canticle Four

First Canon

(**Irmos**) Perceiving the unsearchable purpose of God concerning Thine Incarnation from a Virgin, O Most High, the prophet Habakkuk cried: Glory to Thy power, O Lord.

Today the house of God receives the Gate through which none may pass;[2] so it has brought an end to the worship commanded by the shadow of the Law, and it cries aloud: 'Verily the truth has appeared to those on earth.'

The overshadowed mountain that Habakkuk foresaw[3] and announced prophetically in days of old, has come to dwell within the sanctuary of the temple; there she has put forth flowers of virtue and with her shadow she covers the ends of the earth.

Let us, with all the earth, look upon these marvellous, strange, and wonderful events: how the Virgin, receiving food from an angel, offers us an image of the divine dispensation.

Appearing as a Temple and a Palace and living Heaven, thou art dedicated today in the temple of the Law, to be kept therein, O undefiled Bride of God.

[1] Psalm 44: 14–15.
[2] Ezekiel 44: 1–3.
[3] Habakkuk 3: 3.

Second Canon

(**Irmos**) O prophet Habakkuk, thou hast foreseen in spirit the Incarnation of the Word, and hast proclaimed crying: 'Thou shalt be acknowledged when the years draw nigh; Thou shalt be made manifest when the times come. Glory to Thy power, O Lord.'

O prophet Isaiah, prophesy to us: who is the Virgin that shall conceive?[1] 'It is she who has come forth from the root of Judah and who was born of David the King, glorious fruit of a holy seed.'

O ye virgins, begin your songs, and with lamps in hand praise the advance of the pure Theotokos, who now enters the temple of the Lord, and keep ye feast with us.

Be glad, O Joachim and Ann, who now present unto the Lord in the temple, as a three-year old victim of sacrifice, your daughter that shall be the pure Mother of Christ our God, the King of all.

O venerable Holy of Holies, thou dost love to dwell in the holy temple; and thou abidest, O Virgin, in converse with angels, receiving bread most marvellously from heaven, O thou who dost sustain our life.

When all hope was gone, Joachim and Ann gave birth to the undefiled Virgin, and in piety they promised to offer her to God. Today they fulfil their promise, giving their child as a sacrifice in the house of God.

The rod of Aaron once put forth shoot,[2] prefiguring, O undefiled Virgin, thy divine childbirth. For without seed shalt thou conceive and not suffer corruption; and after bearing child shalt thou remain Virgin, giving suck to a babe who is God of all.

Ye virgins, with piety hasten to the Virgin, and ye mothers to the Mother: together let us honour the Child born to

[1] Isaiah 7:14.
[2] Numbers 17:8.

Joachim and Ann, as a blameless Sanctuary, and the Mother that bore Christ, as a holy Tree bringing forth fruit to God. Let us all joyously keep feast.

Glory be to the Father . . .

Three in Persons, One in nature, in reverence we glorify the true God whose praises the hosts of angels and archangels sing as Master of the Creation; and in faith we all worship Him for ever.

Both now . . .

O pure and undefiled Virgin, pray without ceasing to thy Son and God, whom thou hast conceived in the flesh, that He may deliver all thy servants from the manifold snares of the devil and from every temptation that assails us.

(**Katavasia**) Rod of the root of Jesse, and flower that blossomed from his stem, O Christ, Thou hast sprung from the Virgin. From the Mountain overshadowed by the forest Thou hast come, made flesh from her that knew not wedlock, O God who art not formed from matter. Glory to Thy power, O Lord.[1]

Canticle Five

First Canon

(**Irmos**) The whole world was amazed at thy venerable entry. For thou, O Virgin who hast not known wedlock, thyself a Temple most pure, hast gone within the temple of God, bestowing peace upon all who sing thy praises.

Glorious sanctuary and holy offering, today the most pure Virgin is dedicated in the temple of God; and in ways which He alone understands, she is kept as a dwelling-place for our God, the King of all.

Seeing the beauty of thy soul, O undefiled Virgin, Zacharias cried out with faith: 'Thou art our deliverance, thou art the joy of all. Thou art our restoration, through

[1] Isaiah 11:1; Habakkuk 3:3.

whom the Incomprehensible appears comprehensible to me.'

O Virgin all-undefiled, past understanding are thy wonders! Strange is the manner of thy birth: strange is the manner of thy growing. Strange and most marvellous are all things concerning thee, O Bride of God, and they are beyond the telling of mortal man.

Thou candlestick with many lights,[1] O Bride of God, thou hast shone forth today in the house of the Lord, and thou dost give us light through the holy gifts of grace from thy wonders, O pure and far-famed Theotokos.

Second Canon

(**Irmos**) O Christ our Master and God who lovest man, cause the radiant and everlasting light to shine upon us, who ponder early in the morning upon the judgements of Thy commandments.

Let us, the Orthodox, all hasten together with our lamps and glorify the Mother of God, for today she is offered to the Lord as an acceptable sacrifice.

Let the forefathers rejoice exceedingly today, O Lady, and let her that bore thee make glad with thy father: for their fruit is led unto the Lord.

Let us all, keeping feast in faith, sing the praises of the undefiled Maiden, most glorious and of many names, for she conceived in the flesh the divine Victim and sacrificial Offering.

The contract of thy betrothal, the divine tokens of thy Motherhood past understanding, O pure Virgin, are written today by the Holy Spirit in the house of God.

Let the forecourt of the glory of our God be opened and let it receive, as a victim of sacrifice three years old and without blemish, the Mother of God who was never to know wedlock.

[1] Exodus 25:31.

Let us sing the praises of that greatly venerated and overshadowed mountain,[1] the ever-Virgin who became the Mother of God. For she has made light shine to the ends of the earth.

Glory be to the Father . . .

Let us glorify and worship the one Godhead in three Persons, undivided by nature and equal in glory, that was before the beginning and ever shall be.

Both now . . .

We have thine intercession, O Mother of God, as a fair haven and an unassailable rampart in times of trouble, and we are ever delivered from danger and affliction.

(**Katavasia**) As Thou art God of peace and Father of mercies, Thou hast sent unto us Thine Angel of great counsel,[2] granting us peace. So are we guided towards the light of the knowledge of God, and watching by night we glorify Thee, O Lover of mankind.

Canticle Six

First Canon

(**Irmos**) As we celebrate this sacred and solemn feast of the Mother of God, let us come, clapping our hands, O people of the Lord, and give glory to God who was born of her.

He who supports all things with His word, in His mercy has hearkened unto the prayer of righteous Joachim and Ann: He has loosed them from the disease of barrenness and given them her that is the cause of our joy.

The Lord, wishing to make known to the Gentiles His salvation, has now chosen from among men her that knew not wedlock, to be a sign of reconciliation and renewal.

[1] Habakkuk 3:3.

[2] Isaiah 9:6 (Septuagint).

Being thyself, O Undefiled, a house of grace, in which are laid the treasures of the ineffable dispensation of God, thou dost partake of boundless joy in the temple.

Having received thee as a royal diadem, O Bride of God, the temple shone with beauty and gave place to better things, seeing in thee the fulfilment of the prophecies.

Second Canon

(**Irmos**) With the prophet Jonah I shout: O Thou who art good, deliver my life from corruption and save me, O Saviour of the world, as I cry: Glory to Thee.

Ye faithful, let us feast in spirit the Mother of God, singing her praises with piety. For she is indeed more holy than the heavenly powers.

Ye faithful, let us praise in spiritual songs the Mother of the Light, for today has she been manifested to us as she enters the temple of God.

The ewe-lamb without blemish, the pure dove,[1] is brought as an offering to dwell in the house of God: the undefiled Virgin who was foreordained to become the Mother of God.

The Temple of God, the heavenly Tabernacle, accomplished her entry into the temple of the Law, and from her the Light has shone on us in darkness.

A child in the flesh but perfect in soul, the holy Ark enters into the house of God, there to feed upon divine grace.

By thine intercessions set us free from every temptation and danger of soul, for we run to thee, O far-famed Mother of Christ our God.

Glory be to the Father . . .

Father, Son, and Spirit of righteousness, Unity in three persons and undivided Trinity, have mercy upon those who worship Thy divine power.

Both now . . .

[1] Numbers 6:14; Leviticus 14:10,22.

He whom nothing can contain was contained in thy womb, O undefiled Mother of God, and from thee He has come forth double in nature, God and Man.

(**Katavasia**) The sea monster spat forth Jonah as it had received him, like a babe from the womb: while the Word, having dwelt in the Virgin and taken flesh, came forth from her yet kept her uncorrupt. For being Himself not subject to decay, He preserved His Mother free from harm.

Kontakion

TONE FOUR

The all-pure Temple of the Saviour, the precious Bridal Chamber and Virgin, the sacred treasure of the glory of God, is led today into the house of the Lord, and with her she brings the grace of the divine Spirit. Of her God's angels sing in praise: 'She is indeed the heavenly Tabernacle.'

Ikos

Seeing the grace of the secret mysteries of God made manifest and clearly fulfilled in the Virgin, I rejoice; and I know not how to understand the strange and secret manner whereby the Undefiled has been revealed as alone chosen above all creation, visible and spiritual. Therefore, wishing to praise her, I am struck dumb with amazement in both mind and speech. Yet still I dare to proclaim and magnify her: She is indeed the heavenly Tabernacle.

Canticle Seven

First Canon

(**Irmos**) The Holy Children bravely trampled upon the threatening fire, preferring not to worship created things rather than the Creator, and they sang in joy: 'Blessed art Thou and praised above all, O Lord God of our fathers.'

Lo, a glad springtime has shone now to the ends of the

earth, making our soul and understanding and mind bright through grace: for today is the feast of the Theotokos. Let us rejoice mystically.

Today let all things, heaven and earth, the ranks of angels and the multitude of mortal men, attend the Queen and Mother, and let them cry aloud: 'Joy and deliverance is led into the temple.'

The written Law has passed away and vanished as a shadow, and the rays of grace have shone forth at thine entry into the temple of God, O undefiled Virgin Mother, who art for ever blessed.

O undefiled Lady, heaven and earth and the things beneath the earth have been brought into subjection to thy Son as Maker and God, and all mortal tongues confess that the Lord has appeared, the Saviour of our souls.[1]

Second Canon

(**Irmos**) The furnace was sprinkled with dew, O Saviour, and the Children danced for joy as they sang: 'O God of our fathers, blessed art Thou.'

Let us exult today in the joy of the feast; let us honour, as is meet, Joachim and Ann, and let us sing the praises of the undefiled Virgin.

Let David prophesy, who said in the spirit: 'Virgins shall be brought after thee; they shall be brought into the temple to the Queen and Mother.'[2]

The ranks of angels rejoiced exceedingly and spirits of the righteous were glad, when the Mother of God was led into the sanctuary.

Mary without spot rejoiced in body and spirit, dwelling as a sacred vessel in the temple of the Lord.

Receiving heavenly food, she who was to become the

[1] Philippians 2:10–11.
[2] Psalm 44:15–16.

Mother of Christ the Saviour according to the flesh, increased in wisdom and grace.

Thy wise parents led thee to the innermost part of the temple, O undefiled Virgin, there to be brought up in strange fashion and prepared as dwelling-place for Christ our God.

Glory be to the Father . . .

Let us glorify the undivided Trinity, let us sing the praises of the one Godhead, the Father, the Word, and the Most Holy Spirit.

Both now . . .

Pray the Lord whom thou hast borne, for He is compassionate by nature, to save the souls of those that sing thy praises, O Mother of God.

(**Katavasia**) Scorning the impious decree, the Children brought up together in godliness feared not the threat of fire, but, standing in the midst of the flames, they sang: 'O God of our fathers, blessed art Thou.'

Canticle Eight

First Canon

(**Irmos**) Hearken, O pure Virgin Maid: let Gabriel tell thee the counsel of the Most High that is ancient and true. Make ready to receive God: for through thee the Incomprehensible comes to dwell with mortal men. Therefore I cry rejoicing: O all ye works of the Lord, bless ye the Lord.

As Ann led the undefiled Temple into the house of God, she cried aloud and said with faith to the priest: 'Take the child given to me by God and lead her into the temple of thy Creator, and sing unto Him with joy: O all ye works of the Lord, bless ye the Lord.'

When he saw Ann, Zacharias said to her in spirit: 'Thou dost lead here the true Mother of life, whom the prophets of God heralded from afar as the Theotokos: and how shall the temple contain her? Therefore in wonder I cry: O all ye works of the Lord, bless ye the Lord.'

'I stand here as the suppliant of God,' answered Ann to him, 'calling upon Him with faith and prayer to receive the fruit of my travail. For I promised that after childbirth I would present my child to Him who gave her to me. Therefore, leaping for joy, I cry: O all ye works of the Lord, bless ye the Lord.'

'Truly this act is in accordance with the Law', said the priest to her. 'I perceive that this is a thing wholly strange: for I see led into the house of God her who wondrously surpasses the sanctuary in grace. Therefore I cry in joy: O all ye works of the Lord, bless ye the Lord.'

'Hearing thy words,' said Ann to him, 'I am filled with new strength. For thou dost understand these things by the Spirit of God, and hast clearly announced what shall come to pass in the Virgin. Take, then, the Undefiled into the temple of thy Creator, and sing unto Him in joy: O all ye works of the Lord, bless ye the Lord.'

'A Lamp that gives light has been kindled for us,' cried the priest, 'and has made mighty joy shine in the temple. Let the souls of the prophets make glad with me, as they see strange wonders accomplished in the house of God, and let them now cry out: O all ye works of the Lord, bless ye the Lord.'

Second Canon

(**Irmos**) Him before whom the angels and all the hosts of heaven are afraid, their Creator and Lord, O ye priests praise, O ye children glorify, O ye people bless and exalt above all for ever.

Bright with joy today, Joachim makes glad; and Ann, without reproach, offers unto the Lord God the sacrifice given to her according to the promise, her holy daughter.

The saints David and Jesse exult today and Judah is filled

with pride. For from their root a branch has sprung, the pure Virgin from whom pre-eternal God is to be born.[1]

Today Mary, the undefiled and living Tabernacle, is offered up in the house of God, and Zacharias receives her in his hands as a holy treasure of the Lord.

As a Gate of salvation and a spiritual Mountain, as a living Ladder,[2] let us, the faithful, honour the true Virgin and Mother of God, who is blessed by the hands of the priests.

Prophets, apostles and martyrs of Christ, ranks of angels and all the dwellers upon earth, let us honour with hymns the pure Virgin, for she is the blessed Mother of the Most High.

They that divinely bore thee, O Undefiled and Pure, offered thee in the temple as a spotless sacrifice; and in strange fashion thou dost lodge in the sanctuary of God, there to be prepared as a dwelling-place for the Word.

We bless the Lord, Father, Son, and Holy Spirit.

Let 'Holy, Holy, Holy'[3] be sung to Father, Son, and Holy Spirit, indivisible Unity, one Godhead, that holds all creation in the hollow of the hand unto all ages.

Both now . . .

He who is without beginning, begins: from a Virgin Maid the Word is born in the flesh according to His good pleasure, God and mortal man, and in His extreme compassion He refashions us who had fallen.

We praise, bless, and worship the Lord; we extol and exalt Him above all for ever.

(**Katavasia**) The furnace moist with dew was the image and figure of a wonder past nature. For it burnt not the Children whom it had received, even as the fire of the Godhead consumed not the Virgin's womb into which it had

[1] Isaiah 11:1; Revelation 5:5.
[2] Ezekiel 44:1–3; Daniel 2:45; Genesis 28:12.
[3] Revelation 4:8.

descended. Therefore in praise let us sing: Let the whole creation bless the Lord and exalt Him above all for ever.

Canticle Nine

The Magnificat and Greater in honour than the cherubim *are not sung, but are replaced by the following megalynaria:*

First Canon

Beholding the entry of the All-Pure, the angels were struck with amazement, seeing how the Virgin entered into the Holy of Holies.

(**Irmos**) Let no profane hand touch the living Ark of God, but let the lips of the faithful, singing without ceasing the words of the Angel to the Theotokos, cry aloud in great joy: O pure Virgin, thou art truly high above all.

Beholding the entry of the All-Pure, the angels were struck with amazement, seeing how she entered with glory into the Holy of Holies.

O pure Theotokos, thou hast a clean and shining beauty of soul, and art filled from heaven with the grace of God. Thou dost ever enlighten with eternal light those who cry aloud in gladness: O pure Virgin, thou art truly high above all.

Beholding the entry of the All-Pure, the angels were struck with amazement, seeing how she entered marvellously into the Holy of Holies.

Thy wonders, O pure Theotokos, surpass the power of words. For in thee I see something beyond speech: a body that was never subject to the taint of sin. Therefore in thanksgiving I cry to thee: O pure Virgin, thou art truly high above all.

Angels and men, let us honour the entry of the Virgin, for in glory she has gone into the Holy of Holies.

The Law prefigured thee most wonderfully as tabernacle, jar of manna, strange ark, veil of the temple, rod of Aaron, temple never to be destroyed, and gate of God;[1] and so it teaches us to cry to thee: O pure Virgin, thou art truly high above all.

Beholding the entry of the All-Pure, the angels were struck with wonder, seeing how she entered, by God's good pleasure, into the Holy of Holies.

David sang in honour of thee, calling thee the daughter of the King, for he saw thee in the beauty of the virtues, in raiment of many-coloured needlework, at the right hand of God;[2] therefore in prophecy he cried aloud: O pure Virgin, thou art truly high above all.

O ye angels, dance with the saints: O ye virgins, make glad with them. For the Child of God has entered into the Holy of Holies.

Solomon, foreseeing how thou wast to receive God, spoke of thee in dark sayings as the gate of the King and the living fountain sealed,[3] from which came forth untroubled waters unto us who cry aloud with faith: O pure Virgin, thou art truly high above all.

Angels and men, let us magnify the Virgin in hymns, for she has entered into the Holy of Holies, as was divinely fit.

Grant to my soul, O Theotokos, the calm peace that comes from thy gifts of grace. Thou art a fountain of life unto those that honour thee as is due; thou dost surround, protect, and preserve us that we may cry aloud to thee: O pure Virgin, thou art truly high above all.

[1] Exodus 26:1, 16:33, 25:10; Matthew 27:51; Hebrews 10:20; Numbers 17:8; 1 Kings 8:13 (Hebr.); John 2:19; Ezekiel 44:1–3.

[2] Psalm 44:10,12,14.

[3] Song of Songs 4:12.

Second Canon

Megalynarion (sung before the irmos and the troparia):

O my soul, magnify her who was led into the temple of the Lord and blessed by the hands of the priests.

(**Irmos**) Let us all magnify the radiant cloud, in which the Master of all descended, as dew from heaven upon the fleece,[1] and for our sake took flesh and was made man, He who is without beginning: for she is the pure Mother of our God.

From the righteous Joachim and Ann a fruit came forth according to the promise, Mary the Child of God. A young girl after the flesh, as acceptable incense she is offered in the holy temple, that she who is herself holy may dwell in the Holy Place.

Let us praise in hymns the child by nature who was shown forth as Mother beyond nature. For today she is offered to the Lord in the temple of the Law as a sweet-smelling savour, the spiritual fruit of her righteous parents.

O ye faithful, offering to the Theotokos the salutation of the angel, let us raise our cry: Hail! O Bride most beautiful. Hail! bright cloud; from thee the Lord has shone forth upon us as we sat in the darkness of ignorance. Hail! thou Hope of all.

All the creation joins the angel Gabriel, crying out to the Theotokos in fitting song: Hail! undefiled Mother of God. Through thee we have been delivered from the ancient curse and have become partakers of incorruption.

O Holy of Holies and pure Mother of God, Mary, from the snares of the enemy and from every heresy and affliction, at thine intercessions set us free who venerate with faith the ikon of thy holy form.

Far greater than the cherubim, high above the seraphim, and more spacious than the heavens, art thou shown forth, O

[1] Judges 6:37.

Virgin, for thou hast contained in thy womb our God whom nothing can contain, and hast ineffably borne Him: entreat Him earnestly on our behalf.

O my soul, magnify the power of the indivisible Godhead in three Persons.

Let us glorify the one Nature in three Persons, the one indivisible glory, the undivided Trinity in one Godhead that is praised without ceasing in heaven and on earth; in piety let us worship the Father, with the Son and the Spirit.

O my soul, magnify her who is greater in honour and more glorious than the hosts above.

O Virgin Mother of God, intercede for those who with faith seek refuge beneath thy compassion, and who piously worship thy Son as God and Lord of the world, that they be delivered from corruption and danger and manifold temptations.

Beholding the entry of the All-Pure, the angels were struck with amazement, seeing how the Virgin entered into the Holy of Holies.

(**Katavasia**) A strange and most wonderful mystery do I see: the cave is heaven; the Virgin the throne of the cherubim; the manger a room, in which Christ, the God whom nothing can contain, is laid. Him do we praise and magnify.

Exapostilarion

Let us praise in faith Mary the Child of God, whom long ago the assembly of prophets foretold, speaking of her as jar of manna and Aaron's rod, tablet of the Law and uncut mountain.[1] For she is led today into the Holy of Holies, there to be brought up unto the Lord (*3 times*).

[1] Exodus 16:33; Numbers 17:8; Exodus 31:18; Daniel 2:45.

Lauds. Four stichera are sung:

TONE ONE

(*to the special melody*, O purest Virgin, thou joy of the heavenly hierarchies . . .)

The virgins bearing lamps, who with their light accompany the ever-Virgin, verily prophesy the future in Spirit. For the Temple of God, the Theotokos, with virginal glory enters as a little child into the temple.

The Theotokos, glorious fruit of a sacred promise, is truly revealed unto the world as higher than all creation. Piously led into the house of God, she fulfils the vow of her parents and she is preserved by the Holy Spirit.

O Virgin, fed in faith by heavenly bread in the temple of the Lord, thou hast brought forth unto the world the Bread of life that is the Word; and as His chosen Temple without spot, thou wast betrothed mystically through the Spirit, to be the Bride of God the Father.

Let the gate of the temple wherein God dwells be opened: for Joachim brings within today in glory the Temple and Throne of the King of all, and he consecrates as an offering to God her whom the Lord has chosen to be His Mother.

Glory be to the Father . . . Both now . . .

TONE TWO

(*by Leo the Master*)

Today the Virgin without blemish is led to the temple, to become the habitation of God the King of all, who sustains our life. Today as a three-year-old victim of sacrifice the most pure Sanctuary is led into the Holy of Holies. To her let us cry out with the angel: Hail! thou who alone art blessed among women.[1]

Great Doxology and Dismissal.

[1] Luke 1:28.

Liturgy

The Typika (Psalms 102 and 145) and the Beatitudes. With the Beatitudes are sung four troparia from Canticle Three of the first Canon of the feast (p. 177) and four troparia from Canticle Six of the second Canon (p. 184).

Alternatively, according to the modern Greek practice, the following antiphons may be sung:

Antiphon One

TONE TWO

℣ 1. Great is the Lord and greatly to be praised: in the city of our God and in His holy mountain (*Psalm* 47:2).

At the prayers of the Theotokos, save us, O Saviour.

℣ 2. Glorious things are spoken of thee, O city of God (*Psalm* 86:3).

At the prayers of the Theotokos . . .

℣ 3. God is known in her palaces for a refuge (*Psalm* 47:4).

At the prayers of the Theotokos . . .

℣ 4. As we have heard, so have we seen in the city of the Lord of hosts, in the city of our God (*ibid.*, 9).

At the prayers of the Theotokos . . .
Glory be to the Father . . . Both now . . .
At the prayers of the Theotokos . . .

Antiphon Two

SAME TONE

℣ 1. The Most High hath sanctified His tabernacle (*Psalm* 45:5).

O Son of God, wonderful in Thy saints, save us who sing to Thee: alleluia.

℣ 2. Holiness and majesty are in His sanctuary (*Psalm* 95:6).

O Son of God . . .

℣ 3. This is the gate of the Lord, by which the righteous shall enter (*Psalm* 117:20).

O Son of God . . .

℣ 4. Holy is Thy temple, and wonderful in righteousness (*Psalm* 64:5–6).

O Son of God . . .

Glory be to the Father . . . Both now . . .
O Only-begotten Son and Word of God . . .

Antiphon Three

TONE FOUR

℣ 1. Even the rich among the people shall entreat thy favour (*Psalm* 44:13).

The troparion of the feast, Today is the foreshadowing of the good pleasure (*p. 172*).

℣ 2. The King's daughter is all glorious within: her clothing is of wrought gold (*ibid.*, 14).

The troparion of the feast.

℣ 3. Virgins shall be brought to the King after her: her companions shall be brought unto Thee (*ibid.*, 15).

The troparion of the feast.

After the introit, the troparion of the feast (*p. 172*); Glory be to the Father . . . Both now . . .; *the kontakion of the feast* (*p. 185*).

Prokimenon: *TONE THREE*

My soul doth magnify the Lord, and my spirit hath rejoiced in God my Saviour (*Luke* 1:46–47).

℣. For He hath regarded the low estate of His handmaiden: for, behold, from henceforth all generations shall call me blessed (*ibid.*, 48).

READING FROM THE EPISTLE TO THE HEBREWS (9:1–7).

Brethren, the first covenant had also ordinances of divine service, and a worldly sanctuary. For there was a tabernacle made; the first, wherein was the candlestick, and the table, and the shewbread; which is called the sanctuary. And after the second veil, the tabernacle which is called the Holiest of all; which had the golden censer, and the ark of the covenant overlaid round about with gold, wherein was the golden pot that had manna, and Aaron's rod that budded, and the tables of the covenant; and over it the cherubims of glory shadowing the mercy-seat: of which we cannot now speak particularly. Now when these things were thus ordained, the priests went always into the first tabernacle, accomplishing the service of God. But into the second went the high priest alone once every year, not without blood, which he offered for himself, and for the errors of the people.

Alleluia, TONE EIGHT

℣ 1. Hearken, O daughter, and consider, and incline thine ear (*Psalm* 44:11).

℣ 2. Even the rich among the people shall entreat thy favour (*ibid.*, 13).

READING FROM THE HOLY GOSPEL ACCORDING TO LUKE (10:38–42; 11:27–28. *See p. 129*).

In place of It is meet, *we sing the first megalynarion and the irmos from Canticle Nine of the first Canon (p. 190).*

Communion verse:

I will receive the cup of salvation, and call upon the Name of the Lord (*Psalm* 115:4).

On the day of the feast, fish, wine, and oil are allowed: but since it is the Christmas fast, meat and animal products may not be eaten.

Because it occurs within the Christmas fast, the feast is observed for five days only, the apodosis falling on 25 November. On that day all the office of the feast is repeated, omitting only the entrance, lessons, lity, and blessing of bread at Vespers; and the polyeleos and Gospel at Mattins. In the reading of the Psalter at Vespers, the normal kathisma appointed for the day is used.

24 DECEMBER

THE FOREFEAST OF THE NATIVITY OF CHRIST

Vespers

On Lord, I have cried, *six stichera are sung: three of the Forefeast, and three of the saint of the day, St. Eugenia the Martyr.*

In the Greek use, the stichera of the Forefeast are as follows:

TONE FOUR

Let us sound the cymbals: let us shout aloud in songs. The revelation of Christ is now made manifest: the preachings of the prophets have received their fulfilment. For He of whom they spoke, foretelling His appearance in the flesh to mortal men, is born in a holy cave and is laid as a babe in a manger, and as a child He is wrapped in swaddling clothes.

With uprightness of mind let us lift up our voice in song, celebrating the Forefeast of Christ's Nativity. For He who is equal in honour with the Father and the Spirit, has from compassion clothed Himself in our substance, and makes ready to be born in the city of Bethlehem. The praises of His Nativity past speech the shepherds and the angels sing.

The Virgin was amazed, as she beheld a conception past telling and a birth past utterance. Rejoicing at once and weeping, she raised her voice and said: 'Shall I give my breast to Thee, who givest nourishment to all the world, or shall I sing Thy praise as my Son and my God? What manner of name shall I find to call Thee, O Lord whom none can name?'

But in the Slav use, the following stichera of the Forefeast are sung:[1]

TONE FIVE

Thou dost bear the form of Adam, yet Thou art all-perfect, being in the form of God.[2] Of Thine own will Thou art held in human hands, who in Thy might upholdest all things with Thine hand. To Thee the pure and undefiled Virgin spake aloud: 'How shall I wrap Thee in swaddling clothes like a child, how shall I give Thee suck who givest nourishment to all the world? How shall I not wonder in amazement at Thy poverty beyond understanding! How shall I, who am Thy handmaiden, call Thee my Son? I sing Thy praises and I bless Thee, who dost grant the world great mercy.'

The undefiled Virgin, beholding the pre-eternal God as a child that had taken flesh from her, held Him in her arms and without ceasing she kissed Him. Filled with joy, she said aloud to Him: 'O Most High God, O King unseen, how is it that I look upon Thee? I cannot understand the mystery of Thy poverty without measure. For the smallest of caves, a strange dwelling for Thee, finds room for Thee within itself. Thou hast been born without destroying my virginity, but Thou hast kept my womb as it was before childbirth; and Thou dost grant the world great mercy.'

The pure Virgin spoke in wonder, as she heard the Magi standing together before the cave, and she said to them: 'Whom do ye seek? For I see that ye have come from a far country. Ye have the appearance, but not the thoughts, of Persians; strange has your journey been, and strange your arrival. Ye have come with zeal to worship Him who, journeying as a stranger from on high, has strangely, in ways known to Himself, come to dwell in me, granting the world great mercy.'

1 In the Greek use these stichera are sung at Vespers on 28 December.
2 Philippians 2:6.

Then follow, in both the Greek and the Slav use, the three stichera of St. Eugenia.[1]

Glory be to the Father . . . Both now . . .

TONE TWO

Lo, the time of our salvation is at hand. Make ready, O cave; the Virgin draws nigh to give birth. Be glad and rejoice, O Bethlehem, land of Judah, for from thee our Lord has shone forth as the dawn. Hearken, ye mountains and hills and all ye lands round about Judaea: for Christ comes in His love for mankind, to save the man He fashioned.

Aposticha in the Greek use:[2]

TONE ONE

Let us celebrate, O ye people, the Forefeast of the Nativity of Christ, and raising our minds on high let us go in spirit to Bethlehem; and with the eyes of our soul let us look upon the Virgin, as she hastens to the cave to give birth to our God, the Lord of all. Joseph, when he beheld the greatness of this wonder, thought that he saw a mortal wrapped as a babe in swaddling clothes; but from all that came to pass he understood that it was the true God, who grants the world great mercy.

℣. God shall come from Teman, and the Holy One from the mountain overshadowed by the forest (*Habakkuk* 3 : 3).

Let us celebrate, O ye people, the Forefeast of the Nativity of Christ, and raising our minds on high let us go in spirit to Bethlehem; and let us look upon the great mystery in the cave. For Eden is opened once again, when from a pure Virgin God comes forth, perfect in His divinity as in His manhood. Therefore let us cry: Holy God, Thou Father

[1] The texts of St. Eugenia are not included in the present translation.

[2] The verses that follow are also used as stichera on *Lord, I have cried* at Vespers on 20 December. In the Slav use they are sung only on that day, and not on 24 December.

without beginning: Holy and Mighty, Thou Son made flesh: Holy and Immortal, Thou Spirit the Comforter: Holy Trinity, glory to Thee.

℣. O Lord, I have heard the report of Thee and was afraid: Lord, I considered Thy works and was amazed (*ibid.*, 1–2).

Hearken, O heaven, and give ear, O earth: for behold, the Son and Word of God the Father comes forth to be born of a Maiden who has not known man, by the good pleasure of the Father who begat Him impassibly, and by the co-operation of the Holy Spirit. Make ready, O Bethlehem: throw open thy gate, O Eden. For He who is, comes to be that which He was not, and He who formed all creation takes form, granting the world great mercy.

Glory be to the Father . . . Both now . . .

TONE SIX

Make ready, O cave, for the Ewe Lamb comes, bearing Christ in her womb. And do thou, O manger, accept Him who by His word has loosed us dwellers on earth from acts that are against reason. Ye shepherds abiding in the fields, bear witness to the fearful wonder. And ye, Magi from Persia, offer to the King gold and frankincense and myrrh: for the Lord has appeared from a Virgin Mother. And she, bending over Him like a handmaiden, worshipped Him and said to Him, as He lay in her arms: 'How wast Thou sown as seed in me? And how hast Thou grown within me, O my Deliverer and my God?'

Aposticha in the Slav use:

TONE ONE

'Kings from the east, having learnt that Thou wast to be born as King, are come, bringing Thee gifts, O Son, frankincense and myrrh and gold; and lo, they stand before the doors. Bid them enter and behold Thee, held in my arms as a child, who art older than ancient Adam.'

℣. God shall come from Teman, and the Holy One from the mountain overshadowed by the forest (*Habakkuk* 3 : 3).

'Come ye and make haste to enter,' said the Virgin to the Magi, 'and behold Him who is invisible, now visibly manifest and become a child.' And they came eagerly and worshipped, bringing gifts in fulfilment of the divine prophecy.[1]

℣. O Lord, I have heard the report of Thee and was afraid: Lord, I considered Thy works and was amazed (*ibid.*, 1–2).

'I hold in my arms as a child Thee who dost uphold all, and I am filled with amazement', said she who had not known wedlock. 'How shall I feed with milk Thee who givest food to all, O my Son and my Creator? I glorify Thy measureless condescension towards man, whereby Thou dost save the world that perishes.'

Glory be to the Father . . . Both now . . .

TONE SIX[2]

Triumph, O Zion; make glad, O Jerusalem, city of Christ our God: receive the Creator who is contained within a cave and a manger. Open unto me the gates, and entering within I shall see as a child wrapped in swaddling clothes Him who upholds the creation in the hollow of His hand, whose praises the angels sing with unceasing voice, the Lord and Giver of Life who saves mankind.

Apolytikion (troparion) of the Forefeast:

TONE FOUR

Mary once, with aged Joseph, went to be taxed in Bethlehem, for they were of the lineage of David; and she bore in her womb the fruit that had not been sown. The time of the birth was at hand and there was no room at the inn; but the cave proved a fair palace for the Queen. Christ is born, that

[1] Psalm 67 : 30; Isaiah 60 : 3,6.

[2] This sticheron occurs in the Greek use at Vespers on 21 December.

He may raise up again the image that before was fallen (*3 times*).

And the Dismissal.

Compline

We sing the Canon of the Forefeast:[1]

TONE SIX

Canticle One

(**Irmos**) He who in ancient times hid the pursuing tyrant beneath the waves of the sea, is hidden in a manger and Herod seeks to kill Him. But let us cry out with the Magi in song: Let us sing unto the Lord, for He has been greatly glorified.

O Lord my God, I will sing a birthday hymn, a song on the Forefeast, to Thee who by Thy Nativity givest me a divine rebirth and leadest me up to my first excellence.

The things above the earth and on the earth were amazed at Thy power, as they beheld Thee, O my Saviour, upon Thy throne on high and in the manger below. For beyond our understanding Thou hast appeared in two natures, God and man.

That thou mightest fill all things with Thy glory, Thou hast come and bowed the heavens[2] till they touched the earth. For as rain upon the fleece[3] hast Thou descended into a

[1] The Canon that follows is sung in the Greek use at Mattins, together with the other Canon given below (p. 210), while a third Canon of the Forefeast is provided for Compline. We have followed the Slav use, which gives only two Canons of the Forefeast, one at Compline and one at Mattins. The Canon used by the Greeks at Compline, is used by the Slavs at Mattins on 23 December.

[2] Psalm 17: 10.

[3] Judges 6:36–38.

virgin womb, from which Thou now comest forth to be born in two natures, O God and man.

Canticle Three

(**Irmos**) When the creation beheld Thee born in a cave, who hast hung the whole earth in the void above the waters, it was seized with amazement and cried: 'There is none holy save Thee, O Lord.'

O merciful Lord, making manifest the figures of Thine ineffable Incarnation, Thou hast unfolded visions and breathed forth prophecies; and now Thou art come and hast fulfilled them, being born in the flesh from a pure Maid in the city of David.

Earth has spread out its wide spaces and receives the Creator, as He receives from angels glory, from heaven the star, from the shepherds praise, from the Magi gifts, and acknowledgement from the whole world.

The riddles of Balaam, the soothsayer and diviner, are now fulfilled. For a star has dawned from Jacob and led the Magi, Kings from Persia bringing gifts, towards the Sun of Glory.[1]

Canticle Four

(**Irmos**) Foreseeing Thy coming from the Virgin, Habakkuk cried out marvelling: O Deliverer, Thou art come incarnate from Teman, to call back Adam from his exile.

The Lord now draws nigh and comes, expectation of the nations[2] and salvation of the world. O city of Bethlehem, prepare the cave: and ye shepherds with the Magi, make haste.

In the strength of Thy Godhead Thou hast been joined with mortal men, through a union without confusion, O Saviour,

[1] Numbers 24:17.

[2] Genesis 49:10 (Septuagint).

in the likeness of the flesh of Adam; and in thus assuming human nature Thou dost bestow upon it immortality and salvation.

The Word is made manifest and assumes the material substance of our flesh; and in His ineffable providence He takes up His dwelling among us. Come ye, O faithful, and let us look upon His glory, the glory as of the Only-begotten Son from God the Father.[1]

Canticle Five

(**Irmos**) Isaiah, as he watched by night, beheld the light that knows no evening, the light of Thy Theophany, O Christ, that came to pass from tender love for us; and he cried aloud: 'Behold, a Virgin shall conceive[2] and shall bear the incarnate Word, and all those born on earth shall rejoice exceedingly.'

O Creator, Thou makest new those born on earth by Thyself becoming clay. A manger and swaddling clothes and a cave are the marks of Thy lowliness. The Betrothed of Thy Mother[3] is thought by men to be Thy father according to the flesh, and so he takes the place of the Father who begat Thee by His counsel.

The Kings, first fruits of the Gentiles, bring Thee gifts at Thy birth in a cave in Bethlehem, from a Mother who suffered no pangs of travail: by myrrh they point to Thy death, by gold to Thy royal power, by frankincense to the pre-eminence of Thy divinity.

Coming forth in the flesh, O Word coeternal with the Father, from a Mother who suffered no pangs of birth, Thou hast made Thy dwelling in the cave, using the manger as Thy throne. Through Thy fearful dispensation Thou dost amaze

[1] John 1:14.
[2] Isaiah 7:14.
[3] Joseph.

the Magi and the shepherds, and Thou fillest the angels with awe as they cry, 'Glory to Thy dominion.'

Canticle Six

(**Irmos**) Jonah was compassed but not held fast in the belly of the whale; for serving as a figure of Thy birth and Thine appearing in the flesh, he came forth from the monster as from a chamber. For, born now in the flesh, Thou shalt in the flesh undergo burial and death, and Thou shalt rise again on the third day.

The middle wall of partition of the ancient enmity is now laid low and destroyed by Thy coming in the flesh, O Christ, and the flaming sword[1] now gives way before all who approach. And I partake in faith of the life-giving tree in Eden, becoming once again a husbandman of immortal plants.

Hell reigned with sin from Adam even down to Thee; but their shameless tyranny is brought to naught, now that Thou art born according to the flesh from the tribe of David, O Deliverer. Thou hast set a light upon the throne of his kingdom and Thou reignest unto all ages.

Herod the wicked became a slayer of children but not of Christ. For though he reaped a bitter harvest of children he failed to seize and slay the wheat ear of life. For being the Giver of life, as God He escaped from the pursuer by His divine power.

Canticle Seven

(**Irmos**) Wonder past speech! He who delivered the Holy Children from the flames of the furnace, is laid as a babe in a poor manger, for our salvation who sing: O God our Deliverer, blessed art Thou.

The enemy and deceiver was wounded when he saw God laid in a poor and narrow manger as a babe, and by the hand

[1] Genesis 3:24.

of God was he cast down, for our salvation who sing: O God our Deliverer, blessed art Thou.

O happy manger! Receiving the Creator as a babe, it is made the throne of the cherubim, for our salvation who sing: O God our Deliverer, blessed art Thou.

According to the law of mortal man, appearing as a babe Thou dost accept to be wrapped in swaddling bands: and thereby Thou dost loose the bands of my offences, bestowing freedom on those who cry aloud: O God our Deliverer, blessed art Thou.

In Thy Birth without beginning and in Thy Nativity after the flesh, Thou hast remained, O Christ, one in Godhead with the Father and the Spirit, for our salvation who sing: O God our Deliverer, blessed art Thou.

Canticle Eight

(**Irmos**) Be ye astonished, O ye heavens, be ye horribly afraid, and let the foundations of the earth be shaken.[1] For lo, He who bears the whole world in the hollow of His hand, is wrapped in swaddling clothes and received as guest in a narrow manger. Him do ye children bless, ye priests praise, and ye people exalt above all for ever.

Adam the prisoner has been set loose and freedom has been given to all the faithful, now that Thou art wrapped in swaddling bands, O Saviour, and laid in a small cave and in a manger for dumb beasts. Therefore, rejoicing, we offer Thee in faith a hymn on this the Forefeast of Thy Nativity.

The error of Persia has ceased: for the stargazers, Kings of the east, bring gifts to Christ the King of all at His birth, gold and myrrh and frankincense. Him do ye children bless, ye priests praise, and ye people exalt above all for ever.

O strange wonders! O goodness and infinite forbearance! Behold, He who dwells in the heights is counted as a babe,

[1] Jeremiah 2:12; Psalm 81:5.

and He who is God flees of His own will from Herod. Him do ye children bless, ye priests praise, and ye people exalt above all for ever.

Canticle Nine

(Irmos) 'Be not amazed O Mother, beholding Me now as a babe, whom the Father begat from the womb before the morning star.[1] For I have come openly to restore and glorify with Myself the fallen nature of mortal man, that magnifies thee in faith and love.'

'O Son without beginning, I am blessed beyond words in Thy strange birth, wherein I have been spared all travail. And as I behold Thee fleeing from Herod with his sword of sorrow, I am torn in soul. But do Thou live and save those that honour Thee.'

'I have gone down into the land of Egypt but, O Mother, I have laid low with an earthquake the idols of Egypt made by hand of man. And sending into hell the enemies that seek My life in vain, with the power that I alone possess, I shall lift up and save those that honour thee.'

Let the creation rejoice exceedingly: for the Creator now makes Himself to be created, and He who was before all things now makes Himself known as God newly revealed. Let the Magi with their gifts go out to meet Him, let the shepherds clap their hands in faith at the wonder, and let mortal men join the angels and make glad.

Mattins

After the first reading from the Psalter, sessional hymn:

TONE SIX

The sayings of the prophets are now fulfilled: for our God shall be born tomorrow of the Virgin Mary in fashion past

[1] Psalm 109:3.

words, and yet shall remain such as He was before His birth. The Magi come together bearing gifts, the shepherds abide in the fields, and we also sing: O Lord born of a Virgin, glory to Thee.

Glory be to the Father . . . Both now . . .

Repeat.

After the second reading from the Psalter, sessional hymn:

TONE EIGHT

As shepherds were piping songs a host of angels stopped them and called out, saying: 'Cease now, ye who abide in the fields at the head of your flocks; cry out and sing that Christ the Lord is born, whose pleasure it is as God to save mankind.'

Then follows Psalm 50.

Two Canons are used:[1] *of the Forefeast, in eight troparia, including the irmos; and of the saint, in six troparia, likewise including the irmos. The irmos of the Canon of the saint is repeated as katavasia at the end of Canticles Three, Six, Eight, and Nine.*

Canon of the Forefeast:

TONE TWO

Canticle One

(**Irmos**) A triumphant force once laid low all the armed host of Pharaoh in the deep: even so the glorious Lord, the Word made flesh, has blotted out malignant sin; for He has been greatly glorified.

O King of all, wishing man to be enrolled in the book of life, thou hast enrolled Thyself according to the law of Caesar. As a stranger hast Thou come unto Thine own, calling back to heaven those who were unhappily estranged from Paradise.

[1] In the Greek use, three Canons (see p. 204).

O Bethlehem, receive Christ: for, made flesh, He comes to dwell in thee, opening Eden to me. Make ready, O Cave, to behold most strangely contained in Thee, Him who cannot be contained, who now is made poor in the wealth of His tender mercies.

Christ comes to be born, granting in His goodness a strange rebirth to those sprung from Adam. Be glad, the whole nature of mortal man, thou that art barren and bearest not:[1] the Master has come to make thee a mother of many children.

Canticle Three

(**Irmos**) The desert flowered as a lily at Thy coming, O Lord, even the Church of the Gentiles that was barren: and in that same coming is my heart established.

Redeeming me from bands of evil, O Lord who lovest mankind, Thou comest to be wrapped as a babe in swaddling bands. I venerate Thy divine condescension.

The Virgin draws nigh to bear Thee, O Lord, who, shining timelessly from the Father, hast now come to be in time, setting us loose from the temporal passions of our souls.

O Lord most merciful and full of pity, seeking me who had gone astray in transgression, Thou hast come to dwell in a cave as in heaven, thereby preparing the heavenly mansions for me.

Sessional hymn of the Forefeast:

TONE ONE

Rejoice exceedingly, O Zion: make ready, O Bethlehem. The Upholder of all things, sending a star before Him, has made known His condescension without measure. He before

[1] Isaiah 54:1.

whom the heavenly powers tremble, our Only God, without suffering change is born in very truth from the Virgin.

Glory be to the Father . . .

Sessional hymn of the saint.

Both now . . .

Of the Forefeast:

TONE EIGHT

Let us, the faithful, keep festival, observing the Forefeast of Christ's Nativity, and as is right let us all go forth to meet Him. Like the Magi let us bring as gifts our virtues, and sing the new song of the angels to our God, who is born in Bethlehem without seed from the Child of God and Maiden. Him do all things glorify.

Canticle Four

(**Irmos**) Thou hast come forth from a Virgin, neither angel nor ambassador, but the Lord Himself made flesh, and to me who am man Thou hast brought salvation. Therefore I cry unto Thee: Glory to Thy power, O Lord.

Let the creation now cast off all things old, beholding Thee the Creator made a child. For through Thy birth Thou dost shape all things afresh, making them new once more and leading them back again to their first beauty.

The Magi who had been led on their way by a divine star, stood before Thee in wonder at Thy marvellous birth; and bearing gifts, they see the Sun that rose from the virgin cloud.

Behold, the Virgin comes like a young heifer, bearing in her womb the fatted Calf that takes away the sins of the world. Let the creation as it keeps feast rejoice exceedingly.

The preaching of the prophets, foretelling the manifestation of Christ, has today received its saving fulfilment: for He has come in the flesh to enlighten those in peril of darkness.

Canticle Five

(**Irmos**) Thou art become mediator between God and man, O Christ our God; for through Thee, O Master, we have access from the darkness of ignorance to Thy Father, the Author of light.

Let the people that once sat in darkness see the light shine forth that knows no evening: Him whom the star once made known to kings from Persia who worshipped fire.

The Great King comes in haste to enter a small cave, that He may make me great who had grown small, and that, as transcendent God, by His poverty without measure He may enrich me who had grown poor.[1]

'Now is Christ born of Jacob,' so Balaam said: 'and He shall rule over nations, and His Kingdom shall be exalted in grace and shall remain perpetually.'[2]

Canticle Six

(**Irmos**) Compassed about in an abyss of sin, on the unsearchable abyss of Thy tender mercies do I call: bring me out of corruption, O God.

Christ in strange wise comes to His own. Let us make ourselves strangers to sin, and let us receive Him who dwells in the souls of the meek.

Thou, O Bethlehem, art not least among cities:[3] for in thee is born the King and Lord who shall tend as a shepherd the people that is His own.

How shall a small cave receive Thee, for whom the world cannot find room, O Thou whom none can comprehend! O Thou, who with the Father art without beginning, how shalt Thou appear as a small child!

[1] 2 Corinthians 8:9.
[2] See Numbers 24:19.
[3] Compare Micah 5:2; Matthew 2:6.

Kontakion of the Forefeast:

TONE THREE

Today the Virgin comes to the cave to give birth ineffably to the pre-eternal Word. Hearing this, be of good cheer, O inhabited earth, and with the angels and the shepherds glorify Him whose will it was to be made manifest a young Child, the pre-eternal God.

Ikos of the Forefeast:[1]

The holy sayings of the Prophets[2] have been fulfilled in the city of Bethlehem within a cave. The whole creation is made rich: let it rejoice and be of good cheer. The Master of all has come to live with His servants, and from the bondage of the enemy He delivers us who were made subject to corruption.[3] In swaddling clothes and lying in a manger, He is made manifest a young Child, the pre-eternal God.

Kontakion and ikos of the saint.

Canticle Seven

(**Irmos**) The profane command of a lawless tyrant fanned the flame exceeding high; but Christ cast the dew of the Spirit over the Children who feared God: blessed is He, and exalted above all.

Let clouds drop water from on high; He who in glory makes the clouds His chariot,[4] comes borne upon a cloud, that is the Virgin. The light that knows no evening, He comes to shine on those who before were in darkness and in peril.

O army of divine angels, make ready to sing the praises of the ineffable condescension of the Lord. O ye Magi, come with all speed; O shepherds, make haste. Christ is come, the

[1] In the Slav use only. In the Greek books this ikos is found after Canticle Three of the Canon at Mattins on 20 December.

[2] Isaiah 7:14; Micah 5:2.

[3] Romans 8:20–21.

[4] Psalm 103:3.

predestined expectation of the nations[1] and their deliverance.

'What is this great and strange wonder? How do I uphold Thee who upholdest all the world by Thy word? O my Son who art without beginning, Thy birth is beyond all speech!' So spake the All-Pure, fearfully holding Christ in her arms.

Canticle Eight

(**Irmos**) In Babylon of old by the command of God, the fiery furnace worked in contrary ways: burning the Chaldeans, it refreshed the faithful as they sang: O all ye works of the Lord, bless ye the Lord.

The blameless Lady was amazed at the height of the mystery, in truth past speech, that covered the heavens with knowledge, and she said: 'The heavenly throne is consumed in flames as it holds Thee: how is it, then, that I carry Thee, my Son?'

'Thou dost bear the likeness of Thy Father, O my Son. How then hast Thou become poor and taken upon Thyself the likeness of a servant? How shall I lay Thee in a manger of beasts without reason, who dost deliver all men from unreason? I sing the praises of Thy compassion.'

Be joyful, all the earth: behold, Christ draws nigh to be born in Bethlehem. Be glad, O sea; dance for joy, thou congregation of prophets, seeing today the fulfilment of your words; rejoice, O all ye righteous.

Canticle Nine

(**Irmos**) The Son of the Father without beginning has appeared to us, God the Lord made flesh of the Virgin, to give light to those in darkness, and to gather the dispersed. Therefore the far-famed Theotokos do we magnify.

Let the kings of the whole earth sing rejoicing, and let the companies of the nations be in exceeding joy. Mountains and

[1] Genesis 49:10 (Septuagint).

hills and hollows, rivers and seas, and the whole creation, magnify the Lord who now is born.

As far as it was right, Thou wast seen by the prophets. Made man in the last times, Thou hast appeared to all in Bethlehem, city of Judah, and a star showed Thee to the stargazers, O Thou who passest all interpretation.

Behold, the Most Holy Word comes unto His own in a holy body that is not His. By a strange birth He makes His own the world that was estranged. To Him let us sing in praise, who became poor for us.[1]

'O sweetest child, how shall I feed Thee who givest food to all? How shall I hold Thee who holdest all things in Thy power? How shall I wrap Thee in swaddling clothes, who dost wrap the whole earth in clouds?' So cried the all-pure Lady whom in faith we magnify.

Exapostilarion of the Forefeast:

He who dwells in the light that no man can approach and who upholds all things, in His ineffable compassion is born of a Virgin. He is wrapped in swaddling clothes as a babe, and laid in a cave in a manger of dumb beasts. Let us hasten to Bethlehem to worship Him with the Magi, bringing as our gifts the fruits of our virtuous deeds.

Glory be to the Father . . .

Exapostilarion of the saint.

Both now . . .

Another, of the Forefeast:

Let us, the faithful, offer a hymn to the Virgin Mary: for behold, she now draws nigh to bear Christ the Saviour in the city of Bethlehem. Therefore, ye Magi bringing gifts, press onward swiftly with the star, that we may worship Him together. And ye shepherds, make haste to cry aloud with

[1] Not in the Slav text.

the angels to Him who is born in a cave and in a manger: Glory to Thee!

Lauds. Four stichera are sung, in the Greek use as follows:

TONE SIX

(*to the special melody*, Go ye on before, O ye angelic powers . . .)

What mysteries beyond mind and speech! God in His compassion is born on earth, putting on the form of a servant that He may snatch from servitude to the enemy those who with fervent love cry out: Blessed art Thou, O Saviour who lovest mankind.

Come, Israel slow of heart, cast from thee the mist that lies upon thy soul; recognize the Maker who is born in a cave. He is the expectation of the nations;[1] He shall destroy thy feasts: for thou wilt not consent to cry aloud: Christ the King of Israel is come.

'O Sun, my Son, how shall I wrap Thee in swaddling clothes? How shall I give Thee milk, who givest food to all creation? How shall I hold Thee in my arms who holdest all things? How shall I look upon Thee without fear, on whom the cherubim with many eyes dare not to lift their gaze?' So spake she who knew not wedlock as she held Christ.

O ye shepherds, shout aloud in new songs: O ye Magi, cast away your magic spells. Let the mountains and the hills rejoice exceedingly. O ye daughters of kings, come unto the joy of the Theotokos. O ye people, let us say: Blessed art Thou, our God who now art born: glory to Thee.

But in the Slav use the following stichera are sung:

TONE SIX

(*to the special melody*, Go ye on before, O ye angelic powers . . .)

The star from Jacob[2] has risen within the cave: celebrating

[1] Genesis 49:10 (Septuagint).
[2] Numbers 24:17.

the Forefeast, let us hasten with the Magi and go with shepherds. Let us see God in swaddling clothes: let us see the Virgin feeding Him on milk. O fearful sight! Christ the King of Israel is come.

The choir of angels honours thee with hymns, O radiant Mother, who hast not known wedlock: and rejoicing it makes glad at thy birthgiving, O Most Pure. Hail! Thou hope of the Orthodox. Hail! Thou Advocate of those who sing to thee. Therefore let us cry: Blessed art Thou, our God who hast come: glory to Thee.

A Light shall spring forth from the root of Jesse, as the prophet full of light foretold.[1] For we see a Virgin giving birth, in ways past nature, to a most precious rose in a cave: He who sits in the heights upon the same throne as the Father. O ye people, let us say: Blessed art Thou, our God who hast come: glory to Thee.

Today Adam has been recalled from error and from the dark deceiving of the adversary, for Christ is made flesh as man from a Virgin; and renewing Adam, He has removed the curse that came from the virgin Eve. O ye people, let us say: Blessed art Thou, our God who hast come: glory to Thee.

Then in both the Greek and the Slav practice we sing:

Glory be to the Father . . .

SAME TONE

Come, O Bethlehem, prepare for the birth. Come, Joseph, and be enrolled with Mary. O most sacred manger! O swaddling clothes that carry God! There the Life was wrapped, even Christ our God, who shall tear to pieces the bands of death, and bind fast mortal men to incorruption.

Both now . . .

SAME TONE

O most blessed womb of the Maid of God, thou hast been

[1] Isaiah 11:1.

shown forth as spiritually vaster than the heavens. For Him whom heaven cannot contain, thou dost carry and hold within thee. O most blessed breasts of the Virgin, that Christ has sucked who feeds all that has breath! He has built flesh for Himself in the womb of the Maiden that knew not a man.

Aposticha:

TONE TWO

(*to the special melody*, O house of Ephratah . . .)

O Virgin, thou art become the dwelling of the Maker of all; for having come to dwell in thee, the Lord of glory now draws near His time of birth.

℣. God shall come from Teman, and the Holy One from the mountain overshadowed by the forest (*Habakkuk* 3:3).

In Bethlehem, in a manger of dumb beasts, from a Virgin now is born a young Child who is the pre-eternal God. O what a wonder is this!

℣. O Lord, I have the report of Thee and was afraid: Lord, I considered Thy works and was amazed (*ibid.*, 1–2).

O ye spiritual ranks of angels in the heights, join the shepherds and Magi, and cry ye aloud to God who now is born: Glory to Thee.

In the Greek use we continue:

Glory be to the Father . . . Both now . . .

TONE SIX

O Bethlehem, receive the Mother of God: for she has come to thee to give birth to the Light that never sets. O ye angels, gaze with wonder from heaven; O ye men, give glory on earth. O Magi from Persia, bring your threefold gift; ye shepherds abiding in the fields, sing ye the thrice-holy hymn. Let everything that hath breath praise the Maker of all.

But in the Slav use we sing:

Glory be to the Father . . .

TONE TWO

Glory to Thee, O Father, Son, and Spirit, through whom a fearful mystery is brought to pass unto man's regeneration.

Both now . . .

SAME TONE

Rejoice, O Virgin Theotokos, who of the Holy Spirit hast borne Life unto the world to the deliverance of all.

The rest of the service of Mattins as usual, and the Dismissal.

The Forefeast of Christmas (24 December) is observed as a fast, and neither animal products nor fish may be eaten. In the Greek use, wine and oil are not permitted, except when the Forefeast falls on Saturday or Sunday: but in the Slav use wine and oil may be taken, whatever day of the week it may be.

24 DECEMBER

CHRISTMAS EVE

The Royal Hours

If Christmas Eve falls on Saturday or Sunday, the Royal Hours are read on the preceding Friday. In such a case, the Liturgy is not celebrated on Friday.

The First Hour

After the blessing of the priest, we say Holy God . . ., *and the opening prayers as usual. Then* O come, let us worship . . ., *and the following three Psalms:*

Psalm 5

Give ear to my words, O Lord, consider my meditation. Hearken unto the voice of my cry, my King, and my God: for unto Thee will I pray. My voice shalt Thou hear in the morning, O Lord; in the morning will I direct my prayer unto Thee, and will look up. For Thou art not a God that hath pleasure in wickedness: neither shall evil dwell with Thee. The foolish shall not stand in Thy sight: Thou hatest all workers of iniquity. Thou shalt destroy them that speak leasing: the Lord will abhor the bloody and deceitful man. But as for me, I will come into Thy house in the multitude of Thy mercy: and in Thy fear will I worship toward Thy holy temple. Lead me, O Lord, in Thy righteousness because of mine enemies; make Thy way straight before my face. For there is no faithfulness in their mouth; their inward part is very wickedness; their throat is an open sepulchre; they flatter with their tongue. Destroy Thou them, O God; let them fall by their own counsels; cast them out in the multitude of their transgressions; for they have rebelled against Thee. But let all those that put their trust in Thee rejoice: let them ever shout for joy, because Thou defendest them: let them also that love Thy name be joyful in Thee. For Thou, Lord, wilt bless the righteous; with favour wilt Thou compass him as with a shield.

Psalm 44

My heart is inditing a good matter: I speak of the things which I have made touching the King: my tongue is the pen of a ready writer. Thou art fairer than the children of men: grace is poured into Thy lips: therefore God hath blessed Thee for ever. Gird Thy sword upon Thy thigh, O most Mighty, with Thy glory and Thy majesty. And in Thy majesty ride prosperously because of truth and meekness and righteousness; and Thy right hand shall teach Thee terrible things. Thine arrows are sharp in the heart of the King's enemies; whereby the people fall under Thee. Thy throne, O God, is for ever and ever: the sceptre of Thy kingdom is a right sceptre. Thou lovest righteousness, and hatest wickedness: therefore God, Thy God, hath anointed Thee with the oil of gladness above Thy fellows. All Thy garments smell of myrrh, and aloes, and cassia, out of the ivory palaces, whereby they have made Thee glad. Kings' daughters were among Thy honourable women: upon Thy right hand did stand the queen in gold of Ophir. Hearken, O daughter, and consider, and incline thine ear; forget also thine own people, and thy father's house. So shall the King greatly desire thy beauty; for He is thy Lord; and worship thou Him. And the daughter of Tyre shall be there with a gift; even the rich among the people shall intreat thy favour. The King's daughter is all glorious within: her clothing is of wrought gold. She shall be brought unto the King in raiment of needlework: the virgins her companions that follow her shall be brought unto Thee. With gladness and rejoicing shall they be brought: they shall enter into the King's palace. Instead of thy fathers shall be thy children, whom thou mayest make princes in all the earth. I will make thy name to be remembered in all generations: therefore shall the people praise thee for ever and ever.

Psalm 45

God is our refuge and strength, a very present help in trouble. Therefore will not we fear, though the earth be removed, and though the mountains be carried into the midst of the sea; though the waters thereof roar and be troubled, though the mountains shake with the swelling thereof. There is a river, the streams whereof shall make glad the city of God, the holy place of the tabernacles of the Most High. God is in the midst of her; she shall not be moved: God shall help her, and that right early. The heathen raged, the kingdoms were moved: He uttered His voice, the earth melted. The Lord of hosts is with us; the God of Jacob is our refuge. Come, behold the works of the Lord, what desolations He hath made in the earth. He maketh wars to cease unto the end of the earth; He breaketh the bow, and cutteth the spear in sunder; He burneth the chariot in the fire. Be still, and know that I am God: I will be exalted among the heathen, I will be exalted in the earth. The Lord of hosts is with us; the God of Jacob is our refuge.

Glory be to the Father . . . Both now . . .

Alleluia, alleluia, alleluia, glory be to Thee, O God (*3 times*).

Kyrie eleison (*3 times*).

Then Glory be to the Father . . . *and the troparion of the Forefeast:*

TONE FOUR

Mary once, with aged Joseph, went to be taxed in Bethlehem, for they were of the lineage of David; and she bore in her womb the fruit that had not been sown. The time of the birth was at hand and there was no room at the inn; but the cave proved a fair palace for the Queen. Christ is born, that He may raise up again the image that before was fallen.

Then the reader continues:

Both now . . .

Theotokion

What shall we call thee, O full of grace? Heaven? For thou hast made the Sun of Righteousness shine forth. Paradise? For thou hast put forth the flower of immortality. Virgin? For thou hast remained without corruption. Pure Mother? For thou hast held in thy holy embrace a Son who is God of all. Pray unto Him to save our souls.

Then we sing the following stichera:

TONE EIGHT

(*by Sophronios, Patriarch of Jerusalem*)

Make ready, O Bethlehem: let the manger be prepared, let the cave show its welcome. The truth has come, the shadow has passed away; born of a Virgin, God has appeared to men, formed as we are and making godlike the garment He has put on. Therefore Adam is renewed with Eve, and they call out: 'Thy good pleasure has appeared on earth to save our kind' (*twice*).

℣. God shall come from Teman, and the Holy One from the mountain overshadowed by the forest (*Habakkuk* 3:3).

TONE THREE

Now the prophecy draws near to its fulfilment, which mystically said: 'And thou, Bethlehem, in the land of Judah, who dost prepare the cave, art not the least among the princes:[1] for out of thee shall come forth unto me in the flesh a Governor of the Nations, Christ our God born of a Virgin Maiden, and as a shepherd He shall tend His people, the new Israel.' Let us all give Him glory.

℣. O Lord, I have heard the report of Thee and was afraid (*ibid.*, 1).

Repeat.

Glory be to the Father . . .

TONE EIGHT

Joseph spoke thus to the Virgin: 'What is this doing, O Mary, that I see in thee? I fail to understand and am amazed, and my mind is struck with dismay. Go from my sight, therefore, with all speed. What is this doing, O Mary, that I see in thee? Instead of honour, thou hast brought me shame; instead of gladness, sorrow; instead of praise, reproof. No further shall I bear the reproach of men. I received thee from the priests of the temple, as one blameless before the Lord. And what is this that I now see?'

Both now . . .

Repeat.

Immediately there follows the Prokimenon of the Prophecy:

TONE FOUR

The Lord said unto Me: Thou art my Son, this day have I begotten Thee (*Psalm* 2:7).

℣. Ask of Me, and I shall give Thee the heathen for Thine inheritance (*ibid.*, 8).

Lessons:

Reading from the Prophet Micah (5:2–4).

Thus saith the Lord: But thou, Bethlehem Ephratah, though thou be little among the thousands of Judah, yet out

[1] Micah 5:2; Matthew 2:6.

of thee shall He come forth unto Me that is to be ruler in Israel; whose goings forth have been from of old, from everlasting. Therefore will He give them up, until the time that she which travaileth hath brought forth: then the remnant of his brethren shall return unto the children of Israel. And He shall stand and feed in the strength of the Lord, in the majesty of the name of the Lord His God; and they shall abide: for now shall He be great unto the ends of the earth.

READING FROM THE EPISTLE TO THE HEBREWS (1 : 1–12).

God, who at sundry times and in divers manners spake in time past unto the fathers by the prophets, hath in these last days spoken unto us by His Son, whom He hath appointed heir of all things, by whom also He made the worlds; who being the brightness of His glory, and the express image of His person, and upholding all things by the word of His power, when He had by Himself purged our sins, sat down on the right hand of the Majesty on high; being made so much better than the angels, as He hath by inheritance obtained a more excellent name than they. For unto which of the angels said He at any time, Thou art My Son, this day have I begotten Thee? And again, I will be to Him a Father, and He shall be to Me a Son? And again, when He bringeth in the first begotten into the world, He saith, And let all the angels of God worship Him. And of the angels He saith, Who maketh His angels spirits, and His ministers a flame of fire. But unto the Son He saith, Thy throne, O God, is for ever and ever: a sceptre of righteousness is the sceptre of Thy kingdom: Thou hast loved righteousness, and hated iniquity; therefore God, even Thy God, hath anointed Thee with the oil of gladness above Thy fellows. And, Thou, Lord, in the beginning hast laid the foundation of the earth; and the heavens are the works of Thine hands: they shall perish; but Thou remainest; and they all shall wax old as doth a garment; and as a vesture shalt Thou fold them up, and they shall be changed: but Thou art the same, and Thy years shall not fail.

Reading from the Holy Gospel according to Matthew (1:18–25).

Now the birth of Jesus Christ was on this wise: When as His mother Mary was espoused to Joseph, before they came together, she was found with child of the Holy Ghost. Then Joseph her husband, being a just man, and not willing to make her a public example, was minded to put her away privily. But while he thought on these things, behold, the angel of the Lord appeared unto him in a dream, saying, Joseph, thou son of David, fear not to take unto thee Mary thy wife: for that which is conceived in her is of the Holy Ghost. And she shall bring forth a son, and thou shalt call His name Jesus: for He shall save His people from their sins. Now all this was done, that it might be fulfilled which was spoken of the Lord by the prophet, saying, Behold, a virgin shall be with child, and shall bring forth a son, and they shall call His name Emmanuel, which being interpreted is, God with us. Then Joseph being raised from sleep did as the angel of the Lord had bidden him, and took unto him his wife; and knew her not till she had brought forth her firstborn son: and he called His name Jesus.

After the Gospel the reader says:

Order my steps in Thy word: and let not any iniquity have dominion over me.

Deliver me from the false accusation of men: so will I keep Thy precepts.

Make Thy face to shine upon Thy servant; and teach me Thy statutes (*Psalm* 118:133–135).

Let my mouth be filled with Thy praise, O Lord: that I may sing of Thy glory and majesty all the day long (*Psalm* 70:8).

Then Holy God . . ., *etc., and the Lord's Prayer, followed by the kontakion of the Forefeast:*

TONE THREE

Today the Virgin comes to the cave to give birth ineffably to the pre-eternal Word. Hearing this, be of good cheer, O inhabited earth, and with the angels and the shepherds glorify Him whose will it was to be made manifest a young Child, the pre-eternal God.

Kyrie eleison, *40 times, and the Prayer of the Hours,* Thou who at every season and every hour . . . *Then* Kyrie eleison, *3 times*; Glory be to the Father . . . Both now . . .; Greater in honour than the cherubim . . .; In the Name of the Lord, give the blessing, Father.

The priest: God be merciful unto us . . .

And the prayer:

O Christ, the true Light who dost enlighten and sanctify every man that comes into the world, let the light of Thy countenance be marked upon us, that in it we may see the light unapproachable; and direct our steps in Thy commandments, at the prayers of Thine undefiled Mother and of all Thy saints. Amen.

The Third Hour

O come, let us worship . . ., *and the following three psalms:*

Psalm 66

God be merciful unto us, and bless us; and cause His face to shine upon us; that Thy way may be known upon earth, Thy saving health among all nations. Let the people praise Thee, O God; let all the people praise Thee. O let the nations be glad and sing for joy: for Thou shalt judge the people righteously, and govern the nations upon earth. Let the people praise Thee, O God; let all the people praise Thee. Then shall the earth yield her increase; and God, even our own God, shall bless us. God shall bless us; and all the ends of the earth shall fear Him.

Psalm 86

His foundation is in the holy mountains. The Lord loveth the gates of Zion more than all the dwellings of Jacob. Glorious things are spoken of thee, O city of God. I will make mention of Rahab and Babylon to them that know me: behold Philistia, and Tyre, with Ethiopia; this man was born there. And of Zion it shall be said, This and that man was born in her: and the Highest Himself shall establish her. The Lord shall count, when He writeth up the people, that this man was born there. As well the singers as the players on instruments shall be there: all my springs are in thee.

Psalm 50

Have mercy upon me, O God, according to Thy loving-kindness; according unto the multitude of Thy tender mercies blot out my transgressions. Wash me thoroughly from mine iniquity, and cleanse me from my sin. For I acknowledge my transgressions: and my sin is ever before me. Against Thee, Thee only, have I sinned, and done this evil in Thy sight: that Thou mightest be justified when Thou speakest, and be clear when Thou judgest. Behold, I was shapen in iniquity; and in sin did my mother conceive me. Behold, Thou desirest truth in the inward parts: and in the hidden part Thou shalt make me to know wisdom. Purge me with hyssop, and I shall be clean: wash me, and I shall be whiter than snow. Make me to hear joy and gladness; that the bones which Thou hast broken may rejoice. Hide Thy face from my sins, and blot out all mine iniquities. Create in me a clean heart, O God; and renew a right spirit within me. Cast me not away from Thy presence; and take not Thy Holy Spirit from me. Restore unto me the joy of Thy salvation; and uphold me with Thy free Spirit. Then will I teach transgressors Thy ways; and sinners shall be converted unto Thee. Deliver me from bloodguiltiness, O God, Thou God of my salvation: and my tongue shall sing aloud of Thy righteousness. O Lord, open Thou my lips; and my mouth shall shew forth Thy praise. For Thou desirest not sacrifice, else would I give it: Thou delightest not in burnt offering. The sacrifices of God are a broken spirit: a broken and a contrite heart, O God, Thou wilt not despise. Do good in Thy good pleasure unto Zion: build Thou the walls of Jerusalem. Then shalt Thou be pleased with the sacrifices of righteousness, with burnt offering and whole burnt offering: then shall they offer bullocks upon Thine altar.

Glory be to the Father . . . Both now . . .

Alleluia, alleluia, alleluia, glory be to Thee, O God (*3 times*).

Kyrie eleison (*3 times*).

Then Glory be to the Father . . . *and the troparion*, Mary once, with aged Joseph . . . (*p. 224*). *After this, the reader continues:*

Both now . . .

Theotokion

O Theotokos, thou art the true vine, that hast put forth the fruit of life. We pray thee, O Lady, intercede together with the apostles and all the saints, that mercy may be granted to our souls.

Then we sing the following stichera:

TONE SIX

This is our God: and there shall none other be accounted of in comparison with Him.[1] Born of a Virgin, He comes to dwell among men. Laid in a poor manger, the Only-begotten

[1] Baruch 3:35.

Son appears as mortal man and the Lord of glory is wrapped in swaddling clothes. A star guides the Magi to come and worship Him; and we sing: O Holy Trinity, save our souls (*twice*).

℣. God shall come from Teman, and the Holy One from the mountain overshadowed by the forest (*Habakkuk* 3:3).

TONE EIGHT

Before Thy birth, O Lord, the angelic hosts looked with trembling on this mystery and were struck with wonder: for Thou who hast adorned the vault of heaven with stars hast been well pleased to be born as a babe; and Thou who holdest all the ends of the earth in the hollow of Thy hand art laid in a manger of dumb beasts. For by such a dispensation has Thy compassion been made known, O Christ, and Thy great mercy: glory to Thee.

℣. O Lord, I have heard the report of Thee and was afraid (*ibid.*, 1).

Repeat.

Glory be to the Father . . .

TONE THREE

Tell us, Joseph, how is it that thou bringest to Bethlehem, great with child, the Maiden whom thou hast received from the sanctuary? 'I have searched the prophets,' said he, 'and have been warned by an angel: and I am persuaded that Mary shall give birth to God, in ways surpassing all interpretation. Magi from the east shall come to worship Him with precious gifts.' O Lord, who for our sake hast taken flesh: glory to Thee.

Both now . . .

Repeat.

Immediately there follows the Prokimenon of the Prophecy:

TONE FOUR

For unto us a Child is born, unto us a Son is given (*Isaiah* 9:6).

℣. And the government shall be upon His shoulder (*ibid.*).

Lessons:

READING FROM THE PROPHET JEREMIAH (*Baruch* 3:35–4:4).

This is our God, and there shall none other be accounted of in comparison of Him. He hath found out all the way of knowledge, and hath given it unto Jacob His servant, and to Israel His beloved. Afterward did He shew Himself upon earth, and conversed with men. This is the book of the commandments of God, and the law that endureth for ever: all they that keep it shall come to life; but such as leave it shall die. Turn thee, O Jacob, and take hold of it; walk in the presence of the light thereof, that thou mayest be illuminated. Give not thine honour to another, nor the things that are profitable unto thee to a strange nation. O Israel, happy are we: for things that are pleasing to God are made known unto us.

READING FROM THE EPISTLE OF PAUL TO THE GALATIANS (3:23–29).

Brethren, before faith came, we were kept under the law, shut up unto the faith which should afterwards be revealed. Wherefore the law was our schoolmaster to bring us unto Christ, that we might be justified by faith. But after that faith is come, we are no longer under a schoolmaster. For ye are all the children of God by faith in Christ Jesus. For as many of you as have been baptized into Christ have put on Christ. There is neither Jew nor Greek, there is neither bond nor free, there is neither male nor female: for ye are all one in Christ Jesus. And if ye be Christ's, then are ye Abraham's seed, and heirs according to the promise.

THE THIRD HOUR

Reading from the Holy Gospel according to Luke (2 : 1–20).

And it came to pass in those days, that there went out a decree from Caesar Augustus, that all the world should be taxed. (And this taxing was first made when Cyrenius was governor of Syria.) And all went to be taxed, every one into his own city. And Joseph also went up from Galilee, out of the city of Nazareth, into Judaea, unto the city of David, which is called Bethlehem (because he was of the house and lineage of David), to be taxed with Mary his espoused wife, being great with child. And so it was, that, while they were there, the days were accomplished that she should be delivered. And she brought forth her firstborn son, and wrapped Him in swaddling clothes, and laid Him in a manger; because there was no room for them in the inn. And there were in the same country shepherds abiding in the field, keeping watch over their flock by night. And, lo, the angel of the Lord came upon them, and the glory of the Lord shone round about them: and they were sore afraid. And the angel said unto them, Fear not: for, behold, I bring you good tidings of great joy, which shall be to all people. For unto you is born this day in the city of David a Saviour, which is Christ the Lord. And this shall be a sign unto you: Ye shall find the babe wrapped in swaddling clothes, lying in a manger. And suddenly there was with the angel a multitude of the heavenly host praising God, and saying, Glory to God in the highest, and on earth peace, good will toward men. And it came to pass, as the angels were gone away from them into heaven, the shepherds said one to another, Let us now go even unto Bethlehem, and see this thing which is come to pass, which the Lord hath made known unto us. And they came with haste, and found Mary, and Joseph, and the babe lying in a manger. And when they had seen it, they made known abroad the saying which was told them concerning this child. And all they that heard it wondered at those things which were told them by the shepherds. But Mary kept all these things, and pondered them in her heart. And the shepherds returned, glorifying and praising God for all the things that they had heard and seen, as it was told unto them.

After the Gospel the reader says:

Blessed be the Lord God: blessed be the Lord from day to day, and may the God of our salvation prosper us, for He is our God, the God of salvation (*Psalm* 67:20–21).

Then Holy God . . ., *etc., and the Lord's Prayer, followed by the kontakion,* Today the Virgin comes to the cave . . . (*p. 228*).

Kyrie eleison, *40 times, and the Prayer of the Hours,* Thou who at every season and every hour . . . *Then* Kyrie eleison, *3 times*; Glory be to the Father . . . Both now . . .; Greater in honour than the cherubim . . .; In the Name of the Lord, give the blessing, Father.

The priest: God be merciful unto us . . .

And the Prayer of St. Mardarios:

O God the Master, Father Almighty, O Lord Jesus Christ, the Only-begotten Son, and Thou, O Holy Spirit, one Godhead, one Power, have mercy upon me a sinner, and according to Thy divine judgement save me, Thine unworthy servant: for blessed art Thou unto the ages of ages. Amen.

The Sixth Hour

O come, let us worship . . ., *and the following three psalms:*

Psalm 71

Give the king Thy judgements, O God, and Thy righteousness unto the king's son. He shall judge Thy people with righteousness, and Thy poor with judgement. The mountains shall bring peace to the people, and the little hills, by righteousness. He shall judge the poor of the people, He shall save the children of the needy, and shall break in pieces the oppressor. They shall fear Thee as long as the sun and moon endure, throughout all generations. He shall come down like rain upon the mown grass: as showers that water the earth. In His days shall the righteous flourish; and abundance of peace so long as the moon endureth. He shall have dominion also from sea to sea, and from the river unto the ends of the earth. They that dwell in the wilderness shall bow before Him; and His enemies shall lick the dust. The kings of Tarshish and of the isles shall bring presents: the kings of Sheba and Seba shall offer gifts. Yea, all kings shall fall down before Him: all nations shall serve Him. For He shall deliver the needy when he crieth; the poor also, and him that hath no helper. He shall spare the poor and needy, and shall save the souls of the needy. He shall redeem their soul from deceit and violence: and precious shall their blood be in His sight. And He shall live, and to Him shall be given of the gold of Sheba: prayer also shall be made for Him continually; and daily shall He be praised. There shall be an handful of corn in the earth upon the top of the mountains; the fruit thereof shall shake like Lebanon: and they of the city shall flourish like grass of the earth. His name shall endure for ever: His name shall be continued as long as the sun: and men shall be blessed in Him: all nations shall call Him blessed. Blessed be the Lord God, the God of Israel, who only doeth wondrous things. And blessed be His glorious name for ever: and let the whole earth be filled with His glory. Amen, and Amen.

Psalm 131

Lord, remember David, and all his afflictions; how he sware unto the Lord, and vowed unto the mighty God of Jacob; surely I will not come into the tabernacle of my house, nor go up into my bed; I will not give sleep to mine eyes, or slumber to mine eyelids, until I find out a place for the Lord, an habitation for the mighty God of Jacob. Lo, we heard of it at Ephratah: we found it in the fields of the wood. We will go into His tabernacles: we will worship at His footstool. Arise, O Lord, into Thy rest; Thou, and the ark of Thy strength. Let Thy priests be clothed with righteousness; and let Thy saints shout for joy. For Thy servant David's sake turn not away the face of Thine anointed. The Lord hath sworn in truth unto David; He will not turn from it; Of the fruit of thy body will I set upon thy throne. If thy children will keep My covenant and My testimony that I shall teach them, their children shall also sit upon thy throne for evermore. For the Lord hath chosen Zion; He hath desired it for His habitation. This is My rest for ever: here will I dwell; for I have desired it. I will abundantly bless her provision: I will satisfy her poor with bread. I will also clothe her priests with salvation: and her saints shall shout aloud for joy. There will I make the horn of David to bud: I have ordained a lamp for Mine anointed. His enemies will I clothe with shame: but upon himself shall his crown flourish.

Psalm 90

He that dwelleth in the secret place of the Most High shall abide under the shadow of the Almighty. I will say of the Lord, He is my refuge and my fortress: my God; in Him will I trust. Surely He shall deliver thee from the snare of the fowler, and from the noisome pestilence. He shall cover thee with His feathers, and under His wings shalt thou trust: His truth shall be thy shield and buckler. Thou shalt not be afraid for the terror by night; nor for the arrow that flieth by day; nor for the pestilence that walketh in darkness; nor for the destruction that wasteth at noonday. A thousand shall fall at thy side, and ten thousand at thy right hand; but it shall not come nigh thee. Only with thine eyes shalt thou behold and see the reward of the wicked. Because thou hast made the Lord, which is my refuge, even the Most High, thy habitation; there shall no evil befall thee, neither shall any plague come nigh thy dwelling. For He shall give His angels charge over thee, to keep thee in all thy ways. They shall bear thee up in their hands, lest thou dash thy foot against a stone. Thou shalt tread upon the lion and adder: the young lion and the dragon shalt thou trample under feet. Because he hath set his love upon Me, therefore will I deliver him: I will set him on high, because he hath known My name. He shall call upon Me, and I will answer him: I will be with him in trouble; I will deliver him, and honour him. With long life will I satisfy him, and shew him My salvation.

Glory be to the Father . . . Both now . . .

Alleluia, alleluia, alleluia, glory be to Thee, O God (*3 times*).

Kyrie eleison (*3 times*).

Then Glory be to the Father . . . *and the troparion*, Mary once, with aged Joseph . . . (*p. 224*). *After this, the reader continues:*

Both now . . .

Theotokion

As there is no boldness in us because of the multitude of our sins, do thou, O Virgin Theotokos, intercede with the Son whom thou hast borne, for the entreaty of a mother has great power to win the favour of the Master. Despise not, O all-venerable Lady, the prayers of sinners, for He who took upon Himself to suffer for our sake is merciful and strong to save.

Then we sing the following stichera:

TONE ONE

Come, O ye faithful, inspired by God let us arise and behold the divine condescension from on high that is made manifest to us in Bethlehem. Cleansing our minds, let us offer through our lives virtues instead of myrrh, preparing with faith our entry into the feast of the Nativity, storing up treasure in our souls and crying: Glory in the highest to God in Trinity, whose good pleasure is now revealed to men, that in His love for mankind He may set Adam free from the ancestral curse (*twice*).

℣. God shall come from Teman, and the Holy One from the mountain overshadowed by the forest (*Habakkuk* 3 : 3).

TONE FOUR

Hearken, O heaven, and give ear, O earth. Let the foundations be shaken, and let trembling lay hold upon the nethermost parts of the world. For our God and Creator has clothed Himself in created flesh, and He who with His strong arm fashioned the creation reveals Himself in the womb of her that He formed. O the depth of the riches of the wisdom and knowledge of God! How unsearchable are His judgements, and His ways past finding out![1]

℣. O Lord, I have heard the report of Thee and was afraid (*ibid.*, 1). *Repeat.*

Glory be to the Father . . .

TONE FIVE

Come ye people, bearers of Christ, and let us behold wonders that strike and hold fast every mind with amazement: and in reverent worship let us sing praises with faith. Today a Maiden great with child comes to Bethlehem to give birth to the Lord: and choirs of angels go before her. Seeing these things Joseph, her betrothed, cried out: 'What is this strange mystery in thee, O Virgin? And how shalt thou bring forth child, Calf upon whom the yoke has never come?'[2]

Both now . . .

Repeat.

[1] Romans 11 : 33.
[2] Numbers 19:2.

Immediately there follows the Prokimenon of the Prophecy:

TONE FOUR

From the womb before the morning star have I begotten Thee (*Psalm* 109 : 3).

℣. The Lord said unto my Lord: Sit Thou at My right hand, until I make Thine enemies Thy footstool (*ibid.*, 1).

Lessons:

READING FROM THE PROPHET ISAIAH (7 : 10–16; 8 : 1–4, 9–10).

Moreover the Lord spake again unto Ahaz, saying, Ask thee a sign of the Lord thy God; ask it either in the depth, or in the height above. But Ahaz said, I will not ask, neither will I tempt the Lord. And he[1] said, Hear ye now, O house of David; is it a small thing for you to weary men, but will ye weary my God also? Therefore the Lord Himself shall give you a sign; Behold, a virgin shall conceive, and bear a Son, and shall call His name Immanuel. Butter and honey shall He eat, that He may know to refuse the evil, and choose the good. For before the Child shall know to refuse the evil, and choose the good, the land that thou abhorrest shall be forsaken of both her kings. Moreover the Lord said unto me, Take thee a great roll, and write in it with a man's pen concerning Maher-shalal-hash-baz. And I took unto me faithful witnesses to record, Uriah the priest, and Zechariah the son of Jeberechiah. And I went unto the prophetess; and she conceived, and bare a son. Then said the Lord to me, Call his name Maher-shalal-hash-baz. For before the child shall have knowledge to cry, My father, and my mother, the riches of Damascus and the spoil of Samaria shall be taken away before the king of Assyria. God is with us. Associate yourselves, O ye people, and ye shall be broken in pieces; and give ear, all ye of far countries: gird yourselves, and ye

[1] The prophet Isaiah.

shall be broken in pieces; gird yourselves, and ye shall be broken in pieces. Take counsel together, and it shall come to nought; speak the word, and it shall not stand: for God is with us.

READING FROM THE EPISTLE TO THE HEBREWS (1 : 10–2 : 3).

Thou, Lord, in the beginning hast laid the foundation of the earth; and the heavens are the works of Thine hands: they shall perish; but Thou remainest; and they all shall wax old as doth a garment; and as a vesture shalt Thou fold them up, and they shall be changed: but Thou art the same, and Thy years shall not fail. But to which of the angels said He at any time, 'Sit on my right hand, until I make Thine enemies Thy footstool?' Are they not all ministering spirits, sent forth to minister for them who shall be heirs of salvation? Therefore we ought to give the more earnest heed to the things which we have heard, lest at any time we should let them slip. For if the word spoken by angels was stedfast, and every transgression and disobedience received a just recompense of reward; how shall we escape, if we neglect so great salvation; which at the first began to be spoken by the Lord, and was confirmed unto us by them that heard Him?

READING FROM THE HOLY GOSPEL ACCORDING TO MATTHEW (2 : 1–12).

Now when Jesus was born in Bethlehem of Judaea in the days of Herod the king, behold, there came wise men from the east to Jerusalem, saying, Where is He that is born King of the Jews? for we have seen His star in the east, and are come to worship Him. When Herod the king had heard these things, he was troubled, and all Jerusalem with him. And when he had gathered all the chief priests and scribes of the people together, he demanded of them where Christ should be born. And they said unto him, In Bethlehem of Judaea: for thus it is written by the prophet, And thou Bethlehem, in the land of Judah, art not the least among the princes of Judah: for out of thee shall come a Governor, that shall rule my people Israel. Then Herod, when he had privily called the wise men, inquired of them diligently what time the star appeared. And he sent them to Bethlehem, and said, Go and search diligently for the young child; and when ye have found Him, bring me word again, that I may come and worship Him also. When they had heard the king, they departed; and, lo, the star, which they saw in the east, went before them till it came and stood over where the young child was. When they saw the star, they rejoiced with exceeding great joy. And when they were come into the house, they saw the young child with Mary His mother, and fell down, and worshipped Him; and when they had opened their treasures, they presented unto Him gifts; gold, and frankincense, and myrrh. And being warned of God in a dream that they should not return to Herod, they departed into their own country another way.

After the Gospel the reader says:

Let Thy tender mercies, O Lord, speedily go before us, for we are become exceeding poor. Help us, O God of our salvation, for the glory of Thy Name: O Lord, deliver us and purge away our sins, for Thy Name's sake (*Psalm* 78 : 8–9).

Then Holy God . . ., *etc., and the Lord's Prayer, followed by the kontakion*, Today the Virgin comes to the cave . . . (*p. 228*).

Kyrie eleison, *40 times, and the Prayer of the Hours*, Thou who at every season and every hour . . . *Then* Kyrie eleison, *3 times*; Glory be to the Father . . . Both now . . .; Greater in honour than the cherubim . . .; In the Name of the Lord, give the blessing, Father.

The priest: God be merciful unto us . . .

And the Prayer of St. Basil:

O God, the Lord of hosts, and Author of all creation, who in Thine ineffable tender mercy hast sent down Thine Only-begotten Son, Our Lord Jesus Christ, for the salvation of our kind, and through His Holy Cross hast torn up the hand-writing of our sins and thereby triumphed over the princes and dominions of darkness: do Thou, O Master, who lovest mankind, accept these prayers of thanksgiving and supplication even from us sinners, and deliver us from every deadly and dark transgression and from all the visible and invisible enemies that seek to do us harm. Nail our flesh with the fear of Thee, and let not our hearts incline to evil words or thoughts, but wound our souls with Thy love, that ever gazing upon Thee, guided by Thy light and beholding Thee, the eternal Light that no man can approach, we may send up unceasing praises and thanks unto Thee, the Father without beginning, together with Thine Only-begotten Son and Thy most holy, good, and life-giving Spirit, now, and ever, and unto the ages of ages. Amen.

The Ninth Hour

O come, let us worship . . ., *and the following three psalms:*

Psalm 109

The Lord said unto my Lord, Sit Thou at My right hand, until I make Thine enemies Thy footstool. The Lord shall send the rod of Thy strength out of Zion: rule Thou in the midst of Thine enemies. Thy people shall be willing in the day of Thy power, in the beauties of holiness from the womb of the morning: Thou hast the dew of Thy youth. The Lord hath sworn, and will not repent, Thou art a priest for ever after the order of Melchizedek. The Lord at Thy right hand shall strike through kings in the day of His wrath. He shall judge among the heathen, He shall fill the places with the dead bodies; He shall wound the heads over many countries. He shall drink of the brook in the way: therefore shall He lift up the head.

Psalm 110

Praise ye the Lord. I will praise the Lord with my whole heart, in the assembly of the upright, and in the congregation. The works of the Lord are great, sought out of all them that have pleasure therein. His work is honourable and glorious: and His righteousness endureth for ever. He hath made His wonderful works to be remembered: the Lord is gracious and full of compassion. He hath given meat unto them that fear Him: He will ever be mindful of His covenant. He hath shewed His people the power of His works, that He may give them the heritage of the heathen. The works of His hands are verity and judgement; all His commandments are sure. They stand fast for ever and ever, and are done in truth and uprightness. He sent redemption unto His people: He hath commanded His covenant for ever: holy and reverend is His name. The fear of the Lord is the beginning of wisdom: a good understanding have all they that do His commandments: His praise endureth for ever.

Psalm 85

Bow down Thine ear, O Lord, hear me: for I am poor and needy. Preserve my soul; for I am holy: O Thou my God, save Thy servant that trusteth in Thee. Be merciful unto me, O Lord: for I cry unto Thee daily. Rejoice the soul of Thy servant: for unto Thee, O Lord, do I lift up my soul. For Thou, Lord, art good, and ready to forgive; and plenteous in mercy unto all them that call upon Thee. Give ear, O Lord, unto my prayer; and attend to the voice of my supplications. In the day of my trouble I will call upon Thee: for Thou wilt answer me. Among the gods there is none like unto Thee, O Lord; neither are there any works like unto Thy works. All nations whom Thou hast made shall come and worship before Thee, O Lord; and shall glorify Thy name. For Thou art great, and doest wondrous things: Thou art God alone. Teach me Thy way, O Lord; I will walk in Thy truth: unite my heart to fear Thy name. I will praise Thee, O Lord my God, with all my heart: and I will glorify Thy name for evermore. For great is Thy mercy toward me: and Thou hast delivered my soul from the lowest hell. O God, the proud are risen against me, and the assemblies of violent men have sought after my soul; and have not set Thee before them. But Thou, O Lord, art a God full of compassion, and gracious, longsuffering, and plenteous in mercy and truth. O turn unto me, and have mercy upon me; give Thy strength unto Thy servant, and save the son of Thine handmaid. Shew me a token for good; that they which hate me may see it, and be ashamed: because Thou, Lord, hast holpen me, and comforted me.

Glory be to the Father . . . Both now . . .

Alleluia, alleluia, alleluia, glory be to Thee, O God (*3 times*).

Kyrie eleison (*3 times*).

Then Glory be to the Father . . . *and the troparion*, Mary once, with aged Joseph . . . (*p. 224*). *After this, the reader continues:*

Both now . . .

Theotokion

O good Lord, for our sakes Thou wast born of a Virgin and hast endured Crucifixion, despoiling death by death, and as God Thou hast shown forth the Resurrection. Despise not Thy handiwork: show Thy love for man, O merciful Lord. Accept the intercessions made on our behalf by the Theotokos who bore Thee; and save, O our Saviour, Thy people from despair.

Then we sing the following stichera:

TONE SEVEN

Herod was struck with amazement on beholding the piety of the Magi; and overcome by wrath, he inquired closely when the Child was born. Mothers were bereft of their infants, and by an untimely death their babes were bitterly harvested. Paps grew dry and sources of milk were stopped. Great was this calamity! Therefore let us, the faithful, gathered in godliness, worship the Nativity of Christ (*twice*).

℣. God shall come from Teman, and the Holy One from the mountain overshadowed by the forest (*Habakkuk* 3:3).

TONE TWO

O Virgin, when Joseph went up to Bethlehem wounded by sorrow, thou didst cry to him: 'Why art thou downcast and troubled, seeing me great with child? Why art thou wholly ignorant of the fearful mystery that comes to pass in me? Henceforth, cast every fear aside and understand this strange marvel: for in my womb God now descends upon earth for mercy's sake, and He has taken flesh. Thou shalt see Him according to His good pleasure, when He is born; and filled with joy thou shalt worship Him as Thy Creator. Him the angels praise without ceasing in song and glorify with the Father and the Holy Spirit.'

℣. O Lord, I have heard the report of Thee and was afraid (*ibid*., 1).

Repeat.

Glory be to the Father . . . Both now . . .

TONE SIX

He who holds the whole creation in the hollow of His hand today is born of the Virgin (*3 times*).[1]

He whom in essence none can touch is wrapped in swaddling clothes as a mortal.

[1] In the Slav use, once only.

God who in the beginning founded the heavens lies in a manger.

He who rained manna down on the people in the wilderness is fed on milk from His Mother's breast.

He who is the Bridegroom of the Church calls unto Himself the Magi.

The Son of the Virgin accepts their gifts.

We worship Thy birth, O Christ (*3 times*).

Show us also Thy divine Epiphany.

Immediately there follows the Prokimenon of the Prophecy:

TONE FOUR

Zion is our mother, a man shall say: and such a man was born in her (*Psalm* 86:5).

℣. His foundations are in the holy mountains (*ibid.*, 1).

Lessons:

READING FROM THE PROPHET ISAIAH (9:6–7).

For unto us a Child is born, unto us a Son is given: and the government shall be upon His shoulder: and His name shall be called Wonderful, Counsellor, The mighty God, The everlasting Father, The Prince of Peace. Of the increase of His government and peace there shall be no end, upon the throne of David, and upon his kingdom, to order it, and to establish it with judgement and with justice from henceforth even for ever. The zeal of the Lord of hosts will perform this.

READING FROM THE EPISTLE TO THE HEBREWS (2:11–18).

Brethren, both He that sanctifieth and they who are sanctified are all of one: for which cause He is not ashamed to call them brethren, saying, I will declare Thy name unto My brethren, in the midst of the church will I sing praise unto Thee. And again, I will put my trust in Him. And again,

Behold I and the children which God hath given me. Forasmuch then as the children are partakers of flesh and blood, He also Himself likewise took part of the same; that through death He might destroy him that had the power of death, that is, the devil; and deliver them who through fear of death were all their lifetime subject to bondage. For verily He took not on Him the nature of angels; but He took on Him the seed of Abraham. Wherefore in all things it behoved Him to be made like unto His brethren, that He might be a merciful and faithful high priest in things pertaining to God, to make reconciliation for the sins of the people. For in that He Himself hath suffered being tempted, He is able to succour them that are tempted.

READING FROM THE HOLY GOSPEL ACCORDING TO MATTHEW (2:13–23).

And when the wise men were departed, behold, the angel of the Lord appeareth to Joseph in a dream, saying, Arise, and take the young child and His mother, and flee into Egypt, and be thou there until I bring thee word: for Herod will seek the young child to destroy Him. When he arose, he took the young child and His mother by night, and departed into Egypt: and was there until the death of Herod: that it might be fulfilled which was spoken of the Lord by the prophet, saying, Out of Egypt have I called My son. Then Herod, when he saw that he was mocked of the wise men, was exceeding wroth, and sent forth, and slew all the children that were in Bethlehem, and in all the coasts thereof, from two years old and under, according to the time which he had diligently inquired of the wise men. Then was fulfilled that which was spoken by Jeremiah the prophet, saying, In Rama was there a voice heard, lamentation, and weeping, and great mourning, Rachel weeping for her children, and would not be comforted, because they are not. But when Herod was dead, behold, an angel of the Lord appeareth in a dream to Joseph in Egypt, saying, Arise, and take the young child and His mother, and go into the land of Israel: for they are dead which sought the young child's life. And he arose, and took the young child and His mother, and came into the land of Israel. But when he heard that Archelaus did reign in Judaea in the room of his father Herod, he was afraid to go thither: notwithstanding, being warned of God in a dream, he turned aside into the parts of Galilee: and he came and dwelt in a city called Nazareth: that it might be fulfilled which was spoken by the prophets, He shall be called a Nazarene.

After the Gospel the reader says:

Deliver us not up unto the end, for Thy Holy Name's sake, neither disannul Thou Thy covenant; and cause not Thy mercy to depart from us, for the sake of Abraham Thy beloved, and Isaac Thy servant, and Israel Thy holy one (*Song of the Three Children*, *verses* 11–12).

Then Holy God . . ., *etc.*, *and the Lord's Prayer*, *followed by the kontakion*, Today the Virgin comes to the cave . . . (*p. 228*).

Kyrie eleison, *40 times*, *and the Prayer of the Hours*, Thou who at every season and every hour . . . *Then* Kyrie eleison, *3 times*; Glory be to the Father . . . Both now . . .; Greater in honour than the cherubim . . .; In the Name of the Lord, give the blessing, Father.

The priest: God be merciful unto us . . .

And the Prayer of St. Basil:

O Master and Lord, Jesus Christ our God, who art longsuffering towards our faults and hast brought us even unto this present hour, in which, hanging upon the life-giving Cross, Thou hast opened unto the good thief the way into Paradise, and destroyed death by death: be merciful to us, Thy humble and sinful and unworthy servants. For we have sinned and transgressed, and we are not worthy to lift up our eyes and look at the height of heaven, since we have forsaken the path of Thy righteousness and have walked according to the desires of our own hearts. But we pray Thee of Thy boundless goodness, spare us, O Lord, according to the abundance of Thy mercy, and save us for Thy Holy Name's sake, for our days have been consumed in vanity. Pluck us from the hand of the adversary, forgive us our sins, and kill our fleshly lusts, that putting off the old man, we may put on the new, and may live for Thee our Master and Protector; and that so, following Thine ordinances, we may attain to eternal rest, in the place where all the joyful dwell. For Thou, O Christ our God, art indeed the true joy and gladness of those that love Thee, and unto Thee we ascribe glory, together with Thy Father who is without beginning, and Thy most holy, good, and life-giving Spirit, now, and ever, and unto the ages of ages. Amen.

The Typika

Psalm 102.

Glory be to the Father . . .

Psalm 145.

Both now . . .

O Only-begotten Son and Word of God . . .

In Thy Kingdom remember us, O Lord, when Thou comest in Thy Kingdom, *and the Beatitudes, at the end of which we say:*

Glory be to the Father . . .

Both now . . .

Remember us, O Lord, when Thou comest in Thy Kingdom.

Remember us, O Master, when Thou comest in Thy Kingdom.

Remember us, O Holy One, when Thou comest in Thy Kingdom.

Then we continue:

The heavenly choir sings Thy praises, saying: Holy, Holy, Holy, Lord of Sabaoth, heaven and earth are full of Thy glory.

℣ Draw near to Him and be enlightened, and your faces shall not be ashamed (*Psalm* 33:6).

The heavenly choir sings Thy praises, saying: Holy, Holy, Holy, Lord of Sabaoth, heaven and earth are full of Thy glory.

Glory be to the Father . . .

The choir of the holy angels and archangels with all the powers of heaven sings Thy praises, saying: Holy, Holy, Holy, Lord of Sabaoth, heaven and earth are full of Thy glory.

Both now . . .

If there is no Liturgy, we say:

I believe in one God, the Father Almighty . . .

Then, whether there is a Liturgy or not, we continue:

Forgive, remit, and pardon, O God, our sins both voluntary and involuntary, in deed and in word, in knowledge and in ignorance, committed by night or by day, in intention and in thought: forgive us them all, for Thou art good and lovest mankind.

Our Father . . .

The kontakion, Today the Virgin comes to the cave . . . (*p. 228*).

Kyrie eleison, *40 times.*

O most holy Trinity, consubstantial Power, undivided Kingship, the Cause of all good, be gracious even to me, a sinner. Confirm and instruct my heart and take away from me every defilement. Enlighten my mind, that I may ever glorify, praise, and worship Thee, saying: One is holy, one is Lord, Jesus Christ, to the glory of God the Father. Amen.

If there is a Liturgy, we continue:

It is meet in truth to bless thee, the Theotokos . . .

And the Dismissal.

But if there is no Liturgy, after the prayer, O most holy Trinity . . ., *we say:*

Blessed be the Name of the Lord, from henceforth and for evermore (*3 times*).

Psalm 33.

It is meet in truth to bless thee, the Theotokos . . .

And the Dismissal.

25 DECEMBER

THE NATIVITY ACCORDING TO THE FLESH OF OUR LORD AND GOD AND SAVIOUR JESUS CHRIST

In the Greek practice, the following rules are observed:

1. *If Christmas falls on any day of the week except Sunday or Monday, the order of service is as in the text below. On 24 December, the Royal Hours with the Typika, and then Vespers followed by the Liturgy of St. Basil; at the Vigil, Great Compline, followed by Mattins; on 25 December, the Liturgy of St. John Chrysostom.*

2. *If Christmas falls on Sunday, the Royal Hours with the Typika are said on Friday, 23 December. On Friday evening and Saturday morning, the office of the Forefeast, 24 December, with the Liturgy of St. John Chrysostom. On Saturday evening the Vigil begins with Great Vespers, followed by Mattins: Great Compline is not used. On Sunday, 25 December, the Liturgy of St. Basil. The normal Sunday texts of the Resurrection are omitted.*

3. *If Christmas falls on Monday, the Royal Hours with the Typika are said on Friday, 22 December. On Saturday evening and Sunday morning, the office of the Sunday before Christmas is used, together with the office of the Forefeast for 24 December; on Sunday morning, the Liturgy of St. John Chrysostom. On Sunday evening the Vigil begins with Great Vespers, followed by Mattins: Great Compline is not used. On Monday, 25 December, the Liturgy of St. Basil.*

The rules are the same in Slav practice, except that on Saturday and Sunday, as on other days, the Vigil begins with Great Compline,

Vespers being said immediately after the Liturgy of St. John Chrysostom.

Vespers

On Lord, I have cried, *eight stichera are sung:*

TONE TWO

(*by Germanos*)

Come, let us greatly rejoice in the Lord as we tell of this present mystery. The middle wall of partition has been destroyed; the flaming sword turns back, the cherubim withdraw from the tree of life, and I partake of the delight of Paradise from which I was cast out through disobedience. For the express Image of the Father,[1] the Imprint of His eternity, takes the form of a servant, and without undergoing change He comes forth from a Mother who knew not wedlock. For what He was, He has remained, true God: and what He was not, He has taken upon Himself, becoming man through love for mankind. Unto Him let us cry aloud: God born of a Virgin, have mercy upon us (*twice*).

(*by Anatolios*)

When the Lord Jesus was born of the holy Virgin, all the world was enlightened. The shepherds watched in the fields, the Magi adored and the angels praised in song; but Herod was troubled: for God has appeared in the flesh, the Saviour of our souls (*twice*).

Thy Kingdom, O Christ our God, is a Kingdom of all the ages, and Thy rule is from generation to generation. Made flesh of the Holy Spirit and made man of the ever-Virgin Mary, Thou hast enlightened us by Thy coming. Light of Light, Brightness of the Father,[1] Thou hast made the whole

[1] Hebrews 1:3.

creation shine with joy. All that hath breath praises Thee, the Image of the glory of the Father. O God who art, and who hast ever been, who hast shone forth from a Virgin, have mercy upon us (*twice*).

What shall we offer Thee, O Christ, who for our sakes hast appeared on earth as man? Every creature made by Thee offers Thee thanks. The angels offer Thee a hymn; the heavens a star; the Magi, gifts; the shepherds, their wonder; the earth, its cave; the wilderness, the manger: and we offer Thee a Virgin Mother. O pre-eternal God, have mercy upon us (*twice*).

Glory be to the Father . . . Both now . . .

SAME TONE

(*by Cassia the nun*)

When Augustus reigned alone upon earth, the many kingdoms of men came to end: and when Thou wast made man of the pure Virgin, the many gods of idolatry were destroyed. The cities of the world passed under one single rule; and the nations came to believe in one sovereign Godhead. The peoples were enrolled by the decree of Caesar; and we, the faithful, were enrolled in the Name of the Godhead, when Thou, our God, wast made man. Great is Thy mercy: glory to Thee.

Entrance with the Gospel, O joyful light, *and prokimenon of the day*.[1]

Lessons:

Reading from Genesis (1 : 1–13).

In the beginning God created the heaven and the earth. And the earth was without form, and void; and darkness was upon the face of the deep. And the Spirit of God moved upon

[1] On Friday, the Great Prokimenon, *Who is so great a God as our God?* (p. 290).

the face of the waters. And God said, Let there be light: and there was light. And God saw the light, that it was good: and God divided the light from the darkness. And God called the light Day, and the darkness He called Night. And the evening and the morning were the first day. And God said, Let there be a firmament in the midst of the waters, and let it divide the waters from the waters. And God made the firmament, and divided the waters which were under the firmament from the waters which were above the firmament: and it was so. And God called the firmament Heaven. And the evening and the morning were the second day. And God said, Let the waters under the heaven be gathered together unto one place, and let the dry land appear: and it was so. And God called the dry land Earth; and the gathering together of the waters called He Seas: and God saw that it was good. And God said, Let the earth bring forth grass, the herb yielding seed, and the fruit tree yielding fruit after his kind, whose seed is in itself, upon the earth: and it was so. And the earth brought forth grass, and herb yielding seed after his kind, and the tree yielding fruit, whose seed was in itself, after his kind: and God saw that it was good. And the evening and the morning were the third day.

Reading from Numbers (24:2–3, 5–9, 17–18).

The spirit of God came upon Balaam, and he took up his parable, and said: How goodly are thy tents, O Jacob, and thy tabernacles, O Israel! As the valleys are they spread forth, as gardens by the river's side, as the trees of lign aloes which the Lord hath planted, and as cedar trees beside the waters. He shall pour the water out of his buckets, and his seed shall be in many waters, and his king shall be higher than Agag, and his kingdom shall be exalted. God brought him forth out of Egypt; he hath as it were the strength of an unicorn: he shall eat up the nations his enemies, and shall break their bones, and pierce them through with his arrows.

He couched, he lay down as a lion, and as a great lion: who shall stir him up? Blessed is he that blesseth thee, and cursed is he that curseth thee. There shall come a Star out of Jacob, and a Sceptre shall rise out of Israel, and shall smite the corners of Moab, and destroy all the children of Sheth. And Edom shall be a possession, Seir also shall be a possession for his enemies; and Israel shall do valiantly.

Reading from the Prophet Micah (4:6–7, 5:2–4).

In that day, saith the Lord, will I assemble her that halteth, and I will gather her that is driven out, and her that I have afflicted; and I will make her that halted a remnant, and her that was cast far off a strong nation: and the Lord shall reign over them in mount Zion from henceforth, even for ever. But thou, Bethlehem Ephratah, though thou be little among the thousands of Judah, yet out of thee shall He come forth unto Me that is to be ruler in Israel; whose goings forth have been from of old, from everlasting. Therefore will He give them up, until the time that she which travaileth hath brought forth: then the remnant of his brethren shall return unto the children of Israel. And He shall stand and feed in the strength of the Lord, in the majesty of the name of the Lord His God; and they shall abide: for now shall He be great unto the ends of the earth.

Then is said, standing:

Troparion, TONE SIX

Thou wast born secretly in the cave, but heaven spoke through a star and proclaimed Thee to all, O Saviour. And it brought to Thee Magi, who worshipped Thee with faith: have mercy upon them and upon us.

℣. 1. His foundations are in the holy mountains: the Lord loveth the gates of Zion more than all the dwellings of Jacob (*Psalm* 86:1–2).

And it brought to Thee Magi, who worshipped Thee with faith: have mercy upon them and upon us.

℣. 2. Glorious things are spoken of thee, O city of God. I will make mention of Rahab and Babylon to them that know me (*ibid.*, 3–4).

And it brought to Thee Magi, who worshipped Thee with faith: have mercy upon them and upon us.

℣. 3. Behold Philistia and Tyre and the people of Ethiopia (*ibid.*, 4).

And it brought to Thee Magi, who worshipped Thee with faith: have mercy upon them and upon us.

℣. 4. This and that man were born there. Zion is our mother, a man shall say, and such a man was born in her; and the Most High Himself hath established her (*ibid.*, 4–5).

And it brought to Thee Magi, who worshipped Thee with faith: have mercy upon them and upon us.

℣. 5. The Lord shall recount, when He writeth up the people and the princes born in her. All rejoice to have their dwelling in thee (*ibid.*, 6–7).

And it brought to Thee Magi, who worshipped Thee with faith: have mercy upon them and upon us.

Glory be to the Father . . . Both now . . .

Thou wast born secretly in the cave, but heaven spoke through a star and proclaimed Thee to all, O Saviour. And it brought to Thee Magi, who worshipped Thee with faith: have mercy upon them and upon us.

Lessons:

READING FROM THE PROPHET ISAIAH (11:1–10).

Thus saith the Lord: There shall come forth a rod out of the stem of Jesse, and a Branch shall grow out of his roots: and the Spirit of the Lord shall rest upon Him, the spirit of wisdom and understanding, the spirit of counsel and might, the spirit of knowledge and of the fear of the Lord; and shall make Him of quick understanding in the fear of the Lord: and He shall not judge after the sight of His eyes, neither reprove after the hearing of His ears: but with righteousness shall He judge the poor, and reprove with equity for the meek of the earth: and He shall smite the earth with the rod of His mouth, and with the breath of His lips shall He slay the wicked. And righteousness shall be the girdle of His loins, and faithfulness the girdle of His reins. The wolf also shall dwell with the lamb, and the leopard shall lie down with the kid; and the calf and the young lion and the fatling together; and a little child shall lead them. And the cow and the bear shall feed; their young ones shall lie down together: and the lion shall eat straw like the ox. And the sucking child shall play on the hole of the asp, and the weaned child shall put his hand on the cockatrice' den. They shall not hurt nor destroy in all My holy mountain: for the earth shall be full of the knowledge of the Lord, as the waters cover the sea. And in that day there shall be a root of Jesse, which shall stand for an ensign of the people; to it shall the Gentiles seek: and His rest shall be glorious.

Reading from the Prophet Jeremiah (*Baruch* 3:35–4:4. *See p.* 232).

Reading from the Prophet Daniel (2:31–36, 44–45).

Daniel said to Nebuchadnezzar: Thou, O king, sawest, and behold a great image. This great image, whose brightness was excellent, stood before thee; and the form thereof was terrible. This image's head was of fine gold, his breast and his arms of silver, his belly and his thighs of brass, his legs of iron, his feet part of iron and part of clay. Thou sawest till that a stone was cut out without hands, which smote the image upon his feet that were of iron and clay, and brake them to pieces. Then was the iron, the clay, the brass, the silver, and the gold, broken to pieces together, and became like the chaff of the summer threshingfloors; and the wind carried them away, that no place was found for them: and the stone that smote the image became a great mountain, and filled the whole earth. This is the dream; and we will tell the interpretation thereof before the king. The God of Heaven shall set up a kingdom which shall never be destroyed: and the kingdom shall not be left to other people, but it shall break in pieces and consume all these kingdoms, and it shall stand for ever. Forasmuch as thou sawest that the stone was cut out of the mountain without hands, and that it brake in pieces the iron, the brass, the clay, the silver, and the gold; the great God hath made known to the king what shall come to pass hereafter: and the dream is certain, and the interpretation thereof sure.

Then is said, standing:

Troparion, TONE SIX

Thou hast shone forth from a Virgin, O Christ, Thou spiritual Sun of Righteousness.[1] And a star showed Thee, whom nothing can contain, contained within a cave. Thou hast led Magi to worship Thee, and joining them we magnify Thee: O Giver of life, glory to Thee.

℣. 1. The Lord is King, and hath put on glorious apparel: the Lord hath put on His apparel and girded Himself with strength (*Psalm* 92:1).

Thou hast led Magi to worship Thee, and joining them we magnify Thee: O Giver of life, glory to Thee.

℣. 2. He hath made the world so sure, that it cannot be moved. Thy throne is prepared of old: Thou art from everlasting (*ibid.*, 1–2).

Thou hast led Magi to worship Thee, and joining them we magnify Thee: O Giver of life, glory to Thee.

℣. 3. The floods have lifted up, O Lord, the floods have lifted up their voice: the floods lift up their waves at the voice of many waters (*ibid.*, 3–4).

Thou hast led Magi to worship Thee, and joining them we magnify Thee: O Giver of life, glory to Thee.

℣. 4. Wonderful are the mighty waves of the sea; wonderful is the Lord on high. Thy testimonies are very sure (*ibid.*, 4–5).

Thou hast led Magi to worship Thee, and joining them we magnify Thee: O Giver of life, glory to Thee.

[1] Malachi 4:2.

℣. 5. Holiness becometh Thine house, O Lord, for ever (*ibid.*, 5).

Thou hast led Magi to worship Thee, and joining them we magnify Thee: O Giver of life, glory to Thee.

Glory be to the Father . . . Both now . . .

Thou hast shone forth from a Virgin, O Christ, Thou spiritual Sun of Righteousness. And a star showed Thee, whom nothing can contain, contained within a cave. Thou hast led Magi to worship Thee, and joining them we magnify Thee: O Giver of life, glory to Thee.

Lessons:

Reading from the Prophet Isaiah (9:6–7. *See p. 246*).

Reading from the Prophet Isaiah (7:10–16; 8:1–4, 9–10. *See p. 239*).

Then follows the Small Litany, and after it the trisagion.

Then the Prokimenon before the Epistle:

TONE ONE

The Lord said unto Me: Thou art My Son, this day have I begotten Thee (*Psalm* 2:7).

℣. Ask of Me, and I shall give Thee the heathen for Thine inheritance (*ibid.*, 8).

Reading from the Epistle to the Hebrews (1:1–12. *See p. 226*).

Alleluia, TONE EIGHT[1]

℣ 1. The Lord said unto my Lord: Sit Thou at My right hand, until I make Thine enemies Thy footstool (*Psalm* 109:1).

℣. 2. The Lord shall send Thee a rod of strength out of Zion (*ibid.*, 2).

[1] In the Slav use, Tone Five.

℣. 3. From the womb before the morning star have I begotten Thee (*ibid.*, 3).

READING FROM THE HOLY GOSPEL ACCORDING TO LUKE (2:1–20. *See p. 233*).

And then the Liturgy of St. Basil the Great.

Immediately after the Liturgy, a candle is lit and set in a candlestick in the middle of the church, and we sing:

Troparion of the Feast, TONE FOUR

Thy Nativity, O Christ our God, has shone upon the world with the light of knowledge: for thereby they who adored the stars through a star were taught to worship Thee, the Sun of Righteousness,[1] and to know Thee the Dayspring from on high. O Lord, glory to Thee.

Glory be to the Father . . . Both now . . .

Kontakion of the Feast, TONE THREE

Today the Virgin gives birth to Him who is above all being, and the earth offers a cave to Him whom no man can approach. Angels with shepherds give glory, and Magi journey with a star. For unto us is born a young Child, the pre-eternal God.

The Vigil Service

Great Compline

We begin Great Compline as usual with the opening blessing, Holy God . . ., *etc., and the Lord's Prayer. Then* Kyrie eleison, *12 times*; Glory be to the Father . . . Both now . . .; O come, let us worship . . .; *and the reading from the Psalter:*

[1] Malachi 4:2.

Psalms 4, 6, 12.

Glory be to the Father, *etc.*

Psalms 24, 30, 90.

Glory be to the Father, *etc.*
God is with us . . .
Now that I have passed through the day . . .
The bodiless powers of the cherubim . . .
I believe in one God . . .
O all-holy Lady Theotokos . . .

Then Holy God . . ., *etc., and the Lord's Prayer, followed by the troparion of the feast,* Thy Nativity, O Christ our God . . . (*p. 261*); Kyrie eleison, *40 times*; Glory be to the Father . . . Both now . . .; Greater in honour than the cherubim . . .; In the Name of the Lord, give the blessing, Father.

The priest: At the prayers of our holy Fathers . . .

And the prayer, O Lord, Lord, who deliverest us from all the arrows . . .

Then O come, let us worship . . ., *and the second reading from the Psalter:*

Psalms 50, 101.

The Prayer of Manasses, King of Judah.

Then Holy God . . ., *etc., and the Lord's Prayer, followed by the kontakion of the feast,* Today the Virgin gives birth . . . (*p. 261*); Kyrie eleison, *40 times*; Glory be to the Father . . . Both now . . .; Greater in honour than the cherubim . . .; In the Name of the Lord, give the blessing, Father.

The priest: At the prayers of our holy Fathers . . .

And the prayer, O God the Master, Father Almighty . . .

Then O come, let us worship . . ., *and the third reading from the Psalter:*

Psalms 69, 142.
The Small Doxology.

Immediately after the Doxology there follows the Lity:

TONE ONE

(*by John the Monk*)

Let heaven and earth today make glad prophetically. Angels and men, let us keep spiritual feast. For God, born of a woman, has appeared in the flesh to those that sit in darkness and shadow. A cave and a manger have received Him. Shepherds announce the wonder; Magi from the east offer gifts in Bethlehem. Let us, then, from our unworthy lips offer praise like the angels: Glory to God in the highest, and on earth peace. For the Expectation of the nations[1] has come, He has come and saved us from the bondage of the enemy.

SAME TONE

(*by the same*)

Heaven and earth are united today, for Christ is born. Today has God come upon earth, and man gone up to heaven. Today for man's sake is seen in the flesh He who by nature is invisible. Therefore let us also give glory and cry aloud to Him: Glory to God in the highest, and on earth peace, which Thy coming has bestowed upon us, O Saviour: glory to Thee.

SAME TONE

(*by the same*)

'Glory to God in the highest', I hear today in Bethlehem from the angels, glory to Him whose good pleasure it was that there be peace on earth. The Virgin is now more spacious than the heavens. Light has shone upon those in darkness, and has exalted the lowly who sing like the angels: Glory to God in the highest.

SAME TONE

Beholding him that was in God's image and likeness fallen through the transgression, Jesus bowed the heavens and

[1] Genesis 49:10 (Septuagint).

came down,[1] and without changing He took up His dwelling in a Virgin womb: that thereby He might fashion corrupt Adam anew, who cried to Him: 'Glory to Thine Epiphany, O my Deliverer and my God.'

Glory be to the Father . . .

TONE FIVE

(*by John the Monk*)

The Magi, kings of Persia, knew with assurance that Thou, the heavenly King, wast born on earth. Led by the light of a star they came to Bethlehem, and offered their chosen gifts, gold and frankincense and myrrh. Falling before Thee they worshipped Thee: for they saw Thee who art timeless lying as a babe in the cave.

Both now . . .

TONE SIX

(*by Germanos*)

All the angels in heaven are of good cheer and greatly rejoice today. The whole creation leaps with joy, for the Saviour and Lord is born in Bethlehem. Every error of idolatry has ceased, and Christ reigns unto all ages.

Aposticha:

TONE TWO

(*by Germanos*)

A great and marvellous wonder has come to pass this day. A Virgin bears child, and her womb suffers no corruption. The Word is made flesh, yet ceases not to dwell with the Father. Angels and shepherds give glory, and with them we cry aloud: Glory to God in the highest, and on earth peace.

℣. The Lord said unto my Lord: Sit Thou at My right hand, until I make Thine enemies Thy footstool (*Psalm* 109:1).

[1] Psalm 17:10.

TONE THREE

(by the same)

Today the Virgin gives birth to the Maker of all. Eden offers a cave and a star discloses Christ, the Sun, to those in darkness. Magi, enlightened by faith, worship with gifts: shepherds behold the wonder and angels sing praises, saying: Glory to God in the highest.

℣. From the womb before the morning star have I begotten Thee (*ibid.*, 3).

SAME TONE

(by Anatolios)

When the Lord Jesus was born in Bethlehem of Judah, Magi coming from the east worshipped God made man. And eagerly opening their treasures, they offered to Him precious gifts: refined gold, as to the King of the ages, and frankincense, as to the God of all; and myrrh they offered to the Immortal, as to one three days dead. Come, all ye nations, and let us worship Him, who was born to save our souls.

Glory be to the Father . . .

TONE FOUR

(by John the Monk)

Make glad, O Jerusalem, and all ye who love Zion, keep feast. Today the ancient bond of the condemnation of Adam is loosed. Paradise is opened to us: the serpent is laid low. Of old he deceived the woman in Paradise, but now he sees a woman become Mother of the Creator. O the depth of the riches of the wisdom and knowledge of God![1] The sinful vessel that brought death upon all flesh has through the Theotokos become the first fruits of salvation for the whole world. For God the All-perfect is born a babe of her, and by His birth He sets the seal upon her virginity. Through His

[1] Romans 11:33.

swaddling clothes He looses the bands of sin, and through becoming child He heals Eve's pangs in travail. Therefore let all creation sing and dance for joy, for Christ has come to restore it and to save our souls.

Both now . . .

SAME TONE

(by Anatolios)

Thou hast come to dwell in a cave, O Christ our God, and the manger received Thee; shepherds and Magi worshipped Thee. Then was the preaching of the prophets fulfilled, and the angelic powers marvelled, crying aloud and saying: 'Glory to Thy condescension, O Thou who alone lovest mankind.'

Apolytikion (troparion) of the feast:

TONE FOUR

Thy Nativity, O Christ our God, has shone upon the world with the light of knowledge: for thereby they who adored the stars through a star were taught to worship Thee, the Sun of Righteousness, and to know Thee the Dayspring from on high. O Lord, glory to Thee.

And the Dismissal.

Mattins

After the first reading from the Psalter, sessional hymn:

TONE FOUR

Come, O ye faithful, and let us behold where Christ is born. Let us join the Magi, kings from the east, and follow the guiding star. Angels sing praises there without ceasing, and shepherds abiding in the fields offer a fitting hymn, saying:

'Glory in the highest to Him who in the cave this day is born of the Virgin and Theotokos, in Bethlehem of Judah.'

Glory be to the Father . . . Both now . . .

Repeat.

After the second reading from the Psalter, sessional hymn:

SAME TONE

Why art thou filled with wonder, O Mary? Why art thou amazed at that which is come to pass in thee? 'Because I have given birth in time to the timeless Son, yet understand not how I have conceived Him. I have not known man: how then shall I bear a child? Who has ever seen a birth without seed?' But, as it is written, 'Where God so wills, the order of nature is overcome.' Christ is born of the Virgin in Bethlehem of Judah.

Glory be to the Father . . . Both now . . .

Repeat.

After the polyeleos, the megalynarion:[1]

We magnify Thee, O Christ the Giver of life, who wast born in the flesh for us this day from her that knew not wedlock, the All-Pure Virgin Mary.

℣. Make a joyful noise unto the Lord, all the earth (*Psalm* 65:1).

We magnify Thee . . .

℣. Our God is in heaven and on earth: He hath done whatsoever He hath pleased (*Psalm* 113:11).

We magnify Thee . . .

Glory be to the Father . . . Both now . . .

Alleluia, alleluia, alleluia, glory be to Thee, O God (*3 times*).

We magnify Thee . . .

[1] In the Slav use only.

Sessional hymn:

TONE FOUR

How is He contained in a womb, whom nothing can contain? And how can He who is in the bosom of the Father be held in the arms of His Mother? This is according to His good pleasure, as He knoweth and wisheth. For being without flesh, of His own will has He been made flesh; and He who is, for our sakes has become that which He was not. Without departing from His own nature He has shared in our substance. Desiring to fill the world on high with citizens, Christ has undergone a twofold birth.

Glory be to the Father . . . Both now . . .

Repeat.

The first antiphon of the hymn of degrees in Tone Four.

Prokimenon: *TONE FOUR*

From the womb before the morning star have I begotten Thee: the Lord hath sworn and will not repent (*Psalm* 109:3–4).

℣. The Lord said unto my Lord: Sit Thou at My right hand until I make Thine enemies Thy footstool (*ibid.*, 1).

Let everything that hath breath . . .

READING FROM THE HOLY GOSPEL ACCORDING TO MATTHEW (1:18–25. *See p. 227*).

Psalm 50.

Glory be to the Father . . .

TONE TWO

All things are filled with joy today: Christ is born of the Virgin.

Both now . . .

All things are filled with joy . . .

Have mercy upon me . . .

TONE SIX

Glory to God in the highest, and on earth peace. Today Bethlehem receives Him that at all times ever sits with the Father. Today angels glorify with holy hymns the Babe that is born. Glory to God in the highest, and on earth peace, good will among men.

Two Canons are used: the first by St. Cosmas in eight troparia, including the irmos, and the second by St. John of Damascus in six, likewise including the irmos. The two irmoi are then repeated as katavasia at the end of each canticle. Before the troparia we say, Glory to Thee, our God, glory to Thee.

Canticle One

First Canon

TONE ONE

(**Irmos**) Christ is born, give ye glory. Christ comes from heaven, meet ye Him. Christ is on earth, be ye exalted. O all the earth, sing unto the Lord, and sing praises in gladness, O ye people, for He has been glorified.

Man fell from the divine and better life: though made in the image of God, through transgression he became wholly subject to corruption and decay. But now the wise Creator fashions him anew: for He has been glorified.

The Creator, when He saw man perishing, whom He had made with His own hands, bowed the heavens and came down;[1] and from the divine and pure Virgin did He take all man's substance, being made truly flesh: for He has been glorified.

Wisdom and Word and Power, Christ our God is the Son and the Brightness of the Father; and unknown to the powers both above and upon the earth, He was made man, and so has won us back again: for He has been glorified.[2]

[1] Psalm 17:10.

[2] 1 Corinthians 1:24; Hebrews 1:3; Colossians 1:26.

Second Canon

(*written originally in iambic verse*)

SAME TONE

(**Irmos**) Of old the Master that works wonders saved His people,
Making the watery wave of the sea into dry land;
And now of His own will has He been born from a Maiden,
And so He establishes a path for us whereby we may mount to heaven.
We glorify Him who in essence is equal to the Father and to mortal men.

Plainly foreshadowed by the burning bush that was not consumed,[1]
A hallowed womb has borne the Word.
God is mingled with the form of mortal men,
And so He looses the unhappy womb of Eve from the bitter curse of old.[2]
We men give Him glory.

A star shewed plainly to the Magi
The Word that was before the sun, who has come to make transgression cease.
They saw Thee wrapped in swaddling clothes, within a poor and lowly cave,
Who sharest all our sufferings,
And in joy they gazed upon Thee, who art at once both man and Lord.

Canticle Three

First Canon

(**Irmos**) To the Son who was begotten of the Father without change before all ages, and in the last times was

[1] Exodus 3 : 2.
[2] Genesis 3 : 16.

without seed made flesh of the Virgin, to Christ our God let us cry aloud: Thou hast raised up our horn, holy art Thou, O Lord.

Adam, though formed from dust, shared in the higher breath of life;[1] yet through the beguilement of a woman he slipped and fell into corruption. But now, beholding Christ born of a woman, he cries aloud, 'O Thou who for my sake hast become as I am, holy art Thou, O Lord.'

O Christ, who hast made Thyself in the form of a creature of vile clay, by Thy sharing in that which is worse, even our flesh, Thou hast made us partakers in the divine nature; for Thou hast become mortal man, yet still remainest God. Thou hast raised up our horn, holy art Thou, O Lord.[2]

Be glad, O Bethlehem, for thou art Queen among the princes of Judah;[3] for from thee comes forth, before the sight of all, the Shepherd who tends Israel, He that is seated upon the cherubim,[4] even Christ. He has raised up our horn and reigns over all.

Second Canon

(**Irmos**) Graciously accept, O Benefactor, the praises of Thy servants,
And bring down the despiteful and haughty looks of the enemy.
O blessed Lord who seest all, raise us up far above sin,
And establish Thy singers firm and unshaken
Upon the foundation of the faith.

The choir of shepherds abiding in the fields was overwhelmed
By the strange sight they were counted worthy to behold:

[1] Genesis 2:7.
[2] Job 33:6; Philippians 2:6–9; 2 Peter 1:4.
[3] Micah 5:2; Matthew 2:6.
[4] Psalm 79:1.

For they looked upon the all-blessed Offspring of an all-pure Bride;
And they saw also the ranks of bodiless angels, who sang
In praise of Christ the King, incarnate without seed.

He who rules the heights of heaven, in His compassion,
Has become such as we are, born of a Maiden who has not known man.
The Word who before was wholly outside matter, in these last times
Has assumed the material substance of the flesh
That so He might draw unto Himself fallen Adam, the first-formed man.

Ypakoë

TONE EIGHT

Calling the Magi by a star, heaven brought the first fruits of the Gentiles unto Thee, a Babe lying in the manger: and they were amazed to see neither sceptre nor throne but only utter poverty. For what is meaner than a cave, what is humbler than swaddling clothes? Yet therein shone forth the wealth of Thy divinity: glory to Thee, O Lord.

Or else the sessional hymn:

TONE EIGHT

Greatly rejoice, O heaven; be glad, O earth. For the Lamb of God has been born on earth, granting the world forgiveness.[1] The Word who is in the bosom of the Father has come forth without seed from the Virgin. The Magi were

[1] John 1:29.

struck with wonder, seeing Him born in Bethlehem as a child; and all things give Him glory.

Glory be to the Father . . . Both now . . .

Repeat.

Canticle Four

First Canon

(**Irmos**) Rod of the root of Jesse, and flower that blossomed from his stem, O Christ, Thou hast sprung from the Virgin. From the Mountain overshadowed by the forest Thou hast come, made flesh from her that knew not wedlock, O God who art not formed from matter. Glory to Thy power, O Lord.[1]

O Christ, whom Jacob foretold in days of old, calling Thee the Expectation of the nations, Thou hast shone forth from the tribe of Judah, and Thou hast come to plunder the strength of Damascus and the spoils of Samaria, turning their error into faith beautiful to God. Glory to Thy power, O Lord.[2]

O Master who hast risen as a Star out of Jacob, Thou hast filled with joy the watchers of the stars, who interpreted wisely the words of Balaam, the soothsayer of old. As the first fruits of the Gentiles were they led unto Thee, and Thou hast openly received them, as they brought Thee acceptable gifts. Glory to Thy power, O Lord.[3]

As dew upon the fleece hast Thou descended into the womb of the Virgin, O Christ, and as drops of rain that fall upon the earth. Ethiopia and Tarshish and the isles of Arabia, the kings of Saba, of the Medes and all the earth, fell down before Thee, O Saviour. Glory to Thy power, O Lord.[4]

[1] Isaiah 11:1; Habakkuk 3:3.
[2] Genesis 49:10 (Septuagint); Isaiah 8:4.
[3] Numbers 24:17; Matthew 2:10–11.
[4] Judges 6:37–38; Psalm 71:6, 9–11.

Second Canon

(Irmos) Of old Habakkuk the Prophet was counted worthy
To behold ineffably the figure and symbol of Christ's birth,
And he foretold in song the renewal of mankind.
For a young babe, even the Word, has now come forth from the Mountain that is the Virgin,[1]
Unto the renewal of the peoples.

Of Thine own will, O Most High, Thou hast come forth equal to mortal men,
Taking flesh from the Virgin,
To purge the poison of the serpent's head.[2]
God by nature, Thou leadest all
From the gates that know no sun to the life-giving light.

O ye people that before were sunk in corruption,
But now have escaped wholly from the perdition of the adversary,
Lift up your hands and clap them in songs of praise,
Honouring Christ alone, our Benefactor,
Who in His compassion is come into our midst.

O Virgin, sprung from the root of Jesse,[3]
Thou hast passed beyond the boundaries of human nature,
For Thou hast borne the pre-eternal Word of the Father.
According to His good pleasure, by a strange self-emptying,
He passed through thy womb, yet kept it sealed.

[1] Daniel 2:45.
[2] Genesis 3:15.
[3] Isaiah 11:1.

Canticle Five

First Canon

(Irmos) As Thou art God of peace and Father of mercies, Thou hast sent unto us Thine Angel of great counsel,[1] granting us peace. So are we guided towards the light of the knowledge of God, and watching by night we glorify Thee, O Lover of mankind.

Obedient to the decree of Caesar, Thou wast enrolled among his servants, O Christ, and Thou hast set us free who were servants of the enemy and of sin. Sharing wholly in our poverty, Thou hast made our clay godlike through Thy union and participation in it.[2]

Lo, the Virgin, as it was said in days of old,[3] has conceived in her womb and brought forth God made man; and she has remained still a Virgin. Reconciled to God through her, let us sinners sing her praises, for she is verily the Theotokos.

Second Canon

(Irmos) From the night of deeds of dark error we watch vigilantly,
And sing to Thee, O Christ, as to our Benefactor.
Come to us and grant us cleansing:
Make the path easy for us,
Whereby we may ascend and so attain to glory.

The Master, by His coming in the flesh, has cut clean through
The harsh enmity of the flesh against Him,[4]
And has destroyed the might of the murderer of our souls.

[1] Isaiah 9:6 (Septuagint).
[2] Luke 2:1–5; 2 Corinthians 8:9.
[3] Isaiah 7:14.
[4] Ephesians 2:14–16.

Uniting the world to the immaterial essences,
He has made the Father merciful to the creation.

The people that before walked in darkness
This day have seen a light from the beacon on high.
The Son offers to God the nations as His inheritance,
Bestowing grace past telling
Where sin once flourished more abundantly.[1]

Canticle Six

First Canon

(**Irmos**) The sea monster spat forth Jonah as it had received him, like a babe from the womb: while the Word, having dwelt in the Virgin and taken flesh, came forth from her yet kept her uncorrupt. For being Himself not subject to decay, He preserved His Mother free from harm.

Christ our God, whom the Father begat from the womb before the morning star, has come, made flesh; and He who holds the reins of the undefiled powers, is laid in a manger of dumb beasts. He who looses the tangled cords of sin, is wrapped in swaddling rags.[2]

From the substance of Adam a young child, a Son, is born and given unto the faithful. He is the Father and Prince of the Age to Come, and He is called the Angel of great counsel. He is the mighty God and holds in His dominion the creation.[3]

Second Canon

(**Irmos**) Enclosed in the uttermost depths of the sea,
Jonah entreated Thee to come and still the storm.

[1] Isaiah 9:2; Psalm 2:8; Romans 5:20.
[2] Psalm 109:3; Proverbs 5:22.
[3] Isaiah 9:6 (Septuagint).

And I, O Christ, pricked by the dart of the tyrant,
Call upon Thee, the Slayer of evil,
Beseeching Thee to come quickly and deliver me from my slothfulness.

God the Word, who was in the beginning with God,[1]
Seeing our nature powerless to guard unharmed
Its ancient fellowship with Him, now grants it new strength:
Abasing Himself, in a second act of fellowship
He makes it once again free from the passions.

For our sakes He has come forth from the loins of Abraham,
To raise up as His sons those who were sadly fallen
Into the darkness of sin that bowed them down to the earth;
And He that dwells in light has now been pleased, despite His high dignity,
To dwell in a manger for the salvation of mankind.[2]

Kontakion

TONE THREE

(*by Romanos the Melodist*)

Today the Virgin gives birth to Him who is above all being, and the earth offers a cave to Him whom no man can approach. Angels with shepherds give glory, and Magi journey with a star. For unto us is born a young Child, the pre-eternal God.

[1] John 1:1.
[2] Matthew 1:1; 1 Timothy 6:16.

Ikos

Bethlehem has opened Eden: come, and let us see. We have found joy in secret: come, and let us take possession of the paradise that is within the cave. There the unwatered Root has appeared, from which forgiveness flowers forth: there is found the undug Well, whence David longed to drink of old.[1] There the Virgin has borne a Babe, and made the thirst of Adam and David to cease straightway. Therefore let us hasten to this place where now is born a young Child, the pre-eternal God.

Canticle Seven

First Canon

(**Irmos**) Scorning the impious decree, the Children brought up together in godliness feared not the threat of fire, but, standing in the midst of the flames, they sang: 'O God of our fathers, blessed art Thou.'

The shepherds abiding in the fields received a vision of light that filled them with terror. For the glory of the Lord shone around them and an angel cried aloud: 'Sing praises, for Christ is born. O God of our fathers, blessed art Thou.'[2]

At the word of the angel, the hosts of heaven suddenly cried aloud: 'Glory to God in the highest, and on earth peace, good will among men; Christ has shone forth. O God of our fathers, blessed art Thou.'[3]

'What are these tidings?' said the shepherds. 'Let us go and see this thing which is come to pass, even Christ our God.' And coming to Bethlehem, they worshipped with her who had given Him birth, as they cried aloud: 'O God of our fathers, blessed art Thou.'[4]

[1] 2 Kings (2 Samuel) 23:15.
[2] Luke 2:8–10.
[3] Luke 2:13–14.
[4] Luke 2:15–16.

Second Canon

(Irmos) Caught and held fast by love for the King of all,
The Children despised the impious threats of the tyrant
In his boundless fury;
And as the terrible fire withdrew before them,
They said to the Master, 'Unto all ages blessed art Thou.'

The seething and roaring furnace, heated sevenfold,
In its fury burnt up the servants of the king,
But spared the Children:
For as the flame encircled them, the Lord,
Rewarding their godliness, shed upon them abundant dew.[1]

O Christ our Defender, Thou hast put to shame the adversary of man,
Using as shield Thine ineffable Incarnation.
Taking man's form, Thou hast now bestowed upon him the joy
Of becoming godlike: for it was in hope of this
That of old we fell from on high into the dark depths of the earth.[2]

Thou hast overthrown by Thine almighty power
The fierce sin that raised its head in wanton pride,
And raged with blasphemy throughout a world gone mad.
Those whom in times past it dragged down, today Thou hast delivered from its snares,
O Benefactor, who of Thine own will hast taken flesh.

[1] Daniel 3:19–27.
[2] Genesis 3:5.

Canticle Eight

First Canon

(**Irmos**) The furnace moist with dew was the image and figure of a wonder past nature. For it burnt not the Children whom it had received, even as the fire of the Godhead consumed not the Virgin's womb into which it had descended. Therefore in praise let us sing: Let the whole creation bless the Lord and exalt Him above all for ever.

The daughter of Babylon once led captive from Zion the children of David, whom she had taken with the sword: but now she sends her own children, the Magi bearing gifts, to entreat the Daughter of David in whom God came to dwell.[1] Therefore in praise let us sing: Let the whole creation bless the Lord and exalt Him above all for ever.

Sorrow silenced the harps of the children of Zion, for they sang not among strangers;[2] while Christ, shining forth in Bethlehem, destroys all the error of Babylon and all the music of her instruments. Therefore in praise let us sing: Let the whole creation bless the Lord and exalt Him above all for ever.

Babylon despoiled Zion the Queen and took her wealth captive. But Christ by a guiding star drew to Zion the treasures of Babylon, with her kings who gazed upon the stars. Therefore in praise let us sing: Let the whole creation bless the Lord and exalt Him above all for ever.

Second Canon

(**Irmos**) The Children of the Old Covenant who walked in the fire, yet were not burnt,
Prefigured the womb of the Maiden that remained sealed,

[1] Psalm 136:8; 44:13.
[2] Psalm 136:2–4.

When she gave birth in fashion past nature.
It was the same grace of God that brought both these wonders to pass in a miracle
And rouses the peoples to sing in praise.

Shunning the guilt of its vain attempt to become as God,[1]
The whole creation sings, like the three Children, in praise of the eternal Word, who now empties Himself:
Yet sings with trembling, afraid to bring
A prayer unacceptable to God, for it is subject to decay,
Even though the divine wisdom maintains it ever in being.

Thou hast come, O Resurrection of the nations,
To bring back the nature of man from its wanderings,
Leading it from the hills of the wilderness to a pasture rich in flowers.[2]
Do Thou destroy the violent strength of the murderer of man,
O Thou who in Thy providence hast appeared as man and God.

Canticle Nine

The Magnificat and Greater in honour than the cherubim *are not sung, but are replaced by the following megalynaria:*

First Canon

Magnify, O my soul, her who is greater in honour and more glorious than the hosts on high.

[1] Genesis 3:5.
[2] Exodus 23:4; Luke 15:4.

(**Irmos**) A strange and most wonderful mystery do I see: the cave is heaven; the Virgin the throne of the cherubim; the manger a room, in which Christ, the God whom nothing can contain, is laid. Him do we praise and magnify.

Repeat the megalynarion and the irmos.

Magnify, O my soul, God born in the flesh from the Virgin.

The Magi, beholding the strange course of an unknown and newly shining star that exceeded the brightness of all heavenly light, learnt thereby that Christ the King was born on earth in Bethlehem for our salvation.

Magnify, O my soul, the King born in the cave.

The Magi, beholding the strange course . . .

Magnify, O my soul, God worshipped by the Magi.

'Where is the new-born Child and King, whose star we have seen?' the Magi said. 'For we are come to worship Him.' Herod, the enemy of God, was troubled, and in his wild madness he plotted how to kill Christ.[1]

Magnify, O my soul, Him who was revealed to the Magi by a star.

'Where is the new-born Child . . .'

Magnify, O my soul, the pure Virgin who has given birth to Christ the King.

Herod inquired what time the guiding star appeared, which brought the Magi to Bethlehem, there to worship Christ with gifts. Led back to their own land by that same star, they returned not to Herod, but mocked the wicked slayer of children.[2]

[1] Matthew 2:2–3.
[2] Matthew 2:7–12.

Magi and shepherds came to worship Christ, born in the city of Bethlehem.

Herod inquired what time the guiding star . . .

Second Canon

Today the Virgin bears the Master within the cave.

(**Irmos**) It would be easier for us, because free from all danger,
To keep silence in fear:
While it is hard indeed, O Virgin, in love to devise songs
Harmoniously put together. But do thou, O Mother,
Give us strength that so we may fulfil our good intent.

Today the Master is born as a babe of a Virgin Mother.

It would be easier for us . . .

Today shepherds behold the Saviour wrapped in swaddling clothes and laid in a manger.

Today the Master who cannot be touched is wrapped as a babe in swaddling rags.

We have seen, O pure Mother, the dim figures of the Word
And the shades that are past;
And now that He has newly appeared from the closed gate,[1]
We who are counted worthy to behold the Light of truth,
As is meet and right, bless Thy womb.

Today all creation rejoices greatly and makes glad, for Christ is born of a Virgin Maid.

[1] Ezekiel 44:2.

The Powers of heaven declare unto the world that the Saviour, Lord, and Master has been born.

We have seen, O pure Mother . . .

Magnify, O my soul, the power of the undivided Godhead in three Persons.

The people that delights in Christ has attained its desire,
Being counted worthy of the coming of God,
And now they humbly pray for the regeneration that gives life.
O undefiled Virgin, grant them the grace.
To worship Christ in His glory.[1]

Magnify, O my soul, her that has delivered us from the curse.

The people that delights in Christ . . .

Katavasia

The first megalynarion and the irmos of the first Canon; and likewise the first megalynarion and the irmos of the second Canon.

Exapostilarion

Our Saviour, the Dayspring from the east, has visited us from on high, and we who were in darkness and shadow have found the truth:[2] for the Lord is born of the Virgin (*3 times*).

Lauds. Four stichera are sung:

TONE FOUR

(*by Andrew of Jerusalem*)

Make glad, O ye righteous; greatly rejoice, O ye heavens; ye mountains, dance for joy. Christ is born; and like the cherubim the Virgin makes a throne,[3] carrying at her bosom

[1] This, the last verse of the Christmas Canon, looks forward to the feast of the Epiphany, which is to follow in twelve days.

[2] Luke 1:78.

[3] Psalm 98:1.

God the Word made flesh. Shepherds glorify the new-born Child, Magi offer the Master gifts. Angels sing praises, saying: 'O Lord past understanding, glory to Thee.'

It was the good pleasure of the Father: the Word became flesh, and the Virgin bore God made man. A star spreads abroad the tidings: the Magi worship, the shepherds stand amazed, and the creation is filled with mighty joy.

O Theotokos Virgin who hast borne the Saviour, thou hast overthrown the ancient curse of Eve. For thou hast become the Mother of Him in whom the Father was well pleased, and hast carried at thy bosom God the incarnate Word. We cannot fathom this mystery: but by faith alone we all glorify it, crying with thee and saying: O Lord past all interpretation, glory to Thee.

O come, let us sing the praises of the Mother of the Saviour, who after bearing child still remained Virgin. Rejoice, thou Living City of God the King, in which Christ has dwelt, bringing to pass our salvation. With Gabriel we sing thy praises; with the shepherds we glorify thee, crying: O Theotokos, intercede for our salvation with Him who took flesh from thee.

Glory be to the Father . . .

TONE SIX

(by Germanos)

When it was time for Thy coming upon earth, the first taxation of the world was held;[1] and then Thou madest ready to enrol the names of all who believed in Thy birth. For this cause Caesar published such a decree, since Thy timeless and eternal Kingdom was newly made manifest. Therefore as we pay our earthly tribute money, at the same time we offer Thee the wealth of our Orthodox faith, O God and Saviour of our souls.

Both now . . .

[1] Luke 2:1.

TONE TWO

(by John the Monk)

Today Christ is born of the Virgin in Bethlehem. Today He who knows no beginning now begins to be, and the Word is made flesh. The powers of heaven greatly rejoice, and the earth with mankind makes glad. The Magi offer gifts, the shepherds proclaim the marvel, and we cry aloud without ceasing: Glory to God in the highest, and on earth peace, good will among men.

Great Doxology and Dismissal.

Liturgy

Antiphon One

TONE TWO

℣ 1. I will praise Thee, O Lord, with my whole heart: I will speak of all Thy marvellous works (*Psalm* 9:1).

At the prayers of the Theotokos, save us, O Saviour.

℣ 2. In the assembly of the upright and in the congregation: the works of the Lord are great (*Psalm* 110:1–2).

At the prayers of the Theotokos . . .

℣ 3. They are sought out according to all His purposes (*ibid.*, 2).

At the prayers of the Theotokos . . .

℣ 4. His work is honourable and glorious: and His righteousness endureth for ever (*ibid.*, 3).

At the prayers of the Theotokos . . .

Glory be to the Father . . . Both now . . .

At the prayers of the Theotokos . . .

Antiphon Two

SAME TONE

℣ 1. Blessed is the man that feareth the Lord: that delighteth greatly in His commandments (*Psalm* 111:1).

O Son of God, born of the Virgin, save us who sing to Thee: alleluia.

℣ 2. His seed shall be mighty upon earth: the generation of the upright shall be blessed (*ibid.*, 2).

O Son of God . . .

℣ 3. Glory and riches shall be in his house: and his righteousness endureth for ever (*ibid.*, 3).

O Son of God . . .

℣ 4. Unto the upright there ariseth light in the darkness: he is gracious, full of compassion, and righteous (*ibid.*, 4).

O Son of God . . .

Glory be to the Father . . . Both now . . .
O Only-begotten Son and Word of God . . .

Antiphon Three

TONE FOUR

℣ 1. The Lord said unto my Lord: Sit Thou at My right hand, until I make Thine enemies Thy footstool (*Psalm* 109:1).

The troparion of the feast, Thy Nativity, O Christ our God (*p. 266*).

℣ 2. The Lord shall send Thee a rod of strength out of Zion (*ibid.*, 2).

The troparion of the feast.

℣ 3. With Thee is dominion in the day of Thy power: in the beauties of Thy saints (*ibid.*, 3).

The troparion of the feast.

Introit:

From the womb before the morning star have I begotten Thee. The Lord hath sworn and will not repent: Thou art a priest for ever after the order of Melchizedek (*Psalm* 109:3–4).

O Son of God, born of the Virgin, save us who sing to Thee: alleluia.[1]

Then the troparion of the feast (*p. 266*); Glory be to the Father . . . Both now . . .; *the kontakion of the feast* (*p. 277*).

Instead of the trisagion we sing:

As many of you as were baptized into Christ, have put on Christ. Alleluia.

Prokimenon: TONE EIGHT

Let all the earth worship Thee and sing unto Thee: let them sing unto Thy Name (*Psalm* 65:4).

℣. Make a joyful noise unto the Lord, all the earth: sing forth the honour of His Name; make His praise glorious (*ibid.*, 1–2).

READING FROM THE EPISTLE OF PAUL TO THE GALATIANS (4:4–7).

Brethren, when the fulness of the time was come, God sent forth His Son, made of a woman, made under the law, to redeem them that were under the law, that we might receive the adoption of sons. And because ye are sons, God hath sent forth the Spirit of His Son into your hearts, crying, Abba, Father. Wherefore thou art no more a servant, but a son: and if a son, then an heir of God through Christ.

Alleluia, TONE ONE

℣ 1. The heavens declare the glory of God: and the firmament sheweth His handiwork (*Psalm* 18:2).

℣ 2. Day unto day uttereth speech, and night unto night sheweth knowledge (*ibid.*, 3).

READING FROM THE HOLY GOSPEL ACCORDING TO MATTHEW (2:1–12. *See p. 240*).

[1] In the Slav use, *O Son of God* . . . is sung only at pontifical services.

In place of It is meet, *we sing the megalynarion and irmos from Canticle Nine of the first Canon (pp. 281–2).*

Communion verse:

The Lord hath sent deliverance unto His people (*Psalm* 110:9).

From Christmas Day until 4 January inclusive there is a general dispensation from all fasting.

26 DECEMBER

THE SYNAXIS OF THE MOST HOLY THEOTOKOS

Great Vespers

On Lord, I have cried, *six stichera are sung from Vespers on Christmas Day (pp. 253–4):*

TONE TWO

Come, let us greatly rejoice in the Lord . . . (*twice*)
When the Lord Jesus was born . . . (*twice*)
Thy Kingdom, O Christ our God . . .
What shall we offer Thee . . .
Glory be to the Father . . . Both now . . .

TONE SIX

Glory to God in the highest, and on earth peace . . ., *the sticheron sung at Christmas Mattins after the Gospel (p. 269).*

Entrance, O joyful light.

Great Prokimenon:[1]

TONE SEVEN

Who is so great a God as our God? Thou only art the God that doest wonders (*Psalm* 76:14–15).

℣ 1. Thou hast made known Thy power among the nations (*ibid.*, 15).

Who is so great a God . . .

[1] On Saturday evening, the usual prokimenon of the day is sung, *The Lord is King . . .*

℣ 2. And I said, Now have I begun to understand: this is the change wrought by the right hand of the Most High (*ibid.*, 11).

Who is so great a God . . .

℣ 3. I remembered the works of the Lord: for I will remember Thy wonders from the beginning (*ibid.*, 12).

Who is so great a God . . .

Aposticha:

TONE EIGHT

(*by John the Monk*)

A marvellous wonder has this day come to pass: nature is made new, and God becomes man. That which He was, He has remained; and that which He was not, He has taken on Himself while suffering neither confusion nor division.

℣. The Lord said unto my Lord: Sit Thou at My right hand (*Psalm* 109:1).

O Lord, Thou art come to Bethlehem and hast made Thy dwelling in the cave. Thou who hast heaven as Thy throne art laid in a manger. Thou whom the hosts of angels attend on every side hast come down among shepherds, that in Thy compassion Thou mightest save our kind. Glory to Thee!

℣. From the womb before the morning star have I begotten Thee (*ibid.*, 3).

How shall I tell of this great mystery? He who is without flesh becomes incarnate; the Word puts on a body; the Invisible is seen; He whom no hand can touch is handled; and He who knows no beginning now begins to be. The Son of God becomes the Son of man: Jesus Christ, the same yesterday and today and for ever.[1]

Glory be to the Father . . . Both now . . .

[1] Hebrews 13:8.

SAME TONE

The shepherds hasten to Bethlehem, revealing the true Shepherd, seated upon the cherubim and lying in a manger. For our sakes He has taken upon Himself the form of a child. O Lord, glory to Thee!

Apolytikion (troparion) of the feast, Thy Nativity, O Christ our God . . . *(p. 266)*.

And the Dismissal.

Mattins

Everything as on Christmas Day, except the following:

After Canticle Three of the Canon, the kontakion of the feast, Today the Virgin gives birth . . . *(p. 277)*.

After Canticle Six, the following kontakion:

TONE SIX

(by Romanos the Melodist)

He who before the morning star was begotten without mother of the Father, is today without father made flesh upon earth of thee. A star announces the good tidings to the Magi, while angels with shepherds sing the praises of thine undefiled child-bearing, O thou who art full of grace.

Ikos

The mystical Vine put forth the bunch of grapes that was never husbanded, and with her arms as branches she carried Him, saying: 'Thou art my fruit, Thou art my life: from Thee have I learnt that I remain what I was. Thou art my God: for seeing the seal of my virginity unbroken, I proclaim Thee to be the unchangeable Word, now made incarnate. I have known no seed, and I know that Thou art the destroyer of corruption: for I am pure, yet Thou hast gone forth from me. As Thou hast found my womb, so Thou hast left it. Therefore all creation shares in my joy and cries to me: Hail, thou who art full of grace.'

At Canticle Nine of the Canon we do not sing the Magnificat but the megalynaria and troparia as on Christmas Day.

At Lauds, the stichera as on Christmas Day (p. 284), followed by the doxastikon:

Glory be to the Father . . .

TONE SIX

Today the invisible Nature is joined to mortal men, coming forth from the Virgin. Today the infinite Essence is wrapped in swaddling clothes at Bethlehem. Today God leads the Magi by a star to worship Him, and with gold and frankincense and myrrh they foretell His three-day burial. Therefore we sing: O Christ our God, made flesh of the Virgin, save our souls.

Both now . . .

TONE TWO

Today Christ is born of the Virgin in Bethlehem . . ., *as on the day of the feast (p. 286).*

Great Doxology and Dismissal.

Liturgy

In the Greek practice we sing, as on Christmas Day, the antiphons, introit, troparion, and kontakion of the feast: and in place of the trisagion we sing, As many of you as were baptized into Christ *(pp. 286–8).*

In the Slav practice, we sing the Typika (Psalms 102 and 145) and the Beatitudes, with four troparia from Canticle Three of the first Canon of the feast (p. 271), and four troparia from Canticle Six of the second Canon (p. 277).

At the entry, we sing in the Slav practice:

O Son of God, born of the Virgin, save us who sing to Thee: alleluia.

Then the troparion of the feast, Thy Nativity, O Christ our God . . . *(p. 266), and the kontakion*, He who before the morning star . . . *(p. 292)*.

Prokimenon in both the Greek and the Slav use:

TONE THREE

My soul doth magnify the Lord, and my spirit hath rejoiced in God my Saviour (*Luke* 1:46–47).

℣. For He hath regarded the low estate of His handmaiden: for, behold, from henceforth all generations shall call me blessed (*ibid.*, 48).

READING FROM THE EPISTLE TO THE HEBREWS (2:11–18. *See p. 246*).

Alleluia, TONE EIGHT

℣ 1. Arise, O Lord, into Thy rest: Thou and the Ark of Thy holiness (*Psalm* 131:8).

℣ 2. The Lord hath sworn in truth unto David; and He will not turn from it (*ibid.*, 11).

READING FROM THE HOLY GOSPEL ACCORDING TO MATTHEW (2:13–23. *See p. 247*).

In place of It is meet, *we sing the megalynarion and irmos from Canticle Nine of the second Canon (p. 283)*.

Communion verse:

The Lord hath sent deliverance unto His people (*Psalm* 110:9).

The apodosis of the feast of Christmas falls on 31 December. On that day all the office of the feast for Vespers, Mattins and the Liturgy is repeated, omitting only the entrance, lessons, lity, and blessing of bread at Vespers; and the polyeleos and Gospel at Mattins.

5 JANUARY

THE FOREFEAST OF THE THEOPHANY

Vespers

On Lord, I have cried, *six stichera are sung: three of the martyrs, St. Theopemptos and St. Theonas, and three of St. Synkletika.*[1]

Glory be to the Father . . . Both now . . .

TONE SIX

Make ready, O river Jordan: for behold, Christ our God draws near to be baptized by John, that He may crush with His divinity the invisible heads of the dragons in thy waters.[2] Rejoice, O wilderness of Jordan; dance with gladness, O ye mountains. For the eternal Life has come to call back Adam. O voice that criest in the wilderness, O John the Forerunner, cry out: 'Prepare ye the ways of the Lord, make His paths straight.'[3]

Aposticha:

TONE SIX

O earth and things upon the earth, dance ye and rejoice exceedingly. The River of joy[4] is baptized in the stream: He dries up the fount of evil and pours forth divine remission.

[1] The texts for these three saints, whose feast is observed on this day, have not been included in the present translation.

[2] Psalm 73:13.

[3] Mark 1:3.

[4] Psalm 35:9 (Septuagint).

℣. Therefore will I remember Thee from the land of Jordan and of the Hermonites (*Psalm* 41:7).

Being Himself the Bestower of light, Jesus needs not to be baptized, but in the flesh He descends into the streams of Jordan, wishing to give light to those in darkness. Let us go eagerly in faith to meet Him.

℣. The waters saw Thee, O God, the waters saw Thee and were afraid (*Psalm* 76:17).

Wearing the form of a servant, O Christ, Thou comest forth to be baptized by a servant in the streams of Jordan, granting deliverance from the servitude of the ancient sin, and sanctifying and enlightening us.

Glory be to the Father . . . Both now . . .

SAME TONE

Let the desert of Jordan rejoice exceedingly and blossom as the lily. For the voice of one who cries has been heard within it: 'Prepare ye the way of the Lord.' For He who weighed the mountains in scales and the wooded valleys in a balance, who fills all things as God, is baptized by a servant. He who bestows rich gifts has now become poor. Eve was once told, 'In sorrow shalt thou bring forth children', but now the Virgin hears: 'Hail, thou who art full of grace, the Lord who has great mercy is with thee.'[1]

Apolytikion (troparion) of the Forefeast:

TONE FOUR

The river Jordan once turned back before the mantle of Elisha, after Elijah had been taken up into heaven, and the waters were divided on this side and on that:[2] the stream became a dry path before him, forming a true figure of the baptism whereby we pass over the changeful course of

[1] Isaiah 35:1, 40:3 and 12; 2 Corinthians 8:9; Genesis 3:16; Luke 1:28.

[2] 4 (2) Kings 2:14.

life. Christ has appeared in the Jordan to sanctify the waters (*3 times*).

And the Dismissal.

Compline

We sing the Canon of the Forefeast:

TONE SIX

Canticle One

(**Irmos**) He who in ancient times hid the pursuing tyrant beneath the waves of the sea, now is cloaked and hidden in the stream of Jordan, and as man He is cleansed that I may be made clean: for He has been greatly glorified.

O Lord my God, I will sing on the Forefeast a hymn of light to Thee, who by Thy divine Theophany dost regenerate me mystically, and leadest me up again to godlike brightness.

The things above the earth and on the earth were amazed, O Saviour, as they beheld Thee, who wast manifest above before the ages, now made newly manifest below: and they sing the praises of Thy condescension past telling.

That Thou mightest fill all things with Thy glory, Thou hast emptied Thine own self, even unto the form of a servant.[1] And now as a servant Thou dost bow down Thy head beneath the hand of the servant, granting me restoration and cleansing.

Canticle Three

(**Irmos**) When the creation beheld Thee in the flesh covered by the streams, who hast established the whole earth in the void above the waters, it was seized with great amazement and cried: 'There is none holy save Thee, O Lord.'

[1] Philippians 2:7–8.

Figures of Thy Theophany hast Thou shown in times past to the prophets; but now hast Thou revealed in visible activity and operation the mysteries that were hidden, making Thyself manifest to men today and dispensing a new regeneration.

Jordan in trembling has spread out its waters to receive the Creator, who is baptized in the body and sanctifies all who cry aloud: There is none holy save Thee, O Lord.

Christ grants by baptism succour unto salvation to those who behold His divine brightness as they sing in joy: There is none holy save Thee, O Lord who lovest man.

Canticle Four

(**Irmos**) Foreseeing Thy coming to baptism, Habakkuk cried out marvelling: 'Thou hast ridden through the sea upon Thy horses, O Saviour, troubling many waters.'[1]

At Thine appearing in the body, the earth was sanctified, the waters blessed, the heaven enlightened, and mankind was set loose from the bitter tyranny of the enemy.

At the divine command the Forerunner now comes from the wilderness to Jordan, saying, 'Repent ye, for the Kingdom of heaven is at hand', calling all to the glory of God.

He who formerly turned the sea into dry land and made springs of water gush forth from the rock, now makes the stream of Jordan a furnace wherein our offences are refined by the fire of the Spirit.

Canticle Five

(**Irmos**) Isaiah, as he watched by night, beheld the light that knows no evening, the light of Thy Theophany, O Christ, that came to pass from tender love for us; and he cried aloud:

[1] Habakkuk 3:15.

'O ye who are enlightened, come ye and wash yourselves, make yourselves clean in soul and body through the divine water and the Spirit.'[1]

O Creator, who art the New Adam, Thou makest new those born on earth, and Thou bringest to pass a strange regeneration and a wonderful restoration by fire and Spirit and water: without destruction or melting pot Thou dost renew mankind through the holy sacrament of baptism.

Through the Spirit dost Thou make souls new and through the water dost Thou sanctify our body compounded from the elements, forming man afresh as a living being. For in wise forethought, as physician alike of bodies and of souls, with profit Thou dost minister the remedies befitting both.

Thou hast come forth from a womb that suffered no pangs of childbirth, O Thou who wast begotten of the Father before the ages; Thou goest to him who was born of a barren mother, and as man Thou askest him for baptism. Yet Thou, O Saviour, by water and through the Spirit hast mystically made the Church, that before was barren, Mother of many children.

Canticle Six

(**Irmos**) The divine Baptist was compassed but not held fast by fear. For, though grass draws back before the face of fire, yet when he heard Christ's words 'Suffer it to be so now',[2] he ran, obediently fulfilling the command; and he heard from on high the voice of God bearing testimony to the pre-eternal Son.

Obeying the decree of Caesar, Thou wast enrolled but not enslaved. Thou grantest us comfort from bondage, yet of Thine own will hast Thou subjected Thyself and paid tribute; and now Thou hast set us free, who before were sold to the

[1] Isaiah 1:16.
[2] Matthew 3:15.

law of sin, and hast made us worthy to be sons by adoption.[1]

Thou reignest, but not after the fashion of the world, for Thou art King by nature. Thou wast born of the tribe of David after the flesh, O Saviour, and hast inherited his throne and kingdom; yet Thou art endued with an eternal power, for Thou reignest always with the Father and the Spirit, before all ages and for evermore.

Of old the prince of this world[2] was named king also of all that was in the waters; but by Thy cleansing he is choked and destroyed, as Legion in the lake.[3] With Thy mighty arm Thou hast granted freedom, O Saviour, to Thy creation, which he had enslaved.

Canticle Seven

(**Irmos**) Wonder past speech! He who delivered the Holy Children from the flames of the furnace, bows His head and begs baptism from His servant, cleansing those who cry aloud: O God our Deliverer, blessed art Thou.

The stream of Jordan was formerly cut in two by a mantle,[4] prefiguring Thy baptism whereby the robe of the passions is rent, and a garment of incorruption is woven for those who cry aloud: O Christ our God, blessed art Thou.

O happy stream! For it received in itself the Creator at His baptism and was made a fountain of life-giving water, for our salvation who sing: O God our Deliverer, blessed art Thou.

Figuring in signs a divine dying by a threefold immersion in water, we are buried with Christ by baptism,[5] and participating in His Resurrection on the third day, we cry aloud to Him: Blessed art Thou.

[1] Matthew 17:27; Romans 7:14; Romans 8:15.
[2] John 12:31
[3] Mark 5:9,13.
[4] 4 (2) Kings 2:8,14.
[5] Romans 6:4.

One is the grace of Father, Son, and Spirit, making perfect those who in faith desire the gift of divine baptism and receive the power of adoption unto sonship, that so they may cry aloud: O God, blessed art Thou.

Canticle Eight

(**Irmos**) Be ye astonished, O ye heavens, be ye horribly afraid, and let the foundations of the earth be shaken.[1] For lo, He who once made the sacrifice of His righteous prophet burn most wondrously with water,[2] wraps Himself in the waters of Jordan. Him do ye children bless, ye priests praise, and ye people exalt above all for ever.

Christ comes to grant through baptism deliverance to all the faithful. For thereby He cleanses fallen Adam and lifts him up, putting to shame the tyrant who had laid him low; He opens the heavens, brings down the divine Spirit, and grants man a share of incorruption.

The error of the enemy has ceased. For the voice of one crying in the wilderness calls out: 'Prepare ye the way of the Lord, and make all His paths straight.' For the humble valley, the nature of mortal man, is exalted, while the mountain and hill of the adversary are made low.[3]

O marvellous gifts! O divine grace and forbearance past speech! For behold, the Fashioner and Master now wears my nature in the Jordan, yet without sin; He cleanses me through water, enlightens me through fire, and makes me perfect through the divine Spirit.

Canticle Nine

(**Irmos**) Weep not in vain, O ye mortal men choked by halters of despair and weighed down with guilt, but in

[1] Jeremiah 2:12; Psalm 81:5.
[2] 3 (1) Kings 18:35–36.
[3] Isaiah 40:3–4; Mark 1:3.

compunction of soul let us approach Him who cleanses all mankind, for He alone is clean, and He grants pardon through baptism.

Thou hast filled us with wonder at Thy strange birth from a Virgin in ways past nature, O Word of God, and now Thou dost exalt in glory a great mystery: by Thy holy participation in the waters of baptism, Thou makest the font rich in children through the divine Spirit.

The earth has been sanctified, O Word, by Thy holy birth, and the heavens with the stars declared Thy glory: and now the nature of the waters is blessed by Thy baptism in the flesh, and mankind has been restored once more to its former nobility.

Let the whole earth rejoice exceedingly, let heaven be glad, let the world leap for joy. Let the rivers clap their hands, let the springs and lakes and the deeps of the sea rejoice with them. For Christ is come to cleanse and save Adam by divine baptism.

Mattins

After the first reading from the Psalter, sessional hymn:

TONE ONE

Make glad, O river Jordan, for the Maker of all draws near, desiring in His compassion to receive baptism in thy streams from a servant. O Adam and Eve, the mother of mankind, be of good cheer and rejoice. For the Redeemer of all has come, God who is supreme in goodness.

Glory be to the Father . . . Both now . . .

SAME TONE

The River of joy,[1] the Master, comes forth to be baptized in the waters of the river, wishing to give me to drink from the

[1] Psalm 35:9 (Septuagint).

spring of incorruption. Seeing Him, John cried aloud: 'How shall I stretch out my hand and touch Thy head, before which all things tremble?'

After the second reading from the Psalter, sessional hymn:[1]

TONE THREE

Let us sing together the praises of Him who is beyond all understanding, who was in flesh made poor and came to baptism, working thereby our restoration, for He is God rich in mercy: and let us magnify His condescension, crying aloud in thankfulness of heart, Glory to Thine Epiphany, O Christ.

Glory be to the Father . . . Both now . . .

SAME TONE

O compassionate Saviour, putting on the nakedness of Adam as a garment of glory, Thou makest ready to stand naked in the flesh in the river Jordan. O marvellous wonder! How shall the water receive Thee, O Master and Lord, who, as it is written, hast covered the roof of heaven with waters?[2] O Jesus our Benefactor, we all sing the praises of Thine Epiphany.

[1] The sessional hymns after the second reading from the Psalter are as follows in the Slav use:

O compassionate Saviour . . .
Glory be to the Father . . . Both now . . .

TONE THREE

The Great Sun, Christ our God, who has risen from the Virgin as from a cloud, has come to shine forth in the Jordan, driving out the darkness of sin and enlightening the ends of the world. In piety let us pray to receive this His Brightness and to be granted great mercy.

[2] Psalm 103: 3.

Then follows Psalm 50.

Three Canons are used: of the Forefeast, in six troparia, including the irmos; of St. Synkletika, in four troparia; and of the Martyrs, also in four troparia. The irmos of the Canon of the Martyrs is repeated as katavasia at the end of Canticles Three, Six, Eight, and Nine.

Canon of the Forefeast, by Joseph:

TONE ONE

Canticle One

(**Irmos**) Delivered from bitter bondage, Israel crossed over the waters as if they were dry land; and seeing the enemy drowning, in gladness they sang a song to God who works wonders with His mighty arm: for He has been glorified.

Christ comes to baptism; Christ approaches Jordan; Christ now buries our sins in the waters, for He is good. In exceeding joy let us sing His praises, for He has been glorified.

Let the clouds, rejoicing, drop down eternal gladness.[1] Jesus Christ comes forth to drown the rivers of sin in the streams of Jordan, granting enlightenment to all.

Behold, the Light is made manifest; behold, our propitiation is revealed; behold, the Saviour approaches to give the light of divine brightness to those in darkness. With pure minds let us welcome Him in joy.

Canticle Three

(**Irmos**) Let no mortal boast of his wisdom and his wealth, but with right faith in the Lord and giving true glory, let him cry to Christ our God and ever sing: Upon the rock of Thy commandments establish me, O Master.

[1] Isaiah 45:8.

He who was enthroned before the ages with the Father and the Spirit, and who has now in the last times been made flesh of a Virgin, in ways that He alone understands, even Christ, comes to baptism, and through the divine washing He grants immortality unto all.

Wishing to bury our sins with water in the streams of Jordan, Christ our God comes forth in His compassionate mercy, and through baptism He forms us anew who had grown corrupt.

Thou who once hast clothed the shameful nakedness of our forefather Adam,[1] art now of Thine own will stripped bare; and Thou who coverest the roof of heaven with waters,[2] wrappest Thine own self in the streams of Jordan, O Christ who alone art full of mercy.

Sessional hymn of St. Synkletika.

Glory be to the Father . . .

Sessional hymn to the Martyrs.

Both now . . .

Sessional hymn of the Forefeast:

TONE ONE

The mighty Rain comes forth in the flesh to the streams of the river, desiring baptism. Filled with amazement the divine Forerunner said to Him: 'How shall I baptize Thee, who hast no stain at all? How shall I stretch out my right hand upon Thy head, before which all things tremble?'

Canticle Four

(**Irmos**) Habakkuk the wonderful heard Thy voice in ancient times, and he cried out in fear: 'God shall come from Teman and the Holy One from the mountain overshadowed

[1] Genesis 3:21.
[2] Psalm 103:3.

by the forest, to save His anointed. Glory to Thy might, O Lord.'

Draw ye from the water of life. Behold, the true River of peace now approaches, to dry up the troubled waters of unbelief and to pour forth enlightenment on those who sing to Him: Glory to Thy might, O Lord.

Let the whole nature of man make glad, that formerly was barren as the wilderness and thirsty. The River of joy[1] has now appeared in the waters of Jordan, setting loose the drought of sin. To Him let us sing with faith: Glory to Thy might, O Lord.

The voice of one crying prophetically sounded in the minds that were barren as the wilderness: 'Prepare ye the ways and make them straight for Christ who comes, that by baptism He may shape us anew who were grown old, loosing us from the ancient sentence.'[2]

Canticle Five

(**Irmos**) With Thy light that never sets, shine forth, O Christ, in the hearts of those who in faith sing Thy praises, and grant us Thy peace that passeth understanding: that so, running from the night of ignorance towards the day of Thy commandments, we may glorify Thee who lovest mankind.

O Christ the King of peace, Thou hast appeared on earth in the likeness of the flesh[3] and hast destroyed the middle wall of partition and enmity.[4] Therefore John, seeing Thy coming, was seized with fear when Thou hast commanded him to lay his hand on Thee.

Christ now comes in haste to the waters, to crush the heads of the dragons,[5] and He cries to the trembling Baptist:

[1] Psalm 35:9 (Septuagint).
[2] Isaiah 40:3; Matthew 3:3.
[3] Romans 8:3.
[4] Ephesians 2:14.
[5] Psalm 73:13

'Stretch out thine hand and touch my head; and cast fear aside, fulfilling that which I command thee.'

The prophet once disclosed the grace of baptism in the Holy Spirit, when he struck the streams of Jordan with his mantle.[1] Its waters now are parted once again, for Christ has appeared in them and makes a path for us unto divine regeneration.

Canticle Six

(**Irmos**) I am utterly compassed by passions without measure, and I am swallowed up by the sea monster of wickedness. But lead me up from corruption, O God, as Thou hast once led Jonah, and grant me by faith freedom from passion: that with a voice of praise and in the spirit of truth, I may sacrifice to Thee.

Though Thou art changeless, O Christ, yet in Thy compassionate mercy Thou comest to Thy servant in the form of a servant, asking for baptism and snatching mankind from bondage: and struck with wonder at this Thy coming, he is afraid and draws back in fear.

How shall the streams of the river receive Thee, the unbearable fire that now approaches? How shall the angels of heaven look upon this stripping? How shall John stretch out his hand upon Thee, O Word of God who wast before all things began and who hast fashioned him from earth?

The waters divided in two and fled, revealing to the new people a path across the stream, which the Lord has made, coming to the river in the flesh, He who once by a miracle caused springs to gush forth from the rock. Let us glorify Him as God, for He has fashioned anew our broken nature.

Kontakion of the Forefeast:

TONE FOUR

When the Lord descended today into the waters of the

[1] 4 (2) Kings 2:8.

Jordan, He cried aloud to John: 'Be not afraid to baptize me: for I am come to save Adam the first-formed man.'

Ikos

(*by Romanos the Melodist*)

'I ask thee not, O Baptist, to step over the boundaries: I tell thee not, "Say to Me what thou dost say to the transgressors, the counsel that thou givest to sinners". Only baptize Me in silence and in expectation of all that shall come from this My baptism. For this cause shalt thou have such honour as belongs not to the angels, and I shall make thee greater than all the prophets.[1] Not one of them saw Me openly, but only in figures and shades and dreams, while thou hast seen Me standing of Mine own will before thee. For I am come to save Adam the first-formed man.'

Canticle Seven

(**Irmos**) Made manifest in God's sight through their piety, the Holy Children entered the unquenchable flames of the furnace as if it were a bridal chamber, and singing with one accord they raised their hymn: 'O God of our fathers, blessed art Thou.'

Christ our salvation has appeared, granting enlightenment. Let the heavens rejoice exceedingly, and let the clouds truly pour down righteousness[2] on those who cry: O God of our fathers, blessed art Thou.

The fleece that Gideon saw prophetically, from which he wringed a bowl full of water,[3] clearly disclosed the baptism, O Christ, which, having been Thyself baptized, Thou wast to grant unto those who sing: O God of our fathers, blessed art Thou.

[1] Matthew 11:9.
[2] Isaiah 45:8.
[3] Judges 6:38.

Elisha, healing the barren waters with salt,[1] prefigured the many children which the precious Font should bear mystically for those who sing: O God of our fathers, blessed art Thou.

Canticle Eight

(**Irmos**) The furnace in ancient times whose flames were moist with dew prefigured a wonder past nature. For the fire burnt not the young Children, thus foretelling the divine birth of Christ without seed from a Virgin. Therefore, raising hymns of praise let us sing: Let the whole creation bless the Lord and exalt Him above all for ever.

With mighty voice let us ascribe praise to the Master. He is come and is made manifest, He goes down into the waters; He who covers the heaven with clouds[2] is stripped bare and baptized, cleansing us who sing: Let the whole creation bless the Lord and exalt Him above all for ever.

Come ye, and let us go in spirit to the Jordan, there to see a great sight. For Jesus our Enlightenment approaches and bows His head beneath the hand of a servant, who sings with trembling: Let the whole creation bless the Lord and exalt Him above all for ever.

The living coal that Isaiah foresaw[3] is kindled in the waters of the Jordan, and He will burn up the whole substance of sin and grant restoration to the broken. Therefore, raising hymns of praise, let us sing: Let the whole creation bless the Lord and exalt Him above all for ever.

Canticle Nine

(**Irmos**) The mystery of the Virgin is past speech: for she had been shown forth as Heaven and Throne of the

[1] 4 (2) Kings 2:19–22.
[2] Psalm 146:8.
[3] Isaiah 6:6.

cherubim, and as the light-bearing Bridal Chamber of God the Almighty. Let us magnify her in piety as Theotokos.

A strange and most wonderful mystery do I see! Jesus comes of His own will to the river Jordan, crying aloud to John: 'O friend, lend Me thy right hand: for fearful things must I perform that I may claim My people for Mine own.'[1]

Let the wilderness of Jordan blossom with flowers; and ye that lie in darkness, leap for joy, for a great light has now appeared to you. Christ, coming from Galilee, suffers Himself to be baptized in the flesh by a servant.

Be glad now and dance, O Jordan; leap for joy, O John, and let the whole inhabited earth rejoice exceedingly. Behold, Christ has appeared: He is stripped bare and baptized, wrapping human nature in a garment of incorruption.

Theotokion

O spotless Maiden, thou hast conceived without corruption Him whom no mind can comprehend. Thou hast borne, beyond nature and words, Him who by a word in wisdom upholds all things through His will. Do thou ever entreat Him as God for our salvation.

Exapostilarion[2]

Seeing Thee stripped naked, with fear Jordan said to him who had been born of a barren womb: 'Suffer the Lord, who cleanses the whole creation by fire and Spirit, to be baptized, O John. For behold, for this cause He has come to sanctify the elements of earth and water.'

Glory be to the Father . . . Both now . . .

Thou who in Bethlehem hast shone forth in the flesh from a Virgin, dost now hasten towards Jordan to wash clean the filth of those born on earth, through holy baptism leading those in darkness to the light.

[1] 1 Peter 2:9.

[2] The first exapostilarion is not found in the Greek books, its place being taken by an exapostilarion to the Martyrs.

Lauds. Four stichera are sung:

TONE SIX

(*to the special melody*, Go ye on before, O ye angelic powers . . .)

'Why dost thou doubt, O Baptist, concerning the dispensation that I fulfil for the salvation of all? Set now aside the old and think of the new. Believe in God who has come down to earth, and drawing near, obey Me. For I have come as God, to cleanse in My compassion fallen Adam.'

'Taking our sins upon Thy shoulders, Thou art come, O Jesus, to the streams of Jordan: and I am afraid at Thy dread coming. How, then, dost Thou bid me baptize Thee? Thou Thyself hast come to cleanse me, and how dost Thou, the Cleanser of all, seek baptism of me?'

'My nature is beyond all understanding: but clothed in the form of a servant have I come forth to Jordan. Doubt not at all concerning me. Come, fear not, draw near me. Place thy right hand upon my head and cry aloud, Blessed art Thou, our God made manifest: glory to Thee.'

Beyond all thought and without measure is Thy poverty, O Word of God! I know that, for my sake who am fallen, Thou hast from pity clothed Thyself in Adam, and all the posterity of Adam Thou makest new again. Obeying Thy command I cry to Thee in faith, Blessed art Thou, our God made manifest: glory to Thee.

Glory be to the Father . . .

SAME TONE

O John, who dost minister in trembling to the Master, be joyful in soul and cry with gladness: 'Rejoice with me, O all ye generations of the Forefather. For our expectation has come: Christ has drawn nigh to Jordan to cleanse all from the sin of Adam, for He is full of lovingkindness.'

Both now . . .

SAME TONE

O ye peoples, let us sing to Him who was born of a Virgin, and baptized in the river Jordan, and let us cry to Him: O King of all the creation, grant us uncondemned, with a clear conscience, to attain in faith Thy holy Resurrection from the dead on the third day.

Aposticha:

TONE TWO

(*to the special melody*, O house of Ephratah . . .)

Behold the King: lo, the expectation of Israel is at hand. O ye people, rejoice exceedingly. For the Light is made manifest.

℣. Therefore will I remember Thee from the land of Jordan and of the Hermonites (*Psalm* 41:7).

The Godhead has appeared in the flesh to the dwellers upon earth: light has now shone on those in darkness, and grace has shed its bright rays upon all.[1]

℣. The waters saw Thee, O God, the waters saw Thee and were afraid (*Psalm* 76:17).

O Candlestick of the Light, Ray of the Sun, Forerunner of the Word, Friend of the Bridegroom, fulfil thy ministry, O Prophet.

Glory be to the Father . . . Both now . . .

TONE EIGHT

'O John the Baptist, who from the womb hast known Me as the Lamb,[2] minister to Me in the river, serving Me with the angels. Stretch out thy hand and touch My undefiled head; and when thou seest the mountains tremble and Jordan turn back, do thou cry aloud with them: O Lord who hast been made flesh of a Virgin for our salvation, glory to Thee.'

[1] Baruch 3:37; Isaiah 9:2; Titus 2:11.

[2] Luke 1:44.

The rest of the service of Mattins as usual, and the Dismissal.

The Forefeast of the Theophany (5 January) is observed as a fast, and neither animal products nor fish may be eaten. In the Greek use, wine and oil are not permitted, except when the Forefeast falls on Saturday or Sunday: but in the Slav use wine and oil may be taken, whatever day of the week it may be.

5 JANUARY

THE EVE OF THE THEOPHANY

The Royal Hours

If the Eve of the Theophany falls on Saturday or Sunday, the Royal Hours are read on the preceding Friday. In such a case, the Liturgy is not celebrated on Friday.

The First Hour

After the blessing by the priest, we say Holy God . . ., *and the opening prayers as usual. Then* O come, let us worship . . ., *and the following three psalms:*

Psalm 5 (p. 221)

Psalm 22

The Lord is my shepherd; I shall not want. He maketh me to lie down in green pastures: He leadeth me beside the still waters. He restoreth my soul: He leadeth me in the paths of righteousness for His name's sake. Yea, though I walk through the valley of the shadow of death, I will fear no evil: for Thou art with me; Thy rod and Thy staff they comfort me. Thou preparest a table before me in the presence of mine enemies: Thou anointest my head with oil; my cup runneth over. Surely goodness and mercy shall follow me all the days of my life: and I will dwell in the house of the Lord for ever.

Psalm 26

The Lord is my light and my salvation; whom shall I fear? the Lord is the strength of my life; of whom shall I be afraid?

When the wicked, even mine enemies and my foes, came upon me to eat up my flesh, they stumbled and fell. Though an host should encamp against me, my heart shall not fear: though war should rise against me, in this will I be confident. One thing have I desired of the Lord, that will I seek after; that I may dwell in the house of the Lord all the days of my life, to behold the beauty of the Lord, and to inquire in His temple. For in the time of trouble He shall hide me in His pavilion: in the secret of His tabernacle shall He hide me; He shall set me up upon a rock. And now shall mine head be lifted up above mine enemies round about me: therefore will I offer in His tabernacle sacrifices of joy; I will sing, yea, I will sing praises unto the Lord. Hear, O Lord, when I cry with my voice: have mercy also upon me, and answer me. When Thou saidst, Seek ye My face; my heart said unto Thee, Thy face, Lord, will I seek. Hide not Thy face far from me; put not Thy servant away in anger: Thou hast been my help; leave me not, neither forsake me, O God of my salvation. When my father and my mother forsake me, then the Lord will take me up. Teach me Thy way, O Lord, and lead me in a plain path, because of mine enemies. Deliver me not over unto the will of mine enemies: for false witnesses are risen up against me, and such as breathe out cruelty. I had fainted, unless I had believed to see the goodness of the Lord in the land of the living. Wait on the Lord: be of good courage, and He shall strengthen thine heart: wait, I say, on the Lord.

Glory be to the Father . . . Both now . . .

Alleluia, alleluia, alleluia, glory be to Thee, O God (*3 times*).

Kyrie eleison (*3 times*).

Then Glory be to the Father . . . *and the troparion of the Forefeast:*

TONE FOUR

The river Jordan once turned back before the mantle of

Elisha, after Elijah had been taken up into heaven, and the waters were divided on this side and on that: the stream became a dry path before him, forming a true figure of the baptism whereby we pass over the changeful course of life. Christ has appeared in the Jordan to sanctify the waters.

Then the reader continues:

Both now . . .

Theotokion

What shall we call thee, O full of grace? . . . (*p. 224*).

Then we sing the following stichera:

TONE EIGHT

(by Sophronios, Patriarch of Jerusalem)

Today the nature of the waters is sanctified, and the Jordan is parted in two: it holds back the stream of its own waters, seeing the Master wash Himself (*twice*).

℣. Therefore will I remember Thee from the land of Jordan and of the Hermonites (*Psalm* 41:7).

SAME TONE

O Christ the King, Thou hast come unto the river as a man, and in Thy goodness Thou dost make haste to receive the baptism of a servant at the hands of the Forerunner, for the sake of our sins, O Thou who lovest mankind.

℣. The waters saw Thee, O God, the waters saw Thee and were afraid (*Psalm* 76:17).

Repeat.

Glory be to the Father . . .

SAME TONE

At the voice of one crying in the wilderness, 'Prepare ye the way of the Lord',[1] Thou hast come, O Lord, taking the form of a servant,[2] and Thou who knowest not sin dost ask

[1] Mark 1:3.
[2] Philippians 2:7.

for baptism. The waters saw Thee and were afraid;[1] the Forerunner was seized with trembling and cried aloud, saying: 'How shall the lamp illuminate the Light? How shall the servant set his hand upon the Master? O Saviour who takest away the sin of the world, sanctify both me and the waters.'

Both now . . .

Repeat.

Immediately there follows the Prokimenon:

TONE FOUR

The Lord thundered upon many waters: the voice of Thy thunder was in the heaven.[2]

℣. I will love Thee, O Lord my strength: the Lord is my support, my refuge, and my deliverer (*Psalm* 17: 2–3).

Lessons:

READING FROM THE PROPHET ISAIAH (35: 1–10).

Thus saith the Lord: The wilderness and the solitary place shall be glad for them; and the desert shall rejoice, and blossom as the rose. It shall blossom abundantly, and rejoice even with joy and singing: the glory of Lebanon shall be given unto it, the excellency of Carmel and Sharon, they shall see the glory of the Lord, and the excellency of our God. Strengthen ye the weak hands, and confirm the feeble knees. Say to them that are of a fearful heart, Be strong, fear not: behold, your God will come with vengeance, even God with a recompence; He will come and save you. Then the eyes of the blind shall be opened, and the ears of the deaf shall be unstopped. Then shall the lame man leap as an hart, and the

[1] Psalm 76: 17.
[2] See Psalms 28: 3; 76: 19.

tongue of the dumb sing: for in the wilderness shall waters break out, and streams in the desert. And the parched ground shall become a pool, and the thirsty land springs of water: in the habitation of dragons, where each lay, shall be grass with reeds and rushes. And an highway shall be there, and a way, and it shall be called The way of holiness; the unclean shall not pass over it; but it shall be for those: the wayfaring men, though fools, shall not err therein. No lion shall be there, nor any ravenous beast shall go up thereon, it shall not be found there; but the redeemed shall walk there: and the ransomed of the Lord shall return, and come to Zion with songs and everlasting joy upon their heads: they shall obtain joy and gladness, and sorrow and sighing shall flee away.

Reading from the Acts of the Apostles (13:25–33).

In those days, as John fulfilled his course, he said, Whom think ye that I am? I am not He. But, behold, there cometh One after me, whose shoes of His feet I am not worthy to loose. Men and brethren, children of the stock of Abraham, and whosoever among you feareth God, to you is the word of this salvation sent. For they that dwell at Jerusalem, and their rulers, because they knew Him not, nor yet the voices of the prophets which are read every sabbath day, they have fulfilled them in condemning Him. And though they found no cause of death in Him, yet desired they Pilate that He should be slain. And when they had fulfilled all that was written of Him, they took Him down from the tree, and laid Him in a sepulchre. But God raised Him from the dead: and He was seen many days of them which came up with Him from Galilee to Jerusalem, who are His witnesses unto the people. And we declare unto you glad tidings, how that the promise which was made unto the fathers, God hath fulfilled the same unto us their children, in that He hath raised up Jesus again.

READING FROM THE HOLY GOSPEL ACCORDING TO MATTHEW (3 : 1–6).

In those days came John the Baptist, preaching in the wilderness of Judaea, and saying, Repent ye: for the kingdom of heaven is at hand. For this is he that was spoken of by the prophet Isaiah, saying, The voice of one crying in the wilderness, Prepare ye the way of the Lord, make His paths straight. And the same John had his raiment of camel's hair, and a leathern girdle about his loins; and his meat was locusts and wild honey. Then went out to him Jerusalem, and all Judaea, and all the region round about Jordan, and were baptized of him in Jordan, confessing their sins.

After the Gospel the reader says:

Order my steps in Thy word . . . (*p. 227*).

Then Holy God . . ., *etc., and the Lord's Prayer, followed by the kontakion of the Forefeast:*

TONE FOUR

When the Lord descended today into the waters of the Jordan, He cried aloud to John: 'Be not afraid to baptize me: for I am come to save Adam the first-formed man.'

Kyrie eleison, *40 times, and the Prayer of the Hours,* Thou who at every season and every hour . . . *Then* Kyrie eleison, *3 times*; Glory be to the Father . . . Both now. . .; Greater in honour than the cherubim . . .; In the Name of the Lord, give the blessing, Father.

The priest: God be merciful unto us . . .

And the prayer O Christ, the true Light . . . (*p. 228*).

The Third Hour

O come, let us worship . . ., *and the following three psalms:*

Psalm 28

Give unto the Lord, O ye mighty, give unto the Lord glory and strength. Give unto the Lord the glory due unto His name; worship the Lord in the beauty of holiness. The voice of the Lord is upon the waters: the God of glory thundereth: the Lord is upon many waters. The voice of the Lord is powerful; the voice of the Lord is full of majesty. The voice of the Lord breaketh the cedars; yea, the Lord breaketh the cedars of Lebanon. He maketh them also to skip like a calf; Lebanon and Sirion like a young unicorn. The voice of the Lord divideth the flames of fire. The voice of the Lord shaketh the wilderness; the Lord shaketh the wilderness of Kadesh. The voice of the Lord maketh the hinds to calve, and discovereth the forests: and in His temple doth every one speak of His glory. The Lord sitteth upon the flood; yea, the Lord sitteth King for ever. The Lord will give strength unto His people; the Lord will bless His people with peace.

Psalm 41

As the hart panteth after the water brooks, so panteth my soul after Thee, O God. My soul thirsteth for God, for the living God: when shall I come and appear before God? My tears have been my meat day and night, while they continually say unto me, Where is thy God? When I remember these things, I pour out my soul in me: for I had gone with the multitude, I went with them to the house of God, with the voice of joy and praise, with a multitude that kept holyday. Why art thou cast down, O my soul? and why art thou disquieted in me? hope thou in God: for I shall yet praise Him for the help of His countenance. O my God, my soul is cast down within me: therefore will I remember Thee from the land of Jordan, and of the Hermonites, from the hill Mizar. Deep calleth unto deep at the noise of Thy water-spouts: all Thy waves and Thy billows are gone over me. Yet the Lord will command His lovingkindness in the daytime, and in the night His song shall be with me, and my prayer unto the God of my life. I will say unto God my rock, Why hast Thou forgotten me? why go I mourning because of the oppression of the enemy? As with a sword in my bones, mine enemies reproach me; while they say daily unto me, Where is thy God? Why art thou cast down, O my soul? and why art thou disquieted within me? hope thou in God: for I shall yet praise Him, who is the health of my countenance, and my God.

Psalm 50 (*p. 229*)

Glory be to the Father . . . Both now . . .

Alleluia, alleluia, alleluia, glory be to Thee, O God (*3 times*).

Kyrie eleison (*3 times*).

Then Glory be to the Father . . . *and the troparion*, The river Jordan once turned back . . . (*p. 315*). *After this the reader continues:*

Both now . . .

Theotokion

O Theotokos, thou art the true vine (*p. 230*).

Then we sing the following stichera:

TONE EIGHT

The right hand of the Forerunner and Baptist, the prophet honoured above all the prophets,[1] trembled as he beheld Thee, the Lamb of God who cleanses the sins of the world.[2] Seized with agony, he cried: 'I dare not touch Thy head, O Word. Do Thou Thyself in Thy mercy sanctify and enlighten me: for Thou art the life and the light and the peace of the world' (*twice*).

[1] Matthew 11:9.
[2] John 1:29.

℣. Therefore will I remember Thee from the land of Jordan and of the Hermonites (*Psalm* 41 : 7).

TONE FOUR

The Trinity, our God, today has made Itself indivisibly manifest to us. For the Father in a loud voice bore clear witness to His Son; the Spirit in the form of a dove came down from the sky; while the Son bent His immaculate head before the Forerunner, and by receiving baptism He delivered us from bondage, in His love for mankind.

℣. The waters saw Thee, O God, the waters saw Thee and were afraid (*Psalm* 76 : 17).

Repeat.

Glory be to the Father . . .

TONE FIVE

Desiring to receive baptism, O Lord, Thou hast come with Thy flesh in man's form to the Jordan, O Giver of life, to enlighten us who were gone astray, delivering us in Thy compassion from every device and snare of the dragon. Then the Father bore witness to Thee, and the divine Spirit in the form of a dove came down upon Thee. Make Thy dwelling in our souls, O Thou who lovest mankind.

Both now . . .

Repeat.

Immediately there follows the Prokimenon:

TONE SIX

The waters saw Thee, O God, the waters saw Thee and were afraid (*Psalm* 76 : 17).

℣. The voice of the Lord is upon the waters: the God of glory thundered, the Lord is upon many waters (*Psalm* 28 : 3).[1]

[1] In the Slavonic books this verse is replaced by the following: *I cried unto the Lord with my voice, even unto God with my voice, and He gave ear unto me* (Psalm 76 : 2).

Lessons:

READING FROM THE PROPHET ISAIAH (1:16–20).

Thus saith the Lord: Wash you, make you clean; put away the evil of your doings from before Mine eyes; cease to do evil; learn to do well; seek judgement, relieve the oppressed, judge the fatherless, plead for the widow. Come now, and let us reason together, saith the Lord: though your sins be as scarlet, they shall be as white as snow; though they be red like crimson, they shall be as wool. If ye be willing and obedient, ye shall eat the good of the land: but if ye refuse and rebel, ye shall be devoured with the sword: for the mouth of the Lord hath spoken it.

READING FROM THE ACTS OF THE APOSTLES (19:1–8).

In those days it came to pass, that, while Apollos was at Corinth, Paul having passed through the upper coasts came to Ephesus: and finding certain disciples, he said unto them, Have ye received the Holy Ghost since ye believed? And they said unto him, We have not so much as heard whether there be any Holy Ghost. And he said unto them, Unto what then were ye baptized? And they said, Unto John's baptism. Then said Paul, John verily baptized with the baptism of repentance, saying unto the people, that they should believe on Him which should come after him, that is, on Christ Jesus. When they heard this, they were baptized in the name of the Lord Jesus. And when Paul had laid his hands upon them, the Holy Ghost came on them; and they spake with tongues, and prophesied. And all the men were about twelve. And he went into the synagogue, and spake boldly for the space of three months, disputing and persuading the things concerning the kingdom of God.

READING FROM THE HOLY GOSPEL ACCORDING TO MARK (1:1–8).

The beginning of the Gospel of Jesus Christ, the Son of God; as it is written in the prophets, Behold, I send My messenger before Thy face, which shall prepare Thy way before Thee. The voice of one crying in the wilderness, Prepare ye the way of the Lord, make His paths straight. John did baptize in the wilderness, and preach the baptism of repentance for the remission of sins. And there went out unto him all the land of Judaea, and they of Jerusalem, and were all baptized of him in the river of Jordan, confessing their sins. And John was clothed with camel's hair, and with a girdle of a skin about his loins; and he did eat locusts and wild honey; and preached, saying, There cometh One mightier than I after me, the latchet of whose shoes I am not worthy to stoop down and unloose. I indeed have baptized you with water: but He shall baptize you with the Holy Ghost.

After the Gospel the reader says:

Blessed be the Lord God . . . *(p. 234)*.

Then Holy God . . ., *etc., and the Lord's Prayer, followed by the kontakion,* When the Lord descended today into the waters of the Jordan . . . *(p. 319)*.

Kyrie eleison, *40 times, and the Prayer of the Hours,* Thou who at every season and every hour . . . *Then* Kyrie eleison, *3 times;* Glory be to the Father . . . Both now . . .; Greater in honour than the cherubim . . .; In the Name of the Lord, give the blessing, Father.

The priest: God be merciful unto us . . .

And the prayer O God the Master, Father Almighty . . . *(p. 234)*.

The Sixth Hour

O come, let us worship . . ., *and the following three psalms:*

Psalm 73

O God, why hast Thou cast us off for ever? why doth Thine anger smoke against the sheep of Thy pasture?

Remember Thy congregation, which Thou hast purchased of old; the rod of Thine inheritance, which Thou hast redeemed; this mount Zion, wherein Thou hast dwelt. Lift up Thy feet unto the perpetual desolations; even all that the enemy hath done wickedly in the sanctuary. Thine enemies roar in the midst of Thy congregations; they set up their ensigns for signs. A man was famous according as he had lifted up axes upon the thick trees. But now they break down the carved work thereof at once with axes and hammers. They have cast fire into Thy sanctuary, they have defiled by casting down the dwelling place of Thy name to the ground. They said in their hearts, Let us destroy them together: they have burned up all the synagogues of God in the land. We see not our signs: there is no more any prophet: neither is there among us any that knoweth how long. O God, how long shall the adversary reproach? Shall the enemy blaspheme Thy name for ever? Why withdrawest Thou Thy hand, even Thy right hand? pluck it out of Thy bosom. For God is my King of old, working salvation in the midst of the earth. Thou didst divide the sea by Thy strength: Thou brakest the heads of the dragons in the waters. Thou brakest the heads of leviathan in pieces, and gavest him to be meat to the people inhabiting the wilderness. Thou didst cleave the fountain and the flood: Thou driedst up mighty rivers. The day is Thine, the night also is Thine: Thou hast prepared the light and the sun. Thou hast set all the borders of the earth: Thou hast made summer and winter. Remember this, that the enemy hath reproached, O Lord, and that the foolish people have blasphemed Thy name. O deliver not the soul of Thy turtledove unto the multitude of the wicked: forget not the congregation of Thy poor for ever. Have respect unto the covenant: for the dark places of the earth are full of the habitations of cruelty. O let not the oppressed return ashamed: let the poor and needy praise Thy name. Arise, O God, plead Thine own cause: remember how the foolish man reproacheth Thee daily. Forget not the voice of Thine enemies: the tumult of those that rise up against Thee increaseth continually.

Psalm 76

I cried unto God with my voice, even unto God with my voice; and He gave ear unto me. In the day of my trouble I sought the Lord: my sore ran in the night, and ceased not: my soul refused to be comforted. I remembered God, and was troubled: I complained, and my spirit was overwhelmed. Thou holdest mine eyes waking: I am so troubled that I cannot speak. I have considered the days of old, the years of ancient times. I call to remembrance my song in the night: I commune with mine own heart: and my spirit made diligent search. Will the Lord cast off for ever? and will He be favourable no more? Is His mercy clean gone for ever? doth His promise fail for evermore? Hath God forgotten to be gracious? hath He in anger shut up His tender mercies? And I said, This is my infirmity: but I will remember the years of the right hand of the most High. I will remember the works of the Lord: surely I will remember Thy wonders of old. I will meditate also of all Thy work, and talk of Thy doings. Thy way, O God, is in the sanctuary: who is so great a God as our God? Thou art the God that doest wonders: Thou hast declared Thy strength among the people. Thou hast with Thine arm redeemed Thy people, the sons of Jacob and Joseph. The waters saw Thee, O God, the waters saw Thee; they were afraid: the depths also were troubled. The clouds poured out water: the skies sent out a sound: Thine arrows also went abroad. The voice of Thy thunder was in the heaven: the lightnings lightened the world: the earth trembled and shook. Thy way is in the sea, and Thy path in the great waters, and Thy footsteps are not known. Thou leddest Thy people like a flock by the hand of Moses and Aaron.

Psalm 90 (p. 236)

Glory be to the Father . . . Both now . . .

Alleluia, alleluia, alleluia, glory be to Thee, O God (*3 times*).

Kyrie eleison (*3 times*).

Then Glory be to the Father . . . *and the troparion*, The river Jordan once turned back . . . (*p. 315*). *After this, the reader continues:*

Both now . . .

Theotokion

As there is no boldness in us . . . (*p. 237*).

Then we sing the following stichera:

TONE EIGHT

Thus spake the Lord to John: 'O Prophet, come and baptize Me who created thee, for I enlighten all men by grace and cleanse them. Touch My divine head and doubt not. O Prophet, suffer it to be so now: for I have come to fulfil all righteousness.[1] Be in no doubt at all: for I am in haste to slay the enemy hidden in the waters, the prince of darkness, that I may now deliver the world from his snares, granting eternal life in my love for mankind' (*twice*).

℣. Therefore will I remember Thee from the land of Jordan and of the Hermonites (*Psalm* 41:7).

TONE SIX

Today the prophecy of the psalms[2] swiftly approaches its fulfilment: The sea saw it and fled: Jordan was driven back, before the face of the Lord, before the face of the God of Jacob, when He came to receive baptism from His servant, that we, washed clean from the defilement of idolatry, through Him might be enlightened in our souls.

[1] Matthew 3:15.

[2] Psalm 113:3,7.

℣. The waters saw Thee, O God, the waters saw Thee and were afraid (*Psalm* 76:17).

Repeat.

Glory be to the Father . . .

TONE FIVE

Why dost thou turn back thy waters, O Jordan? Why dost thou stop thy streams, and why dost thou not proceed upon thy natural course? 'I cannot bear', said he, 'the Fire that consumes me. I am filled with wonder and with dread before His extreme condescension. For I am not used to wash him that is clean: I have not learnt to bathe the sinless, but to purge the filthy vessels. Christ who is baptized in me teaches me to burn the thorns of sin. John, the voice of the Word, bears witness with me and cries: "Behold the Lamb of God, who takes away the sin of the world."'[1] Unto Him let us the faithful cry aloud: O God who art made manifest for our salvation, glory to Thee.

Both now . . .

Repeat.

Immediately there follows the Prokimenon:[2]

TONE FOUR

The voice of the Lord is upon the waters: the God of glory thundered, the Lord is upon many waters (*Psalm* 28:3).

℣. Bring unto the Lord, ye sons of God, bring unto the Lord young rams (*ibid.*, 1).

Lessons:

READING FROM THE PROPHET ISAIAH (12:3–6).

Thus saith the Lord: With joy shall ye draw water out of

[1] John 1:29.

[2] In the Slav use, the prokimenon is as follows: *Thy ways are in the sea, and Thy paths in the great waters* (Psalm 76:20).

℣. *The voice of Thy thunder was heard in the whirlwind* (*ibid.*, 19).

the wells of salvation. And in that day shall ye say, Praise the Lord, call upon His name, declare His doings among the people, make mention that His name is exalted. Sing unto the Lord; for He hath done excellent things: this is known in all the earth. Cry out and shout, thou inhabitant of Zion: for great is the Holy One of Israel in the midst of thee.

Reading from the Epistle to the Romans (6:3–11).

Brethren, know ye not, that so many of us as were baptized into Jesus Christ were baptized into His death? Therefore we are buried with Him by baptism into death: that like as Christ was raised up from the dead by the glory of the Father, even so we also should walk in newness of life. For if we have been planted together in the likeness of His death, we shall be also in the likeness of His resurrection: knowing this, that our old man is crucified with Him, that the body of sin might be destroyed, that henceforth we should not serve sin. For he that is dead is freed from sin. Now if we be dead with Christ, we believe that we shall also live with Him: knowing that Christ being raised from the dead dieth no more; death hath no more dominion over Him. For in that He died, He died unto sin once: but in that He liveth, He liveth unto God. Likewise reckon ye also yourselves to be dead indeed unto sin, but alive unto God through Jesus Christ our Lord.

Reading from the Holy Gospel according to Mark (1:9–11).[1]

And it came to pass in those days, that Jesus came from Nazareth of Galilee, and was baptized of John in Jordan. And straightway coming up out of the water, He saw the heavens opened, and the Spirit like a dove descending upon Him: and there came a voice from heaven, saying, Thou art My beloved Son, in whom I am well pleased.

[1] In the Slav use, continue to verse 15.

After the Gospel the reader says:

Let Thy tender mercies, O Lord . . . (*p. 241*).

Then Holy God . . ., *etc., and the Lord's Prayer, followed by the kontakion* When the Lord descended today . . . (*p. 319*).

Kyrie eleison, *40 times, and the Prayer of the Hours,* Thou who at every season and every hour . . . *Then* Kyrie eleison, *3 times*; Glory be to the Father . . . Both now . . .; Greater in honour than the cherubim . . .; In the Name of the Lord, give the blessing, Father.

The priest: God be merciful unto us . . .
And the prayer, O God, the Lord of hosts . . . (*p. 242*).

The Ninth Hour

O come, let us worship . . ., *and the following three psalms:*

Psalm 92

The Lord reigneth, He is clothed with majesty; the Lord is clothed with strength, wherewith He hath girded Himself: the world also is stablished, that it cannot be moved. Thy throne is established of old: Thou art from everlasting. The floods have lifted up, O Lord, the floods have lifted up their voice; the floods lift up their waves. The Lord on high is mightier than the noise of many waters, yea, than the mighty waves of the sea. Thy testimonies are very sure: holiness becometh Thine house, O Lord, for ever.

Psalm 113

When Israel went out of Egypt, the house of Jacob from a people of strange language: Judah was his sanctuary, and Israel his dominion. The sea saw it, and fled: Jordan was driven back. The mountains skipped like rams, and the little hills like lambs. What ailed thee, O thou sea, that thou fleddest? thou Jordan that thou wast driven back? Ye mountains, that ye skipped like rams; and ye little hills, like lambs? Tremble, thou earth, at the presence of the Lord, at the presence of the God of Jacob; which turned the rock into a standing water, the flint into a fountain of waters. Not unto us, O Lord, not unto us, but unto Thy name give glory, for Thy mercy, and for Thy truth's sake. Wherefore should the heathen say, Where is now their God? But our God is in the heavens: He hath done whatsoever He hath pleased. Their idols are silver and gold, the work of men's hands. They have mouths, but they speak not: eyes have they, but they see not: they have ears, but they hear not: noses have they, but they smell not: they have hands, but they handle not: feet have they, but they walk not: neither speak they through their throat. They that make them are like unto them; so is every one that trusteth in them. O Israel, trust thou in the Lord: He is their help and their shield. O house of Aaron, trust in the Lord: He is their help and their shield. Ye that fear the Lord, trust in the Lord: He is their help and their shield. The Lord hath been mindful of us: He will bless us; He will bless the house of Israel; He will bless the house of Aaron. He will bless them that fear the Lord, both small and great. The Lord shall increase you more and more, you and your children. Ye are blessed of the Lord which made heaven and earth. The heaven, even the heavens, are the Lord's; but the earth hath He given to the children of men. The dead praise not the Lord, neither any that go down into silence. But we will bless the Lord from this time forth and for evermore. Praise the Lord.

Psalm 85 (*p. 243*)

Glory be to the Father . . . Both now . . .

Alleluia, alleluia, alleluia, glory be to Thee, O God (*3 times*).

Kyrie eleison (*3 times*).

Then Glory be to the Father . . . *and the troparion*, The river Jordan once turned back . . . (*p. 315*). *After this, the reader continues:*

Both now . . .

Theotokion

O good Lord, for our sakes . . . (*p. 244*).

Then we sing the following stichera:

TONE SEVEN

A strange wonder it was to see the Maker of heaven and earth stand naked in the river, and as a servant receive baptism from a servant, for our salvation. The choirs of angels were filled with amazement, fear, and joy. Joining with them, we worship Thee: O Lord, save us (*twice*).

℣. Therefore will I remember Thee from the land of Jordan and of the Hermonites (*Psalm* 41 : 7).

TONE TWO

When he saw the Lord of glory draw near to him, the Forerunner cried out: 'Lo, here is He who redeems the world from corruption. Lo, here is He who delivers us from affliction. Lo, here is He who in mercy has come forth upon earth from a pure Virgin, granting remission of sins. Instead of servants, He makes us the sons of God; instead of darkness, He gives mankind light, through the water of His divine baptism. Come ye, then, and let us with one accord glorify Him together with the Father and the Holy Spirit.'

℣. The waters saw Thee, O God, the waters saw Thee and were afraid (*Psalm* 76 : 17).

Repeat.

Glory be to the Father . . . Both now . . .

TONE FIVE

With thine hand hast thou touched the immaculate head of the Master (*3 times*).[1]

[1] In the Slav use, once only.

And with the finger of that hand thou hast shown Him to us: on our behalf, O Baptist, stretch out that same hand over Him, for thou hast great boldness before Him. To thee He bore witness, that thou art greater than all the prophets.[1] With thine own eyes hast thou beheld the Holy Spirit descending in the form of a dove. Lift up those same eyes towards Him, O Baptist, and make Him merciful towards us.

Come and stand with us (*3 times*),
Setting the seal upon our song and beginning our feast.

Immediately there follows the Prokimenon:

TONE THREE

The Lord is my light and my salvation: whom shall I fear? (*Psalm* 26:1)

℣. The Lord is the defender of my life: of whom shall I be afraid? (*ibid.*)

Lessons:

Reading from the Prophet Isaiah (49:8–15).

Thus saith the Lord: In an acceptable time have I heard thee, and in a day of salvation have I helped thee: and I will preserve thee, and give thee for a covenant of the people, to establish the earth, to cause to inherit the desolate heritages; that thou mayest say to the prisoners, Go forth; to them that are in darkness, Shew yourselves. They shall feed in the ways, and their pastures shall be in all high places. They shall not hunger nor thirst; neither shall the heat nor sun smite them: for He that hath mercy on them shall lead them, even by the springs of water shall He guide them. And I will make all My mountains a way, and My highways shall be exalted. Behold, these shall come from far: and, lo, these from the north and from the west; and these from the land of Sinim. Sing, O heavens; and be joyful, O earth; and break forth into singing,

[1] Matthew 11:9.

O mountains: for the Lord hath comforted His people, and will have mercy upon His afflicted. But Zion said, The Lord hath forsaken me, and my Lord hath forgotten me. Can a woman forget her sucking child, that she should not have compassion on the son of her womb? yea, they may forget, yet will I not forget thee. Thus saith the Lord Almighty.

READING FROM THE EPISTLE OF PAUL TO TITUS (2:11–14; 3:4–7).

My child Titus, the grace of God that bringeth salvation hath appeared to all men, teaching us that, denying ungodliness and worldly lusts, we should live soberly, righteously, and godly, in this present world; looking for that blessed hope, and the glorious appearing of the great God and our Saviour Jesus Christ; who gave Himself for us, that He might redeem us from all iniquity, and purify unto Himself a peculiar people, zealous of good works. But after that the kindness and love of God our Saviour toward man appeared, not by works of righteousness which we have done, but according to His mercy He saved us, by the washing of regeneration, and renewing of the Holy Ghost; which He shed on us abundantly through Jesus Christ our Saviour; that being justified by His grace, we should be made heirs according to the hope of eternal life.

READING FROM THE HOLY GOSPEL ACCORDING TO LUKE (3:1–18).[1]

Now in the fifteenth year of the reign of Tiberius Caesar, Pontius Pilate being governor of Judaea, and Herod being tetrarch of Galilee, and his brother Philip tetrarch of Ituraea and of the region of Trachonitis, and Lysanias the tetrarch of Abilene, Annas and Caiaphas being the high priests, the word of God came unto John the son of Zacharias in the wilderness. And he came into all the country about Jordan, preaching the

[1] In the Slav use, the Gospel is Matthew 3:13–17 (see p. 387).

baptism of repentance for the remission of sins; as it is written in the book of the words of Isaiah the prophet, saying, The voice of one crying in the wilderness, Prepare ye the way of the Lord, make His paths straight. Every valley shall be filled, and every mountain and hill shall be brought low; and the crooked shall be made straight, and the rough ways shall be made smooth; and all flesh shall see the salvation of God. Then said he to the multitude that came forth to be baptized of him, O generation of vipers, who hath warned you to flee from the wrath to come? Bring forth therefore fruits worthy of repentance, and begin not to say within yourselves, We have Abraham to our father: for I say unto you, That God is able of these stones to raise up children unto Abraham. And now also the axe is laid unto the root of the trees: every tree therefore which bringeth not forth good fruit is hewn down, and cast into the fire. And the people asked him, saying, What shall we do then? He answereth and saith unto them, He that hath two coats, let him impart to him that hath none; and he that hath meat, let him do likewise. Then came also publicans to be baptized, and said unto him, Master, what shall we do? And he said unto them, Exact no more than that which is appointed you. And the soldiers likewise demanded of him, saying, And what shall we do? And he said unto them, Do violence to no man, neither accuse any falsely; and be content with your wages. And as the people were in expectation, and all men mused in their hearts of John, whether he were the Christ, or not; John answered, saying unto them all, I indeed baptize you with water; but One mightier than I cometh, the latchet of whose shoes I am not worthy to unloose: He shall baptize you with the Holy Ghost and with fire: whose fan is in His hand, and He will thoroughly purge His floor, and will gather the wheat into His garner; but the chaff He will burn with fire unquenchable. And many other things in his exhortation preached he unto the people.

After the Gospel the reader says:

Deliver us not up unto the end . . . *(p. 248).*

Then Holy God . . ., *etc., and the Lord's Prayer, followed by the kontakion,* When the Lord descended today . . . *(p. 319).*

Kyrie eleison, *40 times, and the Prayer of the Hours,* Thou who at every season and every hour . . . *Then* Kyrie eleison, *3 times*; Glory be to the Father . . . Both now . . .; Greater in honour than the cherubim . . .; In the Name of the Lord, give the blessing, Father.

The priest: God be merciful unto us . . .

And the prayer, O Master and Lord, Jesus Christ our God . . . *(p. 248).*

The Typika

The same order of the service is followed as on Christmas Eve (p. 249), except that we use the kontakion, When the Lord descended today . . . *(p. 319).*

6 JANUARY

THE HOLY THEOPHANY OF OUR LORD AND GOD AND SAVIOUR JESUS CHRIST

In the Greek practice, the following rules are observed:

1. If the feast of the Theophany falls on any day of the week except Sunday or Monday, the order of service is as in the text below. On 5 January, the Royal Hours with the Typika, and then Vespers followed by the Liturgy of St. Basil and the Blessing of the Waters; at the Vigil, Great Compline, followed by Mattins; on 6 January, the Liturgy of St. John Chrysostom, followed by the second Blessing of the Waters.

2. If the Theophany falls on Sunday, the Royal Hours with the Typika are said on Friday, 4 January. On Friday evening and Saturday morning, the office of the Forefeast, 5 January, with the Liturgy of St. John Chrysostom, followed by the Blessing of the Waters. On Saturday evening the Vigil begins with Great Vespers, followed by Mattins: Great Compline is not used. On Sunday, 6 January, the Liturgy of St. Basil, followed by the second Blessing of the Waters. The normal Sunday texts of the Resurrection are omitted.

3. If the Theophany falls on Monday, the Royal Hours with the Typika are said on Friday, 3 January. On Saturday evening and Sunday morning, the office of the Sunday before the Theophany is used, together with the office of the Forefeast for 5 January; on Sunday morning, the Liturgy of St. John Chrysostom, followed by the Blessing of the Waters. On Sunday evening the Vigil begins with

Great Vespers, followed by Mattins: Great Compline is not used. On Monday, 6 January, the Liturgy of St. Basil followed by the second Blessing of the Waters.

The rules are the same in the Slav practice, except that when 5 January is a Saturday or Sunday, the Liturgy of St. John Chrysostom on that day is followed by Great Vespers of the feast, and then the Blessing of the Waters. The Vigil begins with Great Compline.

Vespers

On Lord, I have cried, *eight stichera are sung:*

TONE TWO

(*by John the Monk*)

The Forerunner beheld our Enlightenment, who has brought light to all mankind, draw near for baptism: and he rejoiced in soul while his hand trembled. And he shewed Him to the people, saying: 'Behold, the Redeemer of Israel, who sets us free from corruption.' O sinless Christ our God, glory to Thee (*twice*).

The hosts of angels were filled with fear, as they saw our Deliverer baptized by a servant and receiving witness through the coming of the Spirit. And the Father's voice was heard from on high: 'He upon whom the Forerunner lays his hand, the same is My beloved Son in whom I am well pleased.'[1] O Christ our God, glory to Thee (*twice*).

The streams of the Jordan received Thee who art the fountain, and the Comforter descended in the form of a dove. He who bowed the heavens,[2] bowed His head, and the clay cried aloud to Him that formed him: 'Why dost Thou command of me what lies beyond my power? For I have need to be baptized of Thee.'[3] O sinless Christ our God, glory to Thee (*twice*).

1 Matthew 3:17.
2 Psalm 17:10.
3 Matthew 3:14.

Wishing to save man gone astray, Thou hast not disdained to clothe Thyself in the form of a servant. For it befitted Thee, as Master and God, to take upon Thyself our nature for our sakes. For Thou, O Deliverer, hast been baptized in the flesh, making us worthy of forgiveness. Therefore we cry unto Thee: O Christ our God and Benefactor, glory to Thee (*twice*).

Glory be to the Father . . . Both now . . .

SAME TONE

(*by Byzas*)

Thou hast bowed Thine head before the Forerunner and hast crushed the heads of the dragons.[1] Thou hast descended into the waters and hast given light to all things, that they may glorify Thee, O Saviour, the Enlightenment of our souls.

Entrance with the Gospel, O joyful light, *and prokimenon of the day*.[2]

Lessons:

READING FROM GENESIS (1 : 1–13. *See p. 254*).

READING FROM EXODUS (14: 15–18, 21–23, 27–29).

And the Lord said unto Moses, Wherefore criest thou unto Me? speak unto the children of Israel, that they go forward: but lift thou up thy rod, and stretch out thine hand over the sea, and divide it: and the children of Israel shall go on dry ground through the midst of the sea. And I, behold, I will harden the hearts of the Egyptians, and they shall follow them: and I will get Me honour upon Pharaoh, and upon all his host, upon his chariots, and upon his horsemen. And the Egyptians shall know that I am the Lord, when I have gotten Me honour upon Pharaoh, upon his chariots, and upon his

[1] Psalm 73:13.

[2] On Friday, the Great Prokimenon, *Our God is in heaven and on earth* (p. 390).

horsemen. And Moses stretched out his hand over the sea; and the Lord caused the sea to go back by a strong east wind all that night, and made the sea dry land, and the waters were divided. And the children of Israel went into the midst of the sea upon the dry ground: and the waters were a wall unto them on their right hand, and on their left. And the Egyptians pursued, and went in after them to the midst of the sea, even all Pharaoh's horses, his chariots, and his horsemen. And Moses stretched forth his hand over the sea, and the sea returned to his strength when the morning appeared; and the Egyptians fled against it; and the Lord overthrew the Egyptians in the midst of the sea. And the waters returned, and covered the chariots, and the horsemen, and all the host of Pharaoh that came into the sea after them; there remained not so much as one of them. But the children of Israel walked upon dry land in the midst of the sea.

READING FROM EXODUS (15:22–16:1. *See p. 135*).

Then is said, standing:

Troparion, TONE FIVE

Thou who hast created the world art made manifest in the world, to give light to those that sit in darkness. Glory to Thee who lovest mankind.

℣. 1. God be merciful unto us, and bless us: and cause His face to shine upon us, and have mercy upon us (*Psalm* 66:2).

To give light to those that sit in darkness. Glory to Thee who lovest mankind.

℣. 2. That Thy way may be known upon earth, Thy salvation among all nations (*ibid.*, 3).

To give light to those that sit in darkness. Glory to Thee who lovest mankind.

℣. 3. Let the people praise Thee, O Lord, let all the people praise Thee: the earth hath given her increase (*ibid.*, 6–7).

To give light to those that sit in darkness. Glory to Thee who lovest mankind.

℣. 4. May God, even our own God, bless us: may God bless us, and let all the ends of the earth fear Him (*ibid.*, 7–8).

To give light to those that sit in darkness. Glory to Thee who lovest mankind.

Glory be to the Father . . . Both now . . .

Thou who hast created the world art made manifest in the world, to give light to those that sit in darkness. Glory to Thee who lovest mankind.

Lessons:

READING FROM JOSHUA THE SON OF NUN (3:7–8, 15–17).

And the Lord said unto Joshua, This day will I begin to magnify thee in the sight of all Israel, that they may know that, as I was with Moses, so I will be with thee. And thou shalt command the priests that bear the ark of the covenant, saying, When ye are come to the brink of the water of Jordan, ye shall stand still in Jordan. And it came to pass, as they that bare the ark were come unto Jordan, and the feet of the priests that bare the ark were dipped in the brim of the water (for Jordan overfloweth all his banks all the time of harvest), that the waters which came down from above stood and rose up upon an heap very far from the city Adam, that is beside Zaretan: and those that came down toward the sea of the plain, even the salt sea, failed, and were cut off: and the people passed over right against Jericho. And the priests that bare the ark of the covenant of the Lord stood firm on dry ground in the midst of Jordan, and all the Israelites passed over on dry ground, until all the people were passed clean over Jordan.

READING FROM THE FOURTH BOOK OF KINGS (2 Kings 2:6–14).

And Elijah said unto Elisha, Tarry, I pray thee, here: for the Lord hath sent me to Jordan. And he said, As the Lord liveth, and as thy soul liveth, I will not leave thee. And they two went on. And fifty men of the sons of the prophets went, and stood to view afar off: and they two stood by Jordan. And Elijah took his mantle, and wrapped it together, and smote the waters, and they were divided hither and thither, so that they two went over on dry ground. And it came to pass, when they were gone over, that Elijah said unto Elisha, Ask what I shall do for thee, before I be taken away from thee. And Elisha said, I pray thee, let a double portion of thy spirit be upon me. And he said, Thou hast asked a hard thing: nevertheless, if thou see me when I am taken from thee, it shall be so unto thee; but if not, it shall not be so. And it came to pass, as they still went on, and talked, that, behold, there appeared a chariot of fire, and horses of fire, and parted them both asunder; and Elijah went up by a whirlwind into heaven. And Elisha saw it, and he cried, My father, my father, the chariot of Israel, and the horsemen thereof. And he saw him no more: and he took hold of his own clothes, and rent them in two pieces. He took up also the mantle of Elijah that fell from him, and went back, and stood by the bank of Jordan; and he took the mantle of Elijah that fell from him, and smote the waters, and said, Where is the Lord God of Elijah? and when he also had smitten the waters, they parted hither and thither: and Elisha went over.

Reading from the Fourth Book of Kings (2 Kings 5:9–14).

So Naaman, captain of the host of the king of Assyria, came with his horses and with his chariot, and stood at the door of the house of Elisha. And Elisha sent a messenger unto him, saying, Go and wash in Jordan seven times, and thy flesh shall come again to thee, and thou shalt be clean. But Naaman was wroth, and went away, and said, Behold, I thought, He will surely come out to me, and stand, and call on the name of the Lord his God, and strike his hand over the place, and recover the leper. Are not Abana and Pharpar, rivers of Damascus, better than all the waters of Israel? may I not wash in them, and be clean? So he turned and went away in a rage. And his servants came near, and spake unto him, and said, My father, if the prophet had bid thee do some great thing, wouldest thou not have done it? How much rather then, when he saith to thee, Wash and be clean? Then went he down, and dipped himself seven times in Jordan, according to the saying of the man of God: and his flesh came again like unto the flesh of a little child, and he was clean.

Then is said, standing:

Troparion, TONE SIX

In the abundance of Thy mercy Thou hast made Thyself manifest to sinners and publicans, O our Saviour. Where indeed should Thy light have shone save upon those that sit in darkness? Glory to Thee.

℣. 1. The Lord is King, and hath put on glorious apparel: the Lord hath put on His apparel and girded Himself with strength (*Psalm* 92:1).

Where indeed should Thy light have shone save upon those that sit in darkness? Glory to Thee.

℣. 2. The floods have lifted up, O Lord, the floods have lifted up their voice: the floods lift up their waves at the voice of many waters (*ibid.*, 3–4).

Where indeed should Thy light have shone save upon those that sit in darkness? Glory to Thee.

℣. 3. Wonderful are the mighty waves of the sea; wonderful is the Lord on high. Thy testimonies are very sure (*ibid.*, 4–5).

Where indeed should Thy light have shone save upon those that sit in darkness? Glory to Thee.

℣. 4. Holiness becometh Thine house, O Lord, for ever (*ibid.*, 5).

Where indeed should Thy light have shone save upon those that sit in darkness? Glory to Thee.

Glory be to the Father . . . Both now . . .

In the abundance of Thy mercy Thou hast made Thyself manifest to sinners and publicans, O our Saviour. Where indeed should Thy light have shone save upon those that sit in darkness? Glory to Thee.

Lessons:

READING FROM THE PROPHET ISAIAH (1:16–20. *See p. 323*).

READING FROM GENESIS (32:1–10).

And Jacob went on his way, and the angels of God met him. And when Jacob saw them, he said, This is God's host: and he called the name of that place Mahanaim. And Jacob sent messengers before him to Esau his brother unto the land of Seir, the country of Edom. And he commanded them, saying, Thus shall ye speak unto my Lord Esau; Thy servant Jacob saith thus, I have sojourned with Laban, and stayed there until now: and I have oxen, and asses, flocks, and menservants, and womenservants: and I have sent to tell my lord, that I may find grace in thy sight. And the messengers returned to Jacob, saying, We came to thy brother Esau, and also he cometh to meet thee, and four hundred men with him. Then Jacob was greatly afraid and distressed: and he divided the people that was with him, and the flocks, and herds, and the camels, into two bands; and said, If Esau come to the one company, and smite it, then the other company which is left shall escape. And Jacob said, O God of my father Abraham, and God of my father Isaac, the Lord which saidst unto me, Return unto thy country, and to thy kindred, and I will deal well with thee: I am not worthy of the least of all the mercies, and of all the truth, which Thou hast shewed unto Thy servant; for with my staff I passed over this Jordan.

READING FROM EXODUS (2:5–10).

And the daughter of Pharaoh came down to wash herself at the river; and her maidens walked along by the river's side; and when she saw the ark among the flags, she sent her maid to fetch it. And when she had opened it, she saw the child: and, behold, the babe wept. And she had compassion on him, and said, This is one of the Hebrews' children. Then said his sister to Pharaoh's daughter, Shall I go and call to thee a nurse of the Hebrew women, that she may nurse the child for thee? And Pharaoh's daughter said to her, Go. And the maid went and called the child's mother. And Pharaoh's daughter said unto her, Take this child away, and nurse it for me, and I will give thee thy wages. And the woman took the child, and nursed it. And the child grew, and she brought him unto Pharaoh's daughter, and he became her son. And she called his name Moses: and she said, Because I drew him out of the water.

Reading from Judges (6:36–40).

And Gideon said unto God, If Thou wilt save Israel by mine hand, as Thou hast said, behold, I will put a fleece of wool in the floor; and if the dew be on the fleece only, and it be dry upon all the earth beside, then shall I know that Thou wilt save Israel by mine hand, as Thou hast said. And it was so: for he rose up early on the morrow, and thrust the fleece together, and wringed the dew out of the fleece, a bowl full of water. And Gideon said unto God, Let not Thine anger be hot against me, and I will speak but this once: let me prove, I pray Thee, but this once with the fleece; let it now be dry only upon the fleece, and upon all the ground let there be dew. And God did so that night: for it was dry upon the fleece only, and there was dew on all the ground.

Reading from the Third Book of Kings (1 Kings 18:30–39).

And Elijah said unto all the people, Come near unto me. And all the people came near unto him. And he repaired the altar of the Lord that was broken down. And Elijah took twelve stones, according to the number of the tribes of the sons of Jacob, unto whom the word of the Lord came, saying, Israel shall be thy name: and with the stones he built an altar in the name of the Lord: and he made a trench about the altar, as great as would contain two measures of seed. And he put the wood in order, and cut the bullock in pieces, and laid him on the wood, and said, Fill four barrels with water, and pour it on the burnt sacrifice, and on the wood. And he said, Do it the second time. And they did it the second time. And he said, Do it the third time. And they did it the third time. And the water ran round about the altar; and he filled the trench also with water. And it came to pass at the time of the offering of the evening sacrifice, that Elijah the prophet came near, and said, Lord God of Abraham, Isaac, and of Israel, let it be known this day that Thou art God in Israel, and that I am Thy servant, and that I have done all these things at Thy word. Hear me, O Lord, hear me, that this people may know that Thou art the Lord God, and that Thou hast turned their heart back again. Then the fire of the Lord fell, and consumed the burnt sacrifice, and the wood, and the stones, and the dust, and licked up the water that was in the trench. And when all the people saw it, they fell on their faces: and they said, The Lord, He is the God; the Lord, He is the God.

Reading from the Fourth Book of Kings (2 Kings 2:19–22).

And the men of the city of Jericho said unto Elisha, Behold, I pray thee, the situation of this city is pleasant, as my lord seeth: but the water is naught, and the ground barren. And he said, Bring me a new cruse, and put salt therein. And they brought it to him. And he went forth unto the spring of the waters, and cast the salt in there, and said, Thus saith the Lord, I have healed these waters; there shall not be from thence any more death or barren land. So the waters were healed unto this day, according to the saying of Elisha which he spake.

READING FROM THE PROPHET ISAIAH (49:8–15. *See p. 333*).

Then follows the Small Litany, and after it the trisagion.

Then the Prokimenon before the Epistle:

TONE THREE

The Lord is my light and my salvation: whom shall I fear? (*Psalm* 26:1)

℣. The Lord is the defender of my life: of whom shall I be afraid? (*ibid.*)

READING FROM THE FIRST EPISTLE OF PAUL TO THE CORINTHIANS (9:19–27).

Brethren: though I be free from all men, yet have I made myself servant unto all, that I might gain the more. And unto the Jews I became as a Jew, that I might gain the Jews; to them that are under the law, as under the law, that I might gain them that are under the law; to them that are without law, as without law (being not without law to God, but under the law to Christ), that I might gain them that are without law. To the weak became I as weak, that I might gain the weak: I am made all things to all men, that I might by all means save some. And this I do for the gospel's sake, that I might be partaker thereof with you. Know ye not that they which run in a race run all, but one receiveth the prize? So run, that ye may obtain. And every man that striveth for the mastery is temperate in all things. Now they do it to obtain a corruptible crown; but we an incorruptible. I therefore so run, not as uncertainly; so fight I, not as one that beateth the air: but I keep under my body, and bring it into subjection: lest that by any means, when I have preached to others, I myself should be a castaway.

Alleluia, TONE SIX

℣ 1. My heart is inditing a good matter: I speak of the things which I have made to the King (*Psalm* 44:2).

℣ 2. Thou art fairer than the children of men (*ibid.*, 3).

READING FROM THE HOLY GOSPEL ACCORDING TO LUKE (3:1–18. *See p. 334*).

And then the Liturgy of St. Basil the Great.

The Great Blessing of the Waters

After the prayer behind the ambon at the end of the Liturgy, the clergy go in procession, with lights and incense, to the place where the Blessing of the Waters is to be held,[1] *the priest holding in his hand the Precious Cross. Meanwhile the following stichera are sung:*

TONE EIGHT

(*by Sophronios, Patriarch of Jerusalem*)

The voice of the Lord upon the waters cries aloud saying: 'Come ye all, and receive the Spirit of wisdom, the Spirit of understanding, the Spirit of the fear of God,[2] from Christ who is made manifest' (*3 times*).

Today the nature of the waters is sanctified, and the Jordan is parted in two; it holds back the stream of its own waters, seeing the Master wash Himself (*twice*).

O Christ the King, Thou hast come unto the river as a man, and in Thy goodness Thou dost make haste to receive the baptism of a servant at the hands of the Forerunner, for the sake of our sins, O Thou who lovest mankind (*twice*).

Glory be to the Father . . . Both now . . .

[1] If there is a permanent font in the church, the Blessing takes place there. In normal practice today, a large vessel of water is prepared on a special table in the centre of the church.

[2] Isaiah 11:2.

SAME TONE

At the voice of one crying in the wilderness, 'Prepare ye the way of the Lord',[1] Thou hast come, O Lord, taking the form of a servant,[2] and Thou who knowest not sin dost ask for baptism. The waters saw Thee and were afraid;[3] the Forerunner was seized with trembling and cried aloud, saying: 'How shall the lamp illuminate the Light? How shall the servant set his hand upon the Master? O Saviour who takest away the sin of the world, sanctify both me and the waters.'

Lessons:

READING FROM THE PROPHET ISAIAH (35:1–10. *See p. 317*).

READING FROM THE PROPHET ISAIAH (55:1–13).

Thus saith the Lord: Ho, every one that thirsteth, come ye to the waters, and he that hath no money; come ye, buy, and eat; yea, come, buy wine and milk without money and without price. Wherefore do ye spend money for that which is not bread? and your labour for that which satisfieth not? hearken diligently unto me, and eat ye that which is good, and let your soul delight itself in fatness. Incline your ear, and come unto me: hear, and your soul shall live; and I will make an everlasting covenant with you, even the sure mercies of David. Behold, I have given him for a witness to the people, a leader and commander to the people. Behold, thou shalt call a nation that thou knowest not, and nations that knew not thee shall run unto thee because of the Lord thy God, and for the Holy One of Israel; for He hath glorified thee. Seek ye the Lord while He may be found, call ye upon Him while He is near: let the wicked forsake his way, and the unrighteous man his thoughts: and let him return unto the Lord, and He will have mercy upon him; and to our God, for

[1] Mark 1:3.
[2] Philippians 2:7.
[3] Psalm 76:17.

He will abundantly pardon. For My thoughts are not your thoughts, neither are your ways My ways, saith the Lord. For as the heavens are higher than the earth, so are My ways higher than your ways, and My thoughts than your thoughts. For as the rain cometh down, and the snow from heaven, and returneth not thither, but watereth the earth, and maketh it bring forth and bud, that it may give seed to the sower, and bread to the eater: so shall My word be that goeth forth out of My mouth: it shall not return unto Me void, but it shall accomplish that which I please, and it shall prosper in the thing whereto I sent it. For ye shall go out with joy, and be led forth with peace: the mountains and the hills shall break forth before you into singing, and all the trees of the field shall clap their hands. Instead of the thorn shall come up the fir tree, and instead of the brier shall come up the myrtle tree: and it shall be to the Lord for a name, for an everlasting sign that shall not be cut off.

READING FROM THE PROPHET ISAIAH (12:3–6. *See p. 328*).

Prokimenon, TONE THREE

The Lord is my light and my salvation: whom shall I fear? (*Psalm* 26:1)

℣. The Lord is the defender of my life: of whom shall I be afraid? (*ibid.*)

READING FROM THE FIRST EPISTLE OF PAUL TO THE CORINTHIANS (10:1–4).

Moreover, brethren, I would not that ye should be ignorant, how that all our fathers were under the cloud, and all passed through the sea; and were all baptized unto Moses in the cloud and in the sea; and did all eat the same spiritual meat; and did all drink the same spiritual drink: for they drank of that spiritual Rock that followed them: and that Rock was Christ.

Alleluia, *TONE FOUR*

℣ 1. The voice of the Lord is upon the waters (*Psalm* 28:3).

℣ 2. The God of glory thundered, the Lord is upon many waters (*ibid*.).

READING FROM THE HOLY GOSPEL ACCORDING TO MARK (1:9–11).

And it came to pass in those days, that Jesus came from Nazareth of Galilee, and was baptized of John in Jordan. And straightway coming up out of the water, He saw the heavens opened, and the Spirit like a dove descending upon Him: and there came a voice from heaven, saying, Thou art My beloved Son, in whom I am well pleased.

Then the deacon sings the Litany, In peace let us pray to the Lord, *as far as the petition* For those that sail the seas, for those that travel . . ., *after which he adds these petitions:*

For this water, that it may be sanctified by the might and operation and descent of the Holy Spirit, let us pray to the Lord.

For these waters, that the cleansing operation of the Trinity supreme in being may come down upon them, let us pray to the Lord.

For these waters, that they may be given the grace of redemption and the blessing of the Jordan [by the power and operation and descent of the Holy Spirit],[1] let us pray to the Lord.

[That Satan may be swiftly crushed beneath our feet, and that every counsel that is directed against us by the Evil One may be made of no effect, let us pray to the Lord.]

[That He will deliver us from every attack and temptation of the Adversary, and make us worthy of the good things that are promised, let us pray to the Lord.]

[1] The portions within brackets are found in the Slav text only.

That we may be enlightened by the light of knowledge and godliness through the descent of the Holy Spirit, let us pray to the Lord.

[That the Lord may send down the blessing of the Jordan and sanctify these waters, let us pray to the Lord.]

For this water, that it may become a gift of sanctification, a remission of sins, for the healing of soul and body and for every purpose that is expedient, let us pray to the Lord.

For this water, that it may become a fountain springing up unto eternal life, let us pray to the Lord.

For this water, that it may serve to the averting of every evil purpose of enemies visible and invisible, let us pray to the Lord.

For those who draw from this water and take it for the sanctification of their dwellings, let us pray to the Lord.

For this water, that it may bestow cleansing of soul and body upon all who draw it with faith and partake of it, let us pray to the Lord.

That we may be deemed worthy to be filled with holiness through partaking of these waters, by the invisible manifestation of the Holy Spirit, let us pray to the Lord.

That the Lord our God may hearken unto the entreaty of us sinners and have mercy upon us, let us pray to the Lord.

For our deliverance from every tribulation, wrath, danger, and necessity, let us pray to the Lord.

Succour and save us, have mercy upon us and protect us, O God, with Thy grace.

Commemorating our all-holy, undefiled, most blessed, and glorified Lady the Theotokos and ever-Virgin Mary, with all the saints, let us commend ourselves and one another and our whole life to Christ our God.

Secret prayer recited by the priest during this Litany:[1]

[1] If there is no deacon, the secret prayer is said by the priest during the reading of the lessons.

O Lord Jesus Christ, the Only-begotten Son, who art in the bosom of the Father, True God, source of life and immortality, Light of Light, who camest into the world to enlighten it, shine upon our understanding with Thy Holy Spirit and accept us who offer unto Thee glory and thanksgiving for all Thy great and wondrous works from all ages, and for Thy saving dispensation in these last times. For Thou hast clothed Thyself in our poor and infirm nature, and hast submitted Thyself to servitude, Thou who art King of all; and moreover Thou hast accepted to be baptized in the Jordan by the hand of a servant, that having sanctified the nature of the waters, O sinless Lord, Thou mightest lead us to a new birth through water and Spirit, and restore us again to our original freedom. Keeping feast in remembrance of this divine mystery, we entreat Thee, O Master who lovest mankind: sprinkle upon us, Thine unworthy servants, according to Thy divine promise, cleansing water, the gift of Thy compassion; grant that the petition of us sinners over this water may be acceptable unto Thy goodness, and that thereby Thy blessing may be granted to us and to all Thy faithful people unto the glory of Thy holy and venerated Name. For unto Thee, together with Thy Father who is without beginning, and Thy most holy, good, and life-giving Spirit, are due all glory, honour, and worship, now, and ever, and unto the ages of ages. Amen.

Then the priest says aloud the following prayer, composed by Sophronios, Patriarch of Jerusalem.[1]

O Trinity supreme in being, in goodness, and in Godhead, almighty, who watchest over all, invisible, incomprehensible, Maker of spiritual beings and rational natures, innate Goodness, Light that none can approach and that lightens every

[1] The first part of this prayer, *O Trinity supreme in being*, is found only in the Greek books: the Slav books begin at the words *Great art Thou, O Lord* (p. 356).

man that comes into the world: Shine also upon me Thine unworthy servant. Enlighten the eyes of my understanding that I may make bold to sing the praises of Thy measureless beneficence and Thy might. May the prayer be acceptable that I offer for the people here present. Let not my faults hinder Thy Holy Spirit from coming to this place, but suffer me now uncondemned to cry to Thee, O most good Lord, and to say:

We glorify Thee, O Master who lovest mankind, almighty, pre-eternal King. We glorify Thee, the Creator and Maker of all. We glorify Thee, O Only-begotten Son of God, born without father from Thy Mother, and without mother from Thy Father.

In the preceding feast we saw Thee as a child, while in the present we behold Thee full-grown, our God made manifest, perfect God from perfect God. For today the time of the feast is at hand for us: the choir of saints assembles with us and angels join with men in keeping festival. Today the grace of the Holy Spirit in the form of a dove descended upon the waters. Today the Sun that never sets has risen and the world is filled with splendour by the light of the Lord. Today the moon shines upon the world with the brightness of its rays. Today the glittering stars make the inhabited earth fair with the radiance of their shining. Today the clouds drop down upon mankind the dew of righteousness from on high. Today the Uncreated of His own will accepts the laying on of hands from His own creature. Today the Prophet and Forerunner approaches the Master, but stands before Him with trembling, seeing the condescension of God towards us. Today the waters of the Jordan are transformed into healing by the coming of the Lord. Today the whole creation is watered by mystical streams. Today the transgressions of men are washed away by the waters of the Jordan. Today Paradise has been opened to men and the Sun of Righteousness shines down upon us. Today the bitter water, as once with Moses and the people of Israel, is changed to sweetness by the coming of the Lord. Today we have been released from our ancient lamentation, and as the new Israel we have found salvation. Today we have been delivered from darkness and illuminated with the light of the knowledge of God. Today the blinding mist of the world is dispersed by the Epiphany of our God. Today the whole creation shines with light from on high. Today error is laid low and the coming of the Master has made for us a way of salvation. Today things above keep feast with things below, and things below commune with things above. Today the triumphant assembly of the Orthodox keeps this holy festival with great joy. Today the Master hastens towards baptism that He may lift man up to the heights. Today He that bows not, bows down to His own servant that He may set us free from bondage. Today we have purchased the Kingdom of Heaven: for the Lord's Kingdom shall have no end. Today earth and sea share the joy of the world, and the world is filled with gladness. The waters saw Thee, O God, the waters saw Thee and were afraid. The Jordan turned back, seeing the fire of the Godhead descending bodily and entering its stream. The Jordan turned back, beholding the Holy Spirit coming down in the form of a dove and flying about Thee. The Jordan turned back, seeing the Invisible made visible, the Creator made flesh, the Master in the form of a servant. The Jordan turned back and the mountains skipped, looking upon God in the flesh; and the clouds gave voice, marvelling at Him who was come, the Light of Light, true God of true God. For today in the Jordan they saw the triumph of the Master; they saw Him drown in the Jordan the death of disobedience, the sting of error, and the chains of hell, and bestow upon the world the baptism of salvation.

Therefore, sinner and unworthy servant though I am, I recount the majesty of Thy wonders and, seized with fear, in compunction I cry aloud to Thee:

The priest then says in a louder voice:

Great art Thou, O Lord, and marvellous are Thy works: no words suffice to sing the praise of Thy wonders (*3 times*).[1]

For Thou by Thine own will hast brought all things out of nothingness into being, by Thy power Thou dost hold together the creation, and by Thy providence Thou dost govern the world. Of four elements hast Thou compounded the creation: with four seasons hast Thou crowned the circuit of the year. All the spiritual powers tremble before Thee. The sun sings Thy praises; the moon glorifies Thee; the stars supplicate before Thee; the light obeys Thee; the deeps are afraid at Thy presence; the fountains are Thy servants. Thou hast stretched out the heavens like a curtain; Thou hast established the earth upon the waters; Thou hast walled about the sea with sand. Thou hast poured forth the air that living things may breathe. The angelic powers minister to Thee; the choirs of archangels worship Thee; the many-eyed cherubim and the six-winged seraphim, standing round Thee and flying about Thee, hide their faces in fear of Thine unapproachable glory. Thou, the uncircumscribed God without beginning and beyond speech, hast come upon earth, taking the form of a servant and being made in the likeness of man. For Thou, O Master, in Thy merciful compassion couldst not bear to see mankind beneath the tyranny of the devil, but Thou hast come and saved us. We confess Thy grace, we proclaim Thy mercy, we hide not Thy beneficence. Thou hast set free the offspring of our kind. Thou hast hallowed a Virgin womb by Thy Nativity. At Thine Epiphany the whole creation sang Thy praises. For Thou, our God, hast appeared on earth and dwelt among men, Thou hast sanctified the streams of Jordan, sending down from on high the most Holy Spirit, and Thou hast broken the heads of the dragons hidden therein.

[1] In the Greek use, each time the priest says these words, the choir sings *Glory to Thee, O Lord, glory to Thee.*

The priest makes the sign of the Cross over the water three times, saying:

Therefore, O King who lovest mankind, do Thou Thyself be present now as then through the descent of Thy Holy Spirit, and sanctify this water (*3 times*).

And confer upon it the grace of redemption, the blessing of the Jordan. Make it a source of incorruption, a gift of sanctification, a remission of sins, a protection against disease, a destruction to demons, inaccessible to the adverse powers and filled with angelic strength: that all who draw from it and partake of it may have it for the cleansing of their soul and body, for the healing of their passions, for the sanctification of their dwellings, and for every purpose that is expedient. For Thou art our God, who hast renewed through water and Spirit our nature grown old through sin. Thou art our God, who hast drowned sin through water in the days of Noah. Thou art our God who, through the waters of the sea, at Moses' hand hast set free the Hebrew nation from the bondage of Pharaoh. Thou art our God who hast cleft the rock in the wilderness: the waters gushed out, the streams overflowed, and Thou hast satisfied Thy thirsty people. Thou art our God who by water and fire through Elijah hast brought back Israel from the error of Baal.

Do Thou Thyself, O Master, now as then sanctify this water by Thy Holy Spirit (*3 times*).

Grant to all those who touch it, who anoint themselves with it or drink from it, sanctification, blessing, cleansing, and health.

And save, O Lord, Thy servants our faithful rulers (*3 times*).

Keep them in peace under Thy protection; put under their feet every enemy and adversary; bestow upon them whatsoever they ask unto salvation and eternal life.

Remember, O Lord, our most holy Patriarch (*name*), our Bishop (*name*), and all the priests, the diaconate in Christ, the whole order of clergy, and the people here present, together with all our brethren absent for a just cause. Have mercy upon them and upon us according to Thy great mercy.

So, by the elements, by the angels and by men, by things visible and invisible, may Thy most holy Name be glorified, together with the Father and the Holy Spirit, now, and ever, and unto the ages of ages. Amen.

Priest: Peace be with you all.

Choir: And with Thy spirit.

Deacon: Bow your heads to the Lord.

Choir: To Thee, O Lord.

The priest says this prayer secretly:

Incline Thine ear and hearken unto us, O Lord who hast accepted baptism in the Jordan and hast sanctified the waters. Bless us all who by the bowing of our heads outwardly show Thee our servitude; and count us worthy to be filled with Thy sanctification through partaking of this water and being sprinkled with it, and may it bring us, O Lord, health of soul and body.

Aloud:

For Thou art the sanctification of our souls and bodies, and unto Thee we ascribe glory, thanksgiving, and worship, with Thy Father without beginning and Thy most holy, good, and life-giving Spirit, now, and ever, and unto the ages of ages. Amen.

The priest now makes the sign of the Cross over the water with the Precious Cross: then, holding the Cross upright in both hands, he plunges it into the water, and lifts it from the water once again. As he does this, he sings the troparion of the feast:[1]

[1] Alternatively, the priest may sing only the opening words of the troparion, which is then taken up by the choir.

TONE ONE

When Thou, O Lord, wast baptized in the Jordan, the worship of the Trinity was made manifest. For the voice of the Father bore witness unto Thee, calling Thee the beloved Son, and the Spirit in the form of a dove confirmed His word as sure and steadfast. O Christ our God who hast appeared and enlightened the world, glory to Thee.

The priest then plunges the Cross a second and a third time in the water, doing as before: and the troparion is repeated a second and a third time. Next he dips a branch of basil in the water and sprinkles the four corners of the church.

The rest of the clergy, and then the people, approach and kiss the Cross, and the priest sprinkles water on the head of each one with the branch of basil. Clergy and people also drink from the water which has been blessed. During this time the choir continues to sing the troparion.

Then the following sticheron is sung:

TONE SIX

Ye faithful, let us praise the greatness of God's dispensation towards us. For, becoming man on account of our transgression, He who alone is clean and undefiled was cleansed in the Jordan that we might be made clean, sanctifying us and the waters, and crushing the heads of the dragons in the water.[1] Let us then draw water in gladness, O brethren:[2] for upon those who draw with faith, the grace of the Spirit is invisibly bestowed by Christ the God and Saviour of our souls.

The choir sings Blessed be the Name of the Lord, *and Psalm 33 is read: and so the Liturgy concludes in the usual way.*

After the Dismissal we sing the megalynarion of the feast.[3]

[1] Psalm 73:13.
[2] Isaiah 12:3.
[3] Slav use only. See p. 364.

The Vigil Service

Great Compline

Great Compline is read as at Christmas (see pp. 261–2). In the first part of the service we sing the troparion of the feast, When Thou, O Lord, wast baptized in the Jordan . . . *(p. 359). In the second part we sing the kontakion of the feast,* Thou hast appeared today to the inhabited earth . . . *(p. 375).*

Immediately after the Doxology there follows the Lity:

TONE FOUR

(by Cosmas the Monk)

He who covers Himself with light as with a garment[1] has vouchsafed for our sakes to become as we are. Today He is covered by the streams of the Jordan, though He has no need to be cleansed by them: but through the cleansing that He Himself receives He bestows regeneration on us. O wonder! Without fire He casts anew and without shattering He refashions; and He saves those who are enlightened in Him, Christ our God, the Saviour of our souls.

SAME TONE

John the Baptist saw Thee draw near, who cleansest by Spirit and by fire the sin of the world, and he cried aloud in fear and trembling, saying: 'I dare not touch Thine immaculate head. Do Thou, O Master, sanctify me by Thine Epiphany, O Thou who alone lovest mankind.'

SAME TONE

Come, let us do as the wise virgins; come, let us go and meet the Master who has appeared: for as a Bridegroom has

[1] Psalm 103:2.

He come forth to John. The Jordan, seeing Thee, crouched in fear and stopped; John cried aloud: 'I dare not touch Thine immortal head.' The Spirit came down in the form of a dove to hallow the waters, and a voice cried from on high: 'This is My Son who is come into the world to save mankind.' O Lord, glory to Thee.

SAME TONE

Christ is baptized: He comes up out of the waters, and with Him He carries up the world. He sees the heavens opened that Adam closed against himself and his posterity. The Spirit bears witness to His divinity, for He hastens towards His like; and a voice sounds from heaven, for it is from heaven that He has come down to whom this testimony is given, and He is the Saviour of our souls.

SAME TONE

The hand of the Baptist trembled, when it touched Thine immaculate head: the river Jordan turned back, not daring to minister to Thee. For how could he that stood in awe of Joshua the son of Nun[1] not be afraid before the Maker of Joshua? But Thou, our Saviour, hast fulfilled all that was appointed, that so Thou mightest save the world by Thine Epiphany, O Thou who alone lovest mankind.

Glory be to the Father . . .

TONE EIGHT

(*by John the Monk*)

O Lord, wishing to fulfil that which Thou hast appointed from eternity, Thou hast received from all the creation ministers at this Thy mystery: Gabriel from among the angels, the Virgin from among men, the Star from among the heavens, and Jordan from among the waters; and in its stream Thou

[1] Joshua 3:7–17.

hast washed away the transgression of the world. O Saviour, glory to Thee.

Both now . . .

SAME TONE

(by Anatolios)

Today the creation is enlightened. Today all nature is glad, things of heaven and things upon earth. Angels and men mingle with one another, for where the King is present, there His army also goes. Let us run, then, to the Jordan; let us all see how John baptizes a sinless and uncreated head. Therefore let us cry aloud with one accord, echoing the voice of the apostle: The grace of God that brings salvation to all men has appeared,[1] shining upon the faithful and granting them great mercy.

Aposticha:

TONE TWO

(by Anatolios)

Seeing Thee, O Christ our God, draw near to him in the river Jordan, John said: 'Why art Thou, who hast no defilement, come to Thy servant, O Lord? In whose name shall I baptize Thee? Of the Father? But Thou dost bear Him in Thyself. Of the Son? But Thou art Thyself this Son made flesh. Of the Holy Spirit? But Thou knowest that through Thine own mouth Thou dost give Him to the faithful.' O God who hast appeared, have mercy upon us.

℣. The sea saw it and fled: Jordan was driven back (*Psalm* 113:3).

The waters saw Thee, O God: the waters saw Thee and were afraid. For the cherubim cannot lift their eyes upon Thy glory, nor can the seraphim gaze upon Thee: but standing by Thee in fear, the first carry Thee and the second glorify Thy might. With them, O merciful Lord, we

[1] Titus 2:11.

proclaim Thy praises and we say: O God who hast appeared, have mercy upon us.

℣. What ailed thee, O thou sea, that thou fleddest? thou Jordan, that thou wast driven back? (*ibid.*, 5)

Today the Maker of heaven and earth comes in the flesh to the Jordan. He who is sinless asks for baptism, that He may cleanse the world from the error of the enemy. He who is the Master of all is baptized by a servant, and He gives mankind cleansing through water. Unto Him let us cry aloud: O God who hast appeared to us, glory to Thee.

Glory be to the Father . . . Both now . . .

TONE SIX

(*by Theophanes*)

Seeing the Sun that came from a Virgin asking for baptism in the Jordan, the shining Lamp that was born of a barren woman cried to Him in fear and joy: 'Sanctify me, O Master, by Thy divine Epiphany.'

Apolytikion (troparion) of the feast:

TONE ONE

When Thou, O Lord, wast baptized in the Jordan, the worship of the Trinity was made manifest. For the voice of the Father bore witness unto Thee, calling Thee the beloved Son, and the Spirit in the form of a dove confirmed His word as sure and steadfast. O Christ our God who hast appeared and enlightened the world, glory to Thee.

And the Dismissal.

Mattins

After the first reading from the Psalter, sessional hymn:

TONE THREE

Thou hast appeared, O Saviour Christ, in the Jordan and wast baptized by the Forerunner: and testimony was borne to

Thee, that Thou art the beloved Son. So wast Thou revealed as coeternal with the Father, and the Holy Spirit descended upon Thee. Enlightened by Thee, we cry: Glory to the God in Trinity.

Glory be to the Father . . . Both now . . .

Repeat.[1]

After the second reading from the Psalter, sessional hymn:

TONE FOUR

O river Jordan, what hast thou seen to be amazed? 'I have seen Him naked who cannot be seen, and I trembled', said he. 'How should I not tremble before Him and turn back?' The angels, beholding Him, were afraid: heaven was filled with wonder and the earth shook, the sea and all things visible and invisible withdrew. Christ has appeared in the Jordan to sanctify the waters.

Glory be to the Father . . . Both now . . .

Repeat.[2]

After the polyeleos, the megalynarion:[3]

We magnify Thee, O Christ the Giver of life, who for our

[1] But in the Slav practice, instead of repeating *Thou hast appeared, O Saviour* . . ., we use the sessional hymn sung by the Greeks after the polyeleos, *Thou hast sanctified the streams of the Jordan* . . . (p. 365).

[2] The Slav use is as follows:

TONE FIVE

Thou hast wrapped Thyself in the streams of Jordan, O Thou who dost gloriously clothe Thyself in light, and Thou hast renewed therein the nature of Adam, broken by evil disobedience, O Word of God. Therefore we praise Thee and glorify Thy holy Epiphany.

Glory be to the Father . . . Both now . . .

TONE FOUR

O river Jordan, what hast thou seen . . .

[3] In the Slav use only.

sakes wast in the flesh this day baptized by John in the waters of the Jordan.

℣. God be merciful unto us, and bless us: and cause His face to shine upon us, and have mercy upon us (*Psalm* 66:2).

We magnify Thee . . .

℣. The voice of the Lord is upon the waters: the God of glory thundered, the Lord is upon many waters (*Psalm* 28:3).

We magnify Thee . . .

Glory be to the Father . . . Both now . . .

Alleluia, alleluia, alleluia, glory be to Thee, O God (*3 times*).

We magnify Thee . . .

Sessional hymn:

TONE FOUR

Thou hast sanctified the streams of the Jordan and crushed the power of sin, O Christ our God. Thou hast bowed Thine head beneath the hand of the Forerunner, and hast delivered mankind from error. Therefore we pray Thee: Save Thy world.

Glory be to the Father . . . Both now . . .

Repeat.[1]

[1] The Slav use is as follows:

TONE FOUR

O ye faithful, come and see where Christ was baptized, that we may further follow Him to the river Jordan, and so may draw near to the voice crying in the wilderness, and behold there how the Creator of Adam suffers His head to be touched by the hand of a servant in His ineffable lovingkindness. And let us cry aloud to Him: Thou art come and hast appeared in Jordan to sanctify the waters.

Glory be to the Father . . . Both now. . .

Repeat.

The first antiphon of the hymn of degrees in Tone Four.

Prokimenon: *TONE FOUR*

The sea saw it and fled: Jordan was driven back (*Psalm* 113:3).

℣. What ailed thee, O thou sea, that thou fleddest? thou Jordan, that thou wast driven back? (*ibid.*, 5)

Let everything that hath breath . . .

Reading from the Holy Gospel according to Mark (1:9–11. *See p. 351*).

Psalm 50.

Glory be to the Father . . .

TONE TWO

Today let all things greatly rejoice: Christ has appeared in Jordan.

Both now . . .

Today let all things . . .

Have mercy upon me . . .

TONE SIX

God the Word appeared to mankind in the flesh. Ready for baptism, He stood in the Jordan and the Forerunner said to Him: 'How shall I stretch forth my hand and touch the head of Him that rules all things? Though Thou art the child of Mary, yet do I know Thee to be the pre-eternal God. Thou whose praises the seraphim sing dost walk upon the earth. And I who am but a servant know not how to baptize the Master.' O Lord past all understanding, glory to Thee.

Two Canons are used: the first by St. Cosmas in eight troparia, including the irmos, and the second by St. John of Damascus in six, likewise including the irmos. The two irmoi are then repeated as katavasia at the end of each canticle. Before the troparia we say, Glory to Thee, our God, glory to Thee.

MATTINS

Canticle One

First Canon

TONE TWO

(**Irmos**) The Lord mighty in battle uncovered the foundations of the deep and led His servants on dry ground; but He covered their adversaries with the waters, for He has been glorified.

The Lord, King of the ages, in the streams of the Jordan formed Adam anew, who was fallen into corruption, and He broke in pieces the heads of the dragons that were hidden there:[1] for He has been glorified.

The Lord, incarnate of the Virgin, having clothed material flesh with the immaterial fire of His divinity, wraps Himself in the waters of Jordan, for He has been glorified.

The Lord who purges away the filth of men was cleansed in Jordan for their sake, having of His own will made Himself like unto them, while still remaining that which He was; and He enlightens those in darkness, for He has been glorified.

Second Canon

(*written originally in iambic verse*)

SAME TONE

(**Irmos**) Israel passed through the storm-tossed deep of the sea,
That God had turned into dry land:
But the dark waters completely covered
The chief captains of Egypt in a watery grave
Through the mighty strength of the right hand of the Master.

When the Light of the Dawn[2] shone forth upon mortal men,

[1] Psalm 73:13.
[2] John the Baptist.

Coming from the desert to the streams of the Jordan,
Thou, the King of the Sun, hast bowed Thy head before him,
That so Thou mightest snatch our forefather from the land of darkness,
And cleanse the creation from all its filth.

O Word without beginning, Thou hast buried man with Thee in the stream:[1]
He was corrupted by error, but Thou makest Him new again.
And the Father testified to Thee ineffably,
Saying with mighty voice:
'This is My beloved Child, equal to Me by nature.'

Canticle Three

First Canon

(**Irmos**) The Lord who gives strength to our kings and exalts the horn of His anointed, is born of a Virgin and comes to baptism. Therefore let us, the faithful, cry aloud: None is holy as our God and none is righteous save Thee, O Lord.

Rejoice today, O Church of Christ, that before wast barren and sadly childless.[2] For through water and the Spirit[3] sons have been born to thee, who raise their cry in faith: None is holy as our God and none is righteous save Thee, O Lord.

With a loud voice the Forerunner cries in the wilderness: 'Prepare ye the way of Christ and make straight the paths for our God,[4] raising your cry in faith: None is holy as our God and none is righteous save Thee, O Lord.'

1 Romans 6:4.
2 Isaiah 54:1.
3 John 3:5.
4 Isaiah 40:3; Matthew 3:3.

Second Canon

(Irmos) From the ancient snares have we all been set loose,
And the jaws of the devouring lions have been broken:[1]
Let us, then, rejoice exceedingly and open wide our mouths,
Weaving with words a melody to the Word
Whose delight it is to bestow gifts upon us.

He who once assumed the appearance of a malignant serpent
And implanted death in the creation,
Is now cast into darkness by Christ's coming in the flesh:
And by assailing the Master, the Dawn that has shone forth upon us,
He crushes his own hateful and loathsome head.

The Master draws to Himself the nature made by God,
Which had been overcome by the tyranny of greed.
A new birth He grants to the dwellers upon earth, fashioning them afresh,
Thereby accomplishing a glorious work:
For He has come to deliver and protect mankind.

Ypakoë

TONE FIVE

When Thou broughtest light to all things by Thine Epiphany, the salt sea of unbelief fled and Jordan was turned back towards its source,[2] thereby exalting us to heaven. By

[1] Psalm 57:7.
[2] Psalm 113:3.

the height of Thy divine commandments, preserve us through the intercessions of the Theotokos, O Christ our God, and have mercy upon us.

Canticle Four

First Canon

(**Irmos**) He whom Thou hast called, O Lord, 'The voice of one crying in the wilderness', heard Thy voice when Thou hast thundered upon many waters, bearing witness to Thy Son. Wholly filled with the Spirit that had come, he cried aloud: 'Thou art Christ, the wisdom and the power of God.'[1]

'Who has ever seen the sun that is bright by nature being cleansed?' the Preacher cried. 'How, then, shall I wash Thee in the waters, who art the Brightness of the Glory, the Image of the everlasting Father?[2] How shall I that am grass touch with my hand the fire of Thy divinity? For Thou art Christ, the wisdom and the power of God.'

'Moses, when he came upon Thee, displayed the holy reverence that he felt: perceiving that it was Thy voice that spoke from the bush, he forthwith turned away his gaze.[3] How then shall I behold Thee openly, how shall I lay my hand upon Thee? For Thou art Christ, the wisdom and the power of God.'

'Endowed with an understanding soul and honoured with the power of reason, I yet respect the things that have no soul. For if I baptize Thee, I shall have as my accusers the mountain that smoked with fire,[4] the sea which fled on either side,[5] and this same Jordan which turned back.[6] For

[1] Isaiah 40:3; Matthew 3:3, 6–17; Psalm 28:3; 1 Corinthians 1:24.
[2] Hebrews 1:3.
[3] Exodus 3:6.
[4] Sinai (Exodus 19:18).
[5] The Red Sea.
[6] Psalm 113:5.

Thou art Christ, the wisdom and the power of God.'

Second Canon

(**Irmos**) Cleansed by the fire of a mystic vision
The Prophet sang the praises of the renewal of mortal man.
Filled with the inspiration of the Spirit, he raised his voice,
Telling of the Incarnation of the ineffable Word,
Who has shattered the dominion of the strong.

O Word all-shining, sent forth from the Father,
Thou art come to dispel utterly the dark and evil night
And the sins of mortal men,
And by Thy baptism to draw up with Thee, O blessed Lord,
Bright sons from the streams of Jordan.

When he saw in very truth the glorious Word,
The Preacher cried out plainly to the creation:
'This is He who was before me, though He comes after me according to the flesh.[1]
Like us in form, He has shone forth in the strength of the Godhead,
To drive away our hateful sin.'

That He may lead us back to the live-giving pastures of Paradise,
God the Word goes searching for us in the lairs of the dragons.
Destroying the terrible snares which the enemy had laid for man,
He makes a prisoner of him who bruised all mankind in the heel,[2]
And so He saves the creation.

[1] John 1:15.
[2] Genesis 3:15.

Canticle Five

First Canon

(**Irmos**) Jesus, the Prince of Life, has come to set loose from condemnation Adam the first-formed man; and though as God He needs no cleansing, yet for the sake of fallen man He is cleansed in the Jordan. In its streams He slew the enmity and grants the peace that passes all understanding.[1]

A multitude without number came to be baptized by John; and standing in their midst he raised his voice, saying: 'Ye disobedient, who has warned you to shun the wrath to come? Offer worthy fruits to Christ,[2] for He is present now and grants peace.'

The Husbandman and Creator stands in men's midst as one of them[3] and searches their hearts. In His hand He has taken the winnowing fan, and in the fullness of His wisdom He cleanses the threshing floor of the whole world, dividing wheat from chaff, burning the barren and granting eternal life to those that bring forth good fruit.[4]

Second Canon

(**Irmos**) By the cleansing of the Spirit have we been washed
From the poison of the dark and unclean enemy,
And we have set out upon a new path free from error,
That leads to gladness of heart past all attainment,
Which only they attain whom God has reconciled unto Himself.

The Maker saw in the obscurity of sin, in bonds that knew no escape,

[1] Acts 3:15; Ephesians 2:16; Philippians 4:7.
[2] Matthew 3:7–8.
[3] John 1:26.
[4] Matthew 3:11–12.

The man whom He had formed with His own
hand.
Raising him up, He laid him on His shoulders,[1]
And now in abundant floods He washes him clean
From the ancient shame of Adam's sinfulness.

In piety and eagerness let us run
To the undefiled fountains of the stream of
salvation,
And let us look upon the Word who gives us to
drink
From pure waters that satisfy our holy thirst:
And gently He heals the disease of the world.

Canticle Six

First Canon

(**Irmos**) The Voice[2] of the Word, the Candlestick of the Light, the Morning Star and Forerunner of the Sun, cried in the wilderness to all the peoples: 'Repent and be cleansed while there is yet time. For lo, Christ is at hand, who delivers the world from corruption.'

Christ was begotten without change from God the Father, and made flesh without defilement from the Virgin: and as the Forerunner teaches, it is not possible to loose the latchet of His shoes,[3] the bond that joins the Word to our nature. He it is who delivers those born on earth from error.

Christ baptizes in the fire of the Last Day those who are disobedient and believe not that He is God: but through the Spirit and by the grace that comes through water He grants a

[1] Luke 15:5.
[2] John the Baptist.
[3] Mark 1:7.

new birth to all who acknowledge His divinity, delivering them from their faults.

(**Irmos**) The Father in a voice full of joy
Made manifest His Beloved whom He had begotten from the womb.[1]
'Verily,' said He, 'this is My offspring, of the same nature as Myself:
Bearing light, He has come forth from mankind,
My living Word, in divine providence made a mortal man.'

The Prophet, mysteriously swallowed up for the space of three nights
In the belly of the sea monster,
Came forth again, making manifest beforehand to all
Our regeneration at the last times[2]
And our deliverance from the dragon that slays mankind.

When the shining vaults of heaven were opened,
He who knew the mysteries[3] saw the Spirit,
Who proceeds from the Father and rests on the immaculate Word,
Descending in ways past speech in the form of a dove:[4]
And he commanded the multitudes to hasten to the Master.

[1] Psalm 109:3.

[2] It is not clear whether 'regeneration' (παλιγγενεσία) here refers to baptism (Titus 3:5) or to the resurrection from the dead (Matthew 19:28).

[3] John the Baptist.

[4] Matthew 3:16; John 1:33.

Kontakion

TONE FOUR

(by Romanos the Melodist)

Thou hast appeared today to the inhabited earth, and Thy light, O Lord, has been marked upon us,[1] who with knowledge sing Thy praise: Thou hast come, Thou art made manifest, the Light that no man can approach.

Ikos

Upon Galilee of the Gentiles, upon the land of Zabulon and the land of Nephthalim, as the prophet said,[2] a great light has shone, even Christ. To those that sat in darkness a bright dawn has appeared as lightning from Bethlehem. The Lord born from Mary, the Sun of Righteousness,[3] sheds His rays upon the whole inhabited earth. Come then, naked children of Adam, and let us clothe ourselves in Him, that we may warm ourselves. Thou who art a protection and veil to the naked, a light to those in darkness, Thou hast come, Thou art made manifest, the Light that no man can approach.

Canticle Seven

First Canon

(**Irmos**) The breath of the wind heavy with dew and the descent of the angel of God preserved the Holy Children from all harm, as they walked in the fiery furnace. Refreshed with dew in the flames, they sang in thanksgiving: 'Blessed art Thou and praised above all, O Lord God of our fathers.'

In trembling and wonder as if in heaven, the angelic powers stood by the Jordan, watching the great condescension of

[1] Psalm 4:7.
[2] Isaiah 9:1; Matthew 4:15–16.
[3] Malachi 4:2.

God: how He who holds dominion over the waters that are above the firmament stood in the waters in bodily form, He who is the God of our fathers.

The sea and cloud in which the people of Israel were once baptized by Moses the Lawgiver, as they journeyed from Egypt,[1] prefigured the wonder of the baptism of God. The sea was an image of the water and the cloud an image of the Spirit, whereby we are initiated and cry aloud: Blessed art Thou, O God of our fathers.

O let us all, the faithful, discoursing on divine things, join the angels in never-silent hymns to glorify the God in whom we have received initiation, Father, Son, and Holy Spirit, the Trinity, consubstantial in Persons yet one God, to whom we sing: Blessed art Thou, O Lord God of our fathers.

Second Canon

(**Irmos**) He who stilled the heat of the flame of the furnace
That mounted high in the air and encircled the godly Children,
Burnt the heads of the dragons in the stream of the Jordan:[2]
And with the dew of the Spirit He washes away
All the stubborn obscurity of sin.

The fierce Assyrian flame that prefigured Thee
Hast Thou quenched, changing it to dew:
And now Thou hast clothed Thyself in water, O Christ, and so dost burn up
The evil spoiler hidden in its depths,
Who calls men to follow the path that leads to destruction.

[1] 1 Corinthians 10:2.
[2] Psalm 73:13.

Of old the Jordan was parted in two,
And the people of Israel passed over on a narrow piece of dry land,[1]
Prefiguring Thee, O Lord most powerful,
Who now makest haste to bear the creation down into the stream,
Bringing it to a better and a changeless path.

We know that in the beginning Thou hast brought upon the world the all-ruining flood,
Unto the lamentable destruction of all things,[2]
O God who revealest wonders most great and strange:
And now, O Christ, Thou hast drowned sin in the waters
Unto the comfort and salvation of mortal men.

Canticle Eight

First Canon

(**Irmos**) The Babylonian furnace, as it poured forth dew, foreshadowed a marvellous mystery: how the Jordan should receive in its streams the immaterial fire, and should encompass the Creator, when He was baptized in the flesh. Him do ye peoples bless and exalt above all for ever.

The Deliverer said to the Forerunner: 'Cast aside all fear and, obedient to My command, draw near Me, for by nature I am good and full of love.[3] Yield to My ordinance and baptize Me, who have come down in condescension, whom the peoples bless and exalt above all for ever.'

When the Baptist heard the Master's words, he stretched

[1] Joshua 3:16.
[2] Genesis 7:4.
[3] In place of *χρηστῷ*, some Greek books read *Χριστῷ*: 'Draw near to me as to Christ: for He I am by nature.'

out his hand in trembling; and as he touched the head of his Creator, he cried aloud to Him who was baptized: 'Sanctify me, for Thou art my God, whom the peoples bless and exalt above all for ever.'

The Trinity was made manifest in the Jordan. For, supreme in Godhead, the Father proclaimed, saying, 'He who is here baptized is My beloved Son', and the Spirit rested upon His Equal in Godhead, whom the peoples bless and exalt above all for ever.

Second Canon

(Irmos) The creation finds itself set free,
And those in darkness are now made sons of light:
Alone the prince of darkness groans.
Let all the inheritance of the nations, that was before in misery,
Now bless with eagerness Him who has wrought this change.

The three godly Children who were sprinkled with dew in the fire
Plainly prefigured how the Most High God,
Who shines with the bright rays of a threefold holiness,
Should mingle with mortal men, to their great blessing,
Consuming all deadly error in the fire of dew.

Let the whole earthly creation clothe itself in white,
For this day it is raised up from its fall from heaven.
The Word who preserves all things
Has cleansed it in the flowing waters:

Washed and resplendent, it has escaped from its former sins.

Canticle Nine

The Magnificat and Greater in honour than the cherubim *are not sung, but are replaced by the following megalynaria:*

First Canon

Magnify, O my soul, her who is greater in honour than the hosts on high.

(Irmos) Every tongue is at a loss to praise thee as is due: even a spirit from the world above is filled with dizziness, when it seeks to sing thy praises, O Theotokos. But since Thou art good, accept our faith: Thou knowest well our love inspired by God, for thou art the Protector of Christians and we magnify thee.

Repeat the megalynarion and the irmos.

Magnify, O my soul, Him who is come to be baptized in Jordan.

O David, come in spirit to those who are now to be enlightened[1] and sing: 'Approach ye now to God in faith and receive enlightenment. Fallen Adam, the poor man, cried and the Lord heard him:[2] He has come and in the streams of Jordan He has made him new again, who was sunk in corruption.'

Magnify, O my soul, Him who receives baptism from the Forerunner.

O David, come in spirit . . .

Magnify, O my soul, Him to whom the voice of the Father bore witness.

[1] i.e. baptized.
[2] Psalm 33: 5–7.

'Wash you, make you clean', says Isaiah. 'Put away the evil of your doings from before the Lord. Ho, everyone that thirsteth, come ye to the living waters:[1] for Christ will sprinkle with the water of renewal those who hasten to Him in faith, and He baptizes them with the Spirit unto life that grows not old.'[2]

Magnify, O my soul, one of the Trinity who bowed His head and received baptism.

'Wash you, make you clean . . .

'O Prophet, come to Me: stretch out thine hand and baptize Me swiftly.'

Let us, the faithful, keep ourselves safe through grace and through the seal of baptism. In the past the Hebrews fled destruction by marking the door posts with blood;[3] so also this divine washing unto regeneration[4] shall be our Exodus, and going hence, we shall behold the light of the Trinity that never sets.

'O Prophet, suffer it to be so now, and baptize me as I wish: for I have come to fulfil all righteousness.'

Let us, the faithful, keep ourselves safe through grace . . .

Second Canon

Today the Master bows His head beneath the hand of the Forerunner.

(Irmos) O most pure Bride, O blessed Mother,
The wonders of Thy birthgiving pass all understanding.

[1] Isaiah 1:16; 55:1.
[2] John 4:14.
[3] Exodus 12:7,13.
[4] Titus 3:5.

Through thee we have obtained salvation in all things,
And, as is right and meet, we rejoice before thee our Benefactor,
Bearing as gift a song of thanksgiving.

Today John baptizes the Master in the streams of Jordan.

O most pure Bride . . .

Today the Master buries in the waters the sin of mortal man.

Today the Master receives testimony from on high, that He is the beloved Son.

That which was revealed to Moses in the bush[1]
We see accomplished here in strange manner.
The Virgin bore Fire within her, yet was not consumed,
When she gave birth to the Benefactor who brings us light,
And the streams of Jordan suffered no harm when they received Him.

Today the Master has come to sanctify the nature of the waters.

Today the Master receives baptism at the hand of the Forerunner.

That which was revealed to Moses . . .

Magnify, O my soul, the power of the undivided Godhead in three Persons.

O King without beginning, through the communion of the Spirit
Thou dost anoint and make perfect the nature of mankind.[2]

[1] Exodus 3:2–4.

[2] 2 Corinthians 1:21–22; 1 John 2:27.

Thou hast cleansed it in the undefiled streams,
Putting to shame the arrogant force of darkness,
And now Thou dost translate it unto endless life.

Magnify, O my soul, her that has delivered us from the curse.

O King without beginning . . .

Katavasia

The first megalynarion and the irmos of the first Canon; and likewise the first megalynarion and the irmos of the second Canon.

Exapostilarion

The Saviour, who is grace and truth, has appeared in the streams of the Jordan, and enlightened those that sleep in darkness and shadow. For the Light that no man can approach has come and is made manifest (*3 times*).

Lauds. Six stichera are sung:

TONE ONE

(*by Patriarch Germanos*)

Light from Light, Christ our God has shone upon the world, God made manifest: O ye peoples, let us worship Him (*twice*).

O Christ our Master, how shall we Thy servants give Thee worthy honour? For Thou hast renewed us all in the waters.

Thou, O our Saviour, wast baptized in Jordan and hast sanctified the waters: accepting a servant's hand upon Thine head, Thou healest the passions of the world. Great is the mystery of Thy dispensation: O Lord who lovest mankind, glory to Thee.

The true Light has appeared and bestows enlightenment on all. Christ who is above all purity is baptized with us; He brings sanctification to the water and it becomes a cleansing for our souls. That which is outward and visible is earthly, that which is inwardly understood is higher than heaven. Salvation comes through washing, and through water the Spirit: by descending into the water we ascend to God. Wonderful are Thy works, O Lord: glory to Thee.

He who covers the heaven with clouds[1] is Himself covered today by the streams of Jordan; and He who takes away the sin of the world is cleansed, that I may be made clean. The Only-begotten Son of the Most High Father receives from above the testimony of the consubstantial Spirit. Unto Him let us cry aloud: O Christ our God who hast made Thyself manifest and saved us, glory to Thee.

Glory be to the Father . . .

TONE SIX

(*by Anatolios*)

O Saviour, who clothest Thyself with light as with a garment,[2] Thou hast clothed Thyself in the waters of Jordan; and Thou who hast measured heaven with a span,[3] hast bowed Thine head before the Forerunner, that so Thou mightest turn the world back from error and save our souls.

Both now . . .

TONE TWO

(*by the same*)

Today Christ has come to be baptized in Jordan; today John touches the head of the Master. The powers of heaven are amazed as they behold the marvellous mystery. The sea saw it and fled: Jordan at the sight was driven back.[4] And we who have been enlightened cry aloud: Glory to God

[1] Psalm 146:8.
[2] Psalm 103:2.
[3] Isaiah 40:12.
[4] Psalm 113:3.

made manifest, who has appeared upon earth and brought light to the world.

Great Doxology and Dismissal.[1]

Liturgy

Antiphon One

TONE ONE

℣ 1. When Israel went out of Egypt, the house of Jacob from a people of strange language (*Psalm* 113:1).

At the prayers of the Theotokos, save us, O Saviour.

℣ 2. Judah was his sanctuary, and Israel his dominion (*ibid.*, 2).

At the prayers of the Theotokos . . .

℣ 3. The sea saw it and fled: Jordan was driven back (*ibid.* 3).

At the prayers of the Theotokos . . .

℣ 4. What ailed thee, O thou sea, that thou fleddest? thou Jordan, that thou wast driven back? (*ibid.*, 5)

At the prayers of the Theotokos . . .

Glory be to the Father . . . Both now . . .

At the prayers of the Theotokos . . .

[1] The second Blessing of the Waters is sometimes held at the end of Mattins. The priest puts on all his vestments during Lauds, and the service of Blessing then takes place after the troparion at the end of the Doxology. We begin with the sticheron, *The voice of the Lord upon the waters* . . ., and recite everything as in the text above (pp. 348–59), except that in place of *Ye faithful, let us praise the greatness* . . . (p. 359), we sing *The Trinity was made manifest* . . ., from Canticle Eight of the first Canon (p. 378). Then the deacon sings the Litany of Entreaty and Mattins concludes in the usual way.

But normally this second Blessing takes place at the end of the Liturgy (p. 387).

Antiphon Two

TONE TWO

℣ 1. I am well pleased, for the Lord will hear the voice of my prayer (*Psalm* 114:1).

O Son of God, baptized by John in the Jordan, save us who sing to Thee: alleluia.

℣ 2. He hath inclined His ear unto me: therefore will I call upon Him as long as I live (*ibid.*, 2).

O Son of God . . .

℣ 3. The sorrows of death compassed me, and the pains of hell took hold of me: I found trouble and sorrow, and I called upon the Name of the Lord (*ibid.*, 3–4).

O Son of God . . .

℣ 4. Gracious is the Lord and righteous: yea, our God is merciful (*ibid.*, 5).

O Son of God . . .

Glory be to the Father . . . Both now . . .

O Only-begotten Son and Word of God . . .

Antiphon Three

TONE ONE

℣ 1. O give thanks unto the Lord, for He is good: for His mercy endureth for ever (*Psalm* 117:1).

The troparion of the feast, When Thou, O Lord, wast baptized in the Jordan (*p. 359*).

℣ 2. Let the house of Israel now confess that He is good: for His mercy endureth for ever (*ibid.*, 2).

The troparion of the feast.

℣ 3. Let the house of Aaron now confess that He is good: for His mercy endureth for ever (*ibid.*, 3).

The troparion of the feast.

℣ 4. Let them now that fear the Lord confess that He is good: for His mercy endureth for ever (*ibid.*, 4).

The troparion of the feast.

Introit:

Blessed is He that cometh in the Name of the Lord. The Lord is God and hath appeared unto us (*Psalm* 117:26, 27).

O Son of God, baptized by John in the Jordan, save us who sing to Thee: alleluia.[1]

Then the troparion of the feast (*p. 359*); Glory be to the Father . . . Both now . . .; *the kontakion of the feast* (*p. 375*).

Instead of the trisagion we sing:

As many of you as were baptized into Christ, have put on Christ. Alleluia.

Prokimenon: *TONE FOUR*

Blessed is He that cometh in the Name of the Lord. The Lord is God and hath appeared unto us (*Psalm* 117:26, 27).

℣. O give thanks unto the Lord, for He is good: for His mercy endureth for ever (*ibid.*, 1).

READING FROM THE EPISTLE OF PAUL TO TITUS (2:11–14; 3:4–7. *See p. 334*).

Alleluia, TONE ONE[2]

℣ 1. Bring unto the Lord, ye sons of God, bring unto the Lord young rams (*Psalm* 28:1).

℣ 2. The voice of the Lord is upon the waters: the God of glory thundered, the Lord is upon many waters (*ibid.*, 3).

[1] In the Slav use, *O Son of God* . . . is sung only at pontifical services.

[2] In the Slav use, Tone Four.

READING FROM THE HOLY GOSPEL ACCORDING TO MATTHEW (3:13–17).

Then cometh Jesus from Galilee to Jordan unto John, to be baptized of him. But John forbad Him, saying, I have need to be baptized of Thee, and comest Thou to me? And Jesus answering said unto him, Suffer it to be so now: for thus it becometh us to fulfil all righteousness. Then he suffered Him. And Jesus, when He was baptized, went up straightway out of the water: and, lo, the heavens were opened unto Him, and He saw the Spirit of God descending like a dove, and lighting upon Him: and lo a voice from heaven, saying, This is My beloved Son, in whom I am well pleased.

In place of It is meet, *we sing the first megalynarion and irmos from Canticle Nine of the first Canon (p. 379).*

Communion verse:

The grace of God that bringeth salvation unto all men hath appeared (*Titus* 2:11).

After the prayer behind the ambon, the second Blessing of the Waters takes place.[1] *During the singing of the sticheron,* The voice of the Lord upon the waters, *the clergy and people proceed in procession to a nearby river or spring, or to the sea shore, and the Blessing is held there in the open air.*[2] *The same order of service is followed as on the previous day (pp. 348–59), except that when the procession returns to the church at the end of the ceremony, in place of* Ye faithful, let us praise the greatness . . . *(p. 359), we sing* The Trinity was made manifest . . ., *from Canticle Eight of the first Canon (p. 378). On returning to the church, we sing* Blessed be the Name of the Lord; *Psalm 33 is read, and the Liturgy concludes in the usual way.*

On the day of the feast there is a general dispensation from all fasting, even if it is Wednesday or Friday.

[1] Unless it has been held at the end of Mattins (p. 384).

[2] If there is no convenient place in the open air, the Blessing is held inside the church, as before.

7 JANUARY

THE SYNAXIS OF THE HONOURED AND GLORIOUS PROPHET, FORERUNNER, AND BAPTIST JOHN

Great Vespers

On Lord, I have cried, *six stichera are sung: three of the feast, and three of the Forerunner.*

Stichera of the feast from Vespers of the Theophany *(p. 338)**:*

TONE TWO

The Forerunner beheld our Enlightenment . . .
The hosts of angels were filled with fear . . .
The streams of the Jordan received Thee . . .

Stichera of the Forerunner in the Greek use:

TONE ONE

(*to the special melody*, O ye martyrs praised in all the world . . .)

O Forerunner of Christ, who art praised in all the world, with reverence we call thee blessed, O Baptist inspired by God; and we glorify Christ who bowed His head before thee in the Jordan and sanctified the nature of mortal man. Entreat Him that peace and great mercy may be given to our souls.

O wise John the Forerunner, thou hast looked down from the bank of the river upon the Glory past speech of the Father, even the Son, as He stood in the waters; and thou hast seen the Spirit descend as a dove, cleansing and enlightening the ends of the earth. To thee the mystery of the Trinity was revealed: and to thee we sing, honouring thy divine festival.

O Baptist and Forerunner, strengthened by the divine grace of Christ thou hast shown us the Lamb that takes away all the sins of the world;[1] and with joy thou hast this day brought two disciples to Him.[2] Entreat Him that peace and great mercy may be given to our souls.

But in the Slav use we sing the following stichera:

TONE ONE

(*to the special melody*, O ye martyrs praised in all the world . . .)

When the Forerunner beheld Thee, O Christ, draw near to him and ask for baptism, he cried out in trembling: 'Why dost Thou bid me perform what lies beyond my strength? How shall I touch Thee with my hand, O Lord all-powerful, who with Thy hand dost hold all things? Do Thou rather baptize me Thy servant.'

'I have appeared this day as a complete man; by nature unapproachable, I have become approachable to thee. Being rich, I have of Mine own will made Myself poor, that what has grown poor I may make rich with incorruption and deliverance.[3] Draw near and baptize Him who is not subject to corruption and who delivers the world from decay.'

'I am constrained on every side', said the Forerunner to the Creator, 'and I am at a loss whither to flee. O bountiful Lord, Thou art a stream full of nourishment: how then shall the flowing streams receive Thee, O Word, who art come to pour forth salvation upon all who honour Thy holy Epiphany?'

[1] John 1:29, 35–36.
[2] Andrew and Simon Peter (John 1:35–42).
[3] 2 Corinthians 8:9.

Then both in the Greek and in the Slav use:

Glory be to the Father . . .

TONE SIX

Thou Light in the flesh and Forerunner of the Saviour, offspring of a barren mother and friend of Him who was born of a Virgin, thou hast worshipped Him by leaping in the womb[1] and hast baptized Him in the waters of the Jordan. We entreat thee, intercede with Him, O Prophet, that we may escape from the mighty tempests to come.

Both now . . .

SAME TONE

God the Word appeared to mankind in the flesh . . ., *the sticheron sung at Mattins of the feast after the Gospel* (*p. 366*).

Entrance, O joyful light.

Great Prokimenon:[2]

TONE SEVEN

Our God is in heaven and on earth: He hath done whatsoever He hath pleased (*Psalm* 113:11).

℣ 1. When Israel went out of Egypt, the house of Jacob from a people of strange language (*ibid.*, 1).

Our God is in heaven . . .

℣ 2. The sea saw it and fled: Jordan was driven back (*ibid.*, 3).

Our God is in heaven . . .

℣ 3. What ailed thee, O thou sea, that thou fleddest? thou Jordan, that thou wast driven back? (*ibid.*, 5)

Our God is in heaven . . .

[1] Luke 1:41.

[2] On Saturday evening, the usual prokimenon of the day is sung, *The Lord is King . . .*

Aposticha:

TONE FOUR

(*to the special melody*, Thou hast given an ensign . . .)

When he saw Thee, O Master, draw near to him, John the Forerunner was amazed, and as a faithful servant he cried out in fear: 'What is this humility, O Saviour? What is this poverty that Thou hast put on? In the wealth of Thy goodness and compassion Thou hast raised up man from his humiliation, by clothing Thyself in him.'

℣. The sea saw it and fled: Jordan was driven back (*Psalm* 113:3).

'Come unto me this day,' the Saviour of all replied to the Forerunner, 'for I bring to pass a mystery. Serve Me with trembling, yet draw not back in fear. For I, by nature undefiled, stand now before thee in the waters of the Jordan and am baptized as man: for I make Adam new, who was shattered by sin.'

℣. What ailed thee, O thou sea, that thou fleddest? thou Jordan, that thou wast driven back? (*ibid.*, 5)

'Who among men has seen the sun being cleansed,' replied John, 'and Him that covered the heaven with clouds, stripped naked? Who has seen Him that made the springs and rivers, Himself enter the waters? I stand amazed at Thine ineffable dispensation, O Master. Burden not Thy servant with fearful commands.'

Glory be to the Father . . .

TONE FOUR

(*by Byzas*)

As the lover of the Spirit, the swallow that brings divine tidings of grace, O Forerunner, thou hast clearly made known to mankind the dispensation of the King, who shone forth in brightness from a pure Virgin unto the restoration of men. Thou dost banish the dominion of dark and evil ways, and guidest towards eternal life the hearts of those baptized in repentance, O blessed Prophet inspired by God.

Both now . . .

SAME TONE

Come, let us do as the wise virgins . . ., *the sticheron sung at the Lity of the feast* (*p.* 360).

Apolytikion (*troparion*) *of the feast* (*p.* 359), *and then the apolytikion of the saint:*

TONE TWO[1]

The memory of the just is praised,[2] but thou art well pleased, O Forerunner, with the testimony of the Lord. For thou hast verily been shown forth as more honoured than the prophets,[3] since thou wast counted worthy to baptize in the stream Him whom they foretold. Therefore, having mightily contended and suffered for the truth, with joy thou hast preached also to those in hell the good tidings of God made manifest in the flesh, who takes away the sin of the world and grants us great mercy.

And the Dismissal.

Mattins

After the first reading from the Psalter, sessional hymn:

TONE ONE

When Jesus was born of the Virgin Mary and baptized in the Jordan by John, the Spirit descended visibly upon Him in the form of a dove. Therefore the Prophet cried aloud with the angels, saying: 'Glory to Thy coming, O Christ, glory

[1] In some editions, Tone Four.
[2] Proverbs 10:7.
[3] Matthew 11:9.

to Thy Kingdom: glory to Thy dispensation, O Thou who alone lovest mankind.'

Glory be to the Father . . . Both now . . .

Repeat.

After the second reading from the Psalter, sessional hymn:

TONE FOUR

When the great Forerunner saw Thee, O Christ, seeking baptism in the streams of the Jordan, he cried out in gladness: 'Thou hast come, Thou art made manifest, the light that no man can approach.'

Glory be to the Father . . . Both now . . .

Repeat.

Psalm 50.

The two Canons of the feast are read, in ten troparia, and then the Canon of the Forerunner by Theophanes, in four troparia. The irmoi of the two Canons of the feast are repeated as katavasia at the end of each Canticle. Before the verses of the Canon of the Forerunner we say, Great Saint John, Forerunner of the Lord, pray for us; *or else,* Saint of God, pray for us, *or* Baptist of Christ, pray for us.

TONE TWO

Canticle One

(**Irmos**) Let us sing to the Lord who by His divine command dried up the billowing sea where none might walk, and led the people of Israel across it on foot: for He has been greatly glorified.

I am plunged in the rough sea of the passions: come to me and save me by thine intercessions, O Forerunner. For as an honoured and pure vessel thou wast granted freedom from passion, and wast dedicated to the Lord on high while still a babe.

An angel that stands before God came in great rejoicing to thine honoured father Zacharias, while he was serving in the temple, and brought glad tidings of thee who art the equal of the angels: how thou, O all-blessed, wast to become the Forerunner and friend of the Lord.[1]

While yet within thy mother's womb thou wast filled with the Most Holy Spirit, and leaping with gladness thou hast joyfully announced the fruit of virginity and hast worshipped Him, O venerable Prophet.[2]

Let us praise the divine and holy Forerunner of the Lord. He cut a path for himself where none before had trod, following a strange way of life, and he baptized Christ in the streams of Jordan.

Theotokion

O most sacred Temple of virginity, who hast conceived in thy womb God the Word, save by thine intercessions those who run to thee and call upon thee, O pure and all-blameless Lady, and set them free from every danger that assails them.

Canticle Three

(**Irmos**) On the rock of the faith Thou hast established me, and Thou hast opened wide my mouth against mine enemies. For my spirit has rejoiced to sing: None is holy as our God and none is righteous save Thee, O Lord.

Having released thy parents from the reproach of childlessness, thou hast acknowledged the divine Offspring of the Virgin by leaping with great joy in the womb of thy mother,[3]

[1] Luke 1:11.
[2] Luke 1:41.
[3] Luke 1:41.

O Forerunner of Christ who art praised in all the world, companion of the angels and sharer in the mysteries of grace.

Thou hast prepared the paths of the Lord and hast gone before His face, O prophet.[1] As a lamp that gives light to all, thou hast revealed through the waters of baptism the Brightness of the Father's glory,[2] made manifest in the flesh, O thou who wast chosen above all.

As the dawn hast thou shone forth, revealing the Sun of Righteousness to those in darkness. For thou hast become preacher and Forerunner of the salvation of all, and to all thou hast said: 'Come ye to Christ with faith and be saved.'

Theotokion

Thou wast granted joy beyond speech, O Mother of God, and thou hast conceived thy Master without seed. All that is beneath the sun He calls back to Himself, and unto Him we cry: None is holy save Thee, O Lord.

Kontakion and ikos of the Theophany.

Then the sessional hymn:[3]

TONE ONE

The mighty Rain comes forth in the flesh to the streams of the river, desiring baptism. Filled with amazement, the divine

[1] Malachi 3:1; Mark 1:2.
[2] Hebrews 1:3.
[3] But in the Slav use we sing this sessional hymn:

TONE EIGHT

Jordan ministered with its waters, and John stretched out his mortal hand when Thou, O invisible Lord, hast appeared in the flesh for baptism. But the river was driven back in fear, while the Forerunner straightway trembled, as he set his hand upon Thee who art incorruptible. Thou art in truth the Lamb of God, the everlasting fountain, and Thou hast sanctified the springs and the sea and man: for the Trinity shone from on high, the Father calling Thee the Son, while the Holy Spirit descended upon Thee.

Glory be to the Father . . . Both now . . .

Repeat.

Forerunner said to Him: 'How shall I baptize Thee who hast no stain at all? How shall I stretch out my right hand upon Thy head, before which all things tremble?'

Glory be to the Father . . . Both now . . .

TONE FOUR

Of His own will has God who is beyond all comprehension come down upon earth, and taken flesh for our sake according to His good pleasure; and He who is our Enlightenment has suffered Himself to be baptized. Therefore the Forerunner cried aloud to Him: 'I dare not touch Thy head, O Saviour, for I see how Thou art beyond comprehension, O Lord.' Thou Word, who hast dispensed all things for our benefit, glory to Thee.

Canticle Four

(**Irmos**) I sing of Thee, O Lord, for I have heard the report of Thee and was afraid. Thou hast come and sought me who had gone astray. Therefore I glorify Thine abundant condescension towards me, O Thou who art rich in mercy.

Thou wast sent before the Master, O most venerable John, to wash the filthy clean in the water, preparing them to receive Christ, who takes away sin and drives out error by the light of the knowledge of God.

O blessed John, who hast baptized Christ in the streams of the Jordan, entreat Him that I may be healed from the poison of the serpent's bite. For in these same streams has the Saviour crushed the evil dragons that lurked in hiding.[1]

O preacher of Christ, thou hast come forth adorned with the wisdom of God. Thou hast become the voice of one crying 'Repent', and as a prophet hast thou foretold Him who declared thee to be greater than all men.[2]

[1] Psalm 73:13.
[2] Matthew 11:11.

Following a way of life that was strange and untrodden by men, O Best of all, thou hast come to the waters of Jordan, there to hear the voice of the Father and to see the coming of the Spirit.

Theotokion

The Lord who fashioned all things is Himself fashioned as we are. Having taken up His dwelling in thy most holy womb, O all-pure Lady, He clothed Himself in the form of man and saved His own image.

Canticle Five

(**Irmos**) O Christ my Saviour, the Enlightenment of those that lie in darkness, the Salvation of all in despair, I seek Thee early in the morning: enlighten me with Thy brightness, O King of peace, for I know no other God save Thee.

Adorned, as though from some heavenly initiation, with the radiance of virtue beyond nature, thou art come to the streams of Jordan, O Forerunner: and thou dost baptize and cleanse with water those who draw near to thee in faith.

Since it was thine appointed task to baptize the pure and undefiled Light, thou wast thyself made a vessel of purity. He declared thee greater than all men and more honoured than the prophets:[1] for thou wast counted worthy to see Him of whom they spoke in prophecy.

The Forerunner who was sent before the face of the Lord and who showed unto men His straight paths, touched the head of the Master with trembling, and baptizing Him he said: 'I know no other God save Thee.'

Theotokion

O Virgin, the Son of God was plainly revealed as thy Son, He that accomplished His divine works by the power of His

[1] Matthew 11:9, 11.

will alone. Therefore we all name thee Theotokos verily and in truth: for we know no Mother of God save thee.

Canticle Six

(**Irmos**) Compassed about in an abyss of sin, on the unsearchable abyss of Thy tender mercies do I call: bring me out of corruption, O God.

Thou hast come as the voice of the Word, and as the morning star hast thou risen, O Forerunner, plainly announcing the approach of the Sun of Righteousness.

Thou hast not known earthly cares but wast enriched by heavenly hopes, and as an angel upon earth hast thou passed through life, O most blessed John.

We acknowledge thee to be the seal of the prophets, the mediator between the Old and the New Testament: and we proclaim thee Baptist and Forerunner of the Saviour Christ.

Theotokion

Unsearchable in very truth is thy conceiving: beyond words and past understanding is thy birthgiving: yet it is known and believed by all the faithful, O thou only Bride of God.

Kontakion

TONE SIX

(*by Romanos the Melodist*)

The Jordan, filled with fear at Thy coming in the flesh, was driven back trembling, and John, fulfilling the ministry of the Spirit,[1] drew back in awe. The ranks of angels stood amazed, beholding Thee in the streams baptized in the flesh. And all those in darkness were filled with light, singing the praises of Thee who art made manifest and givest light to all.

[1] In the Slavonic, 'ministry of prophecy' (reading προφητικήν in place of πνευματικήν).

Ikos

Adam became blind in Eden, but now in Bethlehem the Sun has appeared to him and opened his eyes, washing them clean in the waters of Jordan. Unto him that was in black darkness a Light has risen that shall never be put out: there is no more night for him, but all is day. For his sake the hour has now come round to break of day:[1] for, as it is written, it was the cool of evening when he hid.[2] He who fell at evening has found the Brightness that raises him up: he is released from gloom and has come to the Dawn, that is made manifest and giveth light to all.

Canticle Seven

(**Irmos**) The bush on the mountain that was not consumed by fire and the Chaldean furnace that brought refreshment as the dew plainly prefigured thee, O Bride of God. For in a material womb, unconsumed thou hast received the divine and immaterial Fire. Therefore we cry aloud unto Him who was born of thee: O God of our fathers, blessed art Thou.

O Forerunner, thou hast celebrated the rites of baptism and accomplished the mysteries of God that were openly entrusted to thee; and becoming thyself the victim in a rite of sacrifice, thou wast offered as an innocent lamb. Therefore we join thee and sing: O God of our fathers, blessed art Thou.

O thrice-blessed Forerunner, thou hast become a new Elijah, like him displaying before the world an immaterial life; and with boldness thou hast openly reproved the transgressions of the King and Queen.[3] Therefore we sing with thee, O Prophet: O God of our fathers, blessed art Thou.

[1] Psalm 45:6 (Septuagint).
[2] Genesis 3:8.
[3] Matthew 14:3–4.

Thou hast surpassed the prophets. O Forerunner, and hast inherited the godlike honour of the apostles of Christ: thou wast revealed as the fulfilment of the Law and the manifest first fruits of the new Grace. Therefore we join thee, O thrice-blessed, and we sing: O God of our fathers, blessed art Thou.

Theotokion

Let us all, as is right, reverently praise in hymns the all-pure Lady who received the Godhead, for she has conceived the Only-begotten God who was made manifest to us men. Unto Him do we, the faithful, sing with one accord: O God of our fathers, blessed art Thou.

Canticle Eight

(**Irmos**) In Babylon of old by the command of God the fiery furnace worked in contrary ways: burning the Chaldeans, it refreshed the faithful with dew as they sang: O all ye works of the Lord, bless ye the Lord.

Joyfully we honour thee, O John most blessed, who hast appeared on earth as equal of the angels in thine unaccustomed way of life, and high above all men; and we cry, O all ye works of the Lord, bless ye the Lord.

Unto thee was revealed, O prophet, the mystery of the one essence of the Godhead in three consubstantial Persons. For through the voice of the Father and the coming of the Spirit thou hast known Him who was baptized to be the everlasting Word of God.

Child of a barren mother, O most venerable John, thou wast the spiritual dawn announcing the Sun who shone forth from the Virgin; and thou hast proclaimed the Lamb who in His love for mankind takes away the sin of the world.[1]

[1] John 1:29.

Looking down upon us now from on high, O blessed and most happy Forerunner, guard by thine intercessions those who follow thy godly preaching, and who abide steadfastly by thine inspired teachings and thy saving doctrines.

Theotokion

In ways past telling thou hast conceived the pre-eternal Brightness of the glory of the Father, the Word without beginning who was in the beginning; and now without change has He proceeded forth from thee, O all-pure Virgin, and is become the firstborn of all creation.[1]

Canticle Nine

The Magnificat and Greater in honour than the cherubim *are not sung, but are replaced by the two canons of the feast with their megalynaria: after which is read the Canon of the Forerunner, with the following megalynarion:*[2]

Magnify, O my soul, the Forerunner great among the Prophets.

(**Irmos**) From thy virgin womb the Light that was before the sun, even God who has shone forth upon us, took flesh ineffably, coming to dwell among us in the body. Thee, then, O blessed and all-holy Theotokos, do we magnify.

Magnify, O my soul, the Forerunner . . .

The voice of the Forerunner from the wilderness revealed the Word that was come to dwell among us in the flesh: and in exceeding joy he made ready to baptize Christ, who had drawn near and who through faith cleanses our souls from sin.

Magnify, O my soul, the Forerunner . . .

[1] Hebrews 1:3; Colossians 1:15.

[2] The megalynarion here, and that before the Theotokion, are found in the Slav use only. In the Greek practice we say before the troparia, *Saint of God, pray for us*, or *Baptist of Christ, pray for us.*

Thou art a holy mediator between the Law and Grace: thou settest the seal upon the first, and dost make a beginning of the second. The Word honoured thee above all the prophets, and now thou hast passed beyond things visible, O most venerable John.

Magnify, O my Soul, the Forerunner . . .

He who displayed a life which outshone that of the bodiless powers of heaven, now makes glad with the angelic choirs; and standing by the throne of the Master, he rejoices to intercede for the forgiveness and salvation of those who honour his memory.

Magnify, O my soul, the all-pure Virgin Theotokos, who is greater in honour than the hosts above.

Theotokion

In His supreme compassion, the Deliverer of all becomes man: for man's own sake He who loves mankind, whose nature it is to show love towards us, accepts to be born according to the flesh from thy virgin womb, O all-blessed Mother of God.

Exapostilarion

The Master declared thee to be a prophet higher than the prophets and greater than any born of woman.[1] For Him whom all the prophets and the Law foretold, even Christ, thou hast seen in the flesh; and, more honoured than them all, thou hast baptized Him.

Glory be to the Father . . . Both now . . .

The Exapostilarion of the feast (*p.* 382).

Lauds. Six stichera are sung, from lauds of the feast (*p.* 382):

TONE ONE

Light from Light, Christ our God has shone upon the world . . . (*twice*)

[1] Matthew 11:9,11.

O Christ our Master, how shall we Thy servants . . .

Thou, O our Saviour, wast baptized . . .

The true Light has appeared . . .

He who covers the heaven with clouds . . .

Glory be to the Father . . .

TONE SIX

O Baptist, thou hast come forth as a messenger[1] from a barren womb, and from thy very swaddling clothes hast thou gone to dwell in the wilderness. Thou wast made the seal of all the prophets: for Him whom they had seen in many forms and foretold in dark sayings, thou wast counted worthy to baptize in the Jordan. From heaven hast thou heard the voice of the Father testifying to His Son; and thou hast seen the Spirit in the form of a dove descending with the Father's words upon Him who was baptized. O thou who art higher than all the prophets, cease not to intercede for us who celebrate in faith thy memorial.

Both now . . .

Today Christ has come to be baptized in Jordan . . . (*p. 383*).

Great Doxology and Dismissal.

Liturgy

According to the Greek practice we sing, as on 6 January, the antiphons and introit of the feast: then the troparion of the feast, When Thou, O Lord, wast baptized in the Jordan . . . (*p. 359*), *and the troparion of the saint,* The memory of the just . . . (*p. 392*), *followed by the kontakion of the feast,* Thou hast appeared today to the inhabited earth . . . (*p. 375*). *In place of the trisagion we sing* As many of you as were baptized into Christ (*p. 386*).

[1] Or 'angel'.

According to the Slav practice we sing the Typika (Psalms 102 and 145) and the Beatitudes. With the Beatitudes are sung four troparia from Canticle Three of the first Canon of the feast (p. 368), and four troparia from Canticle Six of the Canon of the saint (p. 398). The introit is as follows:

O Son of God, baptized by John in the Jordan, save us who sing to Thee: alleluia.

Prokimenon, in both the Greek and the Slav use:

TONE SEVEN

The righteous shall be glad in the Lord, and shall hope in Him (*Psalm* 63:11).

℣. Hear my voice, O God, when I pray unto Thee: deliver my soul from fear of the enemy (*ibid.*, 1).

READING FROM THE ACTS OF THE APOSTLES (19:1–8. *See p. 323*).

Alleluia, TONE FIVE[1]

℣ 1. Light hath shone forth upon the righteous: and gladness for the upright in heart (*Psalm* 96:11).

℣ 2. Rejoice in the Lord, ye righteous: and give thanks at the remembrance of His holiness (*ibid.*, 12).

READING FROM THE HOLY GOSPEL ACCORDING TO JOHN (1:29–34).

At that time John seeth Jesus coming unto him, and saith, Behold the Lamb of God, which taketh away the sin of the

[1] In some books, the verses on *Alleluia* are as follows:

TONE FOUR

℣ 1. *The righteous shall flourish like a palm-tree: and shall spread abroad like a cedar in Libanus* (Psalm 91:13).

℣ 2. *Such as are planted in the house of the Lord: they shall flourish in the courts of the house of our God* (ibid., 14).

world. This is He of whom I said, After me cometh a man which is preferred before me: for He was before me. And I knew Him not: but that He should be made manifest to Israel, therefore am I come baptizing with water. And John bare record, saying, I saw the Spirit descending from heaven like a dove, and it abode upon Him. And I knew Him not: but He that sent me to baptize with water, the same said unto me, Upon whom thou shalt see the Spirit descending, and remaining on Him, the same is He which baptizeth with the Holy Ghost. And I saw, and bare record that this is the Son of God.

In place of It is meet, *we sing the megalynarion and irmos from Canticle Nine of the second Canon of the feast* (p. *380*).

Communion verse:

The grace of God that bringeth salvation unto all men hath appeared (*Titus* 2:11),

and

The righteous shall be in everlasting remembrance: he shall not be afraid of evil tidings (*Psalm* 111:6–7).

If 7 January falls on Wednesday or Friday, fish, wine, and oil are allowed, but meat and animal products may not be eaten.

The apodosis of the Theophany falls on 14 January. On that day all the office of the feast is repeated, omitting only the entrance, lessons, lity, blessing of bread, and blessing of the waters at Vespers; and the polyeleos and Gospel at Mattins.

2 FEBRUARY

THE MEETING OF OUR LORD AND GOD AND SAVIOUR JESUS CHRIST

Small Vespers

On Lord, I have cried, *four stichera are sung:*

TONE ONE

(*to the special melody*, O purest Virgin, thou joy of the heavenly hierarchies . . .)

Simeon received in his embrace the Word uncircumscribed and supreme in being, who is borne on high in glory upon heavenly thrones; and he cried aloud: 'Now lettest Thou thy servant depart in peace according to Thy word,[1] O Saviour, salvation and delight of the faithful' (*twice*).

Beholding Thee as a babe, O Word begotten of the Father before all ages, Simeon the venerable cried aloud: 'I am distraught by fear at holding Thee, O Master, in my arms. But now, I pray Thee, lettest Thou Thy servant depart in peace, for Thou art compassionate.'

Now let the gate of heaven be opened: for God the Word, begotten timelessly of the Father, has taken flesh and is born of a Virgin. He desires in His goodness to call back mortal nature and to set it at the right hand of the Father.

Glory be to the Father . . . Both now . . .

[1] Luke 2:29.

TONE FOUR

(*by Andrew of Crete*)

Today the holy Mother who is higher than any temple, has come into the temple, disclosing to the world the Maker of the world and Giver of the Law. Simeon the Elder receives Him in his arms and, venerating Him, he cries aloud: 'Now lettest Thou Thy servant depart, for I have seen Thee, the Saviour of our souls.'

Aposticha:

TONE TWO

(*to the special melody*, O house of Ephratah . . .)

Today the Saviour is brought as a babe into the temple of the Lord, and Simeon the Elder receives Him in his aged hands.

℣. Lord, now lettest Thou Thy servant depart in peace according to Thy word: for mine eyes have seen Thy salvation (*Luke* 2:29–30).

Christ the coal of fire, whom holy Isaiah foresaw, now rests in the arms of the Theotokos as in a pair of tongs,[1] and He is given to the Elder.

℣. A light to lighten the Gentiles, and the glory of Thy people Israel (*ibid.*, 32).

In fear and joy Simeon held the Master in his arms, and asked for his release from life, singing the praises of the Mother of God.

Glory be to the Father . . . Both now . . .

SAME TONE

The All-Pure cried aloud, 'O Simeon, receive as a babe in thine embrace the Lord of glory and the Salvation of the world.'

Apolytikion (*troparion*) *of the feast*, Hail, O Theotokos Virgin full of grace (*p. 416*), *and Dismissal.*

[1] Isaiah 6:6.

Great Vespers

We sing Blessed is the man (*the first portion of the first kathisma*).

On Lord, I have cried, *eight stichera are sung:*

TONE ONE

(*by Patriarch Germanos*)

Simeon, tell us: whom dost thou bear in thine arms, that thou dost rejoice so greatly in the temple? To whom dost thou cry and shout: Now am I set free, for I have seen my Saviour? 'This is He who was born of a Virgin: this is He, the Word, God of God, who for our sakes has taken flesh and has saved man.' Let us worship Him (*3 times*).

Receive, O Simeon, Him whom Moses once beheld in darkness granting the Law on Sinai, and who has now become a babe subject to the Law. This is He who spoke through the Law: this is He whose voice was heard in the prophets, who for our sakes has taken flesh and has saved man. Let us worship Him (*3 times*).

Come, and with divine songs let us also go to meet Christ and let us receive Him whose salvation Simeon saw. This is He whom David announced: this is He whose words the prophets uttered, who for our sakes has taken flesh and speaks to us in the Law. Let us worship Him (*twice*).

Glory be to the Father . . . Both now . . .

TONE SIX

(*by John the Monk*)

Let the gate of heaven be opened today: for He who is without beginning, the Word of the Father, has made a beginning in time without forsaking His divinity, and as a babe forty days old He is of His own will brought by the Virgin His Mother as an offering in the temple of the Law.

The Elder received Him in his arms, crying as a servant to the Master: 'Let me depart: for mine eyes have seen Thy salvation.' Glory to Thee, O Lord, who hast come into the world to save mankind.

Entrance, O joyful light, *and prokimenon of the day.*

Lessons:

READING FROM EXODUS.[1]

The Lord spake unto Moses, in the day that He brought the children of Israel out of the land of Egypt, saying, Sanctify unto Me all the firstborn, whatsoever openeth the womb among the children of Israel, both of man and of beast: it is Mine. And Moses said unto the people, Remember this day, in which ye came out from Egypt, out of the house of bondage; for by strength of hand the Lord brought you out from this place. Thou shalt therefore keep His law. And it shall be, when the Lord shall bring thee into the land of the Canaanites, as He sware unto thee and to thy fathers, and shall give it thee, that thou shalt set apart unto the Lord all that openeth the matrix, and every firstling that cometh of a beast which thou hast; the males shall be the Lord's. And it shall be when thy son asketh thee in time to come, saying, What is this? that thou shalt say unto him, By strength of hand the Lord brought us out from Egypt, from the house of bondage: and it came to pass, when Pharaoh would hardly let us go, that the Lord slew all the firstborn in the land of Egypt, both the firstborn of man and the firstborn of beast: therefore I sacrifice to the Lord all that openeth the matrix, being males; but all the firstborn of my children I redeem. And it shall be for a token upon thine hand, and for frontlets between thine eyes. For thus spake the Lord Almighty: The firstborn of your sons ye shall give unto Me. If a woman have conceived

[1] A cento from Exodus 12:51–13:16, Leviticus 12, and Numbers 8, presenting certain peculiarities of text.

seed, and born a man child, in the eighth day the flesh of his foreskin shall be circumcised. And she shall then continue in the blood of her purifying three and thirty days; she shall touch no hallowed thing, nor come into the sanctuary, until the days of her purifying be fulfilled. And when the days of her purifying are fulfilled, for a son, or for a daughter, she shall bring a lamb of the first year for a burnt offering, and a young pigeon, or a turtledove, for a sin offering, unto the door of the tabernacle of the congregation, unto the priest. And if she be not able to bring a lamb, then she shall bring two turtles, or two young pigeons; the one for the burnt offering, and the other for a sin offering: and the priest shall make an atonement for her, and she shall be clean. For they are wholly given unto Me from among all the children of Israel; instead of the first born of the Egyptians have I taken them unto Me and sanctified them for Myself, on the day that I smote every firstborn in the land of Egypt from man to beast, saith the Lord Most High, the Holy One of Israel.

READING FROM THE PROPHET ISAIAH (6:1–12).

In the year that king Uzziah died I saw also the Lord sitting upon a throne, high and lifted up, and His train filled the temple. Above it stood the seraphims: each one had six wings; with twain he covered his face, and with twain he covered his feet, and with twain he did fly. And one cried unto another, and said, Holy, holy, holy, is the Lord of hosts: the whole earth is full of His glory. And the posts of the door moved at the voice of him that cried, and the house was filled with smoke. Then said I, Woe is me! for I am undone; because I am a man of unclean lips, and I dwell in the midst of a people of unclean lips: for mine eyes have seen the King, the Lord of Hosts. Then flew one of the seraphims unto me, having a live coal in his hand, which he had taken with the tongs from off the altar: and he laid it upon my mouth, and said, Lo, this hath touched thy lips; and thine iniquity is taken away, and thy sin purged. Also I heard the voice of the Lord, saying, Whom shall I send, and who will go for us? Then said I, Here am I; send me. And He said, Go, and tell this people, Hear ye indeed, but understand not; and see ye indeed, but perceive not. Make the heart of this people fat, and make their ears heavy, and shut their eyes; lest they see with their eyes, and hear with their ears, and understand with their heart, and convert, and be healed. Then said I, Lord, how long? And He answered, Until the cities be wasted without inhabitant, and the houses without man, and the land be utterly desolate, and the Lord have removed men far away, and there be a great forsaking in the midst of the land. And after this the Lord shall remove these men far away, and the remnant who are left in the land shall be multiplied.

READING FROM THE PROPHET ISAIAH (19:1, 3–5, 12, 16, 19–21).

Behold, the Lord rideth upon a swift cloud, and shall come into Egypt: and the idols of Egypt shall be moved at His presence, and the heart of Egypt shall melt in the midst of it. And the spirit of Egypt shall fail in the midst thereof; and I will destroy the counsel thereof: and the Egyptians will I give over into the hand of a cruel lord, saith the Lord of hosts. And the waters shall fail from the sea, and the river shall be wasted and dried up. Thus saith the Lord: Where are thy wise men? and let them tell thee now, and let them say what the Lord of hosts hath purposed upon Egypt. In that day shall Egypt be like unto women: and it shall be afraid and fear because of the shaking of the hand of the Lord of hosts, which He shaketh over it. In that day shall there be an altar to the Lord in the midst of the land of Egypt, and a pillar at the border thereof to the Lord. And it shall be for a sign and for a witness unto the Lord of hosts in the land of Egypt: for they shall cry unto the Lord because of the oppressors, and

He shall send them a saviour, and a great one, and He shall deliver them. And the Lord shall be known to Egypt, and the Egyptians shall know the Lord in that day, and shall do sacrifice and oblation; yea, they shall vow a vow unto the Lord, and perform it.

At the Lity:

TONE ONE

(*by Anatolios*)

The Ancient of Days, who in times past gave Moses the Law on Sinai, appears this day as a babe. As Maker of the Law He fulfils the Law, and according to the Law He is brought into the temple and given over to the Elder. Simeon the righteous receives Him, and beholding the fulfilment of the divine ordinance now brought to pass, rejoicing he cries aloud: 'Mine eyes have seen the mystery hidden from the ages, made manifest in these latter days,[1] the Light that disperses the dark folly of the Gentiles without faith and the Glory of the newly-chosen Israel. Therefore let Thy servant depart from the bonds of this flesh to the life filled with wonder that knows neither age nor end, O Thou who grantest the world great mercy.'

SAME TONE

(*by John the Monk*)

Today He who once gave the Law to Moses on Sinai submits Himself to the ordinances of the Law, in His compassion becoming for our sakes as we are. Now the God of purity as a holy child has opened a pure womb, and as God He is brought as an offering to Himself, setting us free from the curse of the Law and granting light to our souls.

[1] Colossians 1:26.

TONE TWO

(by Andrew Pyros)

Him whom the Ministers at the Liturgy on high entreat with trembling, Simeon has now received below in his earthly arms, and he proclaims the union of the Godhead with mankind. Seeing the heavenly God as mortal man, he makes ready to withdraw from earthly things, and raises his cry in joy: 'Glory to Thee, O Lord, who hast revealed to those in darkness the Light that knows no evening.'

SAME TONE

(by Germanos)

Today Simeon takes in his arms the Lord of Glory whom Moses saw of old in the darkness, when on Mount Sinai he received the tables of the Law. This is He who speaks through the prophets; He is the Creator of the Law. This is He whom David announced; He is fearful to all, yet has great and abundant mercy.

SAME TONE

(by Germanos or John the Monk)

The holy Virgin offered in the Holy Place Him who is Holy, giving Him to the minister in holy things. And Simeon with exceeding joy received Him in his outstretched arms, and he cried out: 'O Master, now lettest Thou Thy servant depart in peace according to Thy word, O Lord.'

SAME TONE

(by the same)

The Creator of heaven and earth is carried today by holy Simeon the Elder in his arms: and he said in the Holy Spirit: 'Now am I set free, for I have beheld my Saviour.'

SAME TONE

(by Anatolios or Andrew of Jerusalem)

Today Simeon the Elder enters the temple rejoicing in

spirit, to receive in his arms Him who gave the Law to Moses and who Himself fulfils the Law. For Moses was counted worthy to see God through darkness and sounds not clear;[1] and with his face covered[2] he rebuked the unbelieving hearts of the Hebrews. But Simeon carried the pre-eternal Word of the Father in bodily form, and he revealed the Light of the Gentiles, the Cross and the Resurrection; and Ann was proved to be a prophetess, preaching the Saviour and Deliverer of Israel. Unto Him let us cry aloud: O Christ our God, through the Theotokos have mercy upon us.

TONE FOUR

(by Andrew of Crete)

Today the holy Mother who is higher than any temple, has come into the temple, disclosing to the world the Maker of the world and Giver of the Law. Simeon the Elder receives Him in his arms and, venerating Him, he cries aloud: 'Now lettest Thou Thy servant depart, for I have seen Thee, the Saviour of our souls.'

Glory be to the Father . . .

TONE FIVE

(by the same)

Search the Scriptures, as Christ our God said in the Gospels.[3] For in them we find Him born as a child and bound in swaddling clothes, laid in a manger and fed upon milk, receiving circumcision and carried by Simeon: not in fancy nor in imagination but in very truth has He appeared unto the world. To Him let us cry aloud: Glory to Thee, O pre-eternal God.

Both now . . .

[1] Exodus 19:16–19.
[2] Exodus 34:29–33.
[3] John 5:39.

SAME TONE

(by Germanos or Anatolios)

The Ancient of Days, a young child in the flesh, was brought to the temple by His Mother the Virgin, fulfilling the ordinance of His own Law. Receiving Him, Simeon said: 'Now lettest Thou Thy servant depart in peace according to Thy word, for mine eyes have seen Thy salvation, O Lord.'

Aposticha:

TONE SEVEN

(by Cosmas the Monk)

Adorn Thy bridal chamber, O Zion, and welcome Christ the King; salute Mary, the heavenly gate. For she has been made as the throne of the cherubim,[1] and she carries the King of glory. A cloud of light is the Virgin, who has borne in the flesh the Son begotten before the morning star.[2] Simeon, taking Him in his arms, proclaimed to the peoples: 'This is the Lord of life and death and the Saviour of the world.'

℣. Lord, now lettest Thou Thy servant depart in peace according to Thy word: for mine eyes have seen Thy salvation (*Luke* 2:29–30).

The Mother who has never known wedlock has brought into the temple Him who shone forth before the ages from the Father, and who in the latter times was born from a virgin womb. He who gave the Law upon Mount Sinai, makes Himself obedient to the ordinance of the Law; and she has brought Him to the priest and righteous Elder, whose appointed lot it was to see Christ the Lord. Simeon, receiving Him in his arms, greatly rejoiced, crying aloud: 'This is God coeternal with the Father, and the Deliverer of our souls.'

℣. A light to lighten the Gentiles, and the glory of Thy people Israel (*ibid.*, 32).

[1] Psalm 79:2.
[2] Psalm 109:3 (Septuagint).

The Theotokos Mary carried in her arms Him who is borne aloft upon the chariot of the cherubim[1] and praised in song by the seraphim, who was made flesh of her without her knowing wedlock, the Giver of the Law who fulfils the commandment of the Law. She gave Him into the arms of the priest and Elder; and holding the Life, he asked to be released from life, saying: 'Now, O Master, let me depart to declare to Adam that I have seen the pre-eternal God and the Saviour of the world made a babe without undergoing change.'

Glory be to the Father . . . Both now . . .

TONE EIGHT

(by Andrew of Crete)

He who is borne on high by the cherubim and praised in hymns by the seraphim, is brought today according to the Law into the holy temple and rests in the arms of the Elder as on a throne. From Joseph He receives gifts fitting for God: a pair of doves, symbol of the spotless Church and of the newly-chosen people of the Gentiles; and two young pigeons,[2] for He is the Originator of the two Covenants, both Old and New. Simeon, having now been granted the fulfilment of the prophecies concerning himself, blesses the Virgin and Theotokos Mary, and foretells in figures the Passion of her Son. From Him he begs release, crying aloud: 'Now let me depart, O Master, as Thou hast before promised to me: for I have seen Thee the pre-eternal Light, the Lord and Saviour of the people that bear the name of Christ.'

Apolytikion (troparion) of the feast:

TONE ONE

Hail, O Theotokos Virgin full of grace: for from thee has shone forth the Sun of Righteousness, Christ our God, giving

[1] Ecclesiasticus 49:8.

[2] Leviticus 12:8; Luke 2:24.

light to those in darkness. Be glad also, thou righteous Elder, for thou hast received in thine arms the Deliverer of our souls, who bestows upon us resurrection.

And the Dismissal.

Mattins

After the first reading from the Psalter, sessional hymn:

TONE ONE

Let the choir of angels be amazed at this wonder, and let us mortal men raise our voices in song, beholding the ineffable condescension of God. Aged arms now embrace Him before whom the powers of heaven tremble, He who alone loves mankind.

Glory be to the Father . . . Both now . . .

Repeat.

After the second reading from the Psalter, sessional hymn:

TONE ONE

He who is with the Father upon the holy throne, coming to earth is born of a Virgin; and He who is uncircumscribed by time becomes a babe. Simeon received Him in his arms and said rejoicing: 'Now, O merciful Lord, let me depart in peace, for Thou hast made glad Thy servant.'

Glory be to the Father . . . Both now . . .

Repeat.

After the polyeleos, the megalynarion:[1]

We magnify Thee, O Christ the Giver of life, and we venerate Thy most pure Mother, who this day according to the Law has brought Thee into the temple of the Lord.

[1] In the Slav use only.

℣. My heart is inditing a good matter (*Psalm* 44:2).

We magnify Thee . . .

℣. The Lord is in His holy temple: the Lord's throne is in heaven (*Psalm* 10:4).

We magnify Thee . . .

Glory be to the Father . . . Both now . . .

Alleluia, alleluia, alleluia, glory be to Thee, O God (*3 times*).

We magnify Thee . . .

Sessional hymn:

TONE FOUR

The Ancient of Days for my sake becomes a child; God the most pure receives purification, that He may confirm the reality of the human flesh which He took from the Virgin. Simeon, initiated into this mystery, acknowledged Him as God made manifest in the flesh; he greeted Him as Life and with rejoicing he cried in his old age: 'Let me depart: for I have seen Thee, the Life of all.'

Glory be to the Father . . . Both now . . .

Repeat.

The first antiphon of the hymn of degrees in Tone Four.

Prokimenon: *TONE FOUR*

I will make thy name to be remembered in all generations (*Psalm* 44:18).

℣. My heart is inditing a good matter (*ibid.*, 2).

Let everything that hath breath . . .

READING FROM THE HOLY GOSPEL ACCORDING TO LUKE (2:25–32).

At that time there was a man in Jerusalem, whose name was Simeon; and the same man was just and devout, waiting for the consolation of Israel; and the Holy Ghost was upon him. And it was revealed unto him by the Holy Ghost, that he should not see death, before he had seen the Lord's Christ. And he came by the Spirit into the temple: and when the parents brought in the child Jesus, to do for Him after the custom of the law, then took he Him up in his arms, and blessed God, and said, Lord, now lettest Thou Thy servant depart in peace, according to Thy word: for mine eyes have seen Thy salvation, which Thou hast prepared before the face of all people; a light to lighten the Gentiles, and the glory of Thy people Israel.

Psalm 50.

Glory be to the Father . . .
At the prayers of the Theotokos . . .
Both now . . .
At the prayers of the Theotokos . . .
Have mercy upon me . . .

Let the gate of heaven be opened today, *the troparion sung at Vespers before the Entrance (p. 408).*

Canon of the feast, by St. Cosmas. In each Canticle, the irmos is repeated, and then twelve troparia are read. Before the troparia we say, Most holy Theotokos, save us.

TONE THREE

Canticle One

(**Irmos**) The sun once shone with its rays upon dry land in the midst of the deep. For the water on both sides became firm as a wall while the people crossed the sea on foot, offering this song acceptable to God: Let us sing to the Lord, for He has been greatly glorified.

Let the clouds drop with rain: for Christ the Sun, riding upon a swift cloud,[1] is carried by pure hands as a babe into

[1] Isaiah 19:1.

the temple. Therefore let us, the faithful, cry aloud: Let us sing to the Lord, for He has been greatly glorified.

Ye hands of Simeon, weakened by age, be strong,[1] and ye, the feeble legs of the Elder, run straight to meet Christ. Forming a choir with the bodiless powers, let us sing to the Lord, for He has been greatly glorified.

Be joyful, O heavens stretched out in wisdom, and be ye exceeding glad, O earth.[2] For Christ the Artificer, who came forth from the bosom of the Godhead and who was before all things, as a newborn child is offered to God His Father in the temple by His Mother the Virgin: for He has been greatly glorified.

(**Katavasia**) The sun once shone with its rays . . .

Canticle Three

(**Irmos**) O Lord, the firm foundation of those that put their trust in Thee, do Thou confirm the Church, which Thou hast purchased with Thy precious blood.

The firstborn of the Father before all ages has appeared from an undefiled Maiden as a firstborn child and He stretches out His hands to Adam.

That He might restore the first-formed man, who through beguilement had become childish in his mind,[3] God the Word has appeared as a child.

The Creator, having become a young child without undergoing change, has reshaped according to the form of His divinity our nature, taken from the earth and destined to return to earth once more.

(**Katavasia**) O Lord, the firm foundation . . .

Sessional hymn

TONE FOUR

Moses in days of old saw on Mount Sinai the back parts of

[1] Isaiah 35: 3.
[2] Psalm 135: 5; Isaiah 49: 13.
[3] Ephesians 4: 14.

God and was counted worthy in darkness and a storm of wind faintly to hear the divine voice.[1] But now Simeon has taken in his arms God who for our sakes took flesh without changing; and joyfully has he made haste to depart from hence to the life eternal. Therefore he cried: 'Lord, now lettest Thou Thy servant depart in peace.'

Canticle Four

(**Irmos**) Thy virtue, O Christ, has covered the heavens, for proceeding forth from the Ark of Thy sanctification,[2] from Thine undefiled Mother, Thou hast appeared in the temple of Thy glory as an infant in arms, and the whole world has been filled with Thy praise.

The Theotokos cried: 'O Simeon, knower of mysteries past speech, with rejoicing take in thine arms Christ the Word become a child, concerning whom thou wast told long since by the Holy Spirit;[3] and shout aloud to Him: The whole world has been filled with Thy praise.'

O Simeon, receive with joy Christ in age a babe, the Consolation of God's Israel,[4] for which thou hast hoped, the Maker and Master of the Law who fulfils the order of the Law; and cry unto Him: 'The whole world has been filled with Thy praise.'

Simeon was amazed when he beheld incarnate the Word that is without beginning, carried by the Virgin as on the throne of the cherubim, the Cause of all being, Himself become a babe; and he cried aloud to Him: 'The whole world has been filled with Thy praise.'

(**Katavasia**) Thy virtue, O Christ, has covered the heavens . . .

[1] Exodus 19:16–19; 33:18–23.
[2] Psalm 131:8.
[3] Luke 2:26.
[4] Luke 2:25.

Canticle Five

(**Irmos**) In a figure Isaiah saw God upon a throne, lifted up on high and borne in triumph by angels of glory; and he cried: 'Woe is me! For I have seen beforehand God made flesh, Lord of the light that knows no evening and King of peace.'[1]

The aged servant of God, seeing before him the Word held in the arms of His Mother, understood that this was the Glory made manifest of old to the Prophet;[2] and he cried, 'Rejoice, O holy Lady; for as a throne dost thou carry God, Lord of the light that knows no evening and King of peace.'

The Elder bent down and reverently touched the footprints of the Mother of God who knew not wedlock, and he said: 'O pure Lady, thou dost carry Fire. I am afraid to take God as a babe in my arms, Lord of the light that knows no evening and King of peace.'

'Isaiah was cleansed by receiving the coal from the seraphim',[3] cried the old man to the Mother of God. 'Thou dost fill me with light as thou dost entrust to me, with thy hands as with tongs, Him whom thou holdest, Lord of the light that knows no evening and King of peace.'

(**Katavasia**) In a figure Isaiah saw God . . .

Canticle Six

(**Irmos**) The Elder, having seen with his eyes the salvation that was come to the peoples, cried aloud unto Thee: 'O Christ that comest from God, Thou art my God.'

Thou hast been set up in Zion as a stumbling stone and rock of offence for the disobedient,[4] but unto the faithful Thou art salvation which cannot be broken.

Bearing faithfully the image of Him who begat Thee before

[1] Isaiah 6:1–5.
[2] Isaiah.
[3] Isaiah 6:6.
[4] Isaiah 8:14, 28:16; Luke 2:34; Romans 9:33.

all ages, Thou hast now from pity put on the weakness of mortal man.

Now lettest Thou depart in peace him who worships Thee as Son of the Most High and Son of the Virgin, God become a child.

(**Katavasia**) The Elder, having seen with his eyes . . .

Kontakion

TONE ONE

(*by Romanos the Melodist*)

Thou who hast sanctified by Thy birth a virgin womb and fittingly blessed the hands of Simeon, Thou art come, O Christ our God, and on this day hast saved us. Give peace to Thy commonwealth in time of battle and strengthen the Orthodox people[1] whom Thou hast loved, O Thou who alone lovest mankind.

Ikos

Let us run to the Theotokos, desiring to behold her Son brought to Simeon. The bodiless powers, looking at Him from on high, were filled with amazement, saying 'Now we see wondrous and most marvellous things, past understanding and past telling. He who created Adam is carried as a babe. He who cannot be compassed is compassed by the arms of the Elder. He who rests uncircumscribed in the bosom of His Father, is voluntarily circumscribed in flesh but not in divinity, He who alone loves mankind.

Canticle Seven

(**Irmos**) O Word of God who in the midst of the fire hast dropped dew upon the Children as they discoursed on things divine, and who hast taken up Thy dwelling in the pure Virgin: Thee do we praise as with piety we sing: O God of our fathers, blessed art Thou.

[1] In the original, 'kings'.

'I depart', cried Simeon, 'to declare the good tidings to Adam abiding in hell and to Eve'; and with the prophets he sang rejoicing: O God of our fathers, blessed art Thou.

'To deliver our kind formed from dust, God will go down even unto hell: He will give freedom to all the captives and sight to the blind, and will grant the dumb to cry aloud: O God of our fathers, blessed art Thou.'

'And a sword shall pierce thy heart, O All-Pure Virgin,'[1] Simeon foretold to the Theotokos, 'when thou shalt see thy Son upon the Cross to whom we cry aloud: O God of our fathers, blessed art Thou.'

(**Katavasia**) O Word of God who in the midst of the fire . . .

Canticle Eight

(**Irmos**) Standing together in the unbearable fire yet not harmed by the flame, the Children, champions of godliness, sang a divine hymn: O all ye works of the Lord, bless ye the Lord and exalt Him above all for ever.

O people of Israel, beholding thy Glory, Emmanuel the Child of the Virgin, offered before the Ark of God, dance now and sing together: O all ye works of the Lord, bless ye the Lord and exalt Him above all for ever.

'Lo', cried Simeon, 'this is He who is at once God and a child, who shall become a sign that is spoken against.[2] Unto Him in faith let us sing: O all ye works of the Lord, bless ye the Lord and exalt Him above all for ever.'

He that is Life, God the Word, has here become a little child: and He shall be the fall of the disobedient and the rising again of all those who sing with faith:[3] O all ye works

[1] Luke 2:35.
[2] Luke 2:34.
[3] Luke 2:34.

of the Lord, bless ye the Lord and exalt Him above all for ever.

(**Katavasia**) Standing together in the unbearable fire . . .

Canticle Nine

The Magnificat and Greater in honour than the cherubim *are not sung, but before the irmos and the troparia we sing the following megalynaria:*[1]

(*Greek*) That which is fulfilled in thee is beyond the understanding of angels and mortal men, O pure Virgin Mother.

(*Slav*) O Virgin Theotokos, thou Hope of all Christians, protect, watch over, and guard all those who put their hope in thee.

(**Irmos**) In the shadow and the letter of the Law, let us, the faithful, discern a figure: every male child that opens the womb shall be sanctified to God.[2] Therefore do we magnify the firstborn Word and Son of the Father without beginning, the firstborn Child of a Mother who had not known man.

(*Greek*) Simeon the Elder takes in his arms the Maker of the Law and Master of all.

(*Slav*) O Virgin Theotokos, thou good Helper of the world, protect and preserve us from all necessity and grief.

Repeat the irmos.

(*Greek*) The Creator, wishing to save Adam, took up His dwelling in thy pure and virgin womb.

(*Slav*) O Godbearing Simeon, come thou and lift up Christ, whom the pure Virgin bore.

[1] Since the megalynaria differ widely in the Greek and Slavonic books, the texts of both have been included.

[2] Exodus 13:2.

Of old the people offered a pair of doves and two young pigeons.[1] In their stead the godly Elder and Ann the prophetess, sober in spirit, ministered and gave glory to the Child of the Virgin, the Only-begotten Son of the Father, as He was brought into the temple.

(*Greek*) All mankind blesses thee, O pure Virgin, and in faith glorifies thee as Mother of God.

(*Slav*) Simeon the Elder takes in his arms the Maker of the Law and Master of all.

Of old the people offered . . .

(*Greek*) Come ye and behold Christ the Master of all, whom Simeon carries today in the temple.

(*Slav*) 'It is not the old man who holds Me, but I uphold him: for he begs Me to let him depart.'

Of old the people offered . . .

(*Greek*) 'Thou dost look down upon the earth and make it tremble: how then can I, aged and weary, hold Thee in mine arms?'

(*Slav*) O mystical Tongs,[2] how dost thou bear the Coal? How dost thou feed Him who gives food to all?

Of old the people offered . . .

(*Greek*) Simeon had lived for many years when he beheld Christ and cried aloud to Him: 'Now do I seek my release.'

(*Slav*) O daughter of Phanuel,[3] come and stand with us, and give thanks to Christ our Saviour, the Son of God.

'Thou hast committed to me the exceeding joy of Thy salvation, O Christ', cried Simeon. 'Take Thy servant, who is weary of the shadow, and make him a new preacher of the mystery of grace, as he magnifies Thee in praise.'

[1] Leviticus 12:8.

[2] Isaiah 6:6.

[3] Ann the prophetess (Luke 2:36).

(*Greek*) Mary, thou art the mystic Tongs, who hast conceived in thy womb Christ the live Coal.[1]

(*Slav*) Ann, sober in spirit, makes terrible things known, as she confesses Christ Creator of heaven and earth.

'Thou hast committed to me . . .'

(*Greek*) O God, who wast before all things began, of Thine own will Thou hast become man and art carried, a child forty days old, into the temple.

(*Slav*) O Christ, the King of all, grant Orthodox Christians victory over their enemies.

'Thou hast committed to me . . .'

(*Greek*) Simeon the priest received the Lord of all, come down from heaven.

(*Slav*) That which is fulfilled in thee is beyond the understanding of angels and mortal men, O pure Virgin Mother.

'Thou hast committed to me . . .'

(*Greek*) Illuminate my soul and the light of my senses, that I may see Thee in purity: and I will proclaim that Thou art God.

O pure Virgin Mother, why dost Thou bring into the temple a newborn babe and commit Him into the hands of Simeon?

(*Slav*) The pure Dove, the Ewe without blemish, brings the Lamb and Shepherd into the temple.

Holy Ann, sober in spirit and venerable in years, with reverence confessed the Master freely and openly in the temple; and proclaiming the Theotokos, she magnified her before all who were present.

(*Greek*) 'From Thee, the Creator, I now seek release: for I have seen Thee, O Christ, my Salvation and my Light.'

[1] Isaiah 6:6.

Him whom the Ministers at the Liturgy on high entreat with trembling, here below Simeon now takes in his arms.

(*Slav*) O Christ, the King of all, give me warm tears, that I may weep for my soul which I have lost in evil.

Holy Ann, sober in spirit and venerable . . .

(*Greek*) O Thou by nature One but in Persons Three, watch over Thy servants who put their faith in Thee.

(*Slav*) Let us praise in piety the threefold Light of the Godhead in three Persons.

Holy Ann, sober in spirit and venerable . . .

(*Greek*) O Theotokos, thou Hope of all Christians, protect, watch over, and guard all those who put their hope in thee.

(*Slav*) O Maiden Mary, enlighten my soul which is grievously darkened by the lusts of life.

Holy Ann, sober in spirit and venerable . . .

Katavasia

The first megalynarion and the irmos.

Exapostilarion.

The Elder, brought to the temple by the Spirit, took in his arms the Master of the Law and cried: 'Now let me depart in peace from the bond of the flesh according to Thy word: for mine eyes have seen the revelation that brings light to the Gentiles and the salvation of Israel' (*3 times*).

Lauds. Four stichera are sung:

TONE FOUR

(*to the special melody*, Thou hast given an ensign . . .)

Fulfilling the written Law, He who loves mankind is now brought into the temple; and Simeon receives Him in his aged arms, crying aloud: 'Now let me depart to the blessedness of the world to come: for I have seen today wrapped in mortal flesh Him who is Lord of life and Master of death' (*twice*).

As a light to lighten the Gentiles, hast Thou made Thyself manifest, O Lord: the Sun of Righteousness seated upon a swift cloud,[1] Thou hast fulfilled the shadow of the Law and shown forth the beginning of the new Grace. Therefore, beholding Thee, Simeon raised this cry: 'Let me depart from corruption, for I have seen Thee today.'

Not parted in Thy divinity from the bosom of the Father, Thou wast made flesh according to Thy good pleasure; and upheld in the arms of the ever-Virgin Thou hast been committed to the hands of Simeon, the receiver of God, O Thou who upholdest the whole world with Thine hand. Therefore he cried with joy: 'Now lettest Thou Thy servant depart in peace, for I have seen Thee, O Lord.'

Glory be to the Father . . . Both now . . .

TONE SIX

(*by Germanos*)

O Christ our God, who hast been pleased to rest this day in the arms of the Elder as upon the chariot of the cherubim, from the tyranny of the passions now deliver us who sing Thy praises, and save our souls.

Great Doxology and Dismissal.

Liturgy

The Typika (Psalms 102 and 145) and the Beatitudes. With the Beatitudes are sung four troparia from Canticle Three of the Canon of the feast *(p. 420)**, and four troparia from Canticle Six* *(p. 422)**.*

Alternatively, according to the modern Greek practice, the following antiphons may be sung:

[1] Isaiah 19:1.

Antiphon One

TONE TWO

℣ 1. My heart is inditing a good matter: I speak of the things which I have made to the King (*Psalm* 44:2).

At the prayers of the Theotokos, save us, O Saviour.

℣ 2. My tongue is the pen of a ready writer (*ibid.*).

At the prayers of the Theotokos . . .

℣ 3. Full of grace are thy lips (*ibid.*, 3).

At the prayers of the Theotokos . . .

℣ 4. Therefore God hath blessed thee for ever (*ibid.*).

At the prayers of the Theotokos . . .
Glory be to the Father . . . Both now . . .
At the prayers of the Theotokos . . .

Antiphon Two

SAME TONE

℣ 1. Gird Thy sword upon Thy thigh, O most mighty, in Thy glory and Thy beauty (*ibid.*, 4).

O Son of God, carried in the arms of Simeon the righteous, save us who sing to Thee: alleluia.

℣ 2. Bend Thy bow, and prosper, and reign (*ibid.*, 5).

O Son of God . . .

℣ 3. Thine arrows are sharp, O most mighty, the peoples shall be subdued under Thee: Thou shalt pierce the heart of the King's enemies (*ibid.*, 6).

O Son of God . . .

℣ 4. The sceptre of Thy kingdom is a righteous sceptre (*ibid.*, 7).

O Son of God . . .

Glory be to the Father . . . Both now . . .
O Only-begotten Son and Word of God . . .

Antiphon Three

TONE ONE

℣ 1. Hearken, O daughter, and consider, and incline thine ear: forget also thine own people, and thy father's house (*ibid.*, 11).

The troparion of the feast, Hail, O Theotokos Virgin full of grace (*p. 416*).

℣ 2. Even the rich among the people shall entreat thy favour (*ibid.*, 13).

The troparion of the feast.

℣ 3. I will make thy name to be remembered in all generations (*ibid.*, 18).

The troparion of the feast.

Introit:

The Lord hath made known His salvation: His righteousness hath He revealed in the sight of the Gentiles (*Psalm* 97:2).

O Son of God, carried in the arms of Simeon the righteous, save us who sing to Thee: alleluia.[1]

Then the troparion of the feast (*p. 416*); Glory be to the Father . . . Both now . . .; *the kontakion of the feast* (*p. 423*).

Prokimenon: *TONE THREE*

My soul doth magnify the Lord, and my spirit hath rejoiced in God my Saviour (*Luke* 1:46–47).

℣. For He hath regarded the low estate of His handmaiden: for, behold, from henceforth all generations shall call me blessed (*ibid.*, 48).

[1] In the Slav use, *O Son of God* . . . is sung only at pontifical services.

Reading from the Epistle to the Hebrews (7 : 7–17).

Brethren, without all contradiction the less is blessed of the better. And here men that die receive tithes; but there he receiveth them, of whom it is witnessed that he liveth. And as I may so say, Levi also, who receiveth tithes, payed tithes in Abraham. For he was yet in the loins of his father, when Melchizedek met him. If therefore perfection were by the Levitical priesthood, (for under it the people received the law,) what further need was there that another priest should rise after the order of Melchizedek, and not be called after the order of Aaron? For the priesthood being changed, there is made of necessity a change also of the law. For He of whom these things are spoken pertaineth to another tribe, of which no man gave attendance at the altar. For it is evident that our Lord sprang out of Judah; of which tribe Moses spake nothing concerning priesthood. And it is yet far more evident: for that after the similitude of Melchizedek there ariseth another priest, who is made, not after the law of a carnal commandment, but after the power of an endless life. For he testifieth, Thou art a priest for ever after the order of Melchizedek.

Alleluia, *TONE FOUR*[1]

℣ 1. Lord, now lettest Thou Thy servant depart in peace according to Thy word: for mine eyes have seen Thy salvation (*Luke* 2 : 29–30).

℣ 2. A light to lighten the Gentiles, and the glory of Thy people Israel (*ibid.*, 32).

Reading from the Holy Gospel according to Luke (2 : 22–40).

At that time His parents brought the child Jesus to Jerusalem, to present Him to the Lord; (as it is written in the law of the Lord, Every male that openeth the womb shall be

[1] In the Slav use, Tone Eight.

called holy to the Lord;) and to offer a sacrifice according to that which is said in the law of the Lord, A pair of turtledoves, or two young pigeons. And, behold, there was a man in Jerusalem, whose name was Simeon; and the same man was just and devout, waiting for the consolation of Israel: and the Holy Ghost was upon him. And it was revealed unto him by the Holy Ghost, that he should not see death, before he had seen the Lord's Christ. And he came by the Spirit into the temple: and when the parents brought in the child Jesus, to do for Him after the custom of the law, then took he Him up in his arms, and blessed God, and said, Lord, now lettest Thou Thy servant depart in peace, according to Thy word: for mine eyes have seen Thy salvation, which Thou hast prepared before the face of all people; a light to lighten the Gentiles, and the glory of Thy people Israel. And Joseph and His mother marvelled at those things which were spoken of Him. And Simeon blessed them, and said unto Mary His mother, Behold, this child is set for the fall and rising again of many in Israel; and for a sign which shall be spoken against; (yea, a sword shall pierce through thy own soul also,) that the thoughts of many hearts may be revealed. And there was one Anna, a prophetess, the daughter of Phanuel, of the tribe of Aser: she was of a great age, and had lived with an husband seven years from her virginity; and she was a widow of about fourscore and four years, which departed not from the temple, but served God with fastings and prayers night and day. And she coming in that instant gave thanks likewise unto the Lord, and spake of Him to all them that looked for redemption in Jerusalem. And when they had performed all things according to the law of the Lord, they returned into Galilee, to their own city Nazareth. And the child grew, and waxed strong in spirit, filled with wisdom: and the grace of God was upon Him.

In place of It is meet, *we sing the megalynarion and irmos of Canticle Nine of the Canon (p. 425).*

Communion verse:

I will receive the cup of salvation, and call upon the Name of the Lord (*Psalm* 115:4).

If the feast falls on a day of fasting, fish, wine, and oil are allowed, but meat and animal products may not be eaten.

The apodosis of the feast falls on 9 February. If, however, 2 February occurs on or after the Sunday of the Prodigal Son, on account of the approach of Lent the period of the afterfeast is shortened to a greater or lesser degree. When the feast falls on the Sunday immediately before Lent or the Monday of the first week of Lent, the afterfeast is omitted altogether, the feast closing at Vespers on the same evening (2 February).

On the day of the apodosis all the office of the feast is repeated, omitting only the entrance, lessons, lity, and blessing of bread at Vespers: and the polyeleos and Gospel at Mattins. In the reading of the Psalter at Vespers, the normal kathisma appointed for the day is used.

25 MARCH

THE ANNUNCIATION OF THE MOST HOLY THEOTOKOS AND EVER-VIRGIN MARY

Since the feast of the Annunciation occurs during the Great Fast of Lent or during Easter Week, the texts for the feast are combined with texts from the Triodion or Pentekostarion, according to the rules for the day in question. Note that the feast of the Annunciation is never transferred to another date, but is always to be celebrated on 25 March itself.[1]

The general order of service is as follows:

1. *If the feast of the Annunciation falls on Tuesday, Wednesday, Thursday, or Friday in Lent: on the eve of the feast (24 March), Great Vespers of the feast are sung, followed on Wednesdays by the Liturgy of the Presanctified.*[2] *At the Vigil, Great Compline, followed by Mattins; on 25 March itself, Great Vespers, followed by the Liturgy of St. John Chrysostom.*

2. *If the Annunciation falls on a Saturday in Lent, on the eve of the feast (Friday, 24 March) Great Vespers are sung, followed by the Liturgy of the Presanctified. At the Vigil, Great Compline followed by Mattins. On 25 March, the Liturgy of St. John*

[1] According to the modern Greek practice when Good Friday or Holy Saturday falls on 25 March, the feast of the Annunciation is transferred to Easter Day. Under present circumstances, however, in those Greek churches which observe the fixed feasts by the Gregorian (New Style) Calendar, the Annunciation always occurs before the Saturday of Lazarus.

[2] The Liturgy of the Presanctified is also celebrated when the Thursday of the Great Canon coincides with eve of the feast.

Chrysostom is celebrated at the usual hour, not preceded by Vespers; Great Vespers are sung in the evening, forming part of the Vigil Service of the Sunday following.

3. *If the Annunciation falls on a Sunday in Lent, on Saturday afternoon (24 March) Small Vespers are sung. At the Vigil, Great Vespers followed by Mattins; Great Compline is not said. On Sunday, 25 March, the Liturgy of St. Basil, not preceded by Great Vespers, which are sung later in the usual way.*

4. *If the Annunciation falls on a Monday in Lent or on Monday in Holy Week, on Sunday afternoon (24 March) Small Vespers are sung. At the Vigil, Great Vespers, followed by Mattins: Great Compline is not said. On Monday, 25 March, Great Vespers, followed by the Liturgy of St. John Chrysostom.*

5. *If the Annunciation falls on Tuesday or Wednesday in Holy Week, the order of services is as in (1): on the eve of the feast, 24 March, the Liturgy of the Presanctified follows Vespers.*

6. *If the Annunciation falls on Holy Thursday, the order of services is the same as in (1) above, except that on the day of the feast, 25 March, the Liturgy of St. Basil is used. On the eve of the feast, 24 March, the Liturgy of the Presanctified follows Vespers.*

7. *If the Annunciation falls on Good Friday, on the eve of the feast, Holy Thursday, Great Vespers are sung, followed by the Liturgy of St. Basil. Great Compline is not said: Mattins of the feast are combined with the service of the Twelve Gospels. On the day of the feast, 25 March, Great Vespers, followed by the Liturgy of St. John Chrysostom.*

8. *If the Annunciation falls on Holy Saturday, on the eve of the feast, Good Friday, Great Vespers are sung, but there is no Liturgy. Great Compline is not said: Mattins of the feast are combined with the service of the Epitaphios. On the day of the feast, 25 March, Great Vespers, followed by the Liturgy of St. Basil.*

9. *If the Annunciation falls on Easter Day, on the eve of the feast, Holy Saturday, Great Vespers are sung, followed by the Liturgy of*

St. Basil. Great Compline is not said. Mattins of the feast are combined with Mattins of the Resurrection, followed by the Liturgy of St. John Chrysostom.

10. *If the Annunciation falls on Monday, Tuesday, or Wednesday in Easter Week, on the eve of the feast (24 March) Small Vespers are sung. The Vigil begins with Great Vespers, followed by Mattins: Great Compline is not said. On the day of the feast, the Liturgy of St. John Chrysostom.*

Small Vespers

On Lord, I have cried, *four stichera are sung:*

TONE FOUR

Taking pity upon that which He has made and bending down in His tender mercy, the Maker hastens to dwell in the womb of a Maiden, the Child of God. To her the great Archangel came, saying to her: 'Hail, O thou who art full of divine grace, our God is now with thee.[1] Be not afraid of me, the chief commander of the armies of the King. For thou hast found the grace that thy mother Eve once lost: and thou shalt conceive and bring forth Him who is one in essence with the Father' (*twice*).

Mary said to the Angel: 'Strange is thy speech and strange thine appearance, strange thy sayings and thy disclosures. I am a Maid who knows not wedlock, lead me not astray. Thou sayest that I shall conceive Him who remains uncircumscribed: and how shall my womb contain Him whom the wide spaces of the heavens cannot contain?' 'O Virgin, let the tent of Abraham that once contained God teach thee:[2] for it prefigured thy womb, which now receives the Godhead.'

[1] Luke 1:28.

[2] Genesis 18:1–16.

Having reached the city of Nazareth, Gabriel now salutes thee, the living City of Christ the King, and he cries aloud to thee: 'Hail, thou who art blessed and full of divine grace: thou shalt hold in thy womb God made flesh, and through thee in His compassion He shall call back mankind to its ancient state. Blessed is the divine and immortal fruit of thy womb, who through thee grants the world great mercy.'

Glory be to the Father . . . Both now . . .

TONE ONE

(by Byzas)

In the sixth month the chief of the angelic hosts was sent to thee, pure Virgin, to declare unto thee the word of salvation and to greet thee, saying: 'Hail, thou who art full of grace: the Lord is with thee. Thou shalt bring forth a Son, begotten before the ages from the Father, and He shall save His people from their sins.'[1]

Aposticha:

TONE EIGHT

Gabriel, leader of the powers above, flew down and greeted the Virgin, saying: 'Hail, thou pure chariot of the divinity: God has loved thee from eternity, and He has chosen thee to be His dwelling. As servant of thy Master am I come to proclaim His coming. Thou shalt bring forth the Lord, yet still remain inviolate.'

℣. Tell forth from day to day the glad tidings of the salvation of our God (*Psalm* 95:2).

'Why does thy figure blaze with fire?' said she whom we venerate to Gabriel in her amazement. 'What is thy rank and what the value of thy words? Thou dost announce to me that I shall bring forth child, yet I have no experience of man. Lead me not astray, O man, with crafty words, as the crafty serpent once led astray Eve our mother.'

[1] Matthew 1:21.

℣. Sing unto the Lord a new song: sing unto the Lord, all the earth (*ibid.*, 1).

'The most Holy Spirit of God shall come upon thee, O pure Lady, thou dwelling-place of the divinity, and the power of the Most High shall overshadow thee: and thou shalt bring forth a Child who shall preserve thy virginity unshaken. He is the Son without lineage;[1] and having appeared, in His good pleasure He shall save His people.'

Glory be to the Father . . . Both now . . .

TONE FOUR

In the sixth month the Archangel was sent to the pure Virgin and with his greeting 'Hail!' he brought good tidings, that the Deliverer would come forth from her. And so, accepting his salutation with faith, she conceived Thee, the pre-eternal God, who wast pleased to become man ineffably for the salvation of our souls.

Apolytikion (troparion) of the feast, Today is the crown of our salvation *(p. 445), and Dismissal.*

Great Vespers

No reading from the Psalter.

On Lord, I have cried, *six stichera are sung:*

TONE SIX

(*to the special melody,* Having set all your hope on the things of heaven . . .)

Revealing to thee the pre-eternal counsel, Gabriel came and stood before thee, O Maid; and greeting thee, he said: 'Hail, thou earth that has not been sown; hail, thou burning bush that remains unconsumed; hail, thou unsearchable depth; hail, thou bridge that leads to heaven, and ladder

[1] Hebrews 7:3.

raised on high that Jacob saw; hail, thou divine jar of manna; hail, thou deliverance from the curse; hail, thou restoration of Adam, the Lord is with thee' (*twice*).[1]

'Thou dost appear unto me in the form of a man,' said the undefiled Maid to the chief of the heavenly hosts: 'how then dost thou speak to me of things that pass man's power? For thou hast said that God shall be with me, and shall take up His dwelling in my womb; and how, tell me, shall I become the spacious habitation and the holy place of Him that rides upon the cherubim?[2] Do not beguile me with deceit: for I have not known pleasure, I have not entered into wedlock. How then shall I bear a child?' (*twice*).

'When God so wishes,' said the bodiless angel, 'the order of nature is overcome, and what is beyond man comes to pass. Believe that my sayings are true, O all-holy Lady, utterly without spot.' And she cried aloud, 'Let it be unto me according to thy word: and I shall bear Him that is without flesh, who shall borrow flesh from me, that through this mingling He may lead man up unto his ancient glory, for He alone has power so to do' (*twice*).

Glory be to the Father . . . Both now . . .

SAME TONE

(*by John the Monk*)

Gabriel the Archangel was sent from heaven to announce to the Virgin the glad tidings of her conceiving; and coming to Nazareth he pondered in amazement on this wonder. 'O how shall He who dwelleth in the heights, whom none can comprehend, be born of a Virgin? How shall He whose throne is heaven and whose footstool is the earth[3] be held in the womb of a woman? He upon whom the six-winged seraphim and the many-eyed cherubim cannot gaze has been

[1] Exodus 3:2; Genesis 28:12; Exodus 16:33.
[2] Psalm 17:11.
[3] Isaiah 66:1.

pleased at a single word to be made flesh of this His creature. It is the Word of God who dwells within her. Why then do I stand here, and not say to the Maiden: Hail, thou who art full of grace: the Lord is with thee. Hail, O pure Virgin; hail, Bride unwedded. Hail, Mother of Life: blessed is the fruit of thy womb.'

Entrance, O joyful light, *and prokimenon of the day.*

Lessons:[1]

READING FROM GENESIS (28:10–17).

READING FROM THE PROPHET EZEKIEL (43:27–44:4).

READING FROM PROVERBS (9:1–11).

If the feast falls on Saturday or Sunday, or during Easter Week, two further lessons are added:[2]

READING FROM EXODUS (3:1–8).

READING FROM PROVERBS (8:22–30).

After the lessons, the service proceeds as follows:

If the feast falls on a Thursday or Saturday in Lent, or on Tuesday, Wednesday, or Thursday in Holy Week, we continue with the Liturgy of the Presanctified.

If the feast falls on a Tuesday, Wednesday, or Friday in Lent, we continue with Vespers, saying Vouchsafe, O Lord, *and then the Litany,* Let us complete our evening prayer to the Lord.

If the feast falls on a Sunday or Monday in Lent, on Monday in Holy Week, or on Monday, Tuesday, or Wednesday in Easter Week, we conclude Great Vespers in the normal way, continuing with the Litany of Entreaty and the Lity.[3]

If the feast falls on Good Friday or Easter Sunday, we continue with the Liturgy of St. Basil.

[1] *See* p. 102.
[2] *See* p. 465.
[3] For the Lity, see Great Compline, p. 442, below.

If the feast falls on Holy Saturday, we continue with Great Vespers according to the rules laid down for Good Friday, concluding with the procession of the epitaphios.

The Vigil Service

Great Compline

At the end of the Small Doxology, there follows the Lity:

TONE ONE

(by Byzas)

In the sixth month the chief of the angelic hosts was sent to thee, pure Virgin, to declare unto thee the word of salvation and to greet thee, saying: 'Hail, thou who art full of grace: the Lord is with thee. Thou shalt bring forth a Son, begotten before the ages from the Father, and He shall save His people from their sins.'[1]

SAME TONE

(by Anatolios)

In the sixth month Gabriel the Archangel was sent from heaven to the city of Nazareth in Galilee, to bring to the Maiden glad tidings of joy. And coming before her he cried aloud, saying: 'Hail, thou who art full of grace: the Lord is with thee. Hail, thou vessel containing the Nature that cannot be contained: for thy blessed womb has held Him whom the heavens held not. Hail, O Lady, thou restoration of Adam and deliverance of Eve, thou joy of the world and great rejoicing of our kind.'

SAME TONE

The angel Gabriel was sent from heaven by God to the city of Nazareth in Galilee to an undefiled Virgin, to bring

[1] Matthew 1:21.

her glad tidings of the strange manner of her conceiving. The bodiless servant was sent to the living City and the spiritual Gate, to make known to her the condescension and the coming of the Master. The captain of heaven was sent to the living Pavilion of the Glory, to make ready an everlasting Dwelling for the Maker. And coming before her he cried: 'Hail, fiery throne, more glorious by far than the living creatures with four faces.[1] Hail, thou Seat of the King of Heaven, hail, uncut mountain[2] and precious vessel. For in thee the whole fullness of the Godhead has come to dwell bodily,[3] by the good pleasure of the everlasting Father, and by the joint operation of the Holy Spirit. Hail, thou who art full of grace: the Lord is with thee.'

When the feast falls on Saturday or Sunday we sing:

Glory be to the Father . . .

TONE EIGHT

(*by John the Monk*)

Let the heavens be glad and the earth rejoice:[4] for the Son who is coeternal with the Father, sharing His throne and like Him without beginning, in His compassion and merciful love for mankind has submitted Himself to emptying,[5] according to the good pleasure and the counsel of the Father; and He has gone to dwell in a virgin's womb that was sanctified beforehand by the Spirit. O marvel! God is come among men; He who cannot be contained is contained in a womb; the Timeless enters time; and, strange wonder! His conception is without seed, His emptying is past telling: so great is this mystery! For God empties Himself, takes flesh, and is fashioned as a creature, when the angel tells the pure Virgin

[1] Ezekiel 1:5–6.
[2] Daniel 2:34–35.
[3] Colossians 2:9.
[4] Isaiah 49:13.
[5] Philippians 2:7.

of her conception: 'Hail, thou who art full of grace: the Lord who has great mercy is with thee.'

Both now . . .

TONE TWO

(by Cosmas the Monk)

Gabriel today announces the good tidings to her who is full of grace. 'Hail, O unwedded maiden who hast not known marriage. Be not struck with dismay by my strange form, nor be afraid: I am an archangel. Once the serpent beguiled Eve, but now I announce to thee the good tidings of joy: O Most Pure, thou shalt remain inviolate and yet shalt bear the Lord.'

But if the feast falls on a day of fasting (Monday to Friday inclusive) we sing:

Glory be to the Father . . . Both now . . .
Gabriel today announces . . .

Aposticha:

TONE FOUR

In the sixth month the Archangel was sent to the pure Virgin and with his greeting 'Hail!' he brought good tidings, that the Deliverer would come forth from her. And so, accepting his salutation with faith, she conceived Thee, the pre-eternal God, who wast pleased to become man ineffably, for the salvation of our souls.

℣. Tell forth from day to day the glad tidings of the salvation of our God (*Psalm* 95:2).

The Theotokos heard a voice she knew not, when the Archangel brought her the glad tidings of the Annunciation; and accepting the salutation with faith, she conceived Thee the pre-eternal God. Therefore in great rejoicing we also cry unto Thee: O God, who without change hast been made flesh from her, grant peace unto the world and to our souls great mercy.

℣. Sing unto the Lord a new song: sing unto the Lord, all the earth (*ibid.*, 1).

Lo, our restoration is now made manifest to us: God is ineffably united to men. At the words of the Archangel error is laid low; for the Virgin receives joy, and the things of the earth have become heaven. The world is loosened from the ancient curse. Let the creation rejoice exceedingly and raise its voice to sing: O Lord, our Maker and Deliverer, glory to Thee.

Glory be to the Father . . . Both now . . .

TONE FOUR

(*by Andrew of Jerusalem*)

Today there come glad tidings of joy: it is the feast of the Virgin. Things below are joined to things above. Adam is renewed, and Eve set free from her ancient sorrow; and the Tabernacle of the human nature which the Lord took upon Himself, making divine the substance He assumed, is consecrated as a Temple of God. O mystery! The manner of His emptying is unknown, the fashion of His conceiving is ineffable. An angel ministers at the wonder; a virgin womb receives the Son. The Holy Spirit is sent down; the Father on high gives His consent; and so the covenant is brought to pass by common counsel. In Him and through Him are we saved, and together with Gabriel let us cry aloud unto the Virgin: 'Hail, thou who art full of grace: the Lord is with thee. From thee has Christ our God and our Salvation taken human nature, raising it up unto Himself. Pray to Him that our souls may be saved.'

Apolytikion (troparion) of the feast:

TONE FOUR

Today is the crown of our salvation and the manifestation of the mystery that is from all eternity. The Son of God becomes Son of the Virgin, and Gabriel announces the good tidings of grace. Therefore let us also join him and cry aloud to the Theotokos: Hail, thou who art full of grace: the Lord is with thee.

And the Dismissal.

Mattins

After the first reading from the Psalter, sessional hymn:[1]

TONE ONE

The mighty captain of the companies of angels drew near to the city of Nazareth and announced to thee, O Undefiled, the coming of the King and Lord of the ages, saying to thee: 'Hail, blessed Mary, thou wonder past speech and beyond understanding, who art the restoration of mortal man.'

Glory be to the Father . . . Both now . . .

Repeat.

After the second reading from the Psalter, sessional hymn:

TONE THREE

Today all creation greatly rejoices, for the Archangel says unto thee, 'Hail! Blessed art thou, O Pure and Holy, Undefiled and Spotless.' Today the proud insolence of the serpent is brought low, for the fetters of the curse laid on our forefather are loosened. Therefore with all the world we cry aloud to thee: Hail, thou who art full of grace.

Glory be to the Father . . . Both now . . .

Repeat.

[1] In Slav use the rules are as follows:
After the first reading from the Psalter, the two sessional hymns appointed in the Triodion; no Small Litany.
After the second reading from the Psalter:
The mighty captain of the companies of angels . . .
Glory be to the Father . . . Both now . . .
Today all creation greatly rejoices . . .

After the polyeleos, the megalynarion:[1]

With the voice of the Archangel we cry aloud to thee, O pure Virgin: Hail, thou who art full of grace, the Lord is with thee.

℣. Give the King Thy judgements, O God, and Thy righteousness unto the King's Son (*Psalm* 71 : 1).

With the voice of the Archangel . . .

℣. He shall come down as rain upon a fleece (*ibid.*, 6).

With the voice of the Archangel . . .

Glory be to the Father . . . Both now . . .

Alleluia, alleluia, alleluia, glory be to Thee, O God (*3 times*).

With the voice of the Archangel . . .

Sessional hymn:

TONE FOUR

Gabriel from heaven cried out to her that is holy and pure: 'Hail! For in thy womb thou shalt conceive the pre-eternal God, who by His word has set together the ends of the earth.' 'I know not a man', Mary answered: 'how can I bear a son? Who has ever seen a birth without seed?' Disclosing God's purpose, the angel said to the Theotokos and Virgin: 'The Holy Spirit shall come upon thee and the power of the Most High shall overshadow thee.'[2]

Glory be to the Father . . .

Repeat.

Both now . . .

SAME TONE

Gabriel was sent to the pure Virgin, and disclosed to her joy past telling: 'Thou shalt conceive without seed and shalt

[1] In the Slav use only.
[2] Luke 1 : 35.

remain inviolate. For thou shalt bear a Son who is the pre-eternal God, and He will save His people from their sins.[1] Such is the testimony of Him who sent me to cry aloud to thee, O blessed Lady, "Hail!" As a Virgin shalt thou bear child, and after childbirth thou shalt remain Virgin.'

The first antiphon of the hymn of degrees in Tone Four.

Prokimenon: TONE FOUR

Tell forth from day to day the glad tidings of the salvation of our God (*Psalm* 95:2).

℣. Sing unto the Lord a new song: sing unto the Lord, all the earth (*ibid.*, 1).

Let everything that hath breath . . .

READING FROM THE HOLY GOSPEL ACCORDING TO LUKE (1:39–49, 56. *See p. 109*).

Psalm 50.

Glory be to the Father . . .
At the prayers of the Theotokos . . .
Both now . . .
At the prayers of the Theotokos . . .
Have mercy upon me . . .

Gabriel today announces the good tidings, *the sticheron sung at the end of the Lity (p. 444).*

Canon of the feast, by John the Monk.[2] *In each Canticle the irmos is repeated, and then twelve troparia are used.*

TONE FOUR

Canticle One

(**Irmos**) I shall open my mouth and the Spirit will inspire it, and I shall utter the words of my song to the Queen and

[1] Matthew 1:21.

[2] Some editions of the service books ascribe only Canticles Eight and Nine to John, and the remainder of the Canon to Theophanes.

Mother: I shall be seen radiantly keeping feast and joyfully praising her conceiving.

Most holy Theotokos, save us.

Let thy forefather David sing to thee, O Lady, striking upon the harp of the Spirit: 'Hearken, O Daughter,[1] to the glad voice of the Angel, for he discloses to thee joy past telling.'

The Angel

In gladness I cry to thee: incline thine ear and give heed unto me, as I tell thee of God's conception without seed. For thou, O Most Pure, hast found grace before the Lord such as no other woman ever found.

The Theotokos

O Angel, help me to understand the meaning of thy words. How shall what thou sayest come to pass? Tell me clearly, how shall I conceive, who am a virgin maid? And how shall I become the Mother of my Maker?

The Angel

Thou dost think, so it seems, that I utter words deceitfully; and I rejoice to see thy prudence. But take courage, O Lady: for when God wills, strange wonders are easily accomplished.

(**Katavasia**) I shall open my mouth . . .

Canticle Three

(**Irmos**) O Mother of God, thou living and plentiful fount, give strength to those united in spiritual fellowship, who sing hymns of praise to thee: and on this feast of thy holy conceiving vouchsafe unto them crowns of glory.

The Theotokos

There is no more a prince from Judah's line,[2] but the

[1] Psalm 44:11.
[2] Genesis 49:10.

time is at hand in which Christ, the hope of the Gentiles, shall appear. But do thou make plain to me how I, being a virgin, shall bear Him?

The Angel

O Virgin, thou dost seek to know from me the manner of thy conceiving, but this is beyond all interpretation. The Holy Spirit shall overshadow thee in His creative power and shall make this come to pass.

The Theotokos

My mother Eve, accepting the suggestion of the serpent, was banished from divine delight: and therefore I fear thy strange salutation, for I take heed lest I slip.

The Angel

I am sent as the envoy of God to disclose to thee the divine will. Why art thou, O Undefiled, afraid of me, who rather am afraid of thee? Why, O Lady, dost thou stand in awe of me, who stand in reverent awe of thee?

(**Katavasia**) O Mother of God, thou living and plentiful fount . . .

Sessional hymn

TONE EIGHT

The Word of God is now come down upon earth. The Angel stood before the Virgin and cried aloud: 'Hail, blessed Lady, who alone among women hast preserved the seal of thy virginity, while yet receiving in thy womb the pre-eternal Word and Lord, that He as God may save mankind from error.'

Glory be to the Father . . . Both now . . .

Repeat.

Canticle Four

(**Irmos**) He who sits in glory upon the throne of the Godhead, Jesus the true God, is come in a swift cloud,[1] and with His pure hand He has saved those who cry: Glory to Thy power, O Christ.

The Theotokos

I have learnt from the Prophet, who foretold in times of old the coming of Emmanuel, that a certain holy Virgin should bear a child.[2] But I long to know how the nature of mortal men shall undergo union with the Godhead.

The Angel

The bush that burnt with fire and yet remained unconsumed,[3] disclosed the secret mystery that shall come to pass in thee, O pure Maiden, full of grace. For after childbirth thou shalt remain ever-Virgin.

The Theotokos

O Gabriel, herald of the truth, shining with the radiance of Almighty God, tell me truly: how shall I, my purity remaining untouched, bear in the flesh the Word that has no body?

The Angel

I stand before thee in fear, as a servant before his mistress, and in awe I am afraid to look at thee now, O Maid. In His good pleasure shall the Word of God descend upon Thee, as dew upon the fleece.[4]

(**Katavasia**) He who sits in glory upon the throne of the Godhead . . .

[1] Isaiah 19:1.
[2] Isaiah 7:14.
[3] Exodus 3:2.
[4] Judges 6:38; Psalm 71:6.

Canticle Five

(**Irmos**) The whole world was amazed at thy divine glory: for thou, O Virgin who hast not known wedlock, hast held in thy womb the God of all, and hast given birth to an eternal Son, who rewards with salvation all who sing thy praises.

The Theotokos

I cannot understand the meaning of thy words. For there have often been miracles, wonders worked by the might of God, symbols and figures contained in the Law. But never has a virgin borne child without knowing a man.

The Angel

Thou art amazed, O all-blameless Virgin; and amazing indeed is the wonder that comes to pass in thee: for thou alone shalt receive in thy womb the King of all who is to take flesh. It is thou who art prefigured by the utterances and dark sayings of the prophets and by the symbols of the Law.

The Theotokos

How can He whom nothing can contain, upon whom none can gaze, dwell in the womb of a virgin whom He Himself has formed? And how shall I conceive God the Word, who with the Father and the Spirit has no beginning?

The Angel

He who promised to thy forefather David that of the fruit of his body He would set upon the throne of his kingdom,[1] He it is that has chosen thee, the only excellency of Jacob,[2] as His spiritual dwelling-place.

(**Katavasia**) The whole world was amazed at thy divine glory . . .

[1] Psalm 131:11.
[2] Psalm 46:5.

Canticle Six

(**Irmos**) Prefiguring Thy three-day burial, the prophet Jonah cried out in the belly of the whale: 'Deliver me from corruption, O Jesus, King and Lord of hosts.'

The Theotokos

Receiving thy glad tidings, O Gabriel, I am filled with divine joy. For thou dost speak to me of joy, a joy without end.

The Angel

Divine joy is given to thee, O Mother of God. All creation cries unto thee: 'Hail, O Bride of God.' For thou alone, O pure Virgin, wast foreordained to be the Mother of the Son of God.

The Theotokos

May the condemnation of Eve be now brought to naught through me; and through me may her debt be repaid this day. Through me may the ancient due be rendered up in full.

The Angel

God promised to our forefather Abraham that in his seed the Gentiles would be blest,[1] O pure Lady; and through thee today the promise receives its fulfilment.

(**Katavasia**) As we celebrate this sacred and solemn feast of the Mother of God, let us come, clapping our hands, O people of the Lord, and give glory to God who was born of her.

Kontakion

TONE EIGHT

To thee, O Theotokos, victorious leader of triumphant hosts, we thy servants,[2] delivered from calamity, offer hymns

[1] Genesis 22:18.
[2] In the original, 'city'.

of thanksgiving. In thine invincible power, keep us free from every peril, that we may cry to thee: Hail, thou Bride unwedded.

Ikos

A prince of the angels was sent from heaven to say to the Theotokos, 'Hail!' And seeing Thee, O Lord, take bodily form at the sound of his bodiless voice, he was filled with amazement and stood still, crying to her thus:

Hail, thou through whom joy will shine forth:
Hail, thou through whom the curse will cease.
Hail, thou restoration of fallen Adam:
Hail, thou redemption of the tears of Eve.
Hail, thou Height hard to climb for the thought of man:
Hail, thou Depth hard to perceive even for the eyes of angels.
Hail, thou that art the throne of the King:
Hail, thou who dost hold Him who holdeth all.
Hail, thou Star who dost make the Sun appear:
Hail, thou Womb of the divine incarnation.
Hail, thou through whom the creation is made new:
Hail, thou through whom the Creator becomes a newborn child.
Hail, thou Bride unwedded!

Canticle Seven

(**Irmos**) The Holy Children bravely trampled upon the threatening fire, preferring not to worship created things rather than the Creator, and they sang in joy: 'Blessed art Thou and praised above all, O Lord God of our fathers.'

The Theotokos

Thou dost bring me good tidings of divine joy, that the immaterial Light, in His abundant compassion, will be united to a material body; and now thou criest out to me: 'O All-Pure, blessed is the fruit of thy womb.'

The Angel

Hail, O Lady, hail, O most pure Virgin; hail, thou vessel wherein God is contained, hail, thou candlestick of the Light, the restoration of Adam and the deliverance of Eve, holy Mountain, shining Sanctuary, and Bridal Chamber of immortality.

The Theotokos

The descent of the Holy Spirit has purified my soul and sanctified my body: it has made of me a Temple that contains God, a Tabernacle divinely adorned, a living Sanctuary, and the pure Mother of Life.

The Angel

I see thee as a Lamp with many lights and as a Bridal Chamber made by God. As an Ark of gold, O spotless Maiden, receive now the Giver of the Law, who through thee has been pleased to deliver the corrupt nature of mankind.

(**Katavasia**) The Holy Children bravely trampled upon the threatening fire . . .

Canticle Eight

(**Irmos**)[1] The offspring of the Theotokos saved the Holy Children in the furnace. He who was then prefigured has since been born on earth, and He gathers together all the creation to sing: O all ye works of the Lord, bless ye the Lord and exalt Him above all for ever.

The Angel

'Hearken, O pure Virgin Maid: let Gabriel tell thee the counsel of the Most High that is ancient and true. Make ready

[1] Some books omit *The offspring of the Theotokos*, and proceed at once to the verse that follows, *Hearken, O pure Virgin Maid*.

to receive God: for through thee the Incomprehensible comes to dwell with mortal men. Therefore I cry rejoicing: O all ye works of the Lord, bless ye the Lord.'

The Theotokos

'All mortal thought is overwhelmed,' answered the Virgin, 'as it ponders the strange wonders of which thou tellest me. I am filled with joy at thy words, yet am afraid: I fear lest thou deceive me, as Eve was deceived, and lead me far from God. Yet lo, thou criest out: O all ye works of the Lord, bless ye the Lord.'

The Angel

'See, thy difficulty is resolved', said Gabriel to this. 'Thou hast well said that this matter is hard to grasp. Obey, then, the words of thine own lips: doubt not as though it were deceitful, but believe in this thing as very truth. For I cry rejoicing: O all ye works of the Lord, bless ye the Lord.'

The Theotokos

'Childbirth comes from mutual love: such is the law that God has given to men', said again she who is without reproach. 'I know not at all the pleasure of marriage: how then dost thou say that I shall bear child? I fear lest thou speakest in guile. Yet lo, thou criest out: O all ye works of the Lord, bless ye the Lord.'

The Angel

'O holy Virgin,' replied the Angel, 'thou speakest to me of the customary manner whereby mortal men are born. But I tell thee of the birth of the true God. Beyond words and understanding, in ways that He alone knows, He shall take flesh of thee. Therefore, I cry rejoicing: O all ye works of the Lord, bless ye the Lord.'

The Theotokos

'Thou dost appear to me to speak the truth', answered the Virgin. 'For thou hast come as an angel messenger, bringing joy to all. Since, then, I am purified in soul and body by the Spirit, be it unto me according to thy word: may God dwell in me. Unto Him I cry aloud with thee: O all ye works of the Lord, bless ye the Lord.'

(**Katavasia**) 'Hearken, O pure Virgin Maid . . .'

Canticle Nine

The Magnificat and Greater in honour than the cherubim *are not sung, but before the irmos and the troparia we sing the megalynarion:*

O earth, announce good tidings of great joy: ye heavens, praise the glory of God.

(**Irmos**) Let every mortal born on earth, carrying his torch, in spirit leap for joy; and let the order of the angelic powers celebrate and honour the holy feast of the Mother of God, and let them cry: Hail! Thou blessed and ever Virgin, who gavest birth to God.[1]

Let no profane hand touch the living Ark of God, but let the lips of the faithful, singing without ceasing the words of the Angel to the Theotokos, cry aloud in great joy: Hail, thou who art full of grace: the Lord is with thee.

Having conceived God in ways past understanding, O Maiden, thou hast escaped from the ordinances of nature. For though by nature mortal, thou wast not subject to the established laws of motherhood. Therefore, as is meet, dost thou hear the salutation: 'Hail, thou who art full of grace: the Lord is with thee.'

[1] Some books omit *Let every mortal born on earth*, and proceed at once to the verse that follows, *Let no profane hand*.

How dost thou give milk, O pure Virgin? This the tongue of mortal man cannot make plain. For thou showest forth a thing unknown to nature, that utterly surpasses the usual laws of birth. Therefore, as is meet, dost Thou hear the salutation: 'Hail, thou who art full of grace: the Lord is with thee.'

The Holy Scriptures speak of thee mystically, O Mother of the Most High. For Jacob[1] saw in days of old the ladder that prefigured thee, and said: 'This is the stair on which God shall tread.' Therefore, as is meet, dost thou hear the salutation: 'Hail, thou who art full of grace: the Lord is with thee.'

The bush and the fire showed a strange marvel to Moses, the initiate in sacred things.[2] Seeking its fulfilment in the course of time, he said: 'I shall observe it brought to pass in the pure Virgin. To her as Theotokos shall the salutation come: Hail, thou who art full of grace: the Lord is with thee.'

Daniel called thee a spiritual mountain; Isaiah, the Mother of God; Gideon saw thee as a fleece and David called thee sanctuary; another called thee gate.[3] And Gabriel in his turn cries out to thee: 'Hail, thou who art full of grace, the Lord is with thee.'

(**Katavasia**) Let no profane hand touch the living Ark of God . . .

Exapostilarion

The captain of the angelic hosts was sent by God Almighty to the pure Virgin, to announce the good tidings of a strange and secret wonder: that, as man, God would be born a babe of her without seed, fashioning again the whole race of man.

[1] Genesis 28:12.

[2] Exodus 3:2.

[3] Daniel 2:34; Isaiah 7:14; Judges 6:38; Psalm 95:6 and 131:8 (Septuagint); Ezekiel 44:2.

O ye people, announce the good tidings of the refashioning of the world (*twice*).

Glory be to the Father . . . Both now . . .

Hail, O Theotokos, deliverance from the curse of Adam. Hail, holy Mother of God; hail, living Bush. Hail, Lamp; hail, Throne; hail, Ladder and Gate. Hail, divine Chariot; hail, swift Cloud. Hail, Temple; hail, Vessel of gold. Hail, Mountain; hail, Tabernacle and Table. Hail, thou release of Eve.[1]

Lauds. Four stichera are sung:

TONE ONE

(*to the special melody*, O purest Virgin, thou joy of the heavenly hierarchies . . .)

Gabriel flew down from the vault of heaven and came to Nazareth; and standing before the Virgin Mary, he cried to her: 'Hail! Thou shalt conceive a Son, more ancient than Adam, the Maker of all things and the Deliverer of those who cry to thee: Hail, pure Virgin' (*twice*).

Gabriel brought from heaven good tidings to the Virgin, and he cried out to her: 'Hail! Thou shalt conceive in thy womb Him whom the world cannot contain, who yet shall be contained in thee; and thou shalt be the bearer of Him who shone forth from the Father before the morning star.'[2]

The coeternal Word of the Father without beginning, not being parted from the things on high, has now descended here below, in His infinite compassion taking pity upon fallen men; and assuming the poverty of Adam, He has put on a form that is alien to Him.

Glory be to the Father . . . Both now . . .

[1] Genesis 3:15–17; Exodus 3:2, 25:31; Genesis 28:12,17; Ezekiel 44:2; Isaiah 19:1; Exodus 16:33; Daniel 2:34–35; Exodus 26:1, 25:23.

[2] Psalm 109:3 (Septuagint).

TONE TWO

(by Theophanes)

Today is revealed the mystery that is from all eternity. The Son of God becomes the Son of man, that, sharing in what is worse, He may make me share in what is better. In times of old Adam was once deceived: he sought to become God,[1] but received not his desire. Now God becomes man, that He may make Adam God. Let creation rejoice, let nature exult: for the Archangel stands in fear before the Virgin and, saying to her 'Hail', he brings the joyful greeting whereby our sorrow is assuaged. O Thou who in Thy merciful compassion wast made man, our God, glory to Thee.

Doxology and Dismissal.

Liturgy

On Weekdays during Lent, the Liturgy is celebrated after Vespers (see below, p. 464). But on Saturdays and Sundays during Lent (except for Holy Saturday), and on Monday, Tuesday, or Wednesday during Easter Week, the Liturgy is celebrated before Vespers at the usual hour, as follows:

The Typika (Psalms 102 and 145) and the Beatitudes. With the Beatitudes are sung four troparia from Canticle Three of the Canon of the Feast (p. 449) and four troparia from Canticle Six (p. 453).

Alternatively, according to the modern Greek practice, the following antiphons may be sung:

Antiphon One

TONE TWO

℣ 1. Give the King Thy judgements, O God: and Thy righteousness unto the King's Son (*Psalm* 71:1).

At the prayers of the Theotokos, save us, O Saviour.

[1] Genesis 3:5.

℣ 2. May the mountains bring peace to Thy people: and the little hills righteousness (*ibid.*, 3).

At the prayers of the Theotokos . . .

℣ 3. Tell forth from day to day the glad tidings of the salvation of our God (*Psalm* 95:2).

At the prayers of the Theotokos . . .

℣ 4. The Lord hath sworn in truth unto David; He will not turn from it: of the fruit of thy body will I set upon thy throne (*Psalm* 131:11).

At the prayers of the Theotokos . . .
Glory be to the Father . . . Both now . . .
At the prayers of the Theotokos . . .

Antiphon Two

SAME TONE

℣ 1. He shall come down as rain upon a fleece: and as the dew which falls upon the earth (*Psalm* 71:6).

O Son of God, incarnate of the Virgin,[1] save us who sing to Thee: alleluia.

℣ 2. The Most High hath sanctified His tabernacle (*Psalm* 45:5).

O Son of God . . .

℣ 3. Our God shall plainly come, and shall not keep silence (*Psalm* 49:3).

O Son of God . . .

℣ 4. In His days righteousness shall shine forth: and abundance of peace, so long as the moon endureth (*Psalm* 71:7).

O Son of God . . .

Glory be to the Father . . . Both now . . .
O Only-begotten Son and Word of God . . .

[1] Some editions read, *incarnate for our sake.*

Antiphon Three

TONE FOUR

℣ 1. His Name shall be blessed for ever: His Name shall continue longer than the sun (*Psalm* 71 : 17).

The troparion of the feast, Today is the crown of our salvation (*p. 445*).

℣ 2. Blessed be the Lord, the God of Israel, who only doeth wondrous things (*ibid.*, 18).

The troparion of the feast.

℣ 3. And blessed be His glorious Name unto the ages, and unto the ages of ages (*ibid.*, 19).

The troparion of the feast.

Introit:

Tell forth from day to day the glad tidings of the salvation of our God (*Psalm* 95 : 2).

O Son of God, incarnate of the Virgin, save us who sing to Thee: alleluia.[1]

The troparion of the feast (*p. 445*); Glory be to the Father . . . Both now . . .; *the kontakion of the feast* (*p. 453*).

Prokimenon: *TONE FOUR*

Tell forth from day to day the glad tidings of the salvation of our God (*Psalm* 95 : 2).

℣. Sing unto the Lord a new song: sing unto the Lord, all the earth (*ibid.*, 1).

READING FROM THE EPISTLE TO THE HEBREWS (2 : 11–18. *See p. 246*).

Alleluia, TONE TWO[2]

℣ 1. He shall come down as rain upon a fleece: and as the dew which falls upon the earth (*Psalm* 71 : 6).

[1] In the Slav use, *O Son of God* . . . is sung only at pontifical services.

[2] In the Slav use, Tone One.

℣ 2. His Name shall be blessed for ever: His Name shall continue longer than the sun (*ibid.*, 17).

READING FROM THE HOLY GOSPEL ACCORDING TO LUKE (1:24–38).

After those days Elisabeth the wife of Zacharias conceived, and hid herself five months, saying, Thus hath the Lord dealt with me in the days wherein He looked on me, to take away my reproach among men. And in the sixth month the angel Gabriel was sent from God unto a city of Galilee, named Nazareth, to a virgin espoused to a man whose name was Joseph, of the house of David; and the virgin's name was Mary. And the angel came in unto her, and said, Hail, thou that art highly favoured, the Lord is with thee: blessed art thou among women. And when she saw him, she was troubled at his saying and cast in her mind what manner of salutation this should be. And the angel said unto her, Fear not, Mary: for thou hast found favour with God. And, behold, thou shalt conceive in thy womb, and bring forth a son, and shalt call His name Jesus. He shall be great, and shall be called the Son of the Highest: and the Lord God shall give unto Him the throne of His father David: and He shall reign over the house of Jacob for ever; and of His kingdom there shall be no end. Then said Mary unto the angel, How shall this be, seeing I know not a man? And the angel answered and said unto her, The Holy Ghost shall come upon thee, and the power of the Highest shall overshadow thee: therefore also that holy thing which shall be born of thee shall be called the Son of God. And, behold, thy cousin Elisabeth, she hath also conceived a son in her old age: and this is the sixth month with her, who was called barren. For with God nothing shall be impossible. And Mary said, Behold the handmaid of the Lord; be it unto me according to thy word. And the angel departed from her.

In place of It is meet, *we sing the megalynarion and irmos from Canticle Nine of the Canon* (*p.* 457).

Communion verse:

The Lord hath chosen Zion: He hath desired it for His habitation (*Psalm* 131 : 13).

Great Vespers

On Lord, I have cried, *six stichera are sung, three being of the feast:*

In the sixth month the Archangel was sent to the pure Virgin . . .

The Theotokos heard a voice she knew not . . .

Lo, our restoration is now made manifest to us . . .[1]

Then three stichera of the Archangel:[2]

TONE ONE

Gabriel, the greatest and most godlike of the spiritual powers, shining with heavenly brightness, who with the hosts on high gazes upon the light of the Threefold Sun, came to the Virgin and announced to her the glad tidings of the divine mystery full of awe; and he intercedes for our souls.

To thee alone, O Gabriel, was entrusted the great mystery, till then unknown to the angels and hid from all eternity: coming to Nazareth, thou hast not dared to impart it to any save the pure Virgin alone. Pray with her that our souls may be granted peace and great mercy.

Thou who art ever filled with light, who doest the will and fulfillest the decrees of the Almighty, O Leader of the angels, Gabriel the all-perfect, preserve those who honour thee with

[1] See the aposticha for the Vigil of the feast, pp. 444–5.

[2] 26 March is observed as the Synaxis of the Archangel Gabriel.

love, and ask at all times that our souls may be granted peace and great mercy.

Glory be to the Father . . . Both now . . .

Gabriel the Archangel was sent from heaven . . .[1]

Entrance with the Gospel,[2] O joyful light, *and prokimenon of the day.*

Lessons:

Reading from Exodus (3 : 1–8).

Moses came to the mountain of God, even to Horeb. And the angel of the Lord appeared unto him in a flame of fire out of the midst of a bush: and he looked, and, behold, the bush burned with fire, and the bush was not consumed. And Moses said, I will now turn aside, and see this great sight, why the bush is not burnt. And when the Lord saw that he turned aside to see, God called unto him out of the midst of the bush, and said, Moses, Moses. And he said, Here am I. And He said, Draw not nigh hither: put off thy shoes from off thy feet, for the place whereon thou standest is holy ground. Moreover He said, I am the God of thy father, the God of Abraham, the God of Isaac, and the God of Jacob. And Moses hid his face; for he was afraid to look upon God. And the Lord said, I have surely seen the affliction of My people which are in Egypt, and have heard their cry by reason of their taskmasters; for I know their sorrows; and I am come down to deliver them out of the hand of the Egyptians, and to bring them up out of that land unto a good land and a large, unto a land flowing with milk and honey.

Reading from Proverbs (8 : 22–30).

The Lord possessed me in the beginning of His way, before

[1] The troparion before the entrance in the first Vespers of the feast, p. 440.

[2] On Saturday and Sunday, and during Easter Week, without the Gospel.

His works of old. I was set up from everlasting, from the beginning, or ever the earth was. When there were no depths, I was brought forth; when there were no fountains abounding with water. Before the mountains were settled, before the hills was I brought forth: while as yet He had not made the earth, nor the fields, nor the highest part of the dust of the world. When He prepared the heavens, I was there: when He set a compass upon the face of the depth: when He established the clouds above: when He strengthened the fountains of the deep; when He gave to the sea His decree, that the waters should not pass His commandment: when He appointed the foundations of the earth: then was I by Him, as one brought up with Him: and I was daily His delight, rejoicing always before Him.

On weekdays during Lent, and during Holy Week (except on Good Friday), the Liturgy follows, with the Small Litany, the trisagion, and then the Prokimenon, Epistle, and Gospel given above (p. 462–3).

On Saturdays and Sundays, Vespers continue as usual: we sing the aposticha from Small Vespers, Gabriel, leader of the powers above, *etc.* (*p. 438*).

Apolytikion (troparion) of the Archangel:

TONE FOUR

O chief commander of the heavenly hosts, in our unworthiness unceasingly we pray to thee: surround us with the rampart of thine intercessions. Shelter us beneath the protection of thy wings of spiritual glory, for we fall down before thee, crying earnestly: deliver us from peril, O leader of the powers on high.

If the feast of the Annunciation falls within Lent, fish, wine, and oil are allowed, but meat and animal products may not be eaten.

If it falls in Holy Week, however, wine and oil only are permitted, but not fish, and on Good Friday and Holy Saturday, wine is permitted, but not oil. Within Eastertide, there is a general dispensation from all fasting, as usual during Easter Week.

The feast of the Annunciation closes either at Vespers on 25 March, or else on the day following, 26 March.

6 AUGUST

THE TRANSFIGURATION OF OUR LORD AND GOD AND SAVIOUR JESUS CHRIST

Small Vespers

On Lord, I have cried, *four stichera are sung:*

TONE FOUR

(*to the special melody*, Thou hast given an ensign . . .)

Come, let us rejoice, mounting up from the earth to the highest contemplation of the virtues: let us be transformed this day into a better state and direct our minds to heavenly things, being shaped anew in piety according to the form of Christ.[1] For in His mercy the Saviour of our souls has transfigured disfigured man and made him shine with light upon Mount Tabor (*twice*).

O let us who love to see and hear things past understanding, mystically behold Christ shine as lightning with the rays of divine splendour; and let us make the Father's voice resound, who proclaimed Him as His well-beloved Son.[2] On Mount Tabor He makes bright the weakness of man and bestows enlightenment upon our souls.

Let the assembly of all on earth and in the world above be moved to praise Christ our God, Lord both of the living and the dead.[3] For when He was divinely transfigured on Tabor,

1 Philippians 3:10.
2 Matthew 17:5.
3 Romans 14:9.

the Saviour of our souls was pleased to have at His side the leaders and the preachers of both the Law and Grace.

Glory be to the Father . . . Both now . . .

TONE EIGHT

The shining cloud of the Transfiguration has taken the place of the darkness of the Law. Moses and Elijah were counted worthy of this glory brighter than light and, taken up within it, they said unto God: 'Thou art our God, the King of the ages.'

Aposticha:

TONE TWO

(*to the special melody*, O house of Ephratah . . .)

Today Christ on Mount Tabor has changed the darkened nature of Adam, and filling it with brightness He has made it godlike.

℣. The heavens are Thine, the earth also is Thine: as for the world and the fullness thereof, Thou hast founded them (*Psalm* 88: 12).

Shining forth with the light of the virtues, let us set foot on the holy mountain that we may gaze upon the divine Transfiguration of the Lord.

℣. Tabor and Hermon shall rejoice in Thy Name (*ibid.*, 13).

The sun which makes the earth bright sets once more; but Christ has shone as lightning with glory upon the mountain and has filled the world with light.

Glory be to the Father . . . Both now . . .

SAME TONE

Moses and Elijah saw upon Tabor God, who was made flesh of a virgin Maid for the redemption of mortal men.

Apolytikion (*troparion*) *of the feast*, Thou wast transfigured upon the mountain (*p. 477*), *and Dismissal.*

Great Vespers

No reading from the Psalter.

On Lord, I have cried, *eight stichera are sung:*

TONE FOUR

(*by Cosmas the Monk*)

Before Thy Crucifixion, O Lord, the mountain became as heaven and a cloud spread itself out to form a tabernacle. When Thou wast transfigured and the Father testified unto Thee, Peter with James and John were there, who were to be present with Thee also at the time of Thy betrayal: that, having beheld Thy wonders, they should not be afraid before Thy suffering. Grant in Thy great mercy that we too may be counted worthy to venerate these Thy sufferings in peace (*twice*).

Before Thy Crucifixion, O Lord, taking the disciples up into a high mountain, Thou wast transfigured before them, shining upon them with the bright beams of Thy power: from love of mankind and in Thy sovereign might, Thy desire it was to show them the splendour of the Resurrection. Grant that we too in peace may be counted worthy of this splendour, O God, for Thou art merciful and lovest mankind (*twice*).

When Thou wast transfigured, O Saviour, upon a high mountain, having with Thee the chief disciples, Thou hast shone forth in glorious majesty, proving thereby that those who surpass in the height of their virtues shall be counted worthy of the divine glory. Talking with Christ, Moses and Elijah showed that He is Lord of both the living and the dead,[1] the God who spake of old through the Law and the prophets. And the voice of the Father testified to Him from the cloud

[1] Romans 14:9.

of light saying, 'Hear ye Him, who through His Cross harrows hell and gives the dead eternal life' (*twice*).[1]

The mountain that was once gloomy and veiled in smoke has now become venerable and holy, since Thy feet, O Lord, have stood upon it. For thy dread Transfiguration, the mystery hidden before the ages, has been made manifest in the last times to Peter, John, and James.[2] Unable to endure the shining of Thy countenance and the brightness of Thy garments, they fell to the ground upon their faces. Seized with astonishment and wonder, they saw Moses and Elijah talking with Thee of the things that should befall Thee; and a voice in testimony came from the Father, saying: 'This is my beloved Son in whom I am well-pleased: hear ye Him. He it is who grants the world great mercy' (*twice*).

Glory be to the Father . . . Both now . . .

TONE SIX

(*by Anatolios*)

Prefiguring, O Christ our God, Thy Resurrection, Thou hast taken with Thee in Thy ascent upon Mount Tabor Thy three disciples, Peter, James, and John. When Thou wast transfigured, O Saviour, Mount Tabor was covered with light. Thy disciples, O Word, cast themselves down upon the ground, unable to gaze upon the Form that none may see. The angels ministered in fear and trembling, the heavens shook and the earth quaked, as they beheld upon earth the Lord of glory.

Entrance, O joyful light, *and the prokimenon of the day*.

[1] In the Slavonic books, this and the following sticheron are reversed in order.

[2] Colossians 1:26.

Lessons:

READING FROM EXODUS (24:12–18).

The Lord said unto Moses, Come up to Me into the mount, and be there: and I will give thee tables of stone, and a law, and commandments which I have written; that thou mayest teach them. And Moses rose up, and his minister Joshua; and Moses went up into the mount of God. And he said unto the elders, Tarry ye here for us, until we come again unto you: and, behold, Aaron and Hur are with you: if any man have any matters to do, let him come unto them. And Moses went up into the mount, and a cloud covered the mount. And the glory of the Lord abode upon mount Sinai, and the cloud covered it six days: and the seventh day He called unto Moses out of the midst of the cloud. And the sight of the glory of the Lord was like devouring fire on the top of the mount in the eyes of the children of Israel. And Moses went into the midst of the cloud, and gat him up into the mount: and Moses was in the mount forty days and forty nights.

READING FROM EXODUS (33:11–23; 34:4–6, 8).

The Lord spake unto Moses face to face, as a man speaketh unto his friend. And he turned again into the camp: but his servant Joshua, the son of Nun, a young man, departed not out of the tabernacle. And Moses said unto the Lord, See, Thou sayest unto me, Bring up this people; and Thou hast not let me know whom Thou wilt send with me. Yet, Thou hast said, I know thee by name, and thou hast also found grace in My sight. Now therefore, I pray Thee, if I have found grace in Thy sight, shew me now Thy way, that I may know Thee, that I may find grace in Thy sight; and consider that this nation is Thy people. And He said, My presence shall go with thee, and I will give thee rest. And he said unto Him, If Thy presence go not with me, carry us not up hence. For wherein shall it be known here that I and Thy people have found grace in Thy sight? Is it not in that Thou goest with us? So shall we be separated, I and Thy people, from all the people that are upon the face of the earth. And the Lord said unto Moses, I will do this thing also that thou hast spoken: for thou hast found grace in My sight, and I know thee by name. And he said, I beseech Thee, shew me Thy glory. And He said, I will make all My goodness pass before thee, and I will proclaim the Name of the Lord before thee; and will be gracious to whom I will be gracious, and will shew mercy on whom I will shew mercy. And He said, Thou canst not see My face; for there shall no man see Me, and live. And the Lord said, Behold, there is a place by Me, and thou shalt stand upon a rock: and it shall come to pass, while My glory passeth by, that I will put thee in a clift of the rock, and will cover thee with My hand while I pass by: and I will take away Mine hand, and thou shalt see My back parts; but My face shall not be seen. And Moses rose up early in the morning, and went up unto mount Sinai, as the Lord had commanded him, and the Lord descended in the cloud, and stood with him there, and proclaimed the Name of the Lord. And the Lord passed by before him and proclaimed, The Lord, the Lord God, merciful and gracious, longsuffering, and abundant in goodness and truth. And Moses made haste and bowed his head toward the earth, and worshipped.

Reading from the Third Book of Kings (1 Kings 19:3–9, 11–13, 15–16).

In those days, Elijah came to Beer-sheba which belongeth to Judah, and left his servant there. But he himself went a day's journey into the wilderness, and came and sat down under a juniper tree: and he requested for himself that he might die; and said, It is enough; now, O Lord, take away my life; for I am not better than my fathers. And as he lay and slept under a juniper tree, behold, then an angel touched him, and said unto him, Arise and eat. And he looked, and, behold, there was a cake baken on the coals, and a cruse of water at his head. And he did eat and drink, and laid him down again. And the angel of the Lord came again the second time, and touched him, and said, Arise and eat; because the journey is too great for thee. And he arose, and did eat and drink, and went in the strength of that meat forty days and forty nights unto Horeb the mount of God. And he came thither unto a cave, and lodged there; and, behold, the word of the Lord came to him, and He said unto him: Go forth and stand upon the mount before the Lord. And, behold, the Lord passed by, and a great and strong wind rent the mountains, and brake in pieces the rocks before the Lord; but the Lord was not in the wind: and after the wind an earthquake; but the Lord was not in the earthquake: and after the earthquake a fire; but the Lord was not in the fire: and after the fire a still small voice. And it was so, when Elijah heard it, that he wrapped his face in his mantle, and went out, and stood in the entering in of the cave. And the Lord said unto him, Go, return on thy way to the wilderness of Damascus: and when thou comest, anoint Elisha, the son of Shaphat, to be prophet in thy room.

At the Lity:

TONE TWO

O God, who in Thy goodness hast sanctified with Thy light all the inhabited earth, Thou wast transfigured upon a high mountain, showing Thy might unto Thy disciples: for Thou dost redeem the world from transgression. Therefore we cry aloud to Thee: O Lord of compassion, save our souls.

SAME TONE

O Christ our God, who wast transfigured in glory on Mount Tabor, showing to Thy disciples the splendour of Thy Godhead, do Thou enlighten us also with the light of Thy knowledge and guide us in the path of Thy commandments, for Thou alone art good and lovest man.

SAME TONE

Christ, the Light that shone before the sun, who in the body went about the earth, having fulfilled before His Crucifixion, as befitted His divine majesty, all things pertaining to His fearful dispensation, this day has mystically made known upon Mount Tabor the image of the Trinity. For taking apart the three disciples He had expressly chosen, Peter, James, and John, He led them up into the mountain by themselves; and for a short time He concealed the flesh He had assumed, and was transfigured before them, making manifest the excellence of the original beauty, though not in its full perfection. For while giving them full assurance He also spared them, lest perchance at the sight they should lose their lives: yet they saw as much as their bodily eyes were able to receive. He likewise called before Him the chief prophets Moses and Elijah, who testified to His divinity, that He is indeed the true brightness of the essence of the Father,[1] the Ruler of the living and the dead.[2] Wherefore a cloud wrapped them round like a tent; and out of the cloud from above loudly sounded the voice of the Father, testifying and saying: 'This is my beloved Son, whom I have begotten without change from the womb before the morning star:[3] Him have I sent to save those who are baptized in the Name of Father, Son, and Holy Spirit, and who confess with faith that the One Power of the Godhead is indivisible. Hear ye Him.' And do thou Thyself, O Christ our God, supreme in goodness, who lovest mankind, shine upon us with the light of Thy glory that no man can approach and make us worthy to inherit Thy never-ending Kingdom.

Glory be to the Father . . .

TONE FIVE

Come, let us ascend into the mountain of the Lord, even

[1] Hebrews 1:3.

[2] Romans 14:9.

[3] Psalm 109:3 (Septuagint).

to the house of our God, and behold the glory of His Transfiguration, glory as of the Only-begotten of the Father.[1] Let us receive light from His Light,[2] and with uplifted spirits let us for ever sing the praises of the consubstantial Trinity.

Both now . . .

SAME TONE

Moses who saw God and Elijah who rode in the chariot of fire, passing across the heavens unconsumed, beheld Thee in the cloud at Thy Transfiguration, O Christ, and they testified that Thou art the maker and the fulfilment of the Law and the prophets. With them, count us also worthy of Thy light, O Master, that we may sing Thy praises unto all ages.

Aposticha:

TONE ONE

He who once spoke through symbols to Moses on Mount Sinai, saying, 'I am He who is',[3] was transfigured today upon Mount Tabor before the disciples; and in His own person He showed them the nature of man, arrayed in the original beauty of the Image. Calling Moses and Elijah to be witnesses of this exceeding grace, He made them sharers in His joy, foretelling His decease[4] through the Cross and His saving Resurrection.

℣. The heavens are Thine, the earth also is Thine: as for the world and the fullness thereof, Thou hast founded them (*Psalm* 88:12).

David the ancestor of God, foreseeing in spirit from afar the sojourn with men of the Only-begotten Son in the flesh, called the creation together to rejoice with him, and

[1] John 1:14.
[2] Psalm 35:10.
[3] Exodus 3:14.
[4] Luke 9:31.

prophetically lifted up his voice to cry: 'Tabor and Hermon shall rejoice in Thy name.'[1] For having gone up, O Christ, with Thy disciples into Mount Tabor, Thou wast transfigured, and hast made the nature that had grown dark in Adam to shine again as lightning, transforming it into the glory and splendour of Thine own divinity. Therefore we cry aloud unto Thee: O Lord and Creator of all things, glory to Thee.

℣. Tabor and Hermon shall rejoice in Thy Name (*ibid.*, 13).

When the chosen apostles beheld upon the mountain of the Transfiguration the overwhelming flood of Thy light, O Christ who hast no beginning, and Thy divinity unto which no man may approach, they were caught up into a divine trance. The cloud of light shone around them on every side, and they heard the voice of the Father confirming the mystery of Thine Incarnation: for even after taking flesh Thou dost remain the Only-begotten Son and the Saviour of the world.

Glory be to the Father . . . Both now . . .

TONE SIX

On Mount Tabor, O Lord, Thou hast shown today the glory of Thy divine form unto Thy chosen disciples, Peter, James, and John. For they looked upon Thy garments that gleamed as the light and at Thy face that shone more than the sun; and unable to endure the vision of Thy brightness which none can bear, they fell to the earth, completely powerless to lift up their gaze. For they heard a voice that testified from above: 'This is my beloved Son, who has come into the world to save mankind.'

Apolytikion (troparion) of the feast:

TONE SEVEN

Thou wast transfigured upon the mountain, O Christ our God, showing Thy glory to Thy disciples as far as they were

[1] Psalm 88:13.

able to bear it. At the intercessions of the Theotokos, make Thine everlasting light shine forth also upon us sinners. O Giver of light, glory to Thee.

And the Dismissal.

Mattins

After the first reading from the Psalter, sessional hymn:

TONE FOUR

Thou wast transfigured upon Mount Tabor, showing the exchange mortal men will make with Thy glory at Thy second and fearful coming, O Saviour. Elijah and Moses talked with Thee, and Thou hast called the three disciples to be with Thee. As they gazed upon Thy glory, O Master, they were struck with wonder at Thy blinding brightness. Do Thou who then hast shone upon them with Thy light, give light now to our souls.

Glory be to the Father . . . Both now . . .

Repeat.

After the second reading from the Psalter, sessional hymn:

TONE FOUR

Thou wast transfigured upon Mount Tabor, O Jesus, and a shining cloud, spread out like a tent, covered the apostles with Thy glory. Whereupon their gaze fell to the ground, for they could not bear to look upon the brightness of the unapproachable glory of Thy face, O Saviour Christ, our God who art without beginning. Do Thou who then hast shone upon them with Thy light, give light now to our souls.

Glory be to the Father . . . Both now . . .

Repeat.

After the polyeleos, the megalynarion:[1]

We magnify Thee, O Christ the Giver of life, and we venerate the all-glorious Transfiguration of Thy most pure flesh.

℣. Great is the Lord and greatly to be praised: in the city of our God and in His holy mountain (*Psalm* 47 : 2).

We magnify Thee . . .

℣. Lord, who shall abide in Thy tabernacle? and who shall dwell in Thy holy mountain? (*Psalm* 14 : 1)

We magnify Thee . . .

Glory be to the Father . . . Both now . . .

Alleluia, alleluia, alleluia, glory be to Thee, O God (*3 times*).

We magnify Thee . . .

Sessional hymn:

TONE FOUR

Going up with the disciples into the mountain, Thou hast shone forth with the glory of the Father. Moses and Elijah stood at Thy side, for the Law and the prophets minister to Thee as God. And the Father, acknowledging Thy natural Sonship, called Thee Son. We praise Him in song together with Thee and the Spirit.

Glory be to the Father . . . Both now . . .

Repeat.

But in the Slav use, after Both now . . ., *a further sessional hymn is provided:*

TONE EIGHT

Enlightening the disciples that were with Thee, O Christ our Benefactor, Thou hast shown them upon the holy mountain the hidden and blinding light of Thy nature and of

[1] In the Slav use only.

Thy divine beauty beneath the flesh; and they, understanding that Thy glory could not be borne, loudly cried out, 'Holy art Thou'. For Thou art He whom no man may approach, yet wast Thou seen in the flesh by the world, O Thou who alone lovest mankind.

The first antiphon of the hymn of degrees in Tone Four.

Prokimenon: TONE FOUR

Tabor and Hermon shall rejoice in Thy name (*Psalm* 88 : 13).

℣. The heavens are Thine, the earth also is Thine (*ibid.*, 12).

Let everything that hath breath . . .

READING FROM THE HOLY GOSPEL ACCORDING TO LUKE (9 : 28–36).

At that time Jesus took Peter and John and James, and went up into a mountain to pray. And as He prayed, the fashion of His countenance was altered, and His raiment was white and glistering. And, behold, there talked with Him two men, which were Moses and Elijah: who appeared in glory, and spake of His decease which He should accomplish at Jerusalem. But Peter and they that were with Him were heavy with sleep: and when they were awake, they saw His glory, and the two men that stood with Him. And it came to pass, as they departed from Him, Peter said unto Jesus, Master, it is good for us to be here: and let us make three tabernacles; one for Thee, and one for Moses, and one for Elijah: not knowing what he said. While he thus spake, there came a cloud, and overshadowed them: and they feared as they entered into the cloud. And there came a voice out of the cloud, saying, This is My beloved Son: hear Him. And when the voice was past, Jesus was found alone. And they kept it close, and told no man in those days any of those things which they had seen.

After the Gospel, in the Greek use the following is read and sung:

Psalm 50.

Glory be to the Father . . .
At the prayers of the apostles . . .
Both now . . .
At the prayers of the Theotokos . . .
Have mercy upon me . . .
O God, who in Thy goodness, *the first sticheron at the Lity (p. 474).*

But in the Slav use we say:

Psalm 50.

Glory be to the Father . . .
Today all things are filled with joy: Christ is transfigured before the disciples.
Both now . . .
Today all things are filled with joy . . .
Have mercy upon me . . .

TONE FIVE

Having uncovered, O Saviour, a little of the light of Thy divinity to those who went up with Thee into the mountain, Thou hast made them lovers of Thy heavenly glory. Therefore they cried in awe: 'It is good for us to be here.' With them we also sing unto Thee, O Saviour Christ who wast transfigured.

Two Canons are read: the first, by St. Cosmas, in eight troparia including the irmos, and the second by St. John of Damascus, in six, likewise including the irmos. The irmoi of each Canon are sung twice. Before the troparia we say, Glory to Thee, O God, glory to Thee.

Canticle One

First Canon

TONE FOUR

(**Irmos**) The choirs of Israel passed dry-shod across the Red Sea and the watery deep; and beholding the riders and captains of the enemy swallowed by the waters, they cried out for joy: 'Let us sing unto our God, for He has been glorified.'

Delivering to His friends words of life concerning the Kingdom of God, Christ said to them: 'When I shall shine forth with unapproachable light, ye shall know that the Father is in Me,[1] and shall cry out for joy: Let us sing unto our God, for He has been glorified.'

'O my disciples and friends, ye shall eat the strength of the Gentiles and their riches shall be your boast:[2] for when I shall appear shining brighter than the sun, ye shall be filled with glory and cry out for joy: Let us sing unto our God, for He has been glorified.'

Today as He has promised Christ, shining on Mount Tabor, dimly[3] disclosed to His disciples the image and reflection of the divine brightness; and filled with godlike and light-bearing splendour, they cried out for joy: 'Let us sing unto our God for He has been glorified.'

Second Canon

TONE EIGHT

(**Irmos**) Having crossed the water as though it were dry land, and escaped from the wickedness of Egypt, the children of Israel shouted aloud: 'Let us sing unto our Deliverer and our God.'

[1] John 14:10.
[2] Isaiah 61:6.
[3] In the Slavonic, 'clearly'.

In times past, Moses saw prophetically the glory of the Lord by the Red Sea in the cloud and the pillar of fire,[1] and he shouted aloud: 'Let us sing unto our Deliverer and our God.'

Protected by a godlike body as by a rock[2] and seeing Him who is invisible, Moses who beheld God shouted aloud: 'Let us sing unto our Deliverer and our God.'

Thou hast appeared to Moses both on the Mountain of the Law and on Tabor: of old in darkness, but now in the unapproachable light of the Godhead.

Katavasia,[3] *TONE EIGHT*

Inscribing the invincible weapon of the Cross upon the waters, Moses marked a straight line before him with his staff and divided the Red Sea, opening a path for Israel who went over dry-shod. Then he marked a second line across the waters and united them in one, overwhelming the chariots of Pharaoh.[4] Therefore let us sing to Christ our God, for He has been glorified.

Canticle Three

First Canon

(**Irmos**) The bow of the mighty has waxed feeble and the weak have girded themselves with strength: therefore is my heart established in the Lord.

Thou hast put Adam on entire, O Christ, and changing the nature grown dark in past times, Thou hast filled it with glory and made it godlike by the alteration of Thy form.[5]

[1] Exodus 14:19.

[2] Exodus 33:21–23.

[3] The Katavasia at the end of each canticle is taken from the feast of the Exaltation of the Cross (14 September), for which we now begin to prepare.

[4] Exodus 14:21–29.

[5] Luke 9:29.

In the past Christ led Israel in the wilderness with the pillar of fire and the cloud;[1] and today ineffably He has shone forth in light upon Mount Tabor.

Second Canon

(**Irmos**) O Lord, Thou Builder of the vault of heaven and Founder of the Church, do Thou confirm me in Thy love: for Thou art our supreme desire and the support of the faithful, O Thou who alone lovest mankind.

The Glory that once overshadowed the tabernacle and spake with Thy servant Moses,[2] O Master, was a figure of Thy Transfiguration that ineffably shone forth as lightning upon Tabor.

The leaders of the apostles went up with Thee into Mount Tabor, O Only-begotten Word most high, and Moses and Elijah were both present with Thee as attendants of God, O Thou who alone lovest mankind.

Being complete God, Thou hast become complete man, bringing together manhood and the complete Godhead in Thy Person which Moses and Elijah saw on Mount Tabor in the two natures.

(**Katavasia**) The rod of Aaron is an image of this mystery, when it budded it showed who should be priest.[3] So in the Church, that once was barren, the wood of the Cross has now put forth flower, filling her with strength and steadfastness.

Sessional hymn

TONE FOUR

Thou wast transfigured upon Mount Tabor, O God, between Moses and Elijah the wise, in the presence of James, Peter, and John; and Peter, as he stood there, spake thus to

[1] Exodus 14:19.
[2] Exodus 33:9.
[3] Numbers 17:8.

Thee: 'It would be good to make three tabernacles here: one for Moses, one for Elijah, and one for Thee, O Christ our Master.' Do Thou who then hast shone upon them with Thy light, give light now to our souls.

Glory be to the Father . . . Both now . . .

Repeat.

Canticle Four

First Canon

(**Irmos**) I have heard of Thy glorious Dispensation, O Christ our God: how Thou wast born of the Virgin, that so Thou mightest deliver from error those who cry aloud to Thee: Glory to Thy power, O Lord.

Thou, O Christ our God, hast delivered the written Law upon Mount Sinai, and hast appeared there riding upon the cloud, in the midst of fire and darkness and tempest.[1] Glory to Thy power, O Lord.

As a pledge of Thy glorious dispensation, Thou hast ineffably shone forth on Tabor, O Christ our God, who wast before the ages and whose chariot is the clouds.[2]

Those with whom Thou hast conversed of old in fiery vapour, in darkness and the lightest of winds,[3] stood before Thee in the manner of servants, O Christ our Master, and talked with Thee. Glory to Thy power, O Lord.

Moses who in past times foresaw Thee in the fire of the burning bush,[4] and Elijah who was taken up in a chariot of fire,[5] were present on Tabor and made known there Thy decease upon the Cross.[6]

[1] Exodus 19:16–18, 31:18; Deuteronomy 4:11.
[2] Psalm 103:3.
[3] Exodus 19:18–19; Deut. 4:11; 3 (1) Kings 19:12 (Septuagint).
[4] Exodus 3:2.
[5] 4 (2) Kings 2:11.
[6] Luke 9:31.

Second Canon

(**Irmos**) Lightning flashes of divinity proceeded forth from Thy flesh: therefore the chosen prophets and apostles sang and cried aloud: Glory to Thy power, O Lord.

Thou hast preserved the bush unharmed, O Master, though it was united with fire,[1] and Thou hast shown to Moses Thy flesh shining with divine brightness, while he sang: 'Glory to Thy power, O Lord.'

The visible sun was eclipsed by the rays of Thy divinity, when it saw Thee transfigured on Mount Tabor, O my Jesus. Glory to Thy power, O Lord.

Thou wast revealed as an immaterial fire that burns not the material substance of the body, when Thou hast appeared to Moses and the apostles and Elijah, O Master who art one in two natures and both of them perfect.

(**Katavasia**) O Lord, I have heard the mystery of Thy dispensation: I have considered Thy works, and I have glorified Thy Godhead.

Canticle Five

First Canon

(**Irmos**) Thou hast parted the light from the original chaos, that Thy works might celebrate Thee in light, O Christ, as their Creator: do Thou direct our paths in Thy light.

The seasons[2] bowed down before Thy face: for at Thy feet the sun laid its light and its bright rays which fill the heavens, when Thou, O Christ, vouchsafed to change Thy mortal form.

'Behold the Saviour', cried Moses and Elijah on Tabor the Holy Mountain, and their words rang in the ears of the

[1] Exodus 3:2.

[2] In the Slav text, 'the mountains' (reading ὄρη instead of ὧραι).

disciples. 'Lo, here is Christ whom we in ancient times proclaimed as God.'

The nature that knows no change, being mingled with the mortal nature, shone forth ineffably, unveiling in some small measure to the apostles the light of the immaterial Godhead.

When they saw Thee, O Christ the eternal Light, shining forth in the glory of the Father, the disciples cried aloud to Thee: 'Direct our paths in Thy light.'[1]

Second Canon

(**Irmos**) O Light that never sets, why hast Thou cast me from Thy face? And why has the alien darkness covered me in my wretchedness? But I entreat Thee, cause me to return and direct my paths towards the light of Thy commandments.

No tongue, however eloquent, can declare Thy mighty works. For Thou who art Lord of life and Master of death[2] hast called Moses and Elijah before Thee on Mount Tabor, to bear witness to Thy divinity.

Thou, O Christ, with invisible hands hast fashioned man in Thine image; and Thou hast now displayed the original beauty in this same human body formed by Thee, revealing it, not as in an image, but as Thou art in Thine own self according to Thine essence, being both God and man.

In a union without confusion, Thou hast shown us on Mount Tabor the live coal of the Godhead that consumes sins while it enlighten souls,[3] and Thou hast caught up in ecstasy Moses and Elijah and the chief disciples.

(**Katavasia**) O thrice-blessed Tree, on which Christ the King and Lord was stretched! Through thee the beguiler fell, who tempted mankind with the tree. He was caught in the trap set by God, who was crucified upon thee in the flesh, granting peace unto our souls.

1 Psalm 5:9; 118:105, 133.
2 Romans 14:9.
3 Isaiah 6:6.

Canticle Six

First Canon

(**Irmos**) In my affliction I cried unto the Lord, and the God of my salvation heard me.

The Saviour Christ, Light shining forth on Tabor more brightly than the brilliance of the sun, has enlightened us.

Going up into Mount Tabor Thou wast transfigured, O Christ, and darkening all error Thou hast made Thy Light shine forth.

On Tabor, O Christ, the glorious apostles recognized Thee as God and bent their knees before Thee in their amazement.

Second Canon

(**Irmos**) Be merciful to me, O Saviour, for many are my transgressions, and lead me up, I beseech Thee, from the abyss of evil, for unto Thee have I cried: Hearken unto me, O God of my salvation.

How mighty and fearful is the vision that was seen today! The visible sun shone from heaven, but from the earth there shone upon Mount Tabor the spiritual Sun of Righteousness, past all compare.[1]

'The shadow of the Law has grown exceeding weak and passed away, and Christ the Truth has plainly come', cried Moses as he looked upon Thy Godhead on Tabor.

The pillar of fire plainly showed to Moses Christ transfigured, and the cloud pointed clearly to the grace of the Spirit that overshadowed Mount Tabor.[2]

(**Katavasia**) Jonah stretched out his hands in the form of a cross within the belly of the sea monster, plainly prefiguring the redeeming Passion. Cast out from thence after three days,

[1] Malachi 4:2.
[2] Exodus 13:21.

he foreshadowed the marvellous Resurrection of Christ our God, who was crucified in the flesh and enlightened the world by His Rising on the third day.

Kontakion

TONE SEVEN

Thou wast transfigured upon the mountain, and Thy disciples beheld Thy glory, O Christ our God, as far as they were able so to do: that when they saw Thee crucified, they might know that Thy suffering was voluntary, and might proclaim unto the world that Thou art truly the Brightness of the Father.[1]

Ikos

Awake ye sluggards, lie not for ever on the ground; and ye thoughts that draw my soul towards the earth, arise and go up to the high slope of the divine ascent. Let us run to join Peter and the sons of Zebedee, and go with them to Mount Tabor, that with them we may see the glory of our God and hear the voice they heard from heaven; and they proclaimed that this is the Brightness of the Father.

Canticle Seven

First Canon

(**Irmos**) In Babylon the Children, sons of Abraham, once trampled upon the flame of the fiery furnace, and they sang this song of praise: 'O God of our fathers, blessed art Thou.'

On Mount Tabor, O Christ, the apostles, bathed in the light of Thine unapproachable glory, cried aloud: 'O God of our fathers, blessed art Thou.'

The apostles delighted in the whirlwind of the divine voice, in the cloud that shed dew, and in Thy shining majesty,

[1] Hebrews 1:3.

O Christ; and they sang: 'O God of our fathers, blessed art Thou.'

As Peter looked upon Thee, O Christ, shining forth on Mount Tabor in unapproachable light, he cried aloud: 'O God of our fathers, blessed art Thou.'

The children of Zebedee were with Christ, the Prince of life, when light went forth from His Person, and they thundered out: 'O God of our fathers, blessed art Thou.'

Second Canon

(**Irmos**) The Hebrew Children in the furnace boldly trampled upon the flame, and they changed the fire to dew as they cried aloud: 'Blessed art Thou, O Lord our God, for evermore.'

Now the invisible has become visible to the apostles: on Mount Tabor the Godhead has shone forth before them in the flesh, and they cried aloud: 'Blessed art Thou, O Lord our God, for evermore.'

On Mount Tabor the apostles, struck with wonder, trembled with fear before the beauty of the divine Kingdom, and they cried aloud: 'Blessed art Thou, O Lord our God, for evermore.'

Now the unheard of has been heard. For the Son who came forth without father from the Virgin, receives glorious testimony from His Father's voice, that He is both God and man for evermore.

Not by adoption hast Thou become the beloved Son of the Most High, but Thou wast such by essence before the world began; and without changing Thou hast come to dwell with us who cry to Thee: 'Blessed art Thou, O Lord our God, for evermore.'

(**Katavasia**) The senseless decree of the wicked tyrant, breathing forth threats and blasphemy hateful to God, confused the people. Yet neither the fury of wild beasts nor the roaring of the fire could frighten the three Children:

but standing together in the flame, fanned by the wind that brought refreshment as the dew, they sang: 'Blessed art Thou and praised above all, O our God and the God of our fathers.'

Canticle Eight

First Canon

(**Irmos**) In Babylon the Children, burning with zeal for God, bravely trampled upon the threat of the tyrant and the fire; thrown into the midst of the flames but refreshed with dew, they sang: 'O all ye works of the Lord, bless ye the Lord.'

Thou, who dost uphold all things by Thy will, hast gone up with Thine undefiled feet into Mount Tabor. There Thy face shone with a splendour brighter than the light of the sun, and in its radiance stood the elect of the Law and of Grace, singing: 'O all ye works of the Lord, bless ye the Lord.'

When the infinite Light that knows no evening, even the brightness of the Father[1] that gives splendour to creation, ineffably appeared in unapproachable glory on Mount Tabor, it made men godlike as they sang: 'O all ye works of the Lord, bless ye the Lord.'

Standing in reverence on Mount Tabor, Moses and Elijah clearly beheld the express image[2] of the divine Person, even Christ, shining forth as lightning with the glory of the Father, and they sang: 'O all ye works of the Lord, bless ye the Lord.'

The face of Moses once shone with glory because of the divine voice he heard in the darkness;[3] but Christ covers Himself with light and glory as with a garment.[4] For He, who

[1] Hebrews 1:3.
[2] Hebrews 1:3.
[3] Exodus 34:29.
[4] Psalm 103:2.

is by nature Himself the Author of light, shines upon those who sing: 'O all ye works of the Lord, bless ye the Lord.'

The disciples, looking on Mount Tabor upon Christ wrapped in a cloud of light, fell on their faces to the ground, and with their minds enlightened they sang this hymn of praise to Him, and to the Father and the Spirit: 'O all ye works of the Lord, bless ye the Lord.'

Second Canon

(**Irmos**) The tyrant of the Chaldeans ordered the furnace to be heated seven times more for the three Children who were filled with reverent fear of God: but seeing them saved by a greater power, he cried: 'O ye children, bless ye the Creator and Deliverer; O ye priests, sing His praises; O ye people, exalt Him above all for ever.'

The disciples, O Master, heard the testimony of the Father; and unable to bear the sight of Thy Face whose lightning brightness was too fierce for the eyes of man, they fell to the ground in awe, singing: 'O ye priests, bless ye Christ; O ye people, exalt Him above all for ever.'

O blessed Master, Thou art by nature the fairest King of all Kings and blessed Lord of all Lords, and Thou dwellest in unapproachable light. To Thee the disciples, struck with wonder, cried: 'O ye children, bless ye Christ; O ye priests, sing His praises; O ye people, exalt Him above all for ever.'

Because Thou art Master of heaven and Lord of the earth, and hast dominion over the things under the earth, there stood beside Thee, O Christ, the apostles from the earth, and Elijah the Tishbite as if from heaven, and Moses from the dead, singing with one accord: 'O ye people, exalt Christ above all for ever.'

Thy chosen apostles left all idle cares behind them upon earth, and followed Thee who lovest mankind to the divine way of life that is high above this world. So they were accounted worthy to receive the vision of Thy Godhead, and they sang: 'O ye people, exalt Christ above all for ever.'

(**Katavasia**) O ye Children, equal in number to the Trinity, bless ye God the Father and Creator; sing ye the praises of the Word who descended and changed the fire to dew; and exalt ye above all for ever the most Holy Spirit, who gives life to all.

Canticle Nine

The Magnificat and Greater in honour than the cherubim *are not sung, but before the irmoi and the troparia we sing the megalynarion:*

Magnify, O my soul, the Lord who was transfigured on Tabor.

First Canon

(**Irmos**) Thy birthgiving was undefiled: God came forth from thy womb, and He appeared upon earth wearing flesh and made His dwelling among men; therefore we all magnify thee, O Theotokos.

The disciples, struck with fear and illuminated with the sudden stream of strange light, looked at one another and fell face downwards upon the ground, worshipping Thee the Master of all.

A divine voice came forth from the cloud confirming the wonder. For the Father of lights[1] called to the apostles: 'This is My beloved Son. Hear ye Him.'

On Tabor the ministers of the Word looked upon strange and marvellous wonders, and hearing the voice of the Father, they cried out: 'This is the imprint of the archetype, even our Saviour.'

O unchanged Image of the One Who Is, O Seal that cannot be removed or altered, Son and Word, Wisdom[2] and Arm,[3]

[1] James 1:17.
[2] 1 Corinthians 1:24.
[3] Isaiah 53:1.

Right Hand[1] and Strength of the Most High, Thee do we sing with the Father and the Spirit.

Second Canon

(**Irmos**) Every ear trembled with fear at hearing of the ineffable condescension of God: how the Most High of His own will came down even unto the flesh and was made man from a virgin womb. Therefore we the faithful magnify the undefiled Theotokos.

To show plainly how, at Thy mysterious second coming, Thou wilt appear as the Most High God standing in the midst of gods,[2] on Mount Tabor Thou hast shone in fashion past words upon the apostles and upon Moses and Elijah. Therefore we all magnify Thee, O Christ.

Come and hearken unto me, O ye peoples: going up into the holy and heavenly mountain, let us stand in spirit in the city of the living God, and let us gaze with our minds at the spiritual Godhead of the Father and the Spirit, shining forth in the Only-begotten Son.[3]

Thou hast taken me captive with longing for Thee, O Christ, and hast transformed me with Thy divine love. Burn up my sins with the fire of the Spirit, and count me worthy to take my fill of delight in Thee, that dancing with joy I may magnify both Thy Comings, O Lord who art good.

(**Katavasia**) O Theotokos, thou art a mystical Paradise, who untilled hast brought forth Christ. He has planted upon earth the life-giving Tree of the Cross: therefore at its Exaltation on this day, we worship Him and thee do we magnify.

(**Another Katavasia**) Today the death that came to man through eating of the tree, is made of no effect through the Cross. For the curse of our mother Eve that fell on all man-

[1] Exodus 15:6.
[2] Psalm 81:1 (Septuagint).
[3] Isaiah 2:3; Hebrews 12:22.

kind is destroyed by the fruit of the pure Mother of God, whom all the powers of heaven magnify.

Exapostilarion

Today on Tabor in the manifestation of Thy Light, O Word, Thou unaltered Light from the Light of the unbegotten Father, we have seen the Father as Light and the Spirit as Light, guiding with light the whole creation (*3 times*).

Lauds. Four stichera are sung:

TONE FOUR

Before Thy precious Cross and Thy Passion, taking with Thee those among Thy holy disciples that Thou hadst specially chosen, Thou hast gone up, O Master, into Mount Tabor, wishing to show them Thy glory. And when they saw Thee transfigured and shining more brightly than the sun, falling upon their faces, they were smitten with wonder at Thy power, and cried aloud: 'O Christ, Thou art the timeless Light and Brightness of the Father,[1] yet of Thine own will without changing Thou art made manifest in the flesh' (*twice*).

O Thou who from all eternity art God the Word, who coverest Thyself with light as with a garment,[2] Thou wast transfigured before Thy disciples, shining more brightly than the sun. Moses and Elijah stood by Thy side, making it plain that Thou art Lord both of the dead and of the living:[3] they glorified Thine ineffable dispensation, Thy compassion and Thy great condescension, whereby Thou hast saved the world lost utterly in sin.

O Lord who wast born of a virgin cloud[4] and made flesh, Thou wast transfigured on Mount Tabor, encompassing

[1] Hebrews 1:3.
[2] Psalm 103:2.
[3] Romans 14:9.
[4] Isaiah 19:1.

Thyself with a bright cloud; and the voice of the Father in the presence of the disciples plainly declared Thee to be the beloved Son, one in essence and sharing the same throne. Thereupon Peter spoke with wonder, not knowing what he said: 'It is good for us to be here, O Thou Benefactor rich in mercy.'

Glory be to the Father . . . Both now . . .

TONE EIGHT

(*by Byzas*)

Christ took Peter, James, and John up into a high mountain apart, and was transfigured before them. His face shone as the sun and His raiment became white as the light. There appeared Moses and Elijah talking with Him; a bright cloud overshadowed them, and behold, a voice out of the cloud, saying: 'This is My beloved Son in whom I am well pleased: hear ye Him.'[1]

Great Doxology and Dismissal.

Liturgy

In the Greek use the following antiphons are sung:

Antiphon One

TONE TWO

℣ 1. Great is the Lord and greatly to be praised: in the city of our God and in His holy mountain (*Psalm* 47:2).

At the prayers of the Theotokos, save us, O Saviour.

℣ 2. By His strength He setteth fast the mountains, being girded with power: He troubleth the depths of the sea; who shall endure the noise of its waves? (*Psalm* 64:7–8)

At the prayers of the Theotokos . . .

[1] Matthew 17:1–5.

℣ 3. Thou art clothed with honour and majesty: Thou coverest Thyself with light as with a garment (*Psalm* 103:1–2).

At the prayers of the Theotokos . . .

℣ 4. The mountains shall be joyful before the face of the Lord: for He is come to judge the earth (*Psalm* 97:8–9).

At the prayers of the Theotokos . . .

Glory be to the Father . . . Both now . . .

At the prayers of the Theotokos . . .

Antiphon Two

SAME TONE

℣ 1. His foundations are in the holy mountains (*Psalm* 86:1).

O Son of God, transfigured upon Mount Tabor, save us who sing to Thee: alleluia.

℣ 2. The Lord loveth the gates of Zion more than all the dwellings of Jacob (*ibid.*, 2).

O Son of God . . .

℣ 3. Glorious things are spoken of thee, O city of God (*ibid.*, 3).

O Son of God . . .

℣ 4. Zion is our mother, a man shall say, and such a man was born in her: and the Most High Himself hath established her (*ibid.*, 5).

O Son of God . . .

Glory be to the Father . . . Both now . . .

O Only-begotten Son and Word of God . . .

Antiphon Three

TONE SEVEN

℣ 1. I will sing of Thy mercies for ever, O Lord (*Psalm* 88:2).

The troparion of the feast, Thou wast transfigured upon the mountain (*p. 477*).

℣ 2. The heavens shall praise Thy wonders, O Lord: and Thy truth in the congregation of the saints (*ibid.*, 6).

The troparion of the feast.

℣ 3. Blessed is the people that know the sound of joy (*ibid.*, 16).

The troparion of the feast.

℣ 4. They shall walk, O Lord, in the light of Thy countenance: in Thy Name shall they rejoice all the day, and in Thy righteousness shall they be exalted (*ibid.*, 16–17).

The troparion of the feast.

But in the Slav use the antiphons are as follows:

Antiphon One

TONE TWO

℣ 1. Make a joyful noise unto the Lord, all the earth: sing forth the honour of His Name; make His praise glorious (*Psalm* 65 : 1–2).

At the prayers of the Theotokos, save us, O Saviour.

℣ 2. The voice of Thy thunder was heard in the whirlwind, Thy lightnings shone upon the inhabited earth: the earth trembled and shook (*Psalm* 76 : 19).

At the prayers of the Theotokos . . .

℣ 3. Thou art clothed with honour and majesty: Thou coverest Thyself with light as with a garment (*Psalm* 103 : 1–2).

At the prayers of the Theotokos . . .
Glory be to the Father . . . Both now . . .
At the prayers of the Theotokos . . .

Antiphon Two

SAME TONE

℣ 1. Mount Zion upon the north side is the city of the Great King (*Psalm* 47 : 3).

O Son of God, transfigured upon the mountain, save us who sing to Thee: alleluia.

℣ 2. And He brought them to the mountain of His sanctuary: even to this mountain which His right hand had purchased (*Psalm* 77:54).

O Son of God . . .

℣ 3. He chose the tribe of Judah, the mount Zion which He loved: and He built His sanctuary as the place of the unicorns (*ibid.*, 68–69).

O Son of God . . .

Glory be to the Father . . . Both now . . .

O Only-begotten Son and Word of God . . .

Antiphon Three

TONE SEVEN

℣ 1. They that trust in the Lord shall be as Mount Zion: he that dwells in Jerusalem shall never be shaken (*Psalm* 124:1).

The troparion of the feast, Thou wast transfigured upon the mountain (*p. 477*).

℣ 2. As the mountains are round about Jerusalem, so the Lord is round about His people: from henceforth even for evermore (*ibid.*, 2).

The troparion of the feast.

℣ 3. Lord, who shall abide in Thy tabernacle? and who shall dwell in Thy holy mountain? (*Psalm* 14:1)

The troparion of the feast.

℣ 4. Who shall ascend into the mountain of the Lord: or who shall stand in His holy place? (*Psalm* 23:3)

The troparion of the feast.

Introit in the Greek use:

Tabor and Hermon shall rejoice in Thy Name (*Psalm* 88:13).[1]

O Son of God, transfigured upon Mount Tabor, save us who sing to Thee: alleluia.

But in the Slav use the introit is as follows:

O Lord, send forth Thy light and Thy truth that they may lead me and bring me to Thy holy mountain (*Psalm* 42:3).

Then, in both the Greek and the Slav use, are sung the troparion of the feast (p. 477); Glory be to the Father . . . Both now; *the kontakion of the feast (p. 489).*

Prokimenon: *TONE FOUR*

O Lord, how marvellous are Thy works: in wisdom hast Thou made them all (*Psalm* 103:24).

℣. Bless the Lord, O my soul: O Lord my God, Thou art very great (*ibid.*, 1).

READING FROM THE SECOND EPISTLE GENERAL OF PETER (1:10–19).

Wherefore the rather, brethren, give diligence to make your calling and election sure: for if ye do these things, ye shall never fall: for so an entrance shall be ministered unto you abundantly into the everlasting kingdom of our Lord and Saviour Jesus Christ. Wherefore I will not be negligent to put you always in remembrance of these things, though ye know them, and be established in the present truth. Yea, I think it meet, as long as I am in this tabernacle, to stir you up by putting you in remembrance; knowing that shortly I must

[1] In the Greek use, this is sometimes replaced by the following: *For with Thee is the fountain of life, O Lord: and in Thy light shall we see light* (Psalm 35:10).

put off this my tabernacle, even as our Lord Jesus Christ hath shewed me. Moreover I will endeavour that ye may be able after my decease to have these things always in remembrance. For we have not followed cunningly devised fables, when we made known unto you the power and coming of our Lord Jesus Christ, but were eyewitnesses of His majesty. For He received from God the Father honour and glory, when there came such a voice to Him from the excellent glory, This is My beloved Son, in whom I am well pleased. And this voice which came from heaven we heard, when we were with Him in the holy mount. We have also a more sure word of prophecy; whereunto ye do well that ye take heed, as unto a light that shineth in a dark place, until the day dawn, and the day star arise in your hearts.

In the Greek use, Alleluia, TONE ONE

℣ 1. The heavens shall praise Thy wonders (*Psalm* 88 : 6).

℣ 2. God is glorified in the assembly of the saints (*ibid.*, 8).

In the Slav use,[1] *Alleluia, TONE EIGHT*

℣ 1. The heavens are Thine, the earth also is Thine (*Psalm* 88 : 12).

℣ 2. Blessed is the people that know the sound of joy (*ibid.*, 16).

READING FROM THE HOLY GOSPEL ACCORDING TO MATTHEW (17 : 1–9).

At that time, Jesus taketh Peter, James, and John his brother, and bringeth them up into an high mountain apart, and was transfigured before them: and His face did shine as the sun, and His raiment was white as the light. And, behold, there appeared unto them Moses and Elijah talking with Him. Then answered Peter, and said unto Jesus, Lord, it is good

[1] Also in certain of the Greek books.

for us to be here: if Thou wilt, let us make here three tabernacles; one for Thee, and one for Moses, and one for Elijah. While he yet spake, behold a bright cloud overshadowed them: and behold a voice out of the cloud, which said, This is My beloved Son, in whom I am well pleased; hear ye Him. And when the disciples heard it, they fell on their face, and were sore afraid. And Jesus came and touched them, and said, Arise, and be not afraid. And when they had lifted up their eyes, they saw no man, save Jesus only. And as they came down from the mountain, Jesus charged them, saying, Tell the vision to no man, until the Son of man be risen again from the dead.

In place of It is meet, *we sing the irmos from Canticle Nine of the first Canon (p. 493).*

Communion verse:

We shall walk, O Lord, in the light of the glory of Thy countenance: and in Thy Name shall we rejoice all the day (*Psalm* 88:16–17).

It is the custom to bring grapes to the church on this day. They are placed on a table in the centre of the church and blessed by the priest at the end of the Liturgy. In the Greek use he says the following prayer:

Bless, O Lord, this new fruit of the vine, which Thou hast been pleased to bring to full ripeness through temperate seasons, showers of rain, and calm weather. May we who partake thereof be filled with joy; and upon those who offer this fruit of the vine for use at Thy Holy Table, may it confer forgiveness of sins, through the sacred and holy Body and Blood of Thy Christ, with whom Thou art blessed, together with Thy most holy, good, and life-giving Spirit, now, and ever, and unto the ages of ages. Amen.

But in the Slav use the priest says:

O God our Saviour, who wast pleased to call Thine Only-begotten Son, our Lord and God and Saviour Jesus Christ, the Vine, and in Him hast granted us the fruit of immortality: do Thou now bless this fruit of the vine lying here, and make us Thy servants, who eat of it, partakers of the true Vine. Keep our lives from harm and ever give us peace, and adorn us with the eternal gifts of grace that none can take away: at the intercessions of our most pure Lady, the Theotokos and ever-Virgin Mary, and of all Thy saints who have pleased Thee down the ages. For Thou art a good God who lovest mankind, and unto Thee, Father without beginning, together with Thine Only-begotten Son and Thy most holy, good, and life-giving Spirit, do we ascribe glory, now, and ever, and unto the ages of ages. Amen.

The grapes are then distributed by the priest, together with the blessed bread (antidoron).

On the day of the feast, fish, wine, and oil are allowed, but meat and animal products are not eaten, because it is within the fast before the Dormition of the Theotokos.

The apodosis of the feast falls on 13 August. On that day all the office of the feast is repeated, omitting only the entrance, lessons, lity, and blessing of bread at Vespers; the polyeleos and Gospel at Mattins; and the blessing of grapes at the Liturgy.

15 AUGUST

THE DORMITION OF OUR MOST HOLY LADY THE THEOTOKOS AND EVER-VIRGIN MARY

Small Vespers

On Lord, I have cried, *four stichera are sung:*

TONE TWO

With what lips shall we, poor and worthless, call the Theotokos blessed ? She is more honoured than the creation, and more holy than the cherubim and all the angels. She is the unshaken Throne of the King, the Abode in which the Most High has dwelt. She is the salvation of the world, the Holy Place of God, who richly grants unto the faithful great mercy on this her holy feast (*twice*).

What songs filled with awe did all the apostles of the Word then offer thee, O Virgin, as they stood round thy deathbed and cried aloud in wonder: 'The Palace of the King withdraws: the Ark of holiness is raised on high.[1] Let the gates be opened wide[2] that the Gate of God may enter into abundant joy, she who asks without ceasing for great mercy on the world.'

What spiritual songs shall we now offer thee, O most holy ? For by thy deathless Dormition thou has sanctified the whole world, and then hast been translated to the places above the world, there to perceive the beauty of the Almighty and, as

[1] Psalm 131:8.
[2] Psalm 23:7.

His Mother, to rejoice in it exceedingly. Thou art attended by ranks of angels, O pure Virgin, and by the souls of the just. Join them to ask for us peace and great mercy.

Glory be to the Father . . . Both now . . .

TONE TWO

(*by Anatolios*)

She who is higher than the heavens and more glorious than the cherubim, she who is held in greater honour than all creation, she who by reason of her surpassing purity became the receiver of the everlasting Essence, today commends her most pure soul into the hands of her Son. With her all things are filled with joy and she bestows great mercy upon us.

Aposticha:

TONE TWO

(*to the special melody*, O house of Ephratah . . .)

The assembly of the disciples is gathered together, come at an all-powerful behest from the ends of the earth to bury the Mother and Theotokos.

℣. Arise, O Lord, into Thy rest: Thou and the Ark of Thy holiness (*Psalm* 131:8).

The Bride of God, the Queen and Virgin, the glory of the elect, the pride of virgins, is translated to her Son.

℣. The Lord hath sworn in truth unto David: and He will not turn from it (*ibid.*, 11).

The choir of disciples is most wondrously brought together from the ends of the world, to attend the burial of thy pure and divine body.

Glory be to the Father . . . Both now . . .

SAME TONE

O gracious Lady, raise thy holy hands towards thy Son, the Maker and Lover of our souls, that He may take pity on thy servants.

Apolytikion (troparion) of the feast, In giving birth, O Theotokos *(p. 511), and Dismissal.*

Great Vespers

We sing Blessed is the man *(the first portion of the first kathisma).*

On Lord, I have cried, *eight stichera are sung:*

TONE ONE

O marvellous wonder! The source of life is laid in the tomb, and the tomb itself becomes a ladder to heaven. Make glad, O Gethsemane, thou sacred abode of the Mother of God. Come, O ye faithful, and with Gabriel to lead us let us cry: 'Hail, thou who art full of grace: the Lord is with thee,[1] granting the world through thee great mercy' *(3 times).*

Glorious are thy mysteries, O pure Lady. Thou wast made the Throne of the Most High, and today thou art translated from earth to heaven. Thy glory is full of majesty, shining with grace in divine brightness. O ye virgins, ascend on high with the Mother of the King. Hail, thou who art full of grace: the Lord is with thee, granting the world through thee great mercy *(3 times).*

The dominions and the thrones, the rulers, the principalities, and the powers,[2] the cherubim and the fearful seraphim glorify thy Dormition: and those who dwell on earth rejoice, adorned by thy divine glory. Kings fall down and sing with the archangels and the angels: 'Hail, thou who art full of grace: the Lord is with thee, granting the world through thee great mercy' *(twice).*

Glory be to the Father . . . Both now . . .

[1] Luke 1:28.
[2] Romans 8:38; Colossians 1:16.

TONE ONE

By the royal command of God, the divinely inspired apostles were caught up from over all the world into the clouds on high.

TONE FIVE

Reaching thine immaculate body, the source of Life, they saluted it with mighty honour.

TONE TWO

The highest powers of heaven stood by with their own Master.

TONE SIX

Seized with dread, they accompanied thine inviolate body that had held God, and they went on high before thee, crying, unseen, to the hierarchies above: 'Lo, the Queen of all, the Maid of God, is nigh.'

TONE THREE

Open wide the gates and receive above the world the Mother of the everlasting Light.

TONE SEVEN

For through her the salvation of all mankind has come. We have not the strength to look upon her, and are unable to render honours worthy of her.

TONE FOUR

For her excellence is past all understanding.

TONE EIGHT

Therefore, O most pure Theotokos, who livest for ever with thy Son, the King who brings life, pray without ceasing that thy newborn people be guarded on every side and saved from all adverse assault: for we are under thy protection.

TONE ONE

And we bless thee in beauty and light unto all ages.

Entrance, O joyful light, *and prokimenon of the day.*

Lessons:[1]

READING FROM GENESIS (28: 10–17).

READING FROM THE PROPHET EZEKIEL (43: 27–44: 4).

READING FROM PROVERBS (9: 1–11).

At the Lity:

TONE ONE

It was right that the eye-witnesses and ministers of the Word should see the Dormition of His Mother according to the flesh, even the final mystery concerning her: that so they might be witnesses not only to the Ascension of the Saviour but also to the Translation of her who gave Him birth. Assembled from all parts by divine power, they came to Zion, and sped on her way to heaven the Virgin who is higher than the cherubim. We also venerate her, for she prays for our souls.

TONE TWO

(*by Anatolios*)

She who is higher than the heavens and more glorious than the cherubim, she who is held in greater honour than all creation, she who by reason of her surpassing purity became the receiver of the everlasting Essence, today commends her most pure soul into the hands of her Son. With her all things are filled with joy and she bestows great mercy upon us.

SAME TONE

(*by John*)

The Spotless Bride, the Mother of Him in whom the Father

[1] See p. 102.

was well pleased, she who was foreordained by God to be the dwelling place of His union without confusion, delivers today her blameless soul to her Creator and her God. The spiritual powers receive her with the honours due to God, and she who is truly the Mother of Life departs unto life, the lamp of the Light which no man can approach, the salvation of the faithful and hope of our souls.

TONE THREE

(*by Germanos*)

Come, all ye ends of the earth, let us praise the most holy Translation of the Mother of God: for she has delivered her spotless soul into the hands of her Son. Therefore the world, restored to life by her holy Dormition, in radiant joy celebrates this feast with psalms and hymns and spiritual songs together with the angels and the apostles.

Glory be to the Father . . .

TONE FIVE

(*by Theophanes*)

Come, O gathering of those who love to keep the feasts, come and let us form a choir. Come, let us crown the Church with songs, as the Ark of God goes to her rest.[1] For today is heaven opened wide as it receives the Mother of Him who cannot be contained. The earth, as it yields up the Source of life, is robed in blessing and majesty. The hosts of angels, present with the fellowship of the apostles, gaze in great fear at her who bore the Cause of life, now that she is translated from life to life. Let us all venerate and implore her: Forget not, O Lady, thy ties of kinship with those who commemorate in faith the feast of thine all-holy Dormition.

Both now . . .

[1] Psalm 131:8.

SAME TONE

Sing, O ye people, sing ye the praises of the Mother of our God: for today she delivers her soul, full of light, into the immaculate hands of Him who was made incarnate of her without seed. And she entreats Him without ceasing to grant the inhabited earth peace and great mercy.

Aposticha:

TONE FOUR

Come, O ye people, and let us sing the praises of the pure and most holy Virgin, from whom the Word of the Father ineffably came forth incarnate. Let us cry aloud and say: Blessed art thou among women and blessed is thy womb that held Christ.[1] Having delivered thy soul into His holy hands, do thou, O most pure, entreat Him for the salvation of our souls.

℣. Arise, O Lord, into Thy rest: Thou and the Ark of Thy holiness (*Psalm* 131:8).

O pure and most holy Virgin, the multitude of angels in heaven and mankind on earth extol and venerate thy Dormition: for thou art the Mother of Christ, our God and the Creator of all. Never cease, we entreat thee, to intercede with Him on our behalf: for next to God we have put our hope in thee, O far-famed and unwedded Theotokos.

℣. The Lord hath sworn in truth unto David: and He will not turn from it (*ibid.*, 11).

Come, O ye people, and let us sing today unto Christ our God a song of David: 'The virgins that follow her', he said, 'shall be brought unto the King: with gladness and rejoicing shall they be brought'.[2] For she, through whom we have been made godlike, is of the seed of David: and gloriously and ineffably she commends herself into the hands of her own

[1] Luke 1:42.
[2] Psalm 44:15.

Son and Master. Praising her as the Mother of God, we cry and say: From all distress save us who confess thee, O Theotokos, and grant our souls deliverance from tribulation.

Glory be to the Father . . . Both now . . .

SAME TONE

At thy departing, O Virgin Theotokos, to Him who was ineffably born of thee, James the first bishop and brother of the Lord was there, and so was Peter, the honoured leader and chief of the disciples,[1] and the whole sacred fellowship of the apostles. In discourses that showed forth heavenly things they sang the praises of the divine and amazing mystery of the dispensation of Christ our God; and they rejoiced, O far-famed Virgin, as they buried thy body, the origin of the Life and holder of God. On high the most holy and venerable of the angelic powers bowed in wonder before this marvel, and said one to another: 'Open wide your gates and receive her who bore the Creator of heaven and earth. With songs of praise let us glorify her precious and holy body, dwelling-place of the Lord on whom we may not gaze.' Therefore we too, as we keep thy feast, cry out to thee, O far-famed Lady: Raise up the Christian horn and save our souls.

Apolytikion (troparion) of the feast:

TONE ONE

In giving birth, O Theotokos, thou hast retained thy virginity, and in falling asleep thou hast not forsaken the world. Thou who art the Mother of Life hast passed over into life, and by thy prayers thou dost deliver our souls from death.

And the Dismissal.

[1] Literally, 'the theologians'.

Mattins

After the first reading from the Psalter, sessional hymn:[1]

TONE FOUR

Cry out, O David: what is this present feast? 'Christ,' said he, 'has translated into the heavenly mansions her who bore Him without seed, of whom I sang in the book of Psalms, calling her daughter, child of God, and Virgin.[2] Therefore, mothers and daughters and brides of Christ, rejoice and cry: Hail, thou who art translated into the heavenly Kingdom.'

Glory be to the Father . . . Both now . . .

Repeat.

After the second reading from the Psalter, sessional hymn:

TONE ONE

The honoured choir of the wise apostles was miraculously assembled to bury in glory thy most pure body, O far-famed Theotokos: and with them the multitudes of angels sounded the triumphant praises of thy Translation that we feast in faith.

Glory be to the Father . . . Both now . . .

Repeat.

After the polyeleos, the megalynarion:[3]

We magnify thee, O undefiled Mother of Christ our God, and we praise thine all-glorious Dormition.

℣. Make a joyful noise unto the Lord, all the earth (*Psalm* 65:1).

We magnify thee . . .

[1] In the Slav use, the three sessional hymns are given in this order:
The honoured choir of the wise apostles . . .
In thy giving birth . . .
Cry out, O David . . .

[2] Psalm 44.

[3] In the Slav use only.

℣. Arise, O Lord, into Thy rest: Thou and the Ark of Thy holiness (*Psalm* 131:8).

We magnify thee . . .

Glory be to the Father . . . Both now . . .

Alleluia, alleluia, alleluia, glory be to Thee, O God (*3 times*).

We magnify thee . . .

Sessional hymn:

TONE THREE

In thy giving birth conception was without seed: in thy falling asleep death was without corruption. A second wonder followed swiftly on the first, O Theotokos: how did she who knew not a man give suck while still remaining pure? And how was the Mother of God embalmed and carried to burial as dead? Therefore with the angel we cry aloud to thee: Hail, thou who art full of grace.

Glory be to the Father . . . Both now . . .

Repeat.

The first antiphon of the hymn of degrees in Tone Four.

Prokimenon: *TONE FOUR*

I will make thy name to be remembered in all generations (*Psalm* 44:18).

℣. Hearken, O daughter, and consider, and incline thine ear (*ibid.*, 11).

Let everything that hath breath . . .

READING FROM THE HOLY GOSPEL ACCORDING TO LUKE (1:39–49, 56. *See p. 109*).

Psalm 50.

Glory be to the Father . . .

At the prayers of the Theotokos . . .

Both now . . .
At the prayers of the Theotokos . . .
Have mercy upon me . . .

TONE SIX

(by Byzas)

When the Translation of thy most pure tabernacle was being prepared, the apostles surrounded thy deathbed and looked upon thee with dread, and as they gazed at thy body, they were filled with awe. In tears Peter cried aloud to thee: 'O undefiled Virgin, I see thee who art the life of all mankind lying here outstretched, and I am struck with wonder: for He who is the delight of the future life made His dwelling in thee. Pray, then, fervently to thy Son and God to save thy flock[1] from harm.'

Two Canons are used: the first by St. Cosmas, in eight troparia, including the irmos, and the second, by St. John of Damascus, in six, likewise including the irmos. Before the troparia we say Most holy Theotokos, save us. *The two irmoi are repeated as katavasia.*

Canticle One

First Canon

TONE ONE

(Irmos) Thy sacred and renowned memorial, O Virgin, is clothed in the embroidered raiment of divine glory.[2] It has brought all the faithful together in joy, and led by Miriam, with dances and timbrels,[3] they sing the praises of thine Only-begotten Son: for He has been greatly glorified.

The spiritual hosts that dwell in heaven attended thy divine body in Zion, while the multitude of the apostles, coming

[1] Literally, 'city'.
[2] Psalm 44:14.
[3] Exodus 15:20.

together of a sudden from the ends of the earth, stood beside thee, O Theotokos. With them we too glorify thine august memory, O undefiled Virgin.

O pure Virgin, thou hast won the honour of victory over nature by bringing forth God; yet like thy Son and Creator, thou hast submitted to the laws of nature in a manner above nature. Therefore, dying thou hast risen to live eternally with thy Son.

Second Canon

TONE FOUR

(**Irmos**) I shall open my mouth and the Spirit will inspire it, and I shall utter the words of my song to the Queen and Mother: I shall be seen radiantly keeping feast and joyfully praising her Dormition.

O ye young virgins, raise now with Miriam the prophetess the song of departure. For the Virgin, the only Theotokos, is taken to her appointed dwelling-place in heaven.

The heavenly mansions of God fittingly received thee, O most holy, who art a living Heaven. Joyously adorned as a Bride without spot, thou standest beside our King and God.

Canticle Three

First Canon

(**Irmos**) O Christ, the Wisdom and the Power of God,[1] who dost create and uphold all, establish the Church unshaken and unwavering: for only Thou art holy, who hast Thy resting place among the saints.[2]

The glorious apostles knew thee, O Virgin without spot, to be a mortal woman and at the same time, beyond and

[1] 1 Cor. 1:24.
[2] Isaiah 57:15 (Septuagint).

above nature, the Mother of God: therefore they touched thee with fearful hands, as they gazed upon thee shining with glory, the tabernacle that had held God.

The Lord guarded with the glory of the Godhead the honour due to the living Ark in which the Word took flesh; and in His just vengeance He intervened to cut off the sacrilegious hands of the presumptuous unbeliever.[1]

Second Canon

(**Irmos**) O Mother of God, thou living and plentiful fount, give strength to those united in spiritual fellowship, who sing hymns of praise to thee: and in thy divine glory vouchsafe unto them crowns of glory.

O pure Virgin, sprung from mortal loins, thine end was conformable to nature: but because thou hast borne the true Life, thou hast departed to dwell with the divine Life Himself.

At an all-powerful command, the assembly of the apostles from the ends of the earth, and the multitude of angels from on high, made haste to Zion, there to minister in fitting manner at thy burial, O Lady.

Ypakoë

TONE FIVE

From all generations we call thee blessed, O Virgin Theotokos: for Christ our God who cannot be contained was pleased to be contained in thee. Blessed also are we in having thee as our succour: for day and night thou dost intercede for us, and the sceptres of kings are strengthened by thy supplications. Therefore, singing thy praises we cry aloud to thee: Hail, thou who art full of grace, the Lord is with thee.

[1] Compare 2 Kings (2 Samuel) 6:6–7.

Canticle Four

First Canon

(**Irmos**) The dark sayings and riddles of the prophets[1] foreshadowed Thine Incarnation from a Virgin, O Christ, even the lightning of Thy brightness which was to come as a light to lighten the Gentiles;[2] and the deep utters its voice to Thee in joy: 'Glory to Thy power, O Thou who lovest mankind.'

Come, O ye people, and gaze in wonder: for the holy Mountain of the Lord, in the sight of all, is exalted above the hills of heaven. The earthly Heaven takes up her dwelling in a heavenly and imperishable land.

Thy death, O pure Virgin, was a crossing into a better and eternal life. It translated thee, O undefiled, from this mortal life to that which knows no end and is indeed divine: and so thou dost look in joy upon thy Son and Lord.

The gates of heaven were opened wide and the angels sang, as Christ received the virgin treasure of His own Mother. Cherubim withdrew before thee in thine exultation, while seraphim glorified thee in thy joy.

Second Canon

(**Irmos**) Perceiving the unsearchable purpose of God concerning Thine Incarnation from a Virgin, O Most High, the prophet Habakkuk cried: Glory to Thy power, O Lord.

A strange wonder it was to see the living Heaven of the Ruler of all descend into the hollows of the earth. How marvellous are Thy works! Glory to Thy power, O Lord.

At thy Translation, O Mother of God, the angelic hosts in fear and joy with their holy wings covered thy body, that had been spacious enough to harbour the divinity.

If her Fruit, whom none may comprehend, on whose account she was called a Heaven, submitted of His own will

[1] Isaiah 7:14.

[2] Luke 2:32.

to burial as a mortal, how should she, who gave Him birth without knowing a man, refuse it?

Canticle Five

First Canon

(**Irmos**) I shall declare the divine and ineffable beauty of Thine excellencies, O Christ. For Thou hast shone forth in Thine own Person as the coeternal brightness from the eternal glory, and taking flesh from a virgin's womb, Thou hast arisen as the sun, giving light to those that were in darkness and shadow.[1]

Carried to Zion as it were upon a cloud, the company of the apostles assembled from the ends of the earth to minister to thee, O Virgin. Thou art the swift cloud,[2] from whom the Most High God, the Sun of Righteousness, shone forth upon those that were in darkness and shadow.

The inspired tongues of the apostles rang out louder than trumpets, as they sang in the Spirit the burial hymn to the Theotokos: 'Hail, incorruptible source of God's life-giving Incarnation, that brings salvation unto all.'

Second Canon

(**Irmos**) The whole world was amazed at thy divine glory:[3] for thou, O Virgin who hast not known wedlock, hast been translated from earth to the eternal mansions and to the life without end, bestowing salvation upon all who sing thy praises.

Let the trumpets of the apostles ring out today, and let the voices of men sound praises in many tongues. Let the air re-echo, shining with infinite light, and let the angels honour with hymns the Dormition of the Virgin.

[1] Malachi 4:2; Isaiah 9:2.
[2] Isaiah 19:1.
[3] In the Slavonic, 'Dormition'.

Wholly beside himself, wholly transported, his whole self consecrated to God, the chosen vessel of the Lord surpassed himself in hymns to thee, O far-famed Theotokos and Virgin: and in the sight of all he proved himself to be in the very truth inspired by God.[1]

Canticle Six

First Canon

(**Irmos**) The fire within the whale, the monster dwelling in the salt waters of the sea, was a prefiguring of Thy three days' burial, and Jonah acted as interpreter. For, saved and unharmed, as though he had never been swallowed, he cried aloud: 'I will sacrifice unto Thee with the voice of praise, O Lord.'

The Lord and God of all gave thee as thy portion the things that are above nature. For just as He kept thee virgin in thy childbirth so did He preserve thy body incorrupt in the tomb; and He glorified thee by a divine Translation, showing thee honour as a Son to His Mother.

Thy Son, O Virgin, has truly made thee dwell in the Holy of Holies as a bright candlestick, flaming with immaterial fire, as a golden censer burning with divine coal, as the vessel of manna, the rod of Aaron, and the tablet written by God, as a holy ark and table of the bread of life.

Second Canon

(**Irmos**) As we celebrate this sacred and solemn feast of the Mother of God, let us come, clapping our hands, O people of the Lord, and give glory to God who was born of her.

[1] This refers to St. Hierotheos, the friend of St. Dionysios the Areopagite, who according to tradition was present at the burial of the Holy Virgin. See Dionysios, *The Divine Names*, iii.2.

Life arose from thee without destroying the seals of thy virginity. How then could the spotless tabernacle of thy body, the source of Life, become a partaker of death?

Having become the temple of Life, thou hast obtained the life eternal: for thou who hast borne the Life in Person, hast now passed over through death into life.

Kontakion

TONE TWO[1]

Neither the tomb nor death had power over the Theotokos, who is ever watchful in her prayers and in whose intercession lies unfailing hope. For as the Mother of Life she has been transported into life by Him who dwelt within her ever-virgin womb.

Ikos

Set a rampart about my mind, O my Saviour, for I make bold to sing the praises of Thy most pure Mother, the rampart of the world. Establish me firmly within the fortress of my words and make me strong within the defences of my thoughts: for Thou dost promise to fulfil the petitions of those that entreat Thee with faith. Endue me with a tongue and ready speech, and with thoughts that are without shame: for every gift of enlightenment is sent down from Thee, O guiding Light, who dwelt within her ever-virgin womb.

Canticle Seven

First Canon

(**Irmos**) Divine Love, fighting against cruel wrath and fire, quenched the fire with dew and laughed the wrath to scorn, making the three-stringed harp of the saints inspired by God sing in the midst of the flames in answer to the instruments of

[1] In some Greek editions, Tone Six.

music: 'Blessed art Thou, O most glorious God, our God and the God of our fathers.'

In his anger, Moses broke in pieces the tables made by God and written by the Holy Spirit.[1] But Moses' Master kept His own Mother unharmed in her childbirth, and now He has made her dwell in the heavenly abodes. Dancing with her in her joy, we cry aloud unto Christ: 'Blessed art Thou, O most glorious God, our God and the God of our fathers.'

To the sound of the cymbals of our pure lips, of the harmonious harps of our hearts, of the sweet-sounding trumpets of our uplifted minds, to the clapping of our active hands, let us cry on this solemn and holy day of the Translation of the pure Virgin: 'Blessed art Thou, O most glorious God, our God and the God of our fathers.'

The people inspired by God has gathered together: for the Tabernacle of the glory of God is translated in Zion to a heavenly abode, where the pure voices of those that keep feast are heard with a sound of ineffable joy, shouting in gladness to Christ: 'Blessed art Thou, O most glorious God, our God and the God of our fathers.'

Second Canon

(**Irmos**) The Holy Children bravely trampled upon the threatening fire, preferring not to worship created things rather than the Creator, and they sang in joy: 'Blessed art Thou and praised above all, O Lord God of our fathers.'

O ye young men and virgins, old men and rulers, kings and judges,[2] who honour the memory of the Virgin and Mother of God, sing ye: Blessed art Thou, O Lord God of our fathers.

Let the high mountains[3] ring out to the trumpet of the Spirit: let the hills now rejoice and let the apostles of God

[1] Exodus 32:19.
[2] Psalm 148:11–12.
[3] Psalm 148:9.

dance for joy. The Queen goes to dwell with her Son and to rule with Him for ever.

The all-holy Translation of Thy divine and undefiled Mother has gathered together the heavenly hosts of the powers on high, that they may rejoice with those on earth who sing to Thee: Blessed art Thou, O God.

Canticle Eight

First Canon

(**Irmos**) The all-powerful Angel of God revealed to the Children a flame, that brought refreshment to the holy while it consumed the ungodly. And he made the Theotokos into a life-giving fount, gushing forth to the destruction of death and to the life of those that sing: 'We who have been delivered praise the one and only Creator and exalt Him above all for ever.'

The whole multitude of the apostles accompanied in Zion the divine Ark of holiness,[1] as they sang: 'Whither dost thou now depart, O Tabernacle of the living God? Cease not to watch over those who sing in faith. We who have been delivered praise the one and only Creator and exalt Him above all for ever.'

As she departed the Virgin without spot lifted up her hands —those hands that had held God incarnate in their embrace— and with the boldness of a Mother to her Son she said: 'Keep unto all ages those whom Thou hast made mine and who cry aloud unto Thee: We who have been delivered praise the one and only Creator and exalt Him above all for ever.'

Second Canon

(**Irmos**) The offspring of the Theotokos saved the Holy Children in the furnace. He who was then prefigured has

[1] Psalm 131:8.

since been born on earth, and He gathers together all the creation to sing: O ye works of the Lord, bless ye the Lord and exalt Him above all for ever.

O most pure Virgin, the rulers and dominions and powers, the angels, archangels and thrones, the principalities, cherubim and dread seraphim[1] make thy memory glorious; and we men also sing praises and exalt thee above all for ever.

He who, taking flesh, strangely made His dwelling in thy most pure womb, Himself received thine all-holy spirit, and as a Son paying His due, He gave it rest with Himself. Therefore we sing thy praises, O Virgin, and exalt thee above all for ever.

Beyond and above the understanding are the wonders of the ever-Virgin and Mother of God. Going to dwell in the tomb, she made it a paradise. Standing beside this tomb today, we sing with joy: O ye works of the Lord, bless ye the Lord and exalt Him above all for ever.

Canticle Nine

The Magnificat and Greater in honour than the cherubim *are not sung.*

First Canon

Before the irmos and each of the troparia, we sing the megalynarion:

All generations call thee blessed, O only Theotokos.[2]

(**Irmos**) In thee, O Virgin without spot, the bounds of nature are overcome: for childbirth remains virgin and death is betrothed to life. O Theotokos, Virgin after bearing child and alive after death, do thou ever save thine inheritance.

[1] Romans 8:38; Colossians 1:16.

[2] According to Slav practice we sing here the megalynarion used by the Greeks with the second Canon, *The angels as they looked upon the Dormition.*

The angelic powers were amazed as they looked in Zion upon their own Master, bearing in His hands the soul of a woman: for as befitted a Son, He said to her who without spot had borne Him: 'Come, honoured among women, and be glorified together with thy Son and God.'

Standing round thy body that had held God, the choir of the apostles looked upon it with awe and saluted it, saying with clear voice: 'As thou departest to the heavenly mansions unto thy Son, do thou ever save thine inheritance.'

Second Canon

Megalynarion sung before the irmos and the troparia:

The angels, as they looked upon the Dormition of the Virgin, were struck with wonder, seeing how the Virgin went up from earth to heaven.[1]

(**Irmos**) Let every mortal born on earth, carrying his torch, in spirit leap for joy; and let the order of the angelic powers celebrate and honour the holy feast[2] of the Mother of God, and let them cry: 'Hail, all-blessed Theotokos, pure and ever-Virgin.'

O come to Zion, the divine and fertile mountain[3] of the living God, and let us rejoice as we gaze upon the Theotokos. For Christ translates her, as His own Mother, into a dwelling far better and more divine, the Holy of Holies.

Come, O ye faithful, let us approach the tomb of the Mother of God, and let us embrace it, touching it sincerely with the lips and eyes and foreheads of the heart. Let us draw abundant gifts of healing grace from this ever-flowing fount.

O Mother of the living God, accept from us this burial

[1] In the Slav practice the following megalynarion is used:
O my soul, magnify the holy Translation of the Mother of God from earth to heaven.

[2] In the Slavonic, 'Decease'.

[3] Psalm 67:16.

hymn, and cover us with the shadow of thy light-giving and divine grace. Grant victory to our rulers, peace to the people that loves Christ, and to us who sing, remission of our sins and salvation of soul.

Exapostilarion

TONE THREE

O ye apostles, assembled here from the ends of the earth, bury my body in Gethsemane: and Thou, O my Son and God, receive my spirit (*3 times*).

Lauds. Four stichera are sung:

TONE FOUR

At thy glorious Dormition the heavens rejoice and the armies of angels exult; the whole earth makes glad, singing a hymn of departure unto thee, O Mother of Him who is Lord of all, all-holy Virgin who knewest not wedlock, thou who hast delivered mankind from the ancestral condemnation (*twice*).

At a divine command the chief apostles hastened from the ends of the earth to bury thee, and when they beheld thee taken up from earth to heaven they shouted with joy the words of Gabriel, and cried unto thee: 'Hail, thou bearer of the whole divinity: hail, thou who alone by thy childbirth hast brought together earthly things and things on high.'

By thy holy Dormition, O Virgin Mother and Bride of God, thou who gavest birth to the Life hast been transported into immortal life, attended by angels, principalities, and powers, by apostles, prophets, and the whole creation: and thy Son received into His immaculate hands thy spotless soul.

Glory be to the Father . . . Both now . . .

TONE SIX

At thy deathless Dormition, O Theotokos, Mother of the Life, clouds caught the apostles up into the air: though dispersed throughout the world, they were brought together to form a single choir before thy most pure body. And burying thee with reverence, they sang aloud the words of Gabriel: 'Hail, thou who art full of grace, O Virgin Mother who knewest not wedlock, the Lord is with thee. Entreat Him who is thy Son and our God to save our souls.'

Great Doxology and Dismissal.

Liturgy

The Typika (Psalms 102 and 145) and the Beatitudes. With the Beatitudes are sung four troparia from Canticle Three of the first Canon of the Feast (p. 515) and four troparia from Canticle Six of the second Canon (p. 519).

Alternatively, according to the modern Greek pratice, the following antiphons may be sung:

Antiphon One

TONE ONE

℣ 1. Make a joyful noise unto the Lord, all the earth: sing forth the honour of His name; make His praise glorious (*Psalm* 65:1–2).

At the prayers of the Theotokos, save us, O Saviour.

℣ 2. O give thanks unto the Lord and call upon His Name; make known His deeds among the peoples (*Psalm* 104:1).

At the prayers of the Theotokos . . .

℣ 3. In the city of the Lord of hosts, in the city of our God (*Psalm* 47:9).

At the prayers of the Theotokos . . .

℣ 4. His sanctuary is in peace: and His dwelling in Zion (*Psalm* 75:3).

At the prayers of the Theotokos . . .
Glory be to the Father . . . Both now . . .
At the prayers of the Theotokos . . .

Antiphon Two

TONE TWO

℣ 1. The Lord loveth the gates of Zion more than all the dwellings of Jacob (*Psalm* 86 : 2).

O Son of God, wonderful in Thy saints, save us who sing to Thee: alleluia.

℣ 2. Glorious things are spoken of thee, O city of God (*ibid.*, 3).

O Son of God . . .

℣ 3. God hath established her for ever: we have thought upon Thy mercy, O God, in the midst of Thy people (*Psalm* 47 : 9–10).

O Son of God . . .

℣ 4. The Most High hath sanctified His tabernacle (*Psalm* 45 : 5).

O Son of God . . .
Glory be to the Father . . . Both now . . .
O Only-begotten Son and Word of God . . .

Antiphon Three

TONE ONE

℣ 1. O God, my heart is ready, my heart is ready: I will sing and give praise in my glory (*Psalm* 107 : 2).

The troparion of the feast, In giving birth, O Theotokos (*p. 511*).

℣ 2. What shall I render unto the Lord for all His benefits toward me? (*Psalm* 115 : 3)

The troparion of the feast.

℣ 3. I will receive the cup of salvation, and call upon the Name of the Lord (*ibid.*, 4).

The troparion of the feast.

After the introit, the troparion of the feast (*p. 511*); Glory be to the Father . . . Both now . . .; *the kontakion of the feast* (*p. 520*).

Prokimenon: *TONE THREE*

My soul doth magnify the Lord, and my spirit hath rejoiced in God my Saviour (*Luke* 1:46–47).

℣. For He hath regarded the low estate of His handmaiden: for, behold, from henceforth all generations shall call me blessed (*ibid.*, 48).

READING FROM THE EPISTLE OF PAUL TO THE PHILIPPIANS (2:5–11. *See p. 129*).

Alleluia, TONE EIGHT[1]

℣ 1. Arise, O Lord, into Thy rest: Thou and the Ark of Thy holiness (*Psalm* 131:8).

℣ 2. The Lord hath sworn in truth unto David: and He will not turn from it (*ibid.*, 11).

READING FROM THE HOLY GOSPEL ACCORDING TO LUKE (10:38–42; 11:27–28. *See p. 129*).

In place of It is meet, *we sing the megalynarion*[2] *and irmos from Canticle Nine of the first Canon* (*p. 523*).

Communion verse:

I will receive the cup of salvation, and call upon the Name of the Lord (*Psalm* 115:4).

[1] In the Slav use, Tone Two.

[2] In the Greek use, *All the generations call thee blessed;* in the Slav use, *The angels as they looked.*

If the feast falls on a day of fasting, fish, wine and oil are allowed, but meat and animal products may not be eaten.

The apodosis of the feast falls on 23 August. On that day all the office of the feast is repeated, omitting only the entrance, lessons, lity, and blessing of bread at Vespers; and the polyeleos and Gospel at Mattins. In the reading of the Psalter at Vespers, the normal kathisma appointed for the day is used.

APPENDIX I

The Psalter

(a) Numbering of the Psalms

Between the Septuagint numbering of the Psalms and that given in the Hebrew there is usually a small difference, the Hebrew figure being normally one greater than the Greek. The Vulgate uses the Greek numbering; the Authorised Version and the Book of Common Prayer follow the Hebrew.

Greek	*Hebrew*
1–8	1–8
9	9 and 10
10–112	Add one to the number of each Psalm
113	114 and 115
114	116:1–9
115	116:10–19
116–145	Add one to the number of each Psalm
146	147:1–11
147	147:12–20
148–150	148–150

(b) The division of the Psalter into kathismata

KATHISMA			
I	Stasis (i)	Ps.	1, 2, 3
	(ii)		4, 5, 6
	(iii)		7, 8

II	(i)	9, 10
	(ii)	11, 12, 13
	(iii)	14, 15, 16
III	(i)	17
	(ii)	18, 19, 20
	(iii)	21, 22, 23
IV	(i)	24, 25, 26
	(ii)	27, 28, 29
	(iii)	30,31
V	(i)	32, 33
	(ii)	34, 35
	(iii)	36
VI	(i)	37, 38, 39
	(ii)	40, 41, 42
	(iii)	43, 44, 45
VII	(i)	46, 47, 48
	(ii)	49, 50
	(iii)	51, 52, 53, 54
VIII	(i)	55, 56, 57
	(ii)	58, 59, 60
	(iii)	61, 62, 63
IX	(i)	64, 65, 66
	(ii)	67
	(iii)	68, 69
X	(i)	70, 71
	(ii)	72, 73
	(iii)	74, 75, 76
XI	(i)	77
	(ii)	78, 79, 80
	(iii)	81, 82, 83, 84
XII	(i)	85, 86, 87
	(ii)	88
	(iii)	89, 90

XIII	(i)	91, 92, 93
	(ii)	94, 95, 96
	(iii)	97, 98, 99, 100
XIV	(i)	101, 102
	(ii)	103
	(iii)	104
XV	(i)	105
	(ii)	106
	(iii)	107, 108
XVI	(i)	109, 110, 111
	(ii)	112, 113, 114
	(iii)	115, 116, 117
XVII	(i)	118:1–72
	(ii)	118:73–131
	(iii)	118:132–176
XVIII	(i)	119, 120, 121, 122, 123
	(ii)	124, 125, 126, 127, 128
	(iii)	129, 130, 131, 132, 133
XIX	(i)	134, 135, 136
	(ii)	137, 138, 139
	(iii)	140, 141, 142
XX	(i)	143, 144
	(ii)	145, 146, 147
	(iii)	148, 149, 150

(c) The recitation of the Psalter

The Psalter is read in its entirety once a week, and during Lent twice a week;[1] each week is reckoned as beginning with Vespers on Saturday evening. The kathismata are distributed as follows:

[1] In smaller monasteries, and in almost all parish churches, the prescribed readings of the Psalter are today greatly abbreviated.

(1) *From 22 September to 19 December,*[1] *and from 15 January to the eve of the Sunday of the Prodigal Son (the Sunday falling fifteen days before the beginning of Lent):*

	MATTINS	VESPERS
Sunday	2, 3, 17 or Polyeleos	—
Monday	4, 5, 6	18
Tuesday	7, 8, 9	18
Wednesday	10, 11, 12	18
Thursday	13, 14, 15	18
Friday	19, 20	18
Saturday	16, 17	1

(2) *During Lent, in the 1st, 2nd, 3rd, 4th, and 6th weeks:*

	MATTINS	FIRST HOUR	THIRD HOUR	SIXTH HOUR	NINTH HOUR	VESPERS
Sunday	2, 3, 17 or Polyeleos	—	—	—	—	—
Monday	4, 5, 6	—	7	8	9	18
Tuesday	10, 11, 12	13	14	15	16	18
Wednesday	19, 20, 1	2	3	4	5	18
Thursday	6, 7, 8	9	10	11	12	18
Friday	13, 14, 15	—	19	20	—	18
Saturday	16, 17	—	—	—	—	1

(3) *The 5th week of Lent:*[2]

	MATTINS	FIRST HOUR	THIRD HOUR	SIXTH HOUR	NINTH HOUR	VESPERS
Sunday	2, 3, 17 or Polyeleos	—	—	—	—	—
Monday	4, 5, 6	—	7	8	9	10
Tuesday	11, 12, 13	14	15	16	18	19
Wednesday	20, 1, 2	3	4	5	6	7
Thursday	8	—	9	10	11	12
Friday	13, 14, 15	—	19	20	—	18
Saturday	16, 17	—	—	—	—	1

[1] The dates given throughout this section are *inclusive*.

[2] At Mattins on Thursday of this week, the Great Canon by St. Andrew of Crete is read; and for this reason only one kathisma is appointed for Mattins on that day.

(4) *Holy Week:*[1]

	MATTINS	FIRST HOUR	THIRD HOUR	SIXTH HOUR	NINTH HOUR	VESPERS
Palm Sunday	2, 3, Polyeleos	—	—	—	—	—
Monday	4, 5, 6	—	7	8	—	18
Tuesday	9, 10, 11	—	12	13	—	18
Wednesday	14, 15, 16	—	19	20	—	18
Saturday	17	—	—	—	—	—

(5) *From the Sunday of St. Thomas (the first after Easter) to 21 September; from 20 December to 14 January; and during the two weeks immediately preceding Lent:*

	MATTINS	VESPERS
Sunday	2, 3, 17 or Polyeleos	—
Monday	4, 5	6
Tuesday	7, 8	9
Wednesday	10, 11	12
Thursday	13, 14	15
Friday	19, 20	18
Saturday	16, 17	1

1 The Psalms are read once in their entirety—apart from kathisma 17—during the first four days of Holy Week (Sunday to Wednesday); all reading of the Psalter is then omitted—except at Mattins on Holy Saturday—until Vespers on Saturday in Easter Week.

APPENDIX II

The Service Books of the Orthodox Church

The service books used in the worship of the Orthodox Church may be reckoned as eleven in number, and fall into three main groups.

I. First of all, there are three books containing readings from Holy Scripture:

1. THE BOOK OF THE GOSPELS

(Gk. *Εὐαγγέλιον.*) This contains the text of the four Gospels arranged in sections (Gk. *περικοπαί*; Slavonic, *zachála*), following the order in which they are read throughout the year. The Book of the Gospels rests normally on the centre of the Holy Table, and whenever possible its cover is elaborately decorated with silver or gold: it should on no account be bound in the skins of dead animals (i.e. in vellum or leather). The Gospel Book plays an important part in Orthodox ceremonial: it is carried in procession at the Small Entrance in the Liturgy; and when there is a Gospel reading at Mattins, it is afterwards placed on an analogion in the centre of the church—or held up by the priest—and the congregation approach one by one in order to venerate it. In general the Gospel Book is treated in the same way as the Holy Icons, and is regarded as an icon of the Saviour, more particularly in His teaching ministry.

2. THE BOOK OF THE EPISTLES

(Gk. *'Απόστολος.*) This contains the readings from the Acts of the Apostles and the Epistles for the whole year: as with the Book of the Gospels, it is arranged in extracts according to the order of the daily Epistle readings. It also includes the prokimena which precede the Epistle, and the verses upon *Alleluia* which follow it.

3. THE PSALTER

(Gk. *Ψαλτήριον.*) The 150 Psalms of David, divided into their kathismata,[1] together with the nine Biblical Canticles.

There is no separate book containing the lessons from the Old Testament: these are to be found in the relevant choir book containing the texts for the day in question—the Triodion, Pentekostarion, or Menaia, as the case may be.

II. Next to the Biblical service books there come two volumes devoted primarily to the *fixed* parts of the service: i.e. to those parts which do not vary according to the season or saint, but are recited more or less without change whatever day of the year it may be. The first of these two books is concerned mainly with sacraments and 'sacramentals', the second with the offices.

4. THE EUCHOLOGION

(Gk. *Εὐχολόγιον*, 'Book of Prayers'.) This is a book for the use of the priest—and to a lesser degree, of the deacon—containing the sacraments and other services, together with numerous special prayers and blessings. Its contents and arrangement vary widely. There is in the first place a comprehensive volume known as the Great Euchologion (Gk. *Εὐχολόγιον τὸ μέγα*; Slavonic, *Bolshói Ieréisky Molitvoslóv*). In this are to be found:

(i) The fixed portions of Vespers, Mattins, and the Liturgy (the priest's part in full; that of deacon, choir, and reader usually in an abbreviated form).

[1] See pp. 530–2.

(ii) The six remaining sacraments (Baptism, with related services; Chrismation or Confirmation; Ordination; Confession; Marriage; the Service of the Holy Oil or Anointing of the Sick). Here the text is more or less complete, with the reader's part as well as the priest's.

(iii) Other services and blessings, often known in the west as 'sacramentals' (monastic profession; the consecration of a church; the Great and Small Blessing of the Waters; funeral offices, etc.).[1]

Alongside the Great Euchologion, there exist various shorter books of prayers intended for the use of the clergy. These fall into two categories: (a) prayers for use at the standard public services; (b) prayers for use at services of a more personal character, concerned with the particular needs of one or several individuals. Accordingly there are:

(a) The Ieratikon or Service Book (Gk. *Ἱερατικόν*; Slavonic, *Sluzhébnik*): an altar book, containing the priest's parts at Vespers, Mattins, and the Liturgy, with some supplementary material.

(b) The Small Euchologion or Book of Needs (Gk. *Ἁγιασματάριον, Μικρὸν Εὐχολόγιον*; Slavonic, *Trébnik*) containing five of the sacraments (the Liturgy and Ordination are omitted), the funeral offices, and various other services in common use. Some Greek editions include as well the priest's part at Vespers, Mattins, and the Liturgy.

In addition there is a special book of prayers and blessings for use by the bishop, the Archieratikon or Pontifical (Gk. *Ἀρχιερατικόν*; Slavonic, *Chinóvnik*).

5. THE HOROLOGION OR BOOK OF HOURS

(Gk. *Ὡρολόγιον*; Slavonic, *Chasoslóv*.) The Euchologion is an altar book for the priest; the Horologion, a choir book for

[1] The Euchologion itself draws no distinction between (ii) and (iii).

the reader and the singers. As with the Euchologion, its exact contents vary in different editions. In its comprehensive form—what is termed the Great Horologion (Gk. *Ὡρολόγιον τὸ μέγα*)—it includes:

(i) The fixed portions of the daily offices (Midnight Office; Mattins; the Hours; the Typika; prayers before and after meals; Vespers; Compline, Great and Small). The parts for choir and reader are given in full; most of the priest's and deacon's part is omitted.

(ii) A list of the feasts and saints' days throughout the year. For each day a short account of the feast or life of the saint is given, together with the appropriate apolytikion (troparion) of the day and the kontakion. This is followed by a similar section, covering Sundays and movable feasts within the period of the Triodion and the Pentekostarion. Then follow apolytikia and theotokia for different days of the week.

(iii) Miscellaneous canons and other services in frequent use.

In the Greek Church the Horologion is normally printed in a full form, with all these three sections. Editions in the Russian Church are often shorter, containing (i) in its entirety, but (ii) and (iii) considerably abbreviated.

A reader provided with the Great Horologion will find it possible to recite in full both the fixed and the variable portions of the Hours, the Typika, the Midnight Office, and Compline.[1] But in order to sing Vespers or Mattins, choir and reader must also consult, besides the Horologion, one or more of the books in the section that follows.

III. To supplement the Euchologion and Horologion—which are devoted primarily to the fixed portions of the service—there are four books embracing the special texts which change day by day. These volumes constitute the three

[1] Except when a Canon is appointed to be read at the Midnight Office or at Compline.

'cycles' which make up the Church's year in the Byzantine rite:

(a) the weekly cycle (contained in the Octeochos)

(b) the annual cycle of movable feasts, centring upon Easter (contained in the Triodion and Pentekostarion)

(c) the annual cycle of fixed feasts (contained in the Menaia).[1]

6. THE OCTOECHOS OR BOOK OF EIGHT TONES: also known as the PARAKLETIKE

(Gk. *Ὀκτώηχος*; *Παρακλητική*, from *παρακαλεῖν*, 'to supplicate'.) This contains the variable portions for the daily offices throughout the week. Eight series of offices are provided, one for each of the eight tones; and within each series there are seven sets of services, one for each day of the week. Throughout the year, the services proceed week by week through the various tones: on the Sunday of St. Thomas (the first after Easter) the sequence begins with Tone One, and then through the different tones until Tone Eight is completed; after which the offices for Tone One are resumed, and so once more through the whole sequence.

The texts of the Octoechos are combined with those for the fixed feasts from the Menaia; and more or less of the Octoechos will be read, depending on the status of the feast of the day. During Lent, the Octoechos is used only on Friday evening, Saturday, and Sunday. It is not used at all from Lazarus Saturday (the day before Palm Sunday) until the Sunday of All Saints (the first after Pentecost): any material in the weekly cycle of the eight tones that is used during the period of the Pentekostarion is provided in full in the Pentekostarion itself.

The Octoechos is sometimes published in a smaller edition, containing only the eight Sunday offices, and omitting all those for weekdays.

[1] On these three cycles, see above, p. 40.

7. THE TRIODION

(Gk. *Τριῴδιον*, 'the Book of the Three Odes'. Also termed more specifically *Τριῴδιον κατανυκτικόν*, and in Slavonic *Póstnaya Triód*, the 'Penitential' or 'Fasting' Triodion.) Here are found the texts for the Great Fast of Lent: the book begins with the Sunday of the Publican and Pharisee (the tenth before Easter: twenty-two days before the beginning of Lent), and concludes with Saturday in Holy Week. Many canons in the Triodion contain only three canticles or odes: hence the title of the work.

8. THE PENTEKOSTARION

(Gk. *Πεντηκοστάριον*, or more specifically *Πεντηκοστάριον χαρμόσυνον*, the 'Joyful' Pentekostarion; in Slavonic, *Tsvetnáya Triód*, the 'Flowery' or 'Festal' Triodion.) This is a companion volume to the Lenten Triodion, and contains the services for Eastertide and Pentecost: it covers the period from Easter Sunday until the Sunday of All Saints (the first after Pentecost).

9. THE MENAIA

(Gk. *Μηναῖα*, from *μῆν*, 'month'.) In this are contained the services for the fixed feasts throughout the twelve months, from 1 September (the beginning of the ecclesiastical year) until 31 August: it corresponds to the 'proper of saints' (*proprium sanctorum*) in the west. It is normally divided into twelve volumes, one for each month.

There is also a single volume known as the General Menaia (Slavonic, *Obshchaya Minéya*), containing general offices which may be used on all saints' days of a particular type.

For completeness, two further books should be added, somewhat different in scope from those already described:

10. THE IRMOLOGION

(Gk. *Εἱρμολόγιον.*) This gives the text of the irmoi sung at the beginning of the various canticles of the canon. The larger service books, such as the Menaia and the Triodion, often give only the opening words of the irmos: and so a cantor who does not know the irmoi by heart will need to have the Irmologion ready to hand.

11. THE TYPIKON

(Gk. *Τυπικόν,* from *τύπος,* 'ordinance', 'decree'.) This contains the rules and rubrics governing every aspect of the Church services and their celebration throughout the year.

To explain the principles of arrangement which we have adopted in this present translation, it is necessary to consider briefly the history of the Typikon. It is associated specially with the name of St. Sabas (439–532), abbot of the monastery close to Jerusalem that bears his name. Older Greek editions, for example, are entitled *Typikon of the Church Service of the Holy Lavra at Jerusalem of our God-bearing Father St. Sabas.*[1] According to the traditional account, the Typikon was drawn up by St. Sabas himself, and later revised by St. Sophronios, Patriarch of Jerusalem (*ca.* 560–638), who supplemented it with material from the *ordo* followed by the monastery of St. Catherine at Sinai. A further revision was then undertaken by St. John of Damascus (*ca.* 675–*ca.* 749), himself a monk at the Lavra of St. Sabas.

Modern liturgists, while not accepting this account as historically exact, nevertheless acknowledge that it contains an important element of truth. In the evolution of the ecclesiastical *ordo*, a decisive rôle was played by the rite of

[1] So the edition published at Venice in 1615:
Τυπικὸν τῆς ἐκκλησιαστικῆς ἀκολουθίας τῆς ἐν Ἱεροσολύμοις ἁγίας Λαύρας τοῦ ὁσίου καὶ θεοφόρου πατρὸς ἡμῶν Σάββα.

the Church of Jerusalem, and in particular by the celebrated monastery of St. Sabas. On the other hand the Typikon in its present state is later than the time of St. John of Damascus; and other centres besides the Lavra of St. Sabas have exercised a formative influence upon its development, most notably the monastery of Studion—more correctly, Studios—at Constantinople.

The Typikon as we now have it represents essentially a crystallization in liturgical practice which occurred between the ninth and twelfth centuries. It embodies a synthesis between two traditions, originally distinct: first, the 'cathedral' rite, as observed at the 'Great Church' of Agia Sophia in the imperial capital, and elsewhere; and secondly, the strictly 'monastic' rite. From the ninth century onwards these were normally combined into one. The Orthodox Church of the later Byzantine period, unlike the Roman Catholic Church in the West, usually made no distinction between the monastic and the 'secular' or parochial use: monasteries and parishes since that time have both followed the same Typikon, although in most parishes there are inevitably numerous omissions and abbreviations.[1]

Until the last quarter of the nineteenth century the Typikon observed by the Greek, Slav, and Romanian Churches was substantially the same, apart from minor points of detail. In 1888, however, there appeared at

[1] On the history of the Typikon, the chief work is still the monumental study by A. Dimitrievsky, *Opisanie liturgicheskikh rukopisey khranyashchikhsya v bibliotekakh pravoslavnago vostoka* (3 vols., Kiev, 1895–1917), especially vol. I; in English, consult A. Schmemann, *Introduction to Liturgical Theology* (London, 1966). Important Typika in manuscript, reflecting a use very different from that now followed, may be found in the monastic libraries of St. John, Patmos (cod. 266: 10th cent.) and of Holy Cross, Jerusalem (cod. 40: 10th cent.; now housed in the Patriarchal Library). On the first, see Dimitrievsky, op cit., vol. I; on the second, see J. Mateos, S.J., *Le Typicon de la Grande Église. Ms. Sainte-Croix no. 40, Xe siècle*, 2 vols. (*Orientalia Christiana Analecta*, 165–6, Rome, 1962–3).

Constantinople a new edition of the Typikon, prepared by the *protopsaltis* George Violakis (died 1911), and issued with the approval and blessing of the Ecumenical Patriachate. Violakis made extensive and often ill-advised changes, especially in the order of service for Mattins on Sunday: for example, the katavasiai are appointed to be sung all together at the end of Canticle Eight of the Canon, instead of occurring one at the end of each canticle; and the reading of the Gospel is moved from its old position before the Canon, and awkwardly inserted between Canticles Eight and Nine. Thus Canticle Nine is separated from those which precede it, and the whole structure of the Canon is unhappily obscured.[1]

The new Constantinople Typikon has now been generally adopted throughout the Greek-speaking Orthodox Churches; the Church of Russia, on the other hand, adheres faithfully to the older 'Typikon of St. Sabas'. The remaining Orthodox Churches vary in their practice, some approximating more or less closely to the modern Constantinople use, and others remaining virtually uninfluenced by it. The older Typikon is still followed strictly in most Greek monasteries, particularly those of St. Sabas at Jerusalem, of Mount Athos, and of St. John on Patmos. Thus in Greek Orthodoxy today, there is once more—as in the earlier period—a difference between the monastic and the parochial use, but in the earlier period the divergence was of course far more radical.

In the present translation we have preferred to follow the pre-1888 'Typikon of St. Sabas', and for the most part we have taken no account of the changes made in the Violakis edition.

[1] In making these and other changes, perhaps Violakis was not innovating but simply giving formal approval to practices which had already become established in parishes. Presumably the Gospel was moved nearer to the end of the service because so few of the congregation arrived in time for the earlier parts of Mattins!

APPENDIX III

Glossary

AFTERFEAST (Gk. *μεθεόρτια*; Slavonic, *poprázdnestvo*). The period immediately following a feast, during which the observance of the festival continues. It varies in length: often it lasts for a week (compare the western 'octave'), but it may last only for a single day.

AINOI. See *Lauds*.

AMBON (Gk. *ἄμβων*). In Greek churches, the pulpit. In Russian churches, which in general have no pulpit, the term 'ambon' is applied to the central part of the soleas, i.e. to the space immediately in front of the Royal Doors. Whichever the sense in which ambon is used, it is the place from which the deacon reads the Gospel, and from which the sermon is delivered.

ANALOGION (Gk. *ἀναλόγιον*, from *ἀναλέγειν*, 'to read'). A desk, about four or five feet high, with a sloping top; usually made of wood, and often covered with a cloth made of silk, damask, or the like. Such desks are used: (i) for reading (ii) when an icon or the Book of the Gospels is placed in the body of the church for veneration by the faithful.

ANAVATHMOI. See *Degrees, hymns of*.

ANTIDORON (Gk. *ἀντίδωρον*, 'instead of the gift', i.e. instead of Holy Communion; also known as Evlogia, Gk. *εὐλογία*, 'blessing'). Small pieces of bread distributed to the congregation by the priest at the end of the Holy Liturgy. As material for the antidoron, it is the practice to use what remains of the loaves from which the Eucharistic bread has been cut.

Although sharing in some measure in the Eucharistic blessing, the antidoron is to be distinguished carefully from the bread of the Eucharist itself: the antidoron is blessed, but *not* consecrated. It has, to some extent, a western counterpart in the 'Pain bénit', distributed in some French and Canadian churches at the conclusion of High Mass.

APODOSIS (Gk. *ἀπόδοσις*, 'giving back', 'return'; Slavonic, *otdánie*). The last day of the afterfeast, on which the festival finally closes. The office of the feast is repeated more or less in its entirety on the apodosis.

APOLYSIS. See *Dismissal*.

APOLYTIKION (Gk. *ἀπολυτίκιον*, 'dismissal hymn'; Slavonic, *otpustítelnyi*). The principal troparion of the day, occurring at the end of Vespers (hence its name), and celebrating the particular feast or saint commemorated in the calendar. Also known as the 'troparion of the feast' or the 'troparion of the day'.

On Great Feasts the practice with regard to the apolytikion is as follows:

(i) It is sung three times at the end of Vespers, immediately before the blessing of the bread, while the priest censes the table on which the bread rests.

(ii) It is repeated three times near the beginning of Mattins, after *The Lord is God*.

(iii) It is sung once at the end of Mattins, immediately after the Great Doxology.

(iv) It is sung at the Liturgy, after the Small Entrance and the Introit.

(v) It occurs likewise at Great Compline and at all the Hours.

APOSTICHA (Gk. *ἀπόστιχα*; Slavonic, *stikhíry na stikhóvne*). Stichera accompanied by verses (Gk. *στίχοι*) taken from the Psalms. Aposticha occur:

(i) At the end of Vespers, both on feasts and on ordinary days.

(ii) At the end of Mattins, on ordinary days only (i.e. on days when there is no Great Doxology).

ARTOKLASIA. See *Blessing of Bread*.

BLESSING OF BREAD (Gk. ἀρτοκλασία: literally, 'breaking'—not 'blessing'—'of bread'). A ceremony occurring at the end of Vespers on the eve of Great Feasts, and on certain other days on which there is a Lity. A table is placed in the centre of the church, and on it are set five loaves together with three small vessels, containing respectively wine, oil, and grains of wheat.[1] During the singing of the apolytikion the priest goes round the table censing it, and then he says a prayer of blessing, recalling the five loaves at the feeding of the five thousand in the desert (Matthew 14:15–21). The loaves are then taken into the sanctuary, cut up, and dipped in the wine. The bread is later distributed to the congregation: if there is a Vigil, after the Gospel at Mattins; if there is no Vigil, at the end of Vespers.

BOGORODICHEN. See *Theotokion*.

CANON (Gk. κανών). A series of eight canticles, each made up of a number of troparia. The canon occurs at Mattins after the reading of the Psalter and of Psalm 50 (on Sundays and feasts, after the Litany, *O Lord, save Thy people*). Originally, in Mattins at this point the nine Scriptural canticles or 'odes' were sung, with a short refrain inserted between the verses. St. Andrew of Crete (7th–8th cent.) established the practice of expanding these short refrains into troparia celebrating some particular theme: repentance (as in St. Andrew's own masterpiece, *The Great Canon*); the feast or saint of the day; the Saviour; the Theotokos; the departed; and so on. In course of time the custom of reading the actual Biblical

[1] In the Greek use, there are two vessels only, of wine and oil.

text largely disappeared, although it is still observed by many monastic communities during Lent (also throughout the year in monasteries on Mount Athos, Patmos, and certain other places). As a result the troparia of the canon are now usually recited by themselves, accompanied by a short invocation such as *Glory to Thee, O God, glory to Thee*, or *Most Holy Theotokos, save us*. The sole Biblical canticle still sung in full is the Magnificat: this is never omitted, except on Great Feasts. In present practice there is no second canticle in the canon, save only on various days in Lent: thus the canon, which theoretically contains nine canticles, has in reality only eight. The canons on weekdays in Lent contain as a rule either two, three, or four canticles (διῴδια, τριῴδια, τετραῴδια).

Canons have a varying number of troparia in each canticle. Normally more than one canon is prescribed to be read at Mattins: on Sundays, four; on normal days, three; on Great Feasts usually two, but occasionally only one. In reading the canons, the following rules are observed. Canticle One of the first canon is read; then Canticle One of the second, third, etc. canon; then Canticle Three of the first canon, and so on. The canons should be so combined that the total number of troparia in each canticle amounts always to fourteen. If the canons prescribed to be read have too many troparia, then two troparia are joined together and read as if they were one; or else some of the troparia are omitted. If the troparia are too few, then particular troparia must be repeated twice or even three times to make up the requisite total. In assessing the number of troparia, the first stanza of each canticle (the irmos) is included in the reckoning, but not the katavasia at the end.

Canons are read not only at Mattins, but at Compline, and on Sundays at the Midnight Office; and they occur also in other services, such as the Anointing of the Sick, and the Preparation Service before Holy Communion.

CANTICLE (Gk. ᾠδή, 'ode', 'song'; Slavonic, *pesn*). A title applied:

(a) to certain prayers and poetical compositions of Biblical origin (other than the Psalms);

(b) to the nine (in practice, eight) subdivisions of the canon (originally designed to accompany the reading of the Biblical canticles).

Nine Biblical canticles are appointed for use at Mattins, as follows:

(i) The Song of Moses (Exodus 15:1–19).
(ii) The Song of Moses (Deuteronomy 32:1–43).
(iii) The Prayer of Hannah (1 Kings [1 Samuel] 2:1–10).
(iv) The Prayer of Habakkuk (Habakkuk 3:1–19).
(v) The Prayer of Isaiah (Isaiah 26:9–20).
(vi) The Prayer of Jonah (Jonah 2:3–10).
(vii) The Prayer of the Three Holy Children (Daniel 3:26–56).[1]
(viii) The Song of the Three Holy Children (the Benedicite: Daniel 3:57–88).[2]
(ix) The Song of the Theotokos (the Magnificat: Luke 1:46–55).
The Prayer of Zacharias (the Benedictus: Luke 1:68–79).[3]

Apart from the Magnificat, all these canticles are now usually omitted, except during Lent.

[1] In the Authorised Version and many other English translations of the Old Testament, this is to be found separately from the Book of Daniel, in the so-called Apocrypha: The Song of the Three Holy Children, verses 3–34.

[2] In the Apocrypha, The Song of the Three Children, verses 35–66. At the end of this canticle are added three further verses, not of Biblical origin.

[3] The Magnificat and Benedictus, while in principle constituting two separate canticles, are treated in Byzantine Mattins as if they were one.

CATECHUMENS (Gk. *κατηχούμενοι*, 'those who are being catechised'). In the early Church, those undergoing training and instruction preparatory to baptism. They were assigned a distinctive place in the church, and were sent out before the beginning of the specifically Eucharistic portion of the Liturgy. With the more or less universal adoption of infant baptism, they have long since ceased to exist as a separate class: but the Orthodox Church still retains a special Litany for the Catechumens, which concludes with their dismissal from church and occurs shortly before the Great Entrance.[1]

COMMUNION VERSE (Gk. *κοινωνικόν*; Slavonic, *prichásten*). A verse from Scripture, sung at the Divine Liturgy after the words of the priest, *Holy things for the holy*, and the response, *One is holy*.

DEGREES, HYMNS OF (Gk. *ἀναβαθμοί*, from *βαθμός*, 'step', 'ascent'; Slavonic, *stepénnyi*). Poetical compositions based on the Gradual Psalms or 'Songs of Degrees' (Psalms 119–133). They are sung immediately before the prokimenon and Gospel at Mattins on Sundays and feasts. There is a different hymn of degrees for each of the eight tones. Every hymn of degrees is divided into three antiphons (except that in Tone Eight, which has four); and each antiphon in its turn contains three short troparia. On Great Feasts the first antiphon of the hymn of degrees in Tone Four is sung (based on Psalm 128).

DISMISSAL (Gk. *ἀπόλυσις*; Slavonic, *ótpust*). The final blessing said by the priest at the end of Vespers, Mattins, the Liturgy, and other offices. It takes two main forms: a longer, known as the Great Dismissal, and a shorter, the Small Dismissal.

DOGMATIKON (Gk. *δογματικόν*). A term applied to certain theotokia. Dogmatika are so named because they are

[1] In Greek parish churches today, the Litany for the Catechumens is normally omitted.

specially concerned with the dogma of the two natures of Christ.

DOXASTIKON (Gk. δοξαστικόν, from δόξα, 'glory'; Slavonic, *sláva*). A troparion or sticheron inserted after the verse *Glory be to the Father, and to the Son, and to the Holy Spirit*. On many occasions no doxastikon is prescribed, in which case the second half of the Glory, *Both now* . . ., follows immediately upon the first.

DOXOLOGY (Gk. δοξολογία, 'hymn of glory'; Slavonic, *slavoslóvie*). The hymn of great antiquity at the end of Mattins, that opens with the words of the angels, 'Glory to God in the highest and on earth peace, good will among men' (Luke 2 : 14). It takes two forms:

(i) The Great Doxology, sung on Great Feasts, Sundays, and certain Saints' days.[1]

(ii) The Small Doxology, which is said—not sung—on ordinary days.

EKTENEIA. See *Litany*.

ENTRANCE (Gk. εἴσοδος; Slavonic, *vkhod*). A procession in which the priest and deacon, preceded by one or more processional candles, make their way through the north door of the iconostasis to the centre of the church; after pausing there, they return to the sanctuary through the Royal Doors. Entrances occur as follows:

(i) At Great Vespers: here the deacon carries the censer.
(ii) At the Liturgy. There are two Entrances:
  (a) The Small Entrance: here the deacon carries the Book of the Gospels.
  (b) The Great Entrance: here the clergy bring the bread and wine, set aside for the Eucharistic offering, from the table of Prothesis to the Holy

[1] For the text, see p. 95.

Table. The deacon, holding the censer,[1] carries the paten (diskos), and the priest carries the chalice. Both paten and chalice are covered with veils.

EPICLESIS (Gk. ἐπίκλησις, 'invocation'). The prayer during the Orthodox Liturgy in which the priest asks God to send down His Holy Spirit upon the bread and wine, and to make them the Body and Blood of Christ. Whereas in the Roman Catholic Church the 'Words of Institution' (*This is my Body . . . This is my Blood . . .*) are regarded as the 'moment of consecration', for Orthodox the culminating moment in the Eucharistic prayer is the Epiclesis.

EVLOGIA. See *Antidoron*.

EVLOGITARIA (Gk. εὐλογητάρια, from εὐλογητός, 'blessed'; Slavonic, *neporóchnyi*). Troparia sung at Mattins after the reading of the psalter; they are accompanied by the refrain, *Blessed art Thou, O Lord: teach me Thy statutes*. They take two forms:

(i) Evlogitaria of the Resurrection (*εὐλογητάρια ἀναστάσιμα*), at Sunday Mattins after Psalm 118 or the Polyeleos.

(ii) Funeral Evlogitaria (*εὐλογητάρια νεκρώσιμα*), at Mattins for the dead after Psalm 118.

EXAPOSTILARION (Gk. ἐξαποστειλάριον, from ἐξαποστέλλω, 'dismiss'). A troparion occurring at the conclusion of the canon at Mattins, and frequently developing the theme of Christ as light of the world. It is termed 'exapostilarion' because it 'gives the dismissal', as it were, at the end of the canon. Sometimes it is called 'photagogikon' (Gk. φωταγωγικόν, 'hymn of light'; Slavonic, *svetílen*).

The exapostilarion on Sundays is always linked with the Gospel of the Resurrection, used earlier in the service. The

[1] In practice the censer is often carried in front of the deacon by a server.

exapostilarion is usually read, but on occasion it may be sung (e.g. on 15 August).

EXAPSALMOS. See *Six Psalms*.

EXAPTERYGA (Gk. *ἑξαπτέρυγα*, 'six-winged'). Liturgical fans, set on the end of staffs: so termed because the figure of a seraph appears upon them. They are carried in procession, especially at pontifical services: in particular, they are held over the Gospel while it is being read in the course of Mattins or the Liturgy, and over the Holy Gifts at the Great Entrance in the Liturgy; and they are carried in procession before the Holy Cross on 14 September.

FOREFEAST (Gk. *προεόρτια*; Slavonic, *predprázdnestvo*). One or more days of preparation immediately preceding a feast. Christmas has five days of forefeast, and Theophany four; the remainder of the Great Feasts in this volume have a forefeast of one day only.

HEIRMOS. See *Irmos*.

HEXAPSALMOS. See *Six Psalms*.

HEXAPTERYGA. See *Exapteryga*.

HYPAKOË. See *Ypakoë*.

ICONOSTASIS (Gk. *εἰκονοστάσιον, τέμπλον*). The screen of icons separating the sanctuary from the body of the Church, and pierced by three doors. The central doorway, which is closed by double gates and a curtain, is known as the Royal Doors.

IKOS (Gk. *οἶκος*). The stanza or strophe that follows immediately upon the kontakion, between Canticles Six and Seven of the canon at Mattins.

INTROIT (Gk. *εἰσοδικόν*, from *εἴσοδος*, 'entry'; Slavonic, *vkhódnoe*). The hymn sung at the Small Entrance in the Liturgy, as the priest and deacon enter the sanctuary. There is a standard introit beginning *O come, let us worship*, which is sung on most days; certain Great Feasts have a special introit.

IRMOS (Gk. εἱρμός, 'chain'). A title applied to the opening stanza in each canticle of the canon. In the original Greek text, all the remaining troparia in the canticle follow the same rhythm as the irmos. In content it acts as a 'link' verse (hence its name), joining together:

(a) the theme of the Biblical canticle, which the canticle of the canon was originally designed to accompany;

(b) the theme of the feast or commemoration of the day, which is developed in the troparia that follow.

KATAVASIA (Gk. *καταβασία*, from *καταβαίνω*, 'go down'). The concluding stanza in a canticle of the canon. Sometimes the irmos is repeated as katavasia (when there are several canons, the irmos of the last canon); but on Sundays and certain feasts the katavasia at the end of each canticle is specially appointed according to the time within the liturgical year. On Sundays and feasts there is a katavasia at the end of every canticle, but on ordinary weekdays at the end of the third, sixth, eighth, and ninth canticles only.

The katavasia is so named because originally the members of the choir came down from their stalls on either side and stood in the centre of the church in order to sing it.

KATHISMA (Gk. *κάθισμα*, from *καθῆσθαι*, 'to be seated'). A term signifying:

(i) each of the twenty sections into which the Psalter is subdivided in the Orthodox Church;[1]

(ii) a short troparion sung or read during Mattins at the end of each kathisma of the Psalter.

In Slavonic, (ii) is known as *sedálen* (compare the Latin *sedere*, 'to sit'). To distinguish the two senses, in the present translation 'kathisma' is reserved for (i), while (ii) is always designated 'sessional hymn'.

[1] See pp. 530–2.

KONTAKION (Gk. κοντάκιον, from κοντός, 'pole', 'shaft': hence a vellum roll wound round a stick of wood). Originally the kontakion was a long poem, designed for singing in church. It consisted of a short preliminary stanza, followed by some 18–24 strophes, each known as an ikos (Gk. οἶκος): the preliminary stanza and every ikos concluded with the same refrain. In course of time the kontakion was displaced by the canon, and in the liturgical books today all that remains is the brief preliminary stanza (to which the title 'kontakion' is now more particularly attached), followed by the first ikos. These are to be found between Canticles Six and Seven of the canon at Mattins. The kontakion, without the ikos, is also read or sung at the Liturgy after the Small Entrance, and during the Hours.

The most celebrated among the authors of kontakia is St. Romanos the Melodist (died 556).

LAUDS (Gk. αἶνοι, 'praises'; Slavonic, *khvalítnyi*). The morning psalms—148, 149, and 150—used daily throughout the year towards the end of Mattins. The name is taken from the opening of Psalm 148, 'Praise' (Gk. αἰνεῖτε; Slavonic, *khvalíte*), a word which also recurs constantly throughout the psalms. On Great Feasts, Sundays, and certain other days stichera are inserted between the closing verses of Lauds: these may be ten, eight, six, or four in number, according to the rules of the day.

Lauds have their counterpart in the evening psalms sung daily at Vespers, beginning *Lord, I have cried*. The use of these psalms at morning and evening prayer each day is of the utmost antiquity, and has its roots in the worship of the Jewish synagogue.

LITANY (Gk. συναπτή, ἐκτένεια or ἐκτενής, αἴτησις; Slavonic, *ekteniyá*). A form of prayer in which the deacon calls upon the faithful to pray for various intentions: to each petition the choir responds *Lord, have mercy* (*Kyrie, eleison*), or sometimes *Grant this, O Lord*. Meanwhile, in most cases, the priest reads secretly a prayer provided in the service book, reciting aloud—at the end of the Litany—the final 'exclamation' (Gk. ἐκφώνησις; Slavonic, *vózglas*) to the Holy Trinity with which the prayer concludes. Litanies occur with some frequency throughout Vespers, Mattins, and the Liturgy; and with their strongly pronounced 'dialogue' structure, they confer a distinctive character upon all Orthodox worship.

The chief types of Litany are as follows:

(i) The Great Litany, beginning *In peace let us pray to the Lord*. This occurs at or near the opening of Vespers, Mattins, and the Liturgy.

(ii) The Small Litany, beginning *Again and again in peace let us pray to the Lord*.

(iii) The Litany of Fervent Intercession, in two parts, beginning:

(a) *Let us all say, with all our soul* (sometimes the first two petitions are omitted, and it begins *Have mercy upon us, O God*).

(b) *Let us complete our prayer (morning, evening prayer) to the Lord*.

LITURGY (Gk. λειτουργία: literally, a public duty or office). In the west, this term is often used to signify public worship in general; in the Orthodox Church it denotes specifically the Eucharist.

LITY (Gk. λιτή, 'prayer', 'entreaty'; connected with λιτανεύειν: compare the English 'litany'). A procession and solemn intercession at Vespers on the eve of Great Feasts and on certain other days. At the end of the Litany of Fervent Intercession, during the singing of troparia appointed for the day, the clergy go in procession to the narthex, and the entire church is censed by the deacon. When the troparia are finished a long litany is intoned by the deacon, for all the needs of the Christian people. Then, during the singing of the aposticha, the clergy return to the centre of the church; and after the apolytikion, the blessing of the bread takes place.

The term 'Lity' is likewise applied to the shortened Office of the Dead that is commonly sung at the end of the Liturgy, immediately before the Dismissal. This Office of the Dead is also used daily during Lent at the end of the First Hour, except on Saturdays and Sundays.

LORD, I HAVE CRIED (Gk. Κύριε, ἐκέκραξα; Slavonic, *Góspodi vozzvákh*). The opening words of Psalm 140: applied as a general title to the evening psalms—140, 141, 129, and 116—which are sung daily at Vespers throughout the year, and which have their counterpart at Mattins in the three psalms known as 'Lauds'. Stichera are inserted between the last verses of *Lord, I have cried*: they may be ten, eight, six, or four in number, according to the rules of the day.

MEGALYNARION (Gk. μεγαλυνάριον; Slavonic, *velichánie*). A short verse, usually beginning with the word *Magnify* (Gk. μεγάλυνον; Slavonic, *velichádem*). Megalynaria are sung at Mattins:

(i) after the polyeleos, on Great Feasts and on certain saints' days (Slav use only);

(ii) in place of the Magnificat, on Great Feasts.

NARTHEX (Gk. νάρθηξ; Slavonic, *pritvór*). A vestibule at the west end of the church. In monasteries Compline is usually said here, and sometimes the Midnight Office and the Hours; and the Lity on the eve of Great Feasts takes place here.

ODE. See *Canticle*.

OIKOS. See *Ikos*.

PHOTAGOGIKON. See *Exapostilarion*.

POLYELEOS (Gk. πολυέλεος, from πολύ, 'much', and ἔλεος, 'mercy'). A title applied primarily to Psalms 134 and 135. These two psalms constitute the third appointed reading from the Psalter at Mattins on Great Feasts, on certain Sundays (according to the use in many places, on all Sundays), and on certain saints' days. Usually the two psalms are not sung in full, but only a selection of verses is used: *Alleluia* is sung once or more after each verse. The name 'polyeleos', 'much mercy', arises from the frequent repetition of the word 'mercy' in Psalm 135.

At the polyeleos on the three Sundays immediately preceding the beginning of Lent, Psalm 136 is added to the other two psalms.

In the Greek use only, on feasts of the Mother of God the polyeleos is Psalm 44.

PRESANCTIFIED, LITURGY OF THE (Gk. *λειτουργία τῶν προηγιασμένων*). The form of the Liturgy that is celebrated on days in Lent other than Saturday and Sunday. It is combined with Vespers and contains no consecration, communion being given from the Holy Sacrament consecrated on the previous Sunday.

PROKIMENON (Gk. *προκείμενον*, 'what is set forth', i.e. what is appointed to be read). Verses from the Psalter, sung immediately before readings from Holy Scripture. A prokimenon occurs:

(i) at Vespers, after the hymn, *O joyful light*;[1]
(ii) at Mattins on Sundays and feasts, before the Gospel;
(iii) at the Liturgy, before the Epistle.

PROTHESIS (Gk. *πρόθεσις*, *προσκομιδή*). The service of preparation at the beginning of the Holy Liturgy, in which the priest makes ready the bread and wine to be used in the Eucharist: this is done at a special table.

The term 'prothesis' is also applied to the small room in which this service of preparation is performed. This room—frequently, although incorrectly, styled a 'chapel'—is

[1] Often there are no lessons at Vespers, in which case the prokimenon here does not in fact precede a reading from Scripture, but stands isolated.

situated to the north of the sanctuary. If there is no separate room, the prothesis table stands in the sanctuary itself, on the left side.

ROYAL DOORS. See *Iconostasis*.

SESSIONAL HYMN, SEDÁLEN. See *Kathisma (ii)*.

SIX PSALMS (Gk. *ἑξάψαλμος*; Slavonic, *shestopsálmie*). The psalms read daily at the beginning of Mattins: 3, 37, 62, 87, 102, 142. There should be no movement or noise whatever in the church while they are being recited, and all present are required to remain standing.

SOLEAS (Gk. *σωλέας*). The space immediately in front of the iconostasis; it is raised above the level of the nave floor by one or more steps.

STICHERON (Gk. *στιχηρόν*). Stichera are stanzas inserted between verses (Gk. *στίχοι*) taken from the Psalms. They occur in particular:

(i) at Vespers, between the closing verses of *Lord, I have cried*;

(ii) at Mattins, between the concluding verses of Lauds.

Stitchera also occur at the Lity, but without verses from the Psalter.

SVETILEN. See *Exapostilarion*.

SYNAXARION (Gk. *συναξάριον*; also termed Menológion, Gk. *μηνολόγιον*). A short account of the life of the saint whose feast it is, or a commentary on the meaning of the mystery that is being celebrated. In the Greek use, the Synaxarion is read daily at Mattins between Canticles Six and Seven of the canon, immediately after the kontakion and its ikos. These readings are contained in a special book, with the same name 'Synaxarion': this corresponds approximately to the Roman Martyrology. The Synaxarion readings are also incorporated in the Greek Menaia at the relevant points.

The Synaxarion has been omitted in the present translation.

SYNAXIS (Gk. *σύναξις*, 'assembly'; Slavonic, *sobór*). A title applied, among other things, to certain commemorations falling on the day immediately after a Great Feast, and honouring some personage closely connected with the theme of the Feast itself (e.g. the Mother of God on 26 December; St. John the Baptist on 7 January; the Archangel Gabriel on 26 March). Not every Great Feast is followed by a Synaxis.

In a more general sense, 'synaxis' means an assembly for worship.

THEOPHANY (Gk. *Θεοφάνεια*, 'manifestation of God'; Slavonic, *Bogoyavlénie*). The feast of Christ's Baptism in Jordan (6 January): western Epiphany.

THEOTOKION (Gk. *θεοτοκίον*; Slavonic, *Bogoródichen*). A troparion or sticheron in honour of the Theotokos. The last of any series of troparia or stichera usually takes the form of a theotokion. On Wednesdays and Fridays—days specially dedicated to the memory of Our Lord's Passion—in place of the theotokion there is normally a stavrotheotokion (Gk. *σταυροθεοτοκίον*; Slavonic, *krestobogoródichen*), i.e. a troparion honouring both the Cross and the Theotokos.

THEOTOKOS (Gk. *Θεοτόκος*, 'God-bearer'; Slavonic, *Bogoróditsa*). The chief title ascribed to the Blessed Virgin Mary in the theology and worship of the Orthodox Church: the third Ecumenical Council (Ephesus, 431) solemnly decreed that she should be honoured by this name. Often translated 'Mother of God', although for this there is a different phrase in Greek (*Μήτηρ τοῦ Θεοῦ*).

TONES (Gk. *ἦχοι*; Slavonic, *glásy*). The Church music of the Orthodox Church is based upon eight tones, ranged in two groups of four:

One	Five (or First Plagial)
Two	Six (or Second Plagial)
Three	Seven (Grave Tone)[1]
Four	Eight (or Fourth Plagial).

Each week has its appointed tone. On Saturday evening in Easter Week (the eve of the Sunday of St. Thomas), the cycle of tones commences with Tone One; and so, week by week, the sequence continues through the successive tones from One to Eight, changing to a new tone every Saturday evening. The various texts in the Tone for the week are to be found in the Octoechos.

The special texts for fixed feasts (in the Menaia) and for days during Lent and Eastertide (in the Triodion and Pentekostarion) are set in various tones; and these of course do not, save by coincidence, correspond with the appointed tone of the week.

While all Orthodoxy uses the same division into eight tones, the way in which these tones are sung varies from one Orthodox Church to another: for example, the Russians execute the tones quite differently from the Greeks.

TRIADIKON (Gk. *τριαδικόν*; Slavonic, *troíchen*). A stanza in honour of the Holy Trinity (Gk. *Τριάς*). Often the last but one in a series of troparia takes this form, just as the last troparion is usually a theotokion.

On Sunday at the Midnight Office there is sung a special 'Triadic Canon' (Gk. *τριαδικὸς κανών*) in honour of the Trinity: these canons are eight in number, one for each tone, and are found in the Octoechos.

TRISAGION (Gk. *τρισάγιον*, 'thrice-holy'; Slavonic, *trisvyatóe*). The words 'Holy God, Holy and Mighty, Holy and Immortal, have mercy upon us'. They are usually repeated three or more times, and occur:

[1] Gk. *ἦχος βαρύς*.

(i) in the Liturgy, after the hymns following the Small Entrance, and before the prokimenon;

(ii) in Mattins, at the end of the Great Doxology;

(iii) in almost every office, as part of the short petitions preceding the Lord's Prayer.

TROPARION (Gk. *τροπάριον*). A generic term to designate a stanza of religious poetry. In particular it is applied:

(i) to the apolytikion, which is also known as the 'troparion of the feast' or 'troparion of the day';

(ii) to the stanzas of the canon.

TYPICAL PSALMS. Psalms 102 and 145, which are normally sung at the beginning of the Liturgy: so called because they occur in the service of the Typika.

TYPIKA (Gk. *τυπικά*; Slavonic, *izobrazítelnaya*). An office having no precise equivalent in the west; it is sometimes compared with the 'Dry Mass' (*Missa sicca*) of the Roman Church or with the Anglican office of Ante-Communion, but these parallels are not exact. It consists in hymns, prayers, and readings taken from the Liturgy; and in principle it is a substitute for the Liturgy, to be said on days when there is no celebration of the Eucharist. In modern practice it is occasionally said on days when a Liturgy takes place: this happens, for example, on the eves of Christmas and Theophany.[1] The Typika are always said when there is a Liturgy of the Presanctified.

VELICHANIE. See *Megalynarion*.

YPAKOË (Gk. *ὑπακοή*, from *ὑπακούω*, 'hearken', 'give ear'). A troparion sung at Mattins on Great Feasts and Sundays:

[1] Except when Christmas and Theophany fall on Sunday or Monday. But even when both the Typika and the Liturgy are held on 24 December or 5 January, the rule that the Typika are only said on days without a Liturgy is still followed in theory. For the Liturgy on these days takes place *after Vespers*, and from the technical viewpoint Vespers represent the beginning of a new liturgical day.

(i) On Great Feasts it occurs after Canticle Three of the canon (but sometimes the troparion at this point is designated 'sessional hymn').

(ii) On Sundays it comes at the end of the reading of the Psalter (i.e., after the Evlogitaria of the Resurrection and the Small Litany).

(iii) The Sunday Ypakoë is also read at the Midnight Office on that day, after the Canon to the Trinity.

APPENDIX IV

The Calendar

The Orthodox Church follows at present two different calendars: the Old or Julian Calendar, and the New or Gregorian. Since 1900 the Gregorian Calendar has been thirteen days in advance of the Julian.

The Julian Calendar was devised originally under Julius Caesar in 45–44 B.C., while the Gregorian represents a revision of this, effected by Pope Gregory XIII in 1582. In due course the Gregorian Calendar came to be adopted in all countries of western Europe—by England, for example, in 1752. It was condemned, however, by Orthodox synods at Constantinople in 1583 and 1593; and the entire Orthodox Church continued to follow the Old Style reckoning until 1923. In that year an 'Inter-Orthodox Congress' at Constantinople—several Orthodox Churches, including the Russian, were not in fact properly represented at it—proposed the adoption of the Gregorian Calendar, in a slightly emended form. This suggestion was followed, in 1924 or not long afterwards, by the Churches of Constantinople, Alexandria, Antioch, Cyprus, Greece, Romania, and Poland. On the other hand the Churches of Jerusalem, Russia, Serbia, Bulgaria, and Georgia, together with a substantial minority of the Orthodox in Greece, preferred to retain the Old Calendar, which they have continued to observe up to the present time.[1]

This divergence over calendars has not been allowed to

[1] The Church of Bulgaria changed to the New Calendar in December, 1968.

affect the dating of Easter, which is still kept by virtually the entire Orthodox Church on the same day, no account being taken in this instance of the New Calendar. But in regard to the observance of the fixed feasts in the annual cycle, a discrepancy of thirteen days arises. The Greeks, for example, keep Christmas on 25 December (New Style), the Russians on 7 January (New Style), thirteen days later—although for the Russians, of course, it is only 25 December. In the same way Theophany is kept by the Greeks on 6 January, by the Russians on 19 January; the Annunciation on 25 March and 7 April by the two groups respectively; and so on.

This situation, bewildering for Orthodox and non-Orthodox alike, seems likely to persist for some time. When an Ecumenical Council of the Orthodox Church at length assembles, no doubt the calendar question will be one of the many topics for discussion.